Film and Television

**Recent Titles in the
Reference Sources in the Humanity Series**

The Performing Arts: A Guide to the Reference Literature
Linda Keir Simons

American Popular Culture: A Guide to the Reference Literature
Frank W. Hoffman

Philosophy: A Guide to the Reference Literature, Second Edition
Hans E. Bynagle

Journalism: A Guide to the Reference Literature, Second Edition
Jo A. Cates

Children's Literature: A Guide to Information Sources
Margaret W. Denman-West

Reference Works in British and American Literature, Second Edition
James A. Bracken

Reference Guide to Mystery and Detective Fiction
Richard Bleiler

Linguistics: A Guide to the Reference Literature, Second Edition
Anna L. DeMiller

Reference Guide to Science Fiction, Fantasy, and Horror, Second Edition
Michael Burgess and Lisa R. Bartle

Reference and Research Guide to Mystery and Detective Fiction, Second Edition
Richard Bleiler

Journalism: A Guide to the Reference Literature, Third Edition
Jo A. Cates

Film and Television

A Guide to the Reference Literature

Mark Emmons

Reference Sources in the Humanities

LIBRARIES UNLIMITED

A Member of the Greenwood Publishing Group

Westport, Connecticut • London

Library of Congress Cataloging-in-Publication Data

Emmons, Mark, 1961–
    Film and television : a guide to the reference literature / Mark Emmons.
        p. cm. —(Reference sources in the humanities)
    Includes bibliographical references and indexes.
    ISBN 1–56308–914–9
    1. Motion pictures—Bibliography. 2. Motion pictures—Reference books—
Bibliography. 3. Television broadcasting—Bibliography. 4. Television broadcasting—Reference books—Bibliography. I. Title. II. Series: Reference
sources in the humanities series.
Z5784.M9E47   2006
[PN1994]
016.79143—dc22   2005034358

British Library Cataloguing in Publication Data is available.

Library of Congress Catalog Card Number: 2005034358
ISBN: 1–56308–914–9

First published in 2006

Libraries Unlimited, 88 Post Road West, Westport, CT 06881
A Member of the Greenwood Publishing Group, Inc.
www.lu.com

Printed in the United States of America

The paper used in this book complies with the
Permanent Paper Standard issued by the National
Information Standards Organization (Z39.48–1984).

10 9 8 7 6 5 4 3 2 1

To
ALL MOVIE LOVERS
Especially my wife Loraine
and
my daughters Michelle and Natalie

Contents

Preface

It seemed like a good idea at the time. The last research guide to film and television had been written nearly 20 years earlier. I was a reference and instruction librarian with a passion for movies who had worked in the film industry and written a couple of early chapters on Internet film resources. I contacted the good folks at Libraries Unlimited with a proposal to write a new research guide modeled roughly on a book they had published in 1985 by Kim Fisher entitled *On the Screen: A Film, Television, and Video Research Guide* (see entry 4). They replied with a contract offer.

During the three-and-a-half years I worked on my book, I must admit that there were times I wondered if it was a good idea after all. I held in my hands well over 1,200 books and looked at over 500 Web sites. There were times I dreaded reading through the umpteenth guide to Westerns or perusing yet another fan site listing personal favorite episodes of a long forgotten television series. But there were many more times when my love of movies would sidetrack me for minutes or even hours as I laughed out loud at quotes, added scores of neglected films to my must-see list, or marveled at the fervor authors brought to their works. After three-and-a-half years, I am in awe of authors such as Richard Braff, Tony Harrison, Jerome Holst, Ephraim Katz, Harris Lentz, Frank Manchel, David Shipman, William Stewart, Graham Webb, and R. G. Young, who each spent at least a decade compiling their fine works, and of James Robert Parish, who alone has written nearly 100 reference books on film and filmmakers.

Looking back, I still believe it was a good idea. I have learned more about film and television and the resources that can be used to answer questions about them than I ever anticipated. I developed a deeper appreciation of the work that goes into producing a research guide and bibliography. And, for the most part, I had fun. Looking forward, I hope readers of this book will benefit from my lessons.

Acknowledgments

I would not have been able to write this book without the kind help of my family, friends, and colleagues. In addition to researching and writing around work hours, I spent two summers in Los Angeles and took a six-month sabbatical here in Albuquerque.

I owe many thanks to Kim Fisher, whose book *On the Screen: A Film, Television, and Video Research Guide* was one of the inspirations for this book.

To my colleagues at the University of New Mexico Libraries. To the wonderful reference librarians in Zimmerman and Centennial who picked up extra hours. To the marvelous instruction librarians throughout the library who taught extra classes—special thanks to Carroll Botts, who took on day-to-day operations of instruction while I was away. To the amazing interlibrary loan staff, who, despite the fact that I continually reached the system limit of 100 outstanding loans at any one time (only one person before me had reached such dizzying heights), were unfailingly friendly and remarkably quick.

To the librarians at the UCLA Arts Library, where I set up shop for two summers; with special thanks to Lisa Kernan, the Arts Librarian for Film, Television and Theater.

To my editors at Libraries Unlimited, who patiently accepted not one, not two, but three requests for extensions.

To my friends who put me up in Los Angeles and who put up with me as I wrote the book.

To my wife and children, who gave me unlimited support, who did without me Monday through Friday for two summers, and who must have thought I'd moved into our den during the final three months of the project.

1
Introduction

THE LITERATURE OF FILM AND TELEVISION

Film and television are now widely cited in academia as the defining arts of the twentieth century. This wasn't always the case. As with all innovations, it took time before scholars adopted the media as a legitimate area of study. In the earliest days, when audiences flocked to nickelodeons, the only publications to take notice were newspapers interested in the new technology and alarmed decency censors bemoaning the state of society. As audiences grew and exhibitors began building movie palaces, fan magazines like *Photoplay* took notice with fawning tributes or nasty gossip about the stars. Popular magazines followed suit.

Filmmakers stopped relying exclusively on vaudeville and literary adaptations and began producing original works that took full advantage of the medium of film. In the United States, the early producers moved to California and freedom and began to develop the studio and star systems. As war dampened the once-thriving European film industries, Hollywood prospered, pioneering sound, color, and new genres. People attended movies in record numbers and newspapers and magazines began to write reviews instead of relying on the publicity from studios.

Scholars from around the world became aware of motion pictures as an art form. They wrote articles in art journals and chapters in books. In the 1950s and 1960s, they began publishing scholarly journals devoted exclusively to the critical analysis of film. Libraries and archives began seriously collecting films. By the early 1970s, film schools were formed, reference book writers started to compile bibliographies and guides to the literature, and book publishers launched two major film indexes.

Television got a later start, but followed a similar pattern. As the number of networks and stations expanded and television became pervasive in households, newspapers and popular magazines were the first to take notice. Then scholars began to write articles, chapters, and books about television. This time, much of the reference literature was folded into the existing structure for film or communication studies resources. Because of the more ephemeral nature of broadcasting, libraries and archives were slower to collect television shows.

Film and television scholarship is now a mature field. Scholars use film and television to understand the world in which we live. They use a full range of historical, theoretical, and sociocultural perspectives and a variety of approaches and theoretical frameworks. Scholars analyze individual films and television shows, looking at how narrative, form, and technique make meaning. They study aesthetics, analyzing directing, cinematography, acting, and set and costume design to explain how the parts make the whole and send a message. They compare films and shows to the sources from which they are adapted, looking at author and auteur. They study themes and genres. They take semiotic or psychoanalytic approaches. They take ideological perspectives such as Marxism or feminism. They examine representation and identity with critical theories of gender, sex, race, ethnicity, national, postcolonial, and the "other." They deconstruct or analyze from neoformalist, poststructural, or postmodernist perspectives. They study how audiences receive and interpret media. They look at film and television as a business, considering production, marketing, distribution, and exhibition. And they study how the media reflects and impacts on society.

When scholars working in colleges and universities are not asking their students to make films, they are most likely asking them to examine a single film or filmmaker or to analyze a national cinema, genre, theme, movement, or time period in the context of one of these theoretical frameworks or approaches.

SCOPE AND ORGANIZATION

Film and Television: A Guide to the Reference Literature is intended as a starting point where interested researchers can begin their investigations by using the reference literature. Students, teachers, librarians, neophyte filmmakers, and movie fans may read its pages for brief guides to research directing them to books and Web sites. The focus is on movies and television shows: how they are produced, the people who make and appear in them, their content, their distribution and exhibition, and how they were received by audiences, reviewers, critics, and scholars.

The book does not cover the general media or journalism, which are well represented by two other research guides. *Mass Communication Research Resources* (see entry 10), by Christopher Sterling, James Bracken, and Susan Hill, covers "print journalism and media and the processes by which they communicate messages to their audiences." *Journalism: A Guide to the Reference Literature* (see entry 3), by Jo Ann Cates, covers resources that "focus in some way on gathering, evaluating, displaying, or disseminating news, opinion, or information in print, broadcast, and digital or online formats."

SCOPE

Film and Television is international in scope, covering English-language books published through the end of 2004 and Web sites available at the beginning of 2005. For a resource to be included, it must meet the classical definition of a reference source, meaning that it is not designed to be read from beginning to end, but exists instead to present facts or lead readers to other information sources.

Film and Television does not cover individual works or people. There are a multitude of resources about individual movies, television shows, filmmakers, and actors that would make this book so large as to be unmanageable. Fortunately, it is a simple matter to locate such books and Web sites with simple searches in a catalog or with an Internet search engine.

For the most part, *Film and Television* excludes general reference sources as well. I make exceptions only when all of the resources in a section are out of date and a general source covers film or television well enough to be useful.

Film and Television excludes all memorabilia and most trivia. In a few cases, however, I couldn't resist including sources that most reasonable readers would consider trivial (blueprints of sitcom homes). There are, however, no trivia collections. That is not to say that readers won't be able to use the guide to answer trivia questions. The range of information included in these resources is breathtaking and can be used to answer questions ranging from the trivial to the complex and serious.

The vast majority of the resources listed are either books or Web sites, with a handful of CD-ROMs. Based on the admittedly faulty assumption that publishers and editors weed out the worst, virtually any film or television reference book that fell within the scope as defined above is included. The major exceptions are resources such as directories that are so dated as to be useless. I was much more selective with Web resources. Fans are legion, and they are wont to share their enthusiasm on the Internet, creating personal lists of their favorite movies, television shows, quotes, actors, and more in just about every imaginable format. Many of them fancy themselves, rightly or wrongly, reviewers and critics. I erred on the side of caution, selecting only systematically well-organized resources that seem authoritative and accurate and that are updated regularly. For Web resources that didn't meet my standards, I include Web subject guides that should lead readers to many of the resources I left out.

Perhaps the most difficult decision I made was to exclude foreign-language publications. As a result, some of the most significant works on national cinema have been left out. In that case, the introduction to national cinema points to resources that will lead readers to these works.

PROCESS

A description of my selection process will help explain the organization of *Film and Television*. I began the book by creating a database. As I mentioned in the preface, I was in part inspired to write this guide by Kim Fisher's book *On the Screen: A Film, Television, and Video Research Guide* (see entry 4). Published in 1986, his work gave me a good start by allowing me to include older reference books in my database. I then examined every film and television book in the University of New Mexico and the UCLA library reference collections that fit my scope and added them to the database.

I sorted the database by Library of Congress subject heading (LCSH) and used each heading to search the Online Computer Library Center (OCLC) union catalog of 13,000 libraries using WorldCat for books as well as cataloged Web sites. I conducted roughly equivalent keyword searches of the Web using Google. In addition, I consulted *Books in Print,* book review sources, and research guides. I took advantage of the University of New Mexico's excellent interlibrary loan services to order books. Web-based subject guides were particularly useful in gathering Internet resources.

I anticipated that LCSH would make my task simple, but that was not the case. It turned out that some subject headings were too broad while others were two narrow. While most catalogers were spot on, many applied different subject headings at different time periods and at times seemingly at whim. I had hoped the International Federation of Film Archives (FIAF) *Classification Scheme for Literature on Film and Television* would provide a good template, but the reference portion, like almost every research guide including *On the Screen,* was organized primarily by format. I decided to create my own organization scheme as described below.

ORGANIZATION

Film and Television is organized by topic. After general guides and dictionaries and encyclopedias, the book is divided roughly into filmographies, filmmakers, and filmmaking. The general guides point readers to other resources in all areas of film or television. The general dictionaries and encyclopedias cover the entire range of film or television; specialized dictionaries and encyclopedias are placed in one of the more specific categories listed next. "General Film and Television Filmographies" lists films and television shows in the categories of national cinema and genre, made by studios or filmmakers, or featuring various groups of people. "Filmmakers" includes biographies and credits for filmmakers and actors. "Making Films and Television Programs" includes reference sources on making film and television shows. Each section is further subdivided into three parts: resources that cover both film and television, film only, or television only. See the table of contents for detailed breakdowns of each section.

The table of contents, cross references, and indexes help readers navigate. The table of contents describes the content of the book to three levels. At times it was difficult to select the appropriate category for a resource; in those cases, cross references point to related sections or to individual works. Indexes list authors, titles, and subjects.

A typical entry includes a citation number, standard bibliographic data for books and at least a title and URL for Web-based resources, and an annotation. Unless otherwise noted, I held every book in hand and viewed every Web site to write an annotation that describes the contents of the work with particular attention to elements that make it research worthy, and I make comparisons to other works when appropriate. Words in quotation marks are taken directly from the work, most often from the introductory pages. Although the annotations are not critical, I do include editorial comments.

DEFINITIONS

Film, Movies, Cinema, Motion Pictures, Moving Pictures

The terms *movie, film,* and *cinema* are often used interchangeably. In the book, I have tried to use *film* to indicate an individual work, *cinema* as a collection of films from a region or era, and *movie* as a popular term. Even though it is still the standard Library of Congress subject heading, *motion pictures* and the older *moving pictures* are for the most part obsolete. See Appendix A and Appendix B for more information.

Reviews and Criticism

Reviews and *criticism* are also often used interchangeably. In the book, I make an important distinction between the two.

Reviews are intended for fans deciding on which movies they should spend their hard-earned cash on a Saturday night or whether it is worth adjusting their schedules to tune in to a television program. The reviewer shares an opinion on the quality of the movie or show, discussing the aspects that make it worth screening. The reviewer assumes that readers have not seen the movie or show and try not to spoil the plot or the ending. Reviewers will often give a "thumbs up" or a "thumbs down" or rate the movie on some type of scale. The best reviews provide not only an idea of genre and story, but an idea of the kind of experience viewers will have in the theater. The best reviewers approach the level of criticism, but are held in check by the need to make a recommendation to consumers. Reviews are written when the movie is released or before the television show is aired.

Criticism is intended for scholars who study film and television. The critic analyzes the film in the context of a theoretical framework. The critic presents an argument and supports it with evidence. The critic assumes that readers have seen the film or show and are most interested in becoming part of a formal academic dialogue. Critics and scholars often extend their analysis beyond the text of the film or show, conducting research on the makers and the production, placing the film or show in its cultural and historical context, and responding to how other critics have received the film or show. The best critiques bring a new light to a film or show. The best critics prompt formal responses in the scholarly literature. Criticism can be written at any time after a film is released or a television show is aired.

INVITATION

Despite the amount of time I have spent and the care I have taken, I know that I have missed some resources. I fervently hope, however, that I have not somehow omitted a core resource in film or television. I welcome all comments and recommendations for corrections and additions sent care of Libraries Unlimited or directly to me at emmons@unm.edu.

2
Indexes and Bibliographies

The amount of literature written about film and television can be daunting. All of the resources in this section direct researchers to the full range of writings about film and television. Many of these resources, including all of the indexes and abstracts, cite film reviews and criticism. Resources that specialize in citing reviews include the indexes to magazines and journals by the Bowles and the Hansons and the index to critics' anthologies by Heinzkill.

GUIDES TO RESOURCES AND RESEARCH

Research guides steer researchers through the research process and direct them to the best resources. Although dated, Horak's *Bibliography of Film Bibliographies* contains the largest list of film bibliographies. Although there are many guides to film research, Cassata and Skill's dated *Television, a Guide to the Literature* is the only guide devoted exclusively to television. It is therefore worth consulting both Cates's *Journalism: A Guide to the Reference Literature* and Sterling, Bracken, and Hill's *Mass Communications Research Resources*, because they cover television well from journalism and media perspectives, respectively.

1.   Bukalski, Peter J. 1972. *Film Research; a Critical Bibliography with Annotations and Essay.* Boston: G.K. Hall.

Bukalski has compiled a bibliography for film students. The first third of the book lists essential works, film rental and purchase sources, and periodicals. The second two-thirds of the book lists books about film theory, production, genre, national cinema, biography, and more. Entries include the standard author, title, and publication data. Unfortunately, there are no annotations and there is no index, making this book of even less use when considering how dated it is.

2.   Cassata, Mary B., and Thomas Skill. 1985. *Television, a Guide to the Literature.* Phoenix, Ariz.: Oryx Press.

Cassata and Skill have compiled a bibliography on the literature of television. Divided first into broad sections covering communication, research, and the industry, the book is further divided into chapters on such topics as theory, genre, audience, politics, and criticism. Each chapter consists of a bibliographic essay followed by a bibliography. The essays are interesting but now quite dated. Includes author, title, and subject indexes.

3.   Cates, Jo Ann. 2004. *Journalism: A Guide to the Reference Literature.* 3rd ed. Westport, Conn.: Libraries Unlimited.

Cates, a journalism librarian, has written the premier guide to journalism resources. She selects resources that "focus in some way on gathering, evaluating, displaying, or disseminating news, opinion, or information in print, broadcast, and digital or online formats." Organized by format, she offers 15 chapters in categories such as bibliographies, encyclopedias, Internet sources, handbooks, and core periodicals. Entries include standard bibliographic data and a critical annotation that describes the book and explains how it is useful for research. Includes author/title and subject indexes.

4.   Fisher, Kim N. 1986. *On the Screen: A Film, Television, and Video Research Guide,* Reference Sources in the Humanities Series. Littleton, Colo.: Libraries Unlimited.

Fisher has written a guide to the film and television reference literature. Organized into 14 chapters by format, each entry includes standard bibliographic data and an annotation describing the book and comparing it to similar works. Indexes list author/title and subject.

5.   Gottesman, Ronald, and Harry M. Geduld. 1972. *Guidebook to Film: An Eleven-in-One Reference.* New York: Holt Rinehart and Winston.

Film professors Gottesman and Geduld have compiled a multipurpose reference guide to conducting research in film. The first part consists of an annotated bibliography of books and articles. Toward the end, they list award-winning films and supply a glossary. The middle of the book consists of a series of very dated directories of museums and archives, film schools, equipment suppliers, distributors, bookstores and publishers, organizations, and festivals. There is no index.

6.   Horak, Jan-Christopher. 1987. *Bibliography of Film Bibliographies.* München; New York: K.G. Saur.

Horak has compiled an international list of more than 1,000 bibliographies that cover film and film studies. Resources include not only the standard books, chapters in books, and articles, but also list homegrown "institutional publications" from libraries, archives, and more. Chapters cover formats, research, filmmaking, historiography, genre, national cinemas, people, organizations, and general bibliographies. Part II echoes the structure of Part I, but with an exclusive focus on Eastern Europe. Indexes list authors and subjects.

7.   Limbacher, James L. 1972. *A Reference Guide to Audiovisual Information.* New York: R.R. Bowker.

Limbacher has written a bibliographic guide for audiovisual librarians. He begins the book with recommendations on how to create a ready reference card file and offers his own list of the information most often requested in major audiovisual centers. Organized by format, the rest of the book lists books, periodicals, and reference works by subject and offers a glossary, publisher addresses, and a select bibliography. There is no index. As reflected in this annotation, Limbacher's guide is quite dated.

8.   Samples, Gordon. 1976. *How To Locate Reviews of Plays and Films: A Bibliography of Criticism from the Beginnings to the Present.* Metuchen, N.J.: Scarecrow Press.

Samples has written a reference guide to locating reviews and criticism of plays and films. The second half of the book covers film, with chapters on resources such as study guides, review and newspaper indexes, collected reviews, and film periodicals. Organized by the time period the resources cover, each entry includes standard bibliographic data and an annotation. Includes a title index.

9.   Sheahan, Eileen. 1979. *Moving Pictures: An Annotated Guide to Selected Film Literature, with Suggestions for the Study of Film.* South Brunswick, N.J.: A.S. Barnes.

Sheahan wrote this guide as "a starting place for research in the literature of film" for her college students. Organized by formats such as dictionaries, catalogs, film lists, and biography, each of the 10 chapters begins with a brief description of how the resources may be used for research. Entries include standard bibliographic data and an annotation describing the book and its use. Includes subject and author/title indexes.

10.   Sterling, Christopher H., James K. Bracken, and Susan M. Hill. 1998. *Mass Communications Research Resources: An Annotated Guide,* Lea's Communication Series. Mahwah, N.J.: Erlbaum.

Sterling, Bracken, and Hill have compiled a guide to 1,440 books, magazines and journals, CD-ROMs, and organizations that are useful when studying mass communications. They define mass communications as "print journalism and media and the processes by which they communicate messages to their audiences." The resources are primarily American, with one chapter devoted to international media. Ten chapters cover such topics as history, technology, industry and economics, policy and law, and audiences. Entries for published works include standard bibliographic data and an annotation. Entries for organizations include address, telephone numbers, Web addresses, and a description. Appendixes cover Library of Congress and Dewey Decimal classifications and Library of Congress subject headings useful for mass communication research. Includes an author and main entry index.

BIBLIOGRAPHIES

General bibliographies list resources in film and television. Some cover the full range of publications, while others specialize in formats such as articles, books, or Web sites. The largest and most recent of these is *Film: An International Bibliography* by Hagener and Töteberg, but *The Film Index* produced by the WPA with all of its supplementary and complementary volumes and Manchell's *Film Study* are all excellent resources. Other bibliographies worth consulting include Bowles' *Film Anthologies Index* and the various bibliographies by Rehrauer.

GENERAL

11.   Hagener, Malte, and Michael Töteberg. 2002. *Film: An International Bibliography.* Stuttgart: Metzler.

Hagener and Töteberg have compiled a massive international bibliography of books (and a handful of CDs) written about film between 1895 and 2000. The majority of the works are in German, English, or French. The bibliography is classified by subject, with chapters covering film reference, history, national cinemas, theory and criticism, technology, and social issues, plus one small chapter devoted to television, media, and video. Under each subject, entries are in chronological order and include standard bibliographic data as well as the contents of anthologies. The authors viewed all 12,000 works, writing brief annotations only when the title was not self-explanatory. The authors are German and used German libraries and archives to complete their work, but the international scope, the comprehensive coverage, and the fact that their bibliography fills a multiyear gap in the literature make this an excellent source for surveying the film literature.

12.   Manchel, Frank. 1990. *Film Study: An Analytical Bibliography.* Rutherford, N.J.; London: Fairleigh Dickinson University Press; Associated University Presses.

Over a decade in the making, film scholar Manchell has written the premier bibliography of film studies, covering close to 4,000 books and 5,000 articles. Chapters cover theory, genre, representations, themes, literature, periods, and history. What makes Manchell's bibliography stand above his competitors are his introductions placing every aspect of film study in context and his thoughtful critical annotations. Volume 4 includes a glossary, appendixes listing film critics, the Hays and Production Codes, the Waldorf Conference Statement, other now-dated categories, and indexes to article and book titles and authors, film personalities, subjects, and film titles. Useful to all film researchers, Manchell's is more than a bibliography, as it can also serve as a survey of film studies and is highly recommended to all libraries that serve film scholars.

13.   Writers' Program, Harold Leonard, and Museum of Modern Art. 1941. *The Film Index, a Bibliography.* New York: Museum of Modern Art Film Library and H.W. Wilson Co.

The *Film Index* was published as part of the Writers' Program of the Work Projects Administration in the City of New York for the Museum of Modern Art Film Library. As the first major bibliography of film, the editors succeeded in fairly comprehensively covering films and books as well articles from serious and fan magazines. Published in 1941, Volume 1: *The Film as Art* covers history and technique and types of film. The second and third volumes were published four decades later. Volume 2: *Film as Industry* covers publicity, distribution, exhibition, finance, history, law, and production. Volume 3: *Film in Society* covers censorship, education, and cultural, moral and religious, and social and political aspects. Entries for books and articles include standard bibliographic data and a brief synopsis. Entries for films typically include the year and country of production, a brief synopsis, director and principal cast, and citation to reviews. Volume 1 includes a comprehensive index, but volumes 2 and 3 contain only a combined name index. *The New Film Index* (see entry 15) and *The Literature of the Cinema* (see entry 18) were both designed to supplement Volume 1.

ARTICLES

14.   Gerlach, John C., and Lana Gerlach. 1974. *The Critical Index; a Bibliography of Articles on Film in English, 1946–1973.* New York: Teachers College Press.

The Gerlachs have compiled a bibliography of 5,000 periodical articles about films and filmmakers. Divided into sections on names and topics, it is necessary to consult the film title index to find articles about individual films (there is also an author index). Items are only annotated if the title is not self-explanatory. Appendixes include a bibliography of other film bibliographies, a list of magazines not indexed, and an outline of critical approaches to film current in 1974. The excellent coverage of 22 core film periodicals (as well as others) in a time before they were well indexed makes this a useful bibliography for examining films and filmmakers of the era.

15. MacCann, Richard Dyer, and Ted Perry. 1974. *The New Film Index; a Bibliography of Magazine Articles in English, 1930–1970.* 1st ed. New York: Dutton.

Film professors MacCann and Perry compiled this bibliography to update Volume 1 of *The Film Index* (see entry 13), the seminal film bibliography published in 1941. Unlike *The Film Index, The New Film Index* does not cover books or films, instead gathering articles from film journals and popular magazines published between 1930 and 1970. The bibliography is also organized differently, covering reference, filmmaking, theory, history, biography, industry, society, nonfiction, and case histories. Each entry includes standard bibliographic data and a brief synopsis. Along with *The Literature of the Cinema* (see entry 18), which covers books, *The New Film Index* is useful in covering film literature published between *The Film Index* and the advent of the two film indexes in the early 1970s (see entries 34 and 37). Includes a name index.

16. Post, Joyce A., and Catherine E. Johnson. 1979. *TV Guide 25 Year Index, April 3, 1953–December 31, 1977: By Author and Subject.* Philadelphia: Triangle Publications.

Editor Johnson and *TV Guide* librarian Post have developed an author and subject index to the articles published in *TV Guide* from its inception on April 3, 1953, through 1977. The index, much like *TV Guide* itself, is a microcosm of television history. From news, sports, and politics to business and popular entertainment, it's all here. Note that this is not an accumulation of schedules or a comprehensive list of shows aired. The index is of use not only to researchers and fans searching for articles, but also for those seeking patterns of media interest as reflected in the pages of *TV Guide.*

BOOKS

17. Bowles, Stephen E. 1994. *The Film Anthologies Index.* Metuchen, N.J.: Scarecrow Press.

Film scholar Bowles has compiled an index to 6,563 articles and chapters appearing in 716 film anthologies published through 1991. Bowles lists all essays dealing with film, but excludes articles on other subjects such as television and theater as well as anthologies devoted exclusively to summaries or reviews. The body of the work is organized by author, making it necessary to search the index for film titles, filmmaker names, and keywords. Entries are minimal, including the author's name, essay titles (occasionally including parenthetical clarifications of the title), and anthology title. The anthologies are listed separately at the beginning of the index and include standard publication information. Bowles intended for his index to fill a gap in the film reference literature, and he has succeeded admirably. His index will be of use to all film scholars who hope to supplement their research in books and articles with essays from anthologies.

18.   Dyment, Alan R. 1975. *The Literature of the Cinema: A Bibliographical Guide to the Film as Art and Entertainment, 1936–1970.* London; New York: White Lion Publishers.

Designed to supplement the seminal film bibliography *The Film Index* (see entry 13), Dyment has compiled a bibliography of 1,303 English-language books published from 1936 to the early 1970s that treat film as an art form. The book contains chapters on history, criticism, personalities, screenplays, technique, genre, film and society, and the film industry. Each entry includes standard bibliographic data and a brief annotation. Along with *The New Film Index* (see entry 15), which covers magazine and journal articles, *Literature of the Film* is useful in covering film literature published between *The Film Index* and the advent of the two film indexes in the early 1970s (see entries 34 and 37). Includes a name and title index.

19.   Ellis, Jack C., Charles Derry, and Sharon Kern. 1979. *The Film Book Bibliography, 1940–1975.* Metuchen, N.J.: Scarecrow Press.

The editors have compiled a subject guide to 5,442 "books published in English between 1940 and 1975 which deal with the various aspects of the motion picture." The bibliography is designed to complement *The Film Index* (see entry 13) and *The New Film Index* (see entry 15). The bibliography is classified into ten categories: reference, technique, industry, history, genre, biography, individual films, theory, society, and education. Separate title and name indexes guide readers to the appropriate entry. Although the classification system is indeed useful, it is unfortunate that the editors chose not to annotate the books. Now dated, the guide is still useful in finding books written about film and filmmakers during the days before film was well indexed.

20.   Rehrauer, George. 1972. *Cinema Booklist.* Metuchen, N.J.: Scarecrow Press.

21.   Rehrauer, George. 1974. *Cinema Booklist: Supplement One.* Metuchen, N.J.: Scarecrow Press.

22.   Rehrauer, George. 1977. *Cinema Booklist: Supplement Two.* Metuchen, N.J.: Scarecrow Press.

Rehrauer compiled his bibliography as "an aid for the large general audience that is interested in reading about the cinema" as well as for collection development librarians. With almost 4,000 works listed in the original volume and its two supplements, he does a remarkably good job. Works include books, scripts, memoirs, and just about anything of interest to a film fan except novels. In alphabetical order by title, entries include standard bibliographic data and a brief critical annotation. Appendixes list scripts published for films made through 1945, film periodicals, and study guides. Includes author and subject indexes.

23.   Rehrauer, George. 1982. *The Macmillan Film Bibliography.* New York: Macmillan.

Professor Rehrauer compiled his bibliography to assist readers in the "identification, location, and critical appreciation of books about film." He includes the full range of books written about film, but excludes fiction, novelizations, and scripts. The 6,792 entries are organized alphabetically by title, making it necessary to consult volume 2 for the subject and author indexes. In addition to its comprehensiveness, the best feature of the bibliography are the substantive critical annotations. Along with *Film Study* (see entry 12) and the *Film Book Bibliography* (see entry 19), this is one of the premier bibliographies on film.

WEB SITES

24.   *Cinema Spot* [World Wide Web Resource]. Address: http://www.cinemaspot. com. [Accessed: March 2005].

CinemaSpot.com is a Web directory of resources selected by an editorial team "that make it easy to find reviews, show times, video release dates, award-winners, trivia, history, quotes, celebrity gossip, industry resources and more." The editors have done an excellent job of selecting just a few of the best Web sites in each category, so this is a good place to begin a search.

25.   Deivert, Bert, and Dan Harries. 1996. *Film & Video on the Internet: The Top 500 Sites.* Studio City, Calif.: M.W. Publications.

Begun as a compilation of "cool film sites," Deivert and Harries have compiled a list of Web sites devoted to film and television. Divided into 24 chapters on topics such as actors, film reviews, movie theaters, and research and databases, each entry lists the name of the Web site, the URL, a rating of one to four, and a chatty description and review. There is no true index; instead, they have an Appendix & Cross-References section that is divided into academic, commercial, and professional categories. These are further subdivided by unlabeled subcategories—the only way to tell is that the alphabetical sequence starts again. Published in 1996, the guide is extremely dated.

26.   Finkelstein, Richard. *Film and Media Resources from Artslynx* [World Wide Web Resource]. Address: http://www.artslynx.org/film/index.htm. [Accessed: March 2005].

Finkelstein designed *Artslynx* "as a portal to the best information on the arts available on the web." *Artslynx* is strongest in the areas of theater and dance, but it also offers a very nice subject guide to film. Categories include acting, business, design, equipment, employment, history and research, magazines and journals, "mega-sites," organizations, schools, screen writing, sound and music, and film theory and criticism. Simple links lead to useful sites.

27.   Harris, Dan. *CineMedia: The Internet's Largest Film & Media Directory* [World Wide Web Resource]. CineMedia & Dan Harris. Address: http://www.cinemedia.org. [Accessed: March 2005].

With over 25,000 links, *CineMedia* has a strong claim to being largest Web directory of media resources on the Internet. The site can be searched or browsed in the categories of television, cinema, new media, radio, shows, actors, films, directors, networks, video, studios, theaters, organizations, magazines, schools, festivals, production, and research. Each of these categories is then further subdivided. Links to such a large number of sites can be difficult to maintain, and it is common to come across links to sites that no longer exist, but the sheer size of the directory is beneficial when seeking information that might otherwise be difficult to come by.

28. Madin, Mike. *Film Studies Resources—Academic Info* [World Wide Web Resource]. Address: http://www.academicinfo.net/film.html. [Accessed: March 2005].

Madin maintains *Academic Info,* a subject directory focusing on scholarly Web sites. The headings in the film section cover film history, film reviews, film festivals, international film, online film collections, classic cinema, film theory, genre studies, film archives, societies and organizations, silent movies, and directors. Sponsor and advertiser links dominate the top of each page, so it is necessary to scroll down to find his decent set of annotated links to Web sites.

INDEXES AND ABSTRACTS

Indexes and abstracts list resources published in an established set of magazines, journals, and sometimes books on a regular basis. The two premier film and television indexes are the *Film Literature Index* and the *International Index to Film Periodicals* with its complementary set, the *Retrospective Index to Film Periodicals, 1930–1971.* Indexes in other fields, especially the arts and literature, can also cover film well. Popular magazine and newspaper indexes and aggregators do a particularly good job of citing movie reviews.

FILM AND TELEVISION INDEXES

29. Batty, Linda. 1975. *Retrospective Index to Film Periodicals, 1930–1971.* New York: R.R. Bowker.

Batty has created an index to "fourteen film journals from their beginnings through December 1971." She designed the index to complement FIAF's *International Index to Film Periodicals* (see entry 37), which began publication by covering journals written in 1972. The index is divided into three sections. "Individual Films" includes articles, criticism and reviews, and interviews which devote total or significant space to a particular film. "Film Subjects" includes both filmmakers and FIAF subject headings. The third small section covers book reviews. There is no author index, although Batty does offer some work-arounds in her introduction. With the exception of *Sight and Sound,* which began publication in 1932, most of the journals covered here began publication in either the 1950s or the 1960s, making this an excellent resource for locating articles written on film during this era.

30. Bowles, Stephen E. 1974. *Index to Critical Film Reviews in British and American Film Periodicals, Together With: Index to Critical Reviews of Books About Film.* New York: B. Franklin.

Bowles surveyed American and British film journals to create an index to film and book reviews. Volume 1 provides standard citations to 20,000 film reviews. Volume 2 does the same for 6,000 reviews of books about film. Volume 3 contains the indexes to directors, film reviewers, authors, book reviewers, and book subjects. An appendix lists library journal holdings. The index is most useful for finding film reviews as well as book reviews from the more scholarly film journals in the era before they were well indexed by the two major film indexes.

31. D'Agostino, Annette M. 1995. *An Index to Short and Feature Film Reviews in the Moving Picture World: The Early Years, 1907–1915, Bibliographies and Indexes in the Performing Arts, No. 20.* Westport, Conn.: Greenwood Press.

32. D'Agostino, Annette M. 1997. *Filmmakers in the Moving Picture World: An Index of Articles, 1907–1927.* Jefferson, N.C.: McFarland.

The trade magazine *Moving Picture World* was a precursor to *Variety* and the *Hollywood Reporter.* D'Agostino has compiled indexes to reviews and, in the supplement, to filmmakers and actors mentioned in its pages. Entries for films include title and distributor. Entries for filmmakers include occupation and annotated headlines from the magazine. Both include citations to the article. The appendix in the supplement lists volumes by date. The index is an excellent resource for researching the silent film era.

33. *FIAF International FilmArchive Database* [CD-ROM and World Wide Web Resource]. International Federation of Film Archives (FIAF). 2001. Address: http://www. ovid.com/site/catalog/DataBase/211.jsp?top = 2&mid = 3&bottom = 7&subsection = 10. [Accessed: July 2003].

FIAF, the International Federation of Film Archives, combines several of its publications into the *International FilmArchive Database,* available by subscription via the Internet or on CD-ROM. Most prominent of these is the *International Index to Film Periodicals* (see entry 37), but they also include the *International Index to Television Periodicals* (see entry 38), *Treasures from the Film Archives* (see entry 741), the *International Directory of Film and TV Documentation Collections* (see entry 55), and an annotated bibliography of FIAF member publications published since 1966.

34. *Film Literature Index.* Albany, N.Y.: Filmdex.

Film Literature Index is the most comprehensive index to articles on film and television. First published as a prototype covering 28 film journals published during 1971 and then published regularly beginning in 1973, the quarterly index now comprehensively indexes 150 and selectively indexes 200 scholarly, popular, and trade film journals, excluding periodicals of "purely fan interest, totally technical data and extremely short pieces of press release information." Articles are indexed by author, names of filmmakers and performers, and over 1,000 subject headings. In 1986, the index expanded its coverage by devoting a separate section to television. *Film Literature Index* is the premier film and television index, of use to students, researchers, and fans alike. The index is only available in print as a quarterly soft cover or annual hardcover cumulation. In April of 2002, the National Endowment for the Humanities granted funds to the Indiana University Digital Library Project to convert the print index to a Web format—but as this guide went to press, the project had been halted by the Film and Television Documentation Center "because of editorial and artistic differences." So unless they resolve their differences, the preview version that became available online on January 30, 2005, at <http://webapp1.dlib.indiana.edu/fli>, which covers 1976 to 2001 and claims 700,000 records, will remain incomplete.

35.　　　Hanson, Patricia King, Stephen L. Hanson, and Julia Johnson. 1986. *Film Review Index.* Phoenix, Ariz.: Oryx Press.

The Hansons led a team of scholars and librarians in compiling an index to reviews, histories, and critical commentaries of "pictures that have established themselves as being of continuing importance to film researchers." Volume 1 covers films made from 1882 to 1949, and Volume 2 covers 1950 to 1985. For each film, they list title, country of origin, distributor, and year followed by a list of citations to the review sources with date, volume, and page numbers. Indexes point to films by director, year produced, and country where produced. *Film Review Index* is the most comprehensive list of reviews for the time period and belongs in every library with patrons interested in film.

36.　　　Heinzkill, Richard. 1975. *Film Criticism: An Index to Critics' Anthologies.* Metuchen, N.J.: Scarecrow Press.

Heinzkill has created a cumulative index to essays and reviews in anthologies of individual film critics' work. The index includes not only the films, but also filmmakers, actors, and subjects such as acting, French films, and censorship. The book is of most use to libraries that own the majority of the 40 books indexed and is particularly good for locating criticism from the 1940s through the 1960s.

37.　　　*International Index to Film Periodicals.* New York: R.R. Bowker.

The *International Index to Film Periodicals* (*IIFP*) is one of the two premier indexes to the film literature. Produced by FIAF, the index has a more international emphasis than does the *Film Literature Index* (see entry 34), with a particularly strong emphasis on European journals. Covering more than 300 scholarly and popular film journals, the index is broken into three parts: subjects, individual films, and biographies. FIAF has developed a hierarchical thesaurus of over 20,000 terms (see <http://www.fiafnet.org/pdf/uk/THESAURUS01.pdf>), as well as guides to corporate bodies (<http://www.fiafnet.org/pdf/uk/THESAURUS02.pdf>) and personal names (<http://www.fiafnet.org/pdf/uk/THESAURUS03.pdf>). The index includes separate director and author indexes. The *International Index to Film Periodicals* is available online as part of the FIAF *International FilmArchive* (see entry 33).

38.　　　*International Index to Television Periodicals.* London: International Federation of Film Archives (FIAF).

39.　　　*International Index to Television Periodicals. Subject Headings.* London: International Federation of Film Archives (FIAF).

Published as a biennial index to nearly 100 media magazines and journals beginning in 1979, the *International Index to Television Periodicals* ceased as a print publication and was folded into FIAF's *International FilmArchive Database* (see entry 33) in 1990. The largest section organizes articles by hundreds of general subjects such as "children, effects of TV on" and "pop music on TV." Other sections cite articles on programs, list biographical articles, and index authors. The entire run of the index, from 1979 through 1998, is available as part of the *International FilmArchive Database.* Since 1998, only articles about television that appear in film journals are indexed. Up until that point, the index had been one of the two premier indexes for researchers interested in television. Now, the best index is the *Film Literature Index* (see entry 34), which has a separate section for television. In 1992, FIAF published the fourth and final edition of a thesaurus titled "Subject Headings" used in the index to "facilitate the work of indexers and to increase the usefulness to subscribers." The thesaurus was folded into the *IIFP* thesaurus, which is now available online at <http://www.fiafnet.org/uk/publications/theasaurus.cfm>.

40.   *Media Review Digest.* Ann Arbor, Mich.: Pierian Press.

Since 1970, the *Media Review Digest* has served as an annual index and digest of reviews of non-print media, including not only theatrical, video, and DVD films and documentaries, but also audio books and software. Entries include title, production and technical data, and citations to reviews in magazines, journals, and Web sites. An appendix lists the year's film awards. Includes subject, geographical, and reviewer indexes and a producer and distributor directory. From 1970 to 1972, it was known as the *Multi Media Reviews Index.*

GENERAL INDEXES AND AGGREGATORS

41.   *Academic Search Premier / Academic Search Elite* [Online Article Database]. EBSCO. Address: http://search.epnet.com/login.asp?profile = web. [Accessed: March 2005].

Academic Search Premier indexes and abstracts over 14,000 popular magazines and scholarly journals and offers full-text access to over 4,500 of them. Two dozen of the journals deal with film or television, with only a half dozen available in full text online. Most coverage begins in the 1980s or 1990s, but *Premier* does cover a handful of journals beginning in the 1960s. EBSCO, the host and interface provider, offers searching or browsing by virtually any field. Results include standard bibliographic data and an annotation. Despite the small number of journals, *Academic Search Premier*'s multidisciplinary approach makes it a decent source for scholarly film criticism and, with coverage of popular magazines, an excellent source for movie and television reviews. *Academic Search Elite* is a subset of the larger *Premier,* indexing nearly 3,500 popular magazines and scholarly journals and offering over 2,000 in full text.

42.   *Art Index / Art Abstracts / Art Full Text* [Online Article Database]. H.W. Wilson. http://www.hwwilson.com/dd/art_a.htm. [Accessed: January 2005].

Since 1929, *Art Index* has indexed the full range of art journals. In the early 1960s, it began including core film journals, making it one of the better sources for citations to film literature written in the decade before the launch of indexes devoted specifically to film. H.W. Wilson began offering an online version in 1984, abstracts in the mid-nineties with *Art Abstracts,* and select full-text articles in 1997 with *Art Full Text.* Art Index and Art Abstracts are available online through several database vendors. Recently, the publisher converted the older print indexes to online with *Art Index Retrospective: 1929–1984.* When consulting the print version of the index, keep in mind that the terms "moving pictures" and "moving picture plays" were used before 1978, and the term "motion pictures" has been used since that time.

43. *Expanded Academic ASAP / Academic ASAP* [Online Article Database]. Gale Group. http://www.gale.com/ExpandedAcademic/. [Accessed: March 2005].

Expanded Academic ASAP indexes and abstracts over 3,700 popular magazines and scholarly journals and offers full-text access to over 2,000 of them, with most coverage beginning in the 1980s or 1990s. Gale, the host and interface provider, offers searching by virtually any field and browsing by subject or periodical title. Results include standard bibliographic data and an annotation. Although only 11 of the journals in the database specialize in film and only 4 of those offer full text, *Expanded Academic ASAP*'s multidisciplinary approach makes it an adequate source for scholarly film criticism and, with coverage of popular magazines, an excellent source for movie and television reviews. *Academic ASAP* is a subset of the larger *Expanded* version, indexing 1,200 popular magazines and scholarly journals and offering over 700 in full text.

44. *Ethnic NewsWatch* [Online Article Database]. ProQuest Information and Learning. Address: http://proquest.umi.com. [Accessed: March 2005].

Ethnic NewsWatch provides the full text of articles from 261 newspapers and magazines published by the ethnic, minority, and native U.S. press from 1960 to the present. ProQuest, the host and interface provider, offers searching by virtually any field, including by ethnic group. Results include standard bibliographic data and the full text of the article. For film, the best use of *Ethnic NewsWatch* is to locate movie reviews with alternate perspectives and of movies that might not receive full coverage in the mainstream press.

45. *International Index to the Performing Arts (IIPA)* [Online Article Database]. Chadwyck-Healey. Address: http://iipa.chadwyck.com. [Accessed: March 2005].

IIPA indexes and abstracts performing arts journals. Seventy-one of the journals indexed list film or television as a subject, with the vast majority of these covering film rather than television. Most journals are indexed beginning in the mid- to late 1990s, with a handful indexed back to the first volume. Chadwyck-Healey offers both a simple search and an advanced search form with fields for keyword, subject, document type, and each of the elements of a standard citation. The field for "work as subject" is particularly useful for film. Abstracts are included for all records beginning in 1998. *IIPA* is definitely worth consulting when researching film.

46. *Lexis-Nexis Academic Universe* [Online Article Database]. LexisNexis. Address: http://web.lexis-nexis.com/universe. [Accessed: March 2005].

Lexis-Nexis Academic Universe provides the full text of "5,900 news, business, legal, medical, and reference publications" beginning for the most part in the 1980s. *Lexis-Nexis* arranges its publications into "libraries" gathering similar publications. The most useful search interface for film and television researchers is the "guided news search," which leads to the various news libraries, including a subset called "general news" that offers access to newspapers and popular magazines. *Lexis-Nexis* offers searching of words in the title, full text, and photo captions. The extensive coverage of newspapers and popular magazines make *Lexis-Nexis* an excellent source for movie and television reviews.

47. *MLA International Bibliography of Books and Articles on the Modern Languages and Literatures.* New York: Modern Language Association of America.

Since 1921, the *MLA Bibliography* has indexed literature journals. Today, the MLA indexes over 4,000 journals, books, dissertations, and proceedings in not only literature, but in linguistics, folklore, drama, and film. For film, these include 75 peer reviewed journals, 51 journals that are not peer reviewed, and 5 series that list film as one of the subjects they cover. Entries include standard bibliographic elements and subject headings unique to MLA. MLA is available online back to 1963 through several database vendors. Because of its academic emphasis and the fact that film criticism is often written in literary journals, the *MLA Bibliography* is an excellent place to locate film scholarship.

48. *NewsBank / NewsBank Review of the Arts.* New Canaan, Conn.: NewsBank.

Before 1991, NewsBank selected articles from over 450 newspapers to include on a microfiche set. It published monthly indexes which were then cumulated into an annual index. From 1978 to 1997, the Film and Television Index portion of the *Review of the Arts* included film and television show titles, directors, cast, national origin, genres, and subjects. Entries list the article title and the microfiche number, which readers use to retrieve the article. NewsBank has been available online since 1991.

49. *Readers' Guide to Periodical Literature / Readers' Guide Abstracts / Readers' Guide Full Text* [Online Article Database]. H.W. Wilson. http://www.hwwilson.com/databases/readersg.htm. [Accessed: January 2005].

Since 1890, the *Readers' Guide to Periodical Literature* has indexed the full range of popular magazines. Because popular magazines often review movies, *Readers' Guide* is one of the best sources for citations to movie reviews written in the early days of cinema. H.W. Wilson began offering an online version in 1983, abstracts in the mid-nineties with *Readers' Guide Abstracts,* and select full-text articles in 1994 with *Readers' Guide Full Text.* Both are available online through several database vendors. Recently, the publisher converted the older print indexes to online with *Readers' Guide Retrospective: 1890–1982.* When consulting the print version of the index, keep in mind that the terms "moving pictures" and "moving picture plays" were used before 1978, and the term "motion pictures" has been used since that time.

JOURNALS

The *Union List of Film Periodicals* and *Film, Television, and Video Periodicals* both do an excellent job of listing film periodicals. Because both are dated, I have included *Ulrich's* for the most comprehensive current listings and *Magazines for Libraries* for current descriptions and recommendations. Slide provides excellent historical overviews of journals.

50. Brady, Anna, Richard Wall, and Carolynn Newitt Weiner. 1984. *Union List of Film Periodicals: Holdings of Selected American Collections.* Westport, Conn.: Greenwood Press.

Librarians Brady and Wall surveyed 35 American "libraries and research centers with considerable film periodical holdings," including the Library of Congress. The result is an alphabetical list of film periodicals listing title(s), country and language of publication, ISSN, and publication dates followed by a list of libraries by National Union Catalog (NUC) code with years of holdings. Supplementary materials include a guide to NUC codes, an index of title changes, and a geographical index. Although dated in the online era, the holdings statements can still be useful for historical work, especially as a starting point to see what film periodicals existed and to see who owned them.

51.   LaGuardia, Cheryl, William A. Katz, and Linda Sternberg Katz. 2004. *Magazines for Libraries: For the General Reader and School, Junior College, College, University, and Public Libraries.* 13th ed. New Providence, N.J.: R.R. Bowker.

   Magazines for Libraries recommends nearly 7,000 magazines and journals in dozens of subject areas to which libraries may wish to subscribe. Separate chapters cover films; media and AV; and television, video, and radio. Each chapter begins with an introduction, a recommendation for core periodicals for elementary, high school, general, specialized adult, and academic audiences, and the basic indexes and abstracts. Entries include ISSN, date of publication, price, circulation, publisher address, and a description and history of the magazine or journal. Includes a title and subject index. *Magazines for Libraries* is updated regularly, so it can serve as an update to older reference guides that specialize in film as well as an excellent guide in its own right.

52.   Loughney, Katharine. 1991. *Film, Television, and Video Periodicals: A Comprehensive Annotated List, Garland Reference Library of the Humanities; Vol. 1032.* New York: Garland.

   Loughney has compiled a comprehensive international list of film, television, and video periodicals available in the United States. She includes both scholarly journals and fan magazines that were in print at the time of publication. Entries are in alphabetical order by title, listing publisher, publisher's address, and ISSN when available. An annotation describes the publication and its typical contents. Indexes are geographical; they list film, television, and video periodicals; cover popular, scholarly, and technical periodicals; and name annuals. Despite its age, the catalog is very useful for the journals that still exist and for its annotations.

53.   Slide, Anthony. 1985. *International Film, Radio, and Television Journals, Historical Guides to the World's Periodicals and Newspapers.* Westport, Conn.: Greenwood Press.

   Film researcher Slide has compiled a historical dictionary of over 200 magazines and journals devoted to film and television. Slide writes an essay evaluating each periodical, "offering insights into the journal's critical stance and historical background." He lists where the periodical is indexed, if it has been reprinted, and which libraries own complete runs. A publication history lists title changes, dates published, the publisher, and the editor. Since the body of the work covers magazines and journals of interest to researchers, separate appendixes cover fan club journals, fan magazines, in-house journals, and national film journals. Additional indexes list journals by country and by subject. Although dated, Slide's book is still the best historical guide to film periodicals. Includes an index.

54.   *Ulrich's Periodicals Directory, 2005: Including Irregular Serials & Annuals* (43rd). R.R. Bowker. 2004. Address: http://www.ulrichsweb.com. [Accessed: March 2005].

Ulrich's Periodicals Directory is an international directory of scholarly journals, popular magazines, trade journals, newspapers, newsletters, and indexing and abstracting services from over 200 countries. From its vast database of 186,100 periodicals, 1,727 currently active periodicals list either motion pictures or television as a subject, with 163 of these scholarly. *Ulrich's* is searchable by every element in the record, which includes standard bibliographic data, type of periodical, country, language, subject, and subscription information. The print version is classified by broad subject and includes separate sections for motion pictures and, under the communications section, for television and cable and for video. *Ulrich's* is the best place to find updated comprehensive lists of magazines and journals when the sources designed specifically for film or television are outdated.

ARCHIVES, LIBRARIES, AND MUSEUMS

When studying film and television, the film and the show are the primary source material. Ideally, the researcher has the opportunity to view the film or show in its original format. For film, the best solution is to find a copy in an archive, library, or museum by using one of the catalogs listed below. If this is not possible, then obtaining a copy on DVD or video becomes necessary (see under Portals in the next section for means of purchasing, renting, or downloading films and television shows).

55.   Beauclair, René, Nancy Goldman, and International Federation of Film Archives. 1994. *International Directory of Film and TV Documentation Collections.* London: Fédération Internationale des Archives du Film.

FIAF has compiled a directory of 145 film archives located in 54 countries. Organized by country, the directory includes the archive name, address and phone number, date founded, areas of specialization, staff, and hours. Each entry describes the collections held in various formats. Indexes list institutions, special collections, and individuals. Although dated, the directory is still valuable in its ability to convey the scope of each archive. The directory was updated in 2002 and added to the FIAF *International Filmarchive Database* (see entry 33). The directory of the 127 current affiliates is available at the FIAF Web site <http://www.fiafnet.org/uk/members/directory.cfm> with no description of the collections—offering instead a link to each archive's Web site.

56.   Kirchner, Daniela, Memory Archives Programmes, MEDIA Programme of the European Union, and British Universities Film & Video Council. 1995. *Film and Television Collections in Europe: The Map-TV Guide.* 1st ed. London; New York: Blueprint.

The MEDIA Programme of the European Union has compiled a directory of over 1,900 film and television archives in Europe. The archives are organized by country and include the history and purpose of the archive and a description of the collections, including cataloging, access, and copyright information. An appendix lists research organizations and indexes list collections by country and subject.

57.   Klaue, Wolfgang. 1993. *World Directory of Moving Image and Sound Archives, Film, Television, Sound Archive Series; Vol. 5.* München; New Providence, N.J.: K.G. Saur.

Klaue has compiled a country-by-country directory of audiovisual archives. Each entry includes the address and phone number, an overview of the collections, means of accessing the archives, and fees and copyright details. Because the directory is based on survey results, the information is only as complete and correct as the respondents could make it. And because such directories are dated almost as soon as they are published, it is a good idea to double check online for more updated information on individual archives.

58.   Morgan, Jenny. 1996. *Film Researcher's Handbook: A Guide to Sources in North America, South America, Asia, Australasia and Africa.* London; New York: Routledge.

Film researcher Morgan has compiled a "comprehensive reference guide to international film and video libraries, archives and collections." The handbook excludes Europe, which is covered in a similar fashion by *Film and Television Collections in Europe: The Map-TV Guide* (see entry 56). The first part of the book is organized by country, with sources listed in alphabetical order. The second lists companies by subject. The third part lists national archives. Each entry lists name, subjects, contact information, description, and hours. Additional information includes the type of stock, whether research is allowed by either staff or visitors, and the procedure for accessing the stock. Separate indexes point to subject, source, and place. The handbook will be of most use to researchers and filmmakers seeking footage, and it is recommended that any information obtained here is confirmed online to make sure rules of access have not changed.

59.   *Moving Image Collections (MIC)* [World Wide Web Resource]. Address: http://mic.imtc.gatech.edu. [Accessed: January 2005].

Moving Images Collections (MIC) offers a directory of film and television archives with descriptions of their collections. Sponsored by the Library of Congress and the Association of Moving Image Archivists, most of the archives reside in the United States, Canada, and Great Britain, but Australia, Denmark, Guatemala, Germany, Mexico, the Netherlands, New Zealand, and Puerto Rico are also represented. Each record contains a link to the archive's Web site, a profile of its collections and services, and information on how to obtain images. Both the repositories and their collections may be searched by keyword or located by browsing. Eventually, the archivists' goal is to "create the nation's first integrated online union catalog of moving images."

60.   *The Museum of Broadcast Communications* [World Wide Web Resource]. Museum of Broadcast Communications. Address: http://www.museum.tv/collectionssection.php. [Accessed: March 2005].

The Web site for the Museum of Broadcast Communications offers a searchable database of its 13,000 television programs, 4,000 radio programs, 11,000 television commercials, and 4,500 newscasts. Each record includes series title, program type, air date, network, length, topics and names, and a summary. The museum also hosts the *Encyclopedia of Television* (see entry 139).

61.   Museum of Modern Art (New York), Jon Gartenberg, and Lee Amazonas. 1985. *The Film Catalog: A List of Holdings in the Museum of Modern Art.* Boston: G.K. Hall.

The Film and Video department at New York's Museum of Modern Art has one of the premier international film collections. The Web site <http://www.moma.org/collection/depts/film_media> boasts over 14,000 films. Although the catalog is not available on the Web, this older print catalog of 5,500 of its films is still useful. The collection consists of all genres and dates from the earliest days of filmmaking to 1985. Each entry includes the title, the release date and country of origin, a classification, the producers and production company, and the director. The book includes an extensive producer and director index. The films are now housed at the Celeste Bartos Film Preservation Center in Pennsylvania.

62.   *Public Moving Image Archives and Research Centers* [World Wide Web Resource]. Address: http://www.loc.gov/film/arch.html. [Accessed: January 2005].

The National Film Preservation Board at the Library of Congress provides links to the Web sites of film and television archives. Organized by continent (but the United States and Canada have their own lists), the links are useful for people who already know which archive interests them and who just want to find the Web site.

63.   Research Libraries Group. *RedLightGreen.* [Union Catalog]. RLG. Address: http://www.redlightgreen.com. [Accessed: March 2005].

Libraries and archives that are members of the Research Libraries Group have combined holdings of over 130 million books and other materials. *RedLightGreen* allows anyone on the Internet to freely search the database, locate records with standard bibliographic information, and link to catalogs to see if works are owned by local libraries. Because it is such a large database, it is an excellent supplement to local library catalogs.

64.   *WorldCat* [Union Catalog]. Online Computer Library Center. Address: http://newfirstsearch.oclc.org/dbname = WorldCat;done = http://REFERER/dbs.cfm;FSIP. [Accessed: March 2005].

WorldCat is an international union catalog representing 13,000 libraries and archives with combined holdings of over 57 million books and other materials. Produced by OCLC and available by subscription via the *FirstSearch* system, the database is searchable by virtually all fields, lists standard bibliographic information, and lists libraries that own each item. Because it is such a large database, it is an excellent supplement to local library catalogs.

PORTALS

Portals are Web sites that provide a complete array of resources and services. In film and television, these resources and services tend to fall into the categories of listings of credits, links to official sites and movie trailers for upcoming films, news from the industry, sales and rentals of DVDs and videos, movie show times and ticket sales, and television program listings. Because most portals provide most of these services, they are divided into categories of the service most emphasized by the site.

CREDITS

65.   *All Movie Guide: AMG* [World Wide Web Resource]. All Media Guide. 1991. Address: http://www.allmovie.com. [Accessed: January 2005].

With over 270,000 films and nonfiction titles and over 25,000 biographies, the *All Movie Guide* is one of the premier international film databases available. The opening page offers feature articles, lists of new movies, miscellaneous facts, and daily birthdays, but the real value lies in the database. The simple search box on the main page searches by title or name. Film entries include a one- to five-star rating, director, parental guidance and MPAA rating, box office figures, major awards, production company, and purchase information. Two-thirds of the films receive synopses and 1 in 20 include an in-depth review. Most entries list cast and production credits. Of particular value are the lists of genres, keywords, themes, and the unique categories of tones and moods. Because the database is completely relational, these are used to offer lists of similar and related movies and movies with the same personnel. Biographical entries include date and place of birth and death, occupation, years active, a career biography, a filmography, and awards won. AMG also lists the film-makers and actors with whom they have worked. The advanced search lets users search two people who have films in common, by author or title of an adapted work, by location, by technical process, or by creator. The browser lets users peruse lists by genre, country, or time period. AMG also provides a glossary of 1,400 film terms organized into 18 broad categories. Although best known for its *All Music Guide,* the *All Movie Guide* is every bit as worthy of attention.

66. *The Internet Movie Database: IMDb* [World Wide Web Resource]. Address: http://www.imdb.com. [Accessed: January 2005].

The Internet Move Database (*IMDb*) is one of the premier international film databases available anywhere. In pre-Web days, it began as a credits database put together by movie fans on the rec.arts.movies Usenet forum. Fans from all over the world submitted credits to the server in Cardiff for the films they loved. In 1998, *IMDb* was purchased by Amazon.com (see entry 87) in order to sell videos and DVDs, but much of the information in the database is still provided by fans as well as movie producers. *IMDb* claims to be "Earth's Biggest Movie Database," and with over 300,000 films, 80,000 made-for-TV and direct-to-video movies, 30,000 television series, and 200,000 biographical records, it makes a strong case. The typical record for a movie or television show includes title, director, writer, genre, a plot summary, parental ratings, country, language, and credits for cast and crew. A sidebar offers additional categories such as awards, quotes, locations, box office performance, and links to promotional Web sites and trailers. Users can rate movies on a scale of one to ten and make comments or write reviews. The votes are tallied to create lists of the top 250 films by all time, genre, decade, and gender as well as the worst 100 overall. The typical record for an actor or filmmaker lists date and place of birth and death, a brief biography, and a filmography broken down by occupation. Like most portal sites, *IMDb* also offers industry news, lists upcoming movies and DVD releases, and offers links to movie show times with the option to purchase tickets. *IMDb* offers a subscription service called *IMDbpro* for people working in the industry that features entertainment news and a calendar, production charts, representation and company directories, box office figures, and an advanced search engine that generates custom reports. Because 70 percent of the database is produced by contributors, users should beware that not all fields are available for all records and that mistakes can creep in despite the quality control efforts of the *IMDb* staff. Keeping this caveat in mind, *IMDb* is an excellent database, especially worth consulting for credits. Besides, it retains its spirit from the early days and is loads of fun for movie fans.

67. *Movie Tome* [World Wide Web Resource]. Address: http://www.movietome. com. [Accessed: January 2005].

Volunteer editors and contributors have created the content for this film database. The editor is expected to provide release date, MPAA rating, principal cast and crew credits, and a summary. Editors also volunteer to create biographies for filmmakers and actors that might include date and place of birth, miscellaneous notes, credits, and even a photo gallery. As with any database whose content is provided by the public, *Movie Tome* is only as complete and as accurate as its contributors make it. Older films and actors from earlier days are usually listed, but their records rarely contain anything beyond the most basic information. *Movie Tome* offers a similar site for television entitled *TV.com* (see entry 68).

68. *TV.com* [World Wide Web Resource]. Address: http://www.tv.com. [Accessed: March 2005].

Until recently entitled *TV Tome, TV.com* offers one of the most complete guides to television shows available on the Internet, with over 2,500 complete guides and "an additional 3,500+ guides that are partially complete or under development." Volunteer editors and contributors create the content for the database. An editor is expected to provide credits for the writer, director, stars, and guest stars and to summarize each episode. Editors also volunteer to create biographies for actors and crew that might include date and place of birth, miscellaneous notes, credits, and even a photo gallery. As with any database whose content is provided by the public, *TV.com* is only as complete and as accurate as its contributors make it. Unlike its similar site for movies entitled *Movie Tome* (see entry 67), *TV.com* has done a remarkable job in its range of coverage and comprehensiveness. *TV.com* is partnered with *epguides.com* (see entry 786).

OFFICIAL MOVIE SITES AND TRAILERS

69. *Classic Trailers* [World Wide Web Resource]. Address: http://www.classictrailers.co.uk. [Accessed: January 2005].

At the click of the mouse, *Classic Trailers* shows trailers from over nearly 200 films from classics to modern day releases. Divided into eight genres, each film lists director, principal cast, a synopsis, and the button to click to see the trailer. Requires Windows Media Player.

70. *Movie-List* [World Wide Web Resource]. Address: http://www.movie-list.com. [Accessed: January 2005].

Movie-List hosts trailers from current and upcoming films as well as from classics made between 1939 and the present. For each film, *Movie-List* includes release date, director, cast, plot, links to a review and the official Web site, and several versions of trailers in QuickTime format.

71. *MovieClicks.com* [World Wide Web Resource]. Address: http://www.movieclicks.com/index.shtml. [Accessed: January 2005].

MovieClicks provides links to the official movie Web sites created by the distributors to market their movies. Including current and upcoming movies as well as DVDs, each movie includes a plot summary, release date, cast, director, and a link to the official site.

NEWS

72. *Cinescape and Corona Coming Attractions* [World Wide Web Resource]. Address: http://www.cinescape.com. [Accessed: March 2005].

Cinescape offers news, reviews, and previews for upcoming movies, television shows, music, and games. The news is provided by Patrick Sauriol of Corona's *Coming Attractions,* which used to be a separate Web site.

73. *CNN Entertainment* [World Wide Web Resource]. Address: http://www.cnn.com/SHOWBIZ. [Accessed: January 2005].

News network CNN offers entertainment news and reviews daily for movies, television, music, and books. The current top 10 movie box office and Nielsen ratings are listed each week. Movie reviews are archived for just over a year.

74. *E! Online* [World Wide Web Resource]. E! Online. Address: http://www.eonline.com. [Accessed: March 2005].

E! Online offers celebrity gossip and news, reviews, and previews on the latest in television, movies, and music. E! offers a search box for names, titles, news, and features. Names include brief biographies with credits. Movies and television shows include production information, director for movies, cast, and summary. There is no indication how far back the database extends, but there are actors and films listed as far back as the silent era. Additional information includes weekend box office for current films and listings for the E! Channel's programs.

75. *Excite* [World Wide Web Resource]. Architext Software. Address: http://www.excite.com. [Accessed: March 2005].

Excite is a portal and search engine for the Internet. *Excite Movies* <http://movies.excite.com> offers news, lists show times for new and upcoming theatrical and video releases, and posts box office figures for current movies. *Excite TV* <http://tv.entertainment.excite.com> offers news, lists program schedules with an option to search by title or actor, and posts top Nielsen ratings for the week. Both may be customized to display viewer's favorites.

76. Franklin, Garth. *Dark Horizons* [World Wide Web Resource]. Address: http://darkhorizons.com. [Accessed: January 2005].

Based in Australia, Franklin runs an independent press site examining the media that contains news, interviews, reviews, previews, and trailers from movies and television shows. The movie and DVD databases provide a one- to five-star rating and list cast, director, and production credits, summarize the plot, and offer links to the trailer, the official site, interviews, and to critic's reviews. The TV Guide lists shows currently airing and archives older shows, including casts, air times, episode guides, and links to the official site and *TV.com* (see entry 68). Perhaps most interesting to movie fans are the news and previews about upcoming releases.

77. *Hollywood.com* [World Wide Web Resource]. Hollywood Online Inc. Address: http://hollywood.com. [Accessed: March 2005].

Hollywood.com serves up news and gossip from the entertainment industry, offers reviews, previews, and trailers of movies and DVDs, and lists current top 10 box office and DVD rentals and sales. Using information from *BaselineFT* (see entry 1034), users may search the database of films and celebrities to find production data, cast and crew credits, and plot summaries for films as well as news, interviews, awards, filmography, and biographical milestones for celebrities. E-Guide allows fans to search for local movie times and tickets, events, and television schedules by city or ZIP code without registering.

78. Knowles, Harry. *Ain't It Cool News (AICN)* [World Wide Web Resource]. Address: http://aintitcool.com. [Accessed: January 2005].

Since 1997, Knowles has run an independent press site examining the media. Containing gossip, rumors, news, reviews, and previews (not always authorized), his irreverent approach is sometimes controversial and often interesting. Divided into sections on news, reviews, and television, the site is designed for daily viewing, with readers becoming a part of the site as they share news and respond to articles. It can be difficult to navigate when searching for older materials; a keyword search option is buried deep on the left sidebar, and there is an A–Z browsing option on the reviews page. The site is of most interest to people who need to keep up with media news and fans searching for information on upcoming movies.

79. *Lycos Entertainment* [World Wide Web Resource]. Address: http://entertainment.lycos.com. [Accessed: March 2005].

Lycos Entertainment offers a quick look at the news and offers reviews, previews, and clips and trailers for current movies and television shows. *Lycos Movies* <http://entertainment.lycos.com/movies> presents feature articles, movie show times, and a list of current top 10 box office champs. *Lycos Television* <http://entertainment.lycos.com/television> offers feature articles and local television schedules.

80. *MovieWeb* [World Wide Web Resource]. Millennium Internet Corporation. Address: http://www.movieweb.com. [Accessed: March 2005].

MovieWeb contains news, interviews, reviews, previews, and trailers from movies. Its Movie Vault archive is one of the largest, with nearly 3,000 films and over 100,000 DVDs. A typical record includes movie title, tag line, release date, credits, genre, MPAA rating, and, for newer movies, a link to the official site and press kits.

81. *MSN Entertainment* [World Wide Web Resource]. Address: http://entertainment.sidewalk.msn.com. [Accessed: January 2005].

MSN Entertainment is a portal for movie and television (and music) content. The main page offers show times for films searchable by place or by film title and listings for local television programming. In addition to show times, the *MSN Movies* pages <http://movies.msn.com> offer features, reviews (from *AMG,* see entry 65), previews, new DVDs, and current and all-time top 10 box office champs. In addition to program listings, the *MSN TV* pages <http://tv.msn.com> also show features and top 10 Nielsen ratings for the week.

82. *Reel.com* [World Wide Web Resource]. Address: http://www.reel.com. [Accessed: January 2005].

Hollywood Entertainment, the company that owns Hollywood Video, hosts *Reel. com,* a site "designed to help consumers select and view movies in theaters, at the video store, or for purchase through *Reel.com*'s commerce partner, Amazon.com" (see entry 87). The site offers reviews of movies and DVDs, including a one- to four-star rating, credits for director and cast, trailers for movies in theaters, and lists of similar films through its "movie match" service. Clicking on a director's or star's name pulls up a list of credits. Films may be searched by title, actor, or director and may also be browsed by genre.

83.   Schmitz, Greg Dean. *UpcomingMovies.com* [World Wide Web Resource]. Address: http://movies.yahoo.com/mv/upcoming. [Accessed: March 2005].

Schmitz lists upcoming movies by title, date, director, actor, screenwriter, distributor, and video release date. Now hosted on *Yahoo! Movies* (see entry 84), entries include expected release date, distributor, cast, director, writer, source, premise, genre, filming, current status, news, notes, and comments. Archives extend back to 1999.

84.   *Yahoo! Movies* [World Wide Web Resource]. Address: http://movies.yahoo.com. [Accessed: January 2005].

Yahoo! Movies is a portal for movie content. The site offers news, reviews, and previews for movies and DVDs, lists show times and sells tickets online, shows trailers and clips, and provides weekend and cumulative U.S. box office figures for all movies in release as well as the top 100 all-time box office earners. Reviews include cast and production credits, a synopsis, and a reviewers' consensus graded from A to F. Stars are treated to brief career biographies and filmographies. Yahoo! also hosts parental reviewer *Movie Mom* (see entry 492).

85.   *Yahoo! TV* [World Wide Web Resource]. Address: http://tv.yahoo.com. [Accessed: January 2005].

Yahoo! TV is a portal for television content. The site offers local program listings, news, reviews, top 20 Nielsen ratings, and a database of current television shows searchable by keyword and browsable by show and genre. The database describes each show's premise, lists its cast, and provides show times.

86.   *Zap2it* [World Wide Web Resource]. Address: http://www.zap2it.com. [Accessed: January 2005].

Zap2it merged two popular Web sites, *UltimateTV* and *MovieQuest.* The television portion of the site features news, program listings, directories of networks and stations, and current Nielsen ratings by day, week, and season. The movies portion of the site features news, reviews, previews, local theater show times, and daily, weekly, and year-to-date box office figures. In the movies and the DVD and video sections, entries include the movie premise, credits, and links to reviews. Additional sections report on recent Academy Awards and major festivals, Tribune Media Services hosts *Zap2it* and licenses the same information to clients such as *Yahoo!* and *MovieFone* as well as major newspapers.

PURCHASE

87.   *Amazon.com* [World Wide Web Resource]. Amazon.com. Address: http://www. amazon.com. [Accessed: March 2005].

In addition to books and consumer goods of all kinds, *Amazon.com* sells new and used DVDs and VHS videos. In 1998, Amazon purchased *IMDb* (see entry 66), so the film and television presence on its home site is limited to information on new and upcoming releases.

88. *Facets Video* [World Wide Web Resource]. Facets Multi-Media. Address: http://www.facets.org. [Accessed: March 2005].

Facets offers 60,000 "foreign, classic, cult, art, and hard-to-find videos" and DVDs for sale. It is possible to search the database by title, person, country, and year as well as format or to browse select films in 30 categories by region or genre. Entries include a synopsis naming actors, director, format, country, release year, length, and ordering information. Facets sells the *Facets Video Catalog* (now at issue 16), listing 50,000 videos on 900 pages and offers a smaller video guide for free.

89. *Movies Unlimited* [World Wide Web Resource]. Movies Unlimited. Address: http://www.moviesunlimited.com. [Accessed: March 2005].

Movies Unlimited specializes in hard-to-find videos and DVDs. Its large database is searchable by title, actor, or director. Films may be browsed by genre first and then by subject or decade. Entries include a synopsis, category, director, cast list, production data, and ordering information. *Movies Unlimited* also sells the *Movies Unlimited Video Catalog,* with over 800 pages of "tens of thousands of titles on DVD and VHS."

The Scarecrow Video Movie Guide (see entry 177)

TLA Video & DVD Guide (see entry 150)

RENTALS AND DOWNLOADS

90. *Blockbuster Online* [World Wide Web Resource]. Blockbuster. Address: http://www.blockbuster.com. [Accessed: March 2005].

Best known for its video stores, Blockbuster now rents any three DVDs at a time for a fixed monthly fee, with free shipping, no late fees, and the option to keep movies for any length of time. Blockbuster's database contains over 30,000 movies sorted into 18 broad categories and is searchable by title or name and browsable by genre and subgenre. Each record offers a synopsis and lists cast, director, writer, producer, genre, technical and production data, and language.

91. Harris, Lew. 2002. *The IFILM Internet Movie Guide.* Hollywood, Calif.: Lone Eagle.

The primary purpose of the *IFILM* guide is to list Web sites where people can freely view films on the Internet. The first half of the book does just that, listing 50 films as well as a handful of shorts that double as ads. The second half of the book lists a small selection of reviews, celebrity gossip, and studio Web sites, while the appendixes contain sites for aspiring filmmakers and actors. As with any such guide, many of the sites no longer exist, but the book is recent enough that film buffs will still find the book somewhat useful. The *IFILM* Web site offers over 80,000 films of its own (see entry 92).

92. *IFILM* [World Wide Web Resource]. Address: http://www.ifilm.com. [Accessed: March 2005].

IFILM offers streaming video of over 80,000 "movies, short films, TV clips, video-game trailers, music videos, action sports," clips from news and media events, and a collection of "stupid-sexy-weird-funny clips" called Viral Videos. *IFILM* boasts that it delivers "more than 30 million streams per month." In addition to being a good source for commercial video, *IFILM* is an excellent source for independent films.

93. Internet Archive. *Movie Archive* [World Wide Web Resource]. Internet Archive. Address: http://www.archive.org/details/movies. [Accessed: March 2005].

Internet Archive's mission is to offer "permanent access for researchers, historians, and scholars to historical collections that exist in digital format." It does so by archiving the Web and providing a search mechanism called the Wayback Machine. It does the same with *Movie Archive,* digitizing films and making them freely available to download. The largest collection comes from the Prelinger Archives, providing access to nearly 2,000 ephemeral pieces of advertising, educational, industrial, and amateur films. Users may browse the Prelinger Archive alphabetically or by keyword. A typical record includes title, a summary, credits, and keywords with ratings and reviews by viewers. There is generally a variety of download and streaming options, often with an editable version. One interesting feature is the batting average, which measures how often viewing a record led to a download. Other parts of the *Movie Archive* feature movies, independent news, game videos, youth media, cartoons, movie trailers, and educational lectures. The *Movie Archive* is an excellent source of freely available movies.

94. *MovieFlix.com* [World Wide Web Resource]. Address: http://www.movieflix. com. [Accessed: March 2005].

MovieFlix.com has "over 3,000 full-length movies, short films, independent films, television shows" available for streaming on demand. A small selection of movies is freely available with registration, but most require a small monthly subscription fee. Films are listed under 30 genres and typically include the title, a one- to five-star rating, the stars, the director, the length, a synopsis, and a button to begin streaming.

95. *NetFlix* [World Wide Web Resource]. Address: http://www.netflix.com. [Accessed: January 2005].

NetFlix pioneered the business model of renting any three DVDs at a time for a fixed monthly fee, with free shipping, no late fees, and the option to keep movies for any length of time. The database contains over 30,000 movies sorted into over 250 genres and is searchable by title and browsable by genre. Each record offers a synopsis and lists stars, directors, genre, format, language, and MPAA rating.

SHOW TIMES AND TICKETS

96. *Fandango* [World Wide Web Resource]. Address: http://www.fandango.com. [Accessed: January 2005].

Fandango sells tickets to movies online. Searchable by city, ZIP code, or movie, the results screen brings up show times at local theaters. Selecting a time provides options for purchasing tickets at regular prices plus a small service fee. After purchasing the ticket, the viewer can bypass the ticket line and move straight to the ticket taker. Fandango offers reviews of nearly 200 movies showing in the United States and select theaters in Canada.

97. *Moviefone* [World Wide Web resource]. America Online. Address: http://www. moviefone.com. [Accessed: March 2005].

Moviefone lists movie show times. Searchable by movie, actor, director, ZIP code, or city, the results screen brings up show times at local theaters. Records for films include title, credits, release date, length, genre, MPAA rating, a brief synopsis, and a review from *Entertainment Weekly. Moviefone* also offers previews and trailers.

98. *Movies.com* [World Wide Web Resource]. Address: http://movies.go.com. [Accessed: March 2005].

Movies.com lists movie show times. Searchable by movie or ZIP code, the results screen brings up show times at local theaters. Records for films include title, a one- to five-star rating, credits, genre, length, and MPAA rating, with links to the official Web site and critic and fan reviews. *Movies.com* also offers box office results, previews, and trailers.

TELEVISION PROGRAM LISTINGS

99. *EuroTV* [World Wide Web Resource]. Address: http://www.eurotv.com/main. htm. [Accessed: January 2005].

EuroTV provides a program guide for over 180 European television channels organized by channel, by place, and as a searchable database. The amount of information provided for each show depends on the channel that supplies it, but generally includes title, type of show, air time, and cast, with most also providing a synopsis in the local language. Other features list programs on the air that day and group shows by genre, theme, or actor.

100. *TV-Now* [World Wide Web Resource]. Address: http://www.tv-now.com. [Accessed: January 2005].

TV-Now lists "appearances for over 5,300 stars each month" on U.S. national cable television. Viewers may browse by actor, actress, or director's first name or use the search box. The results list all the shows and movies in which they appear with director and star credits, a brief description of the show or movie, a one- to four-star rating, and where and when it will be shown. *TV-Now* also lists movies showing each month by genre.

101. *TV Zap* [World Wide Web Resource]. Address: http://tvzap.com. [Accessed: January 2005].

TV Zap is a portal for television guides from all over the world. Organized by region, each section provides links to local television programming guides. Most local guides reached via *TV Zap* require registration so that personalization and even customization is possible.

3
Dictionaries and Encyclopedias

Consult dictionaries and encyclopedias for factual information or an overview of a topic. Although the line is often blurred between the two, dictionaries define the meanings of terms, and encyclopedias provide broader explanations of terms and concepts, often including more in-depth definitions, historical overviews, and biographies. Dictionaries tend to stand alone, and encyclopedias tend to have separate indexes.

GENERAL DICTIONARIES AND ENCYCLOPEDIAS

102. Bawden, Liz-Anne. 1976. *The Oxford Companion to Film.* New York: Oxford University Press.

Broad in scope, *The Oxford Companion to Film* is intended "to answer any query which may occur to the amateur of film." Professor Bawden has succeeded in this goal, leading a team of film scholars as they created a dictionary of international scope. Most of the entries are for either films or filmmakers. Entries for films list principal cast and crew, summarize the film, and explain its significance. Entries for filmmakers and performers include a biographical sketch and a selective filmography. Topical entries are longer, giving in-depth coverage to genres, concepts, and theories. Other entries cover film companies and organizations, techniques, and technology. There is no index, but in-text cross-references are plentiful. The book is most useful for film and filmmaking before 1975.

103. Corey, Melinda, George Ochoa, Gene Brown, and American Film Institute. 2002. *The American Film Institute Desk Reference.* 1st American ed. New York: DK.

On behalf of the American Film Institute, reference book writers Corey and Ochoa have compiled an all-in-one fact book "about movies and the people behind them." They have divided cinema into history, basics, crafts, people, films, and sources. "Movie History" is a chronological examination of the significant films, people, and events of each year. "Movie Basics" covers how a film gets made, a glossary of terms, and a discussion of pay. "Movie Crafts" describes the various job specialties along with the tasks they perform, from producers and directors to actors and craftspeople to distributors, exhibitors, and critics. "People in Film" provides career biographies for the most prominent filmmakers with such sidelights as historical and fictional characters portrayed in film, minor roles that launched star careers, and a complete list of foot- and handprint ceremonies at the Mann's Chinese Theatre. "Films" lists the "most significant films ever made" as selected by the AFI, the British Film Institute, Academy Awards and other film awards, and box office. "Films" also features the best films by genre and in the world, and has sections on historical accuracy in movies, movie quotations, and Hong Kong cinema. "Sources" is a descriptive directory of major film companies and organizations, libraries and schools, and bookstores and video stores, as well as a guide to books, periodicals, online resources, and software useful to film researchers. The index misses on occasion, which is unfortunate, as this is otherwise an excellent and well-illustrated one-stop guide to film, filmmakers, and filmmaking.

104. *FilmGlossary* [World Wide Web Resource]. Address: http://video.barnesandnoble.com/search/glossary.asp. [Accessed: March 2005].

Barnes & Noble has licensed the *AMG* glossary (see entry 65) of 1,400 film terms organized into 18 broad categories.

105. Gardner, Garth. 2003. *Gardner's Film, Video & TV Dictionary.* Washington, D.C.: GGC.

Professor Gardner, an artist and animator, has compiled one of the standard dictionaries of the technical and digital terms used in the production of film, video, and television. His definitions are clear and succinct, although in some cases illustrations would have been helpful. Although the best reasons to consult this dictionary are the technical definitions, it is also useful for terms related to genre, aesthetics, and style.

106. Geduld, Harry M., and Ronald Gottesman. 1973. *An Illustrated Glossary of Film Terms.* New York: Holt Rinehart and Winston.

Professors Geduld and Gottesman have written a glossary of film acting, criticism, theory, and technique for students and the nonprofessionals. The authors have grouped a number of subdefinitions under approximately 20 larger terms. Written in 1973, the dictionary is now quite dated but can still be useful for its clear definitions and explanatory illustrations.

107. Jackson, Kevin. 1998. *The Language of Cinema.* New York: Routledge.

Jackson has produced an excellent dictionary to the critical, historical, artistic, technical, and commercial aspects of filmmaking and the production roles and institutions that make films. The definitions are clearly written and include extensive cross-references. What places this dictionary apart from many others is the author's attention to etymology in many of the definitions. Although sloppily edited at times, Jackson's dictionary makes a nice complement to the other dictionaries in this section.

108. Katz, Ephraim, Fred Klein, and Ronald Dean Nolen. 2001. *The Film Encyclopedia.* 4th ed. New York: HarperResource.

Katz spent years compiling his film dictionary. Now in its fourth edition, editors Klein and Nolen have made sure that it remains one of the best, containing almost 8,000 entries. The majority of the entries are on filmmakers, with brief biographical sketches that focus primarily on the career followed by complete filmographies when available. Other entries cover the artistic, technical, and commercial aspects of filmmaking. Definitions are clearly written, and longer entries provide excellent overviews on topics. Although numerous cross-references make a name or subject index unnecessary, a film title index would serve readers well.

109. Konigsberg, Ira. 1997. *The Complete Film Dictionary.* 2nd ed. New York: Penguin Reference.

Film scholar Konigsberg has written one of the premier dictionaries on film, covering every aspect of filmmaking from technique and technology to history, economics, and society to criticism and theory. Entries are clearly written, ranging to a sentence or two for technical articles to several paragraphs for historical or critical terms. Cross-references take the place of an index. This standard dictionary is of use to film students as well as filmmakers.

110. Law, Jonathan, John Wright, and Market House Books Ltd. 1997. *Cassell Companion to Cinema.* Rev. and updated ed. London: Cassell.

Broad in scope, the *Cassell Companion to Cinema* is intended "to cover all aspects of cinema life, language, and legend." Law and Wright have succeeded in their goal, covering not only the artistic, technical, and commercial aspects of filmmaking, but also including essays on the most important films and filmmakers. Film entries describe the plot, characters and actors, and the stories behind its production. Entries for filmmakers and performers cover the basics of personal life but focus on career and principal films. Topical entries provide clearly written definitions. All entries include extensive cross-references. The *Companion* is a revised edition of *Brewer's Cinema,* last published in 1995.

111. Manvell, Roger. 1972. *The International Encyclopedia of Film.* 1st American ed. New York: Crown Publishers.

Written in celebration of the 75th year of film, Manvell and a team of film critics have written an excellent dictionary covering the international history of film. The vast majority of the over 1,000 entries are career biographies of filmmakers and actors, but there are also a handful of national film histories, overviews on topics, and definitions of technical terms. The book is lavishly illustrated with almost 1,000 black-and-white stills and over two dozen color plates. The book begins with an extensive chronology of film history and ends with a substantial bibliography. Indexes cover title changes, film titles, and names.

SPECIALIZED DICTIONARIES AND ENCYCLOPEDIAS (SEE ALSO *FILMMAKERS*)

ACRONYMS

112. Stevens, Matthew. 1993. *Handbook of International Film, Television and Video Acronyms.* Trowbridge, England: Flicks.

Stevens has compiled a unique list of "over 3400 acronyms and abbreviations in common usage in the broad areas of film, television, and video." Acronyms are either for technical terms or organizations. Technical terms merely spell out the words that make up the acronym without providing meaning or context. Organizational acronyms not only spell out the name of the organization, but also provide an address and occasionally describe the purpose of the organization. There is a full name index and country and subject/theme indexes for organizations. A comparison to Gale's *Acronyms, Initialisms & Abbreviations Dictionary* shows very little overlap on the international acronyms.

BUSINESS

113. Cones, John W. 1992. *Film Finance & Distribution: A Dictionary of Terms.* Los Angeles: Silman-James Press.

Cones, a lawyer who specializes in entertainment law for independent producers, has compiled a dictionary describing the terms used in financing and distributing a film. He selected the terms based on his own practice, on conversations he had during seminars he presented, and on research from resources listed in a bibliography. Factoring in his introductory essays on the motion picture industry and film finance, the result is a wide-ranging and clearly written dictionary that will be useful to independent producers and to students trying to understand the movie industry.

114. Delson, Donn, and Stuart Jacob. 1990. *Delson's Dictionary of Motion Picture Marketing Terms.* 2nd ed. West Village, Calif.: Bradson Press.

Delson and Jacob's thin specialized glossary provides clear definitions of marketing terms. It is designed for people who work in the film industry in marketing, distribution, accounting, and law.

MULTILINGUAL

115. Carlson, Verne. 1984. *Translation of Film/Video Terms into French. Translation of Film/Video Terms into German. Translation of Film/Video Terms into Italian. Translation of Film/Video Terms into Japanese. Translation of Film/Video Terms into Spanish.* Burbank, Calif.: Double C.

This five-volume set of dictionaries translates English-language film terms into French, German, Italian, Spanish, and Japanese. All have pronunciation keys and are all divided into 16 chapters reflecting different aspects of filmmaking, including movie personnel and communication on and off the set with directors, cinematographers, editors, grips, and more. The books are intended for use on international film projects and are pocket-sized for easy carrying.

116. Clason, W. E. 1956. *Elsevier's Dictionary of Cinema, Sound, and Music, in Six Languages: English/American, French, Spanish, Italian, Dutch, and German, Elsevier's Multilingual Dictionaries.* Amsterdam, New York: Elsevier.

Published in 1956 under the theory that dictionaries of the day were obsolete, this polyglot dictionary now suffers the same problem. The dictionary lists terms and definitions for film, sound, and music in English, with indexes for French, Spanish, Italian, Dutch, and German. It's not fair to say the dictionary is completely obsolete, because many terms are still in use, but it is fair to say that it won't be of much use for any technologies or terms developed since the fifties.

117. Gartenberg, Jon, and International Federation of Film Archives. 1989. *Glossary of Filmographic Terms.* 2nd ed. Brussels, Belgium: FIAF.

Gartenberg has compiled a multilingual dictionary of film credit terms. The first edition covered five languages: English, French, German, Spanish, and Russian. The second edition covers seven additional languages: Bulgarian, Czech, Dutch, Hungarian, Italian, Portuguese, and Swedish. The entries are grouped by broad job specialty and then in English-language alphabetical order by job title. The terms and definitions are spread across two pages, with the original five languages receiving a column each and the additional seven languages sharing the final two columns and only providing the job title without a definition. The first credit index combines all of the roman languages, indicating the language, page, and column. The second credit index combines the Cyrillic languages. The glossary is of particular use to film aficionados who wish to understand the credits at the end of a foreign film.

118. Heidelbach, Oliver. *Online Film Dictionary* [World Wide Web Resource]. Address: http://home.snafu.de/ohei/ofd/moviedict_e.html. [Accessed: March 2005].

Heidelbach translates film and television job titles and key phrases into Albanian, Brazilian, Portuguese, Croatian, Danish, Dutch, English, Finnish, French, German, Hungarian, Italian, Norwegian, Polish, Portuguese, Russian, Slovene, Serbian, Spanish, Swedish, and Turkish. Users checkmark the languages that interest them before searching by keyword or browsing by broad category. Heidelbach cautions that terms may not be accurate and that English or German are the reference languages so that translations between two other languages may lose some meaning in their transitive relationship. Nevertheless, this online film dictionary is an important resource for filmmakers working overseas or fans watching foreign films.

119. Kent, George. 1980. *Motion Picture and Television Dictionary, English-Russian, Russian-English* = Anglo-Russkii, Russko-Angliiskii Slovar' Po Kinematografii I Po Televideniiu. Hollywood, Calif.: ASC Holding Corp.

Kent has compiled an English-Russian, Russian-English dictionary of terms used in the making of movies and television shows. Readers will have to know both English and Russian, because the English part is written in Roman characters and the Russian part is written in Cyrillic characters—without a pronunciation key in either case.

TECHNIQUE

120. Bognár, Desi K. 1999. *International Dictionary of Broadcasting and Film.* 2nd ed. Boston: Focal Press.

Bognár, a filmmaker, professor, and writer, has written an international dictionary for filmmakers defining English-language film and broadcasting terms and acronyms. The majority of the definitions are for technical terms, but he also describes professional organizations, awards, and festivals. Definitions are clearly written and offer extensive cross-references. Added materials include tables for metric conversion, radio frequency, and film speed conversion and lists of news agencies and television standards and systems.

121. Ensign, Lynne Naylor, and Robyn Knapton. 1985. *The Complete Dictionary of Television and Film.* New York: Stein and Day.

Eight years in the making, this dictionary of terms used by people in the film and television industries is still useful for production terms that predate the computer era.

122. *The Focal Encyclopedia of Film & Television Techniques.* 1969. London, New York: Focal Press.

Once the premier encyclopedia of film and television techniques, the *Focal Encyclopedia* is now too dated to offer more than historical value. Over 100 experts contributed 10,000 definitions of terms, with longer articles describing and illustrating the technical side of filmmaking and television production. Includes a separate index.

123. Ferncase, Richard K. 1995. *Film and Video Lighting Terms and Concepts, Focal Handbooks.* Boston: Focal Press.

Ferncase, a filmmaker and professor, has written a dictionary of "all the terms that cinematographers, lighting directors, camera operators and assistants, gaffers, electricians, and grips may encounter on a typical day on the set." His dictionary is a good resource for students as well, including clear definitions and illustrated when needed.

124. Fitt, Brian. 1999. *A–Z of Lighting Terms.* Woburn, Mass.: Focal Press.

Fitt, a film and television lighting specialist, has compiled a dictionary of lighting terms for use by filmmakers who already know something about lighting. Appendixes describe safety and British regulations and provide lighting charts, tables, formulas, and a guide to lamp construction for use by professionals.

125. Gardner, Garth. 2003. *Gardner's Computer Graphics & Animation Dictionary.* Washington D.C.: Garth Gardner.

Professor Gardner, an artist and animator, has compiled one of the standard dictionaries defining the technical and digital terms used in computer graphics and animation. His definitions are clear and succinct, including illustrations for a handful of terms. *Gardner's* is an excellent dictionary.

126. McAlister, Micheal J. 1993. *The Language of Visual Effects.* Los Angeles: Lone Eagle.

McAlister, a visual effects supervisor, has written a dictionary of visual effects terms used in film and television. Intended for professionals and film students, definitions are clearly written, but in some cases assume knowledge of basic visual effects. Graphics and photos are useful in illustrating various techniques. Indexes divide the dictionary into "terms relating to bluescreen and opticals" and "terms relating to computer graphics."

127. Schneider, Arthur. 1990. *Electronic Post-Production Terms and Concepts, Focal Handbooks.* Boston: Focal Press.

Schneider, an editor and post-production supervisor, has written a dictionary of technological terms used in editing. He "defines and discusses the equipment, concepts, and techniques of electronic post-production." With an intended audience of beginners and students, he often goes beyond basic definitions to provide more in-depth explanations. Photographs and diagrams illustrate terms as needed.

128. Singleton, Ralph S., James A. Conrad, and Janna Wong Healy. 2000. *Filmmaker's Dictionary.* 2nd ed. Hollywood, Calif.: Lone Eagle.

Singleton has worked on virtually every aspect of film production. From his experiences, he has put together a dictionary of terms used by film- and television makers. There is no introduction explaining how terms were selected for inclusion, but most of the terms come from the filmmaking process; only a few refer to such topics as awards, ratings, and unions. There are frequent cross-references under related terms. The definitions are clear and useful.

Film

129. Maitland, Ian. 1990. *Maitland's Film Editing Glossary.* Dubuque, Iowa: Kendall/Hunt.

Maitland, a film editor and professor, has compiled a glossary and reference guide for editors and film students. The bulk of the book is a glossary of terms used by editors. Entries are brief, clearly written definitions and only include illustrations when there is a need to clarify. Additional sections include an editing flow chart, a film footage and time chart, and an explanation of various reports written by other filmmakers designed to guide editors with examples. Maitland's guide is useful for editing with film, but does not cover digital editing at all.

130. McGee, Marty. 2001. *Encyclopedia of Motion Picture Sound.* Jefferson, N.C.: McFarland.

McGee has written an encyclopedia on the role of sound in film, covering "people, processes, innovations, facilities, formats and films." Inclusion in the encyclopedia is based primarily on winning an Academy Award, but other prominent historical figures are also included. The entries for films list the standard production data, cast and crew credits, and plot summary along with sections on the best scenes to watch that feature sound with an overall summary of the sound quality (McGee viewed every film but one). Entries for sound artists provide a brief career biography and a complete filmography. Topical entries clearly explain the sound terminology in lay language. Supplementary materials include Academy Award–winning films, a bibliography, and an index that covers everything but the credits and the filmographies.

131. Mercer, John, James R. Crocker, Patricia Erens, E. Nelson Stanley, and University Film and Video Association. 1986. *Glossary of Film Terms.* Rev. ed. Champaign, Ill.: University Film and Video Association.

Mercer led a team of faculty in adding and updating entries to reflect changes in film production techniques and vocabulary. Many of the new words are taken from the ANSI glossary of *Motion Picture Film Used in Studios and Processing Laboratories.* While the definitions are well written, the glossary suffers from obsolescence, as the computer era has changed filmmaking drastically. Still useful for filmmakers working with older technologies.

132. Miller, Tony, and Patricia George Miller. 1972. *"Cut! Print!" The Language and Structure of Filmmaking.* Los Angeles: Ohara Publications.

The Millers, film professionals both, have compiled a glossary of film terms that is still useful today despite its publication in the days well before computers brought changes to filmmaking. The glossary is intended for film students and filmmakers new to the industry, and as such includes terms everyone on the production might be expected to know. It is not intended as a technical manual. The entries are clearly written and are often illustrated with black-and-white drawings. Brief chapters cover the studio, studio personnel, film production procedures, and film budget breakdown. Although many Los Angeles–based film organizations have not moved, the film industry directory is still too old to be of much use. The 1977 edition is a reprint of the 1972 edition.

133.   Netzley, Patricia D. 2000. *Encyclopedia of Movie Special Effects.* Phoenix, Ariz.: Oryx Press.

Netzley, a popular culture writer, has written a guide to the "visual, mechanical, and makeup special effects" used in film. Three hundred sixty-six entries define special effects techniques, tools, and jargon; provide biographies of special effects artists; and give detailed explanations of the special effects used in "every movie to win a special effect Academy Award" as well as other movies that used groundbreaking special effects techniques. Entries are clearly written for the lay person and contain extensive cross-references and recommendations for further reading. Appendixes list special effects Academy Award nominees and winners, magazines, and production houses. Netzley has written an excellent guide for fans and aspiring filmmakers interested in special effects. Includes an index.

134.   Rickitt, Richard. 2000. *Special Effects: The History and Technique.* New York: Billboard Books.

Rickitt has written a lavishly illustrated glossy encyclopedia covering the history and techniques of special effects in film. Chapters cover optical illusions, models, animation, matte paintings, makeup, physical effects, and sound effects. Each chapter describes techniques in great detail with plentiful illustrations and examples from films. Special effects artists and significant films are treated to lengthy articles. A final chapter lists "forty of the most significant special effects films ever made" with entries listing directors and the effects crew and describing the effect. Supplementary materials include a glossary, a bibliography, and an index. Rickitt's guide is designed primarily for fans but will serve neophyte filmmakers as well.

135.   Schlemowitz, Joel. *A Glossary of Film Terms* [World Wide Web Resource]. Joel Schlemowitz 1999. Address: http://homepage.newschool.edu/~schlemoj/film_courses/glossary_of_film_terms. [Accessed: March 2005].

Schlemowitz, a professor at New School University, has written a glossary covering the production and technical aspects of filmmaking designed to supplement a film production course. Organized alphabetically as well as by subject, each term is clearly defined with hyperlinks in the definitions to terms defined elsewhere in the glossary.

Television

136.   A. C. Nielsen Company. 1981. *Glossary of Cable & TV Terms.* Northbrook, Ill.: Nielsen Media Research.

Media Research Services, best known for its Nielsen television ratings, compiled a guide to the jargon of the television industry. The glossary is an alphabetical list with cross-references. Because the definitions predate the digital era, the glossary is dated, but still useful for terms used in audience measurement.

137.   Brown, Les. 1992. *Les Brown's Encyclopedia of Television.* 3rd ed. Detroit: Gale Research.

Media journalist Les Brown has produced one of the standard dictionaries of television. Now in its third edition, there are over 3,000 entries on television programs, actors, producers, writers, companies, and technology. Entries for shows provide brief descriptions, while other entries go into more depth in describing a person's or company's impact on television. Although international in scope, the primary emphasis is on American and some British television. After a brief bibliography, appendixes list top-rated feature films, sporting events, and network programs, number of households owning television and subscribing to cable, FCC commissioners, worldwide advertising expenditures by country, European satellite broadcasters (United States did not have enough in 1991 to be included), and hours of television viewed per day. The index includes both the main entries as well as names included within entries.

138.   Delson, Donn, and Edwin Michalove. 1983. *Delson's Dictionary of Cable, Video & Satellite Terms.* Thousand Oaks, Calif.: Bradson Press.

Film marketer Delson and film executive Michalove have created a brief dictionary providing "definitions for the most commonly used words and phrases in the cable, satellite programming, and home video industries." Definitions are clear and concise, covering terms in use in the earlier days of nonbroadcast television. Supplementary materials include illustrations and international statistics. Useful in its time, the dictionary is now dated.

Encyclopedia of Television (see entry 766)

THEORY

140.   Beaver, Frank Eugene. 1994. *Dictionary of Film Terms: The Aesthetic Companion to Film Analysis.* Rev. ed. *Twayne's Filmmakers Series.* New York; Toronto: Twayne Publishers and Maxwell Macmillan International; Maxwell Macmillan Canada.

Beaver, a film scholar and writer, has written a dictionary of "techniques, concepts, genres, and styles" used in the analysis of film. His definitions are clear and easy to understand and are often illustrated with stills from films. He includes a term and title index that not only points to main entries, but also to terms used and films mentioned in the definitions. A topical index combines terms into broader categories.

141.   Blandford, Steven, Barry Keith Grant, and Jim Hillier. 2001. *The Film Studies Dictionary, Arnold Student Reference.* London; New York: Arnold; Co-published in the United States by Oxford University Press.

Film professors Blandford, Grant, and Hillier have compiled a dictionary for use by students in higher education that "provides signposts for the specialist film language that has grown up around both the film industry itself and the academic discipline of film studies." They include briefer definitions for filmmaking terms students are likely to encounter and more in-depth discussions of genres, critical theory, and movements. They specifically exclude entries for individual filmmakers, films, and national cinemas. The definitions include extensive cross-references and, for academic terms, recommendations for further reading that are cumulated in a bibliography. The dictionary is of use to anyone interested in studying film.

142.   Hayward, Susan. 2000. *Cinema Studies: The Key Concepts.* 2nd ed. *Routledge Key Guides.* London; New York: Routledge.

Hayward writes in-depth articles on the theory of cinema and "historical over-views of key genres, film theory and film movements." Her articles define terms and then discuss the history and theoretical approaches in great depth. Each article points to one or more entries in an extensive bibliography. There are indexes by film, name, and subject. The dictionary is an impressive individual achievement.

143.   Pearson, Roberta E., and Philip Simpson. 2001. *Critical Dictionary of Film and Television Theory.* London; New York: Routledge.

Film educator Pearson and writer Simpson have edited this excellent dictionary focusing on the "major theoretical approaches and definitions" used in the study of film and television. Major entries are substantial and cover concepts, theories, contexts, media systems, and media studies. Minor entries are much shorter and include relevant terms from other disciplines and biographies. In both cases, the entries have been written and the list of references compiled by international experts. Although the main audience for the dictionary is students, it will also be of interest to anyone studying film and television. Includes an excellent name, title, and subject index.

4
General Film and Television Filmographies

A filmography is a list of films or television programs. The filmographies in this section are general in nature, listing annual collections, cumulations from other sources, best and worst lists including award winners, and some oddball miscellaneous publications.

Because this guide does not include books devoted to an individual film or television show, it is necessary instead to consult local library catalogs or union catalogs such as *WorldCat* (see entry 64) or *RedLightGreen* (see entry 63). In most library catalogs, it is best to search by title.

ANNUALS

Annuals gather lists of films, plot summaries, reviews and criticism, and production information from one year into one or more volumes.

144.   British Film Institute. *Sight and Sound Film Review Volume.* London: BFI.

From 1991 to 1998, the British Film Institute annually cumulated the reviews published in its venerable journal *Sight and Sound.* Each film entry includes complete cast and crew credits, one or more critical reviews, and a still from the film. *Sight and Sound* reviews are also available in the *Film Review Annual* (see entry 147), so unless comprehensive coverage is needed and there is no other access to *Sight and Sound,* this annual is a luxury.

145.   Cowie, Peter. 2003. *Variety International Film Guide 2003: The Ultimate Annual Review of World Cinema.* 40th anniversary ed. London; Los Angeles: Button; Distributed in the United States by Silman-James Press.

Variety produces this annual guide to films released around the world. The annual begins with international award winners, *Variety*'s Directors of the Year, and essays on the film industry, but most of the book is a country-by-country film survey. A different film critic is assigned to each country, so quality and content vary, but for the most part each entry includes a discussion on the state of the film industry; a selective list of recent and forthcoming films; and directories of producers, distributors, and useful addresses. The rest of the book lists festivals, film schools, and film archives. The guide is most useful for otherwise hard-to-find information for countries that don't produce as many films.

146.   Ebert, Roger. 2004. *Roger Ebert's Movie Yearbook 2004.* Kansas City, Mo.; Burnham, England: Andrews McMeel; Derek Searle.

Every year, movie critic Ebert cumulates the reviews he wrote for the *Chicago Sun-Times* over the past 30 months into one volume. The 2005 edition is typical, including

674 reviews he wrote between January 2002 and June 2004. As in other years, he includes a handful of interviews and essays, obituaries, and film festival coverage. The reviews include a one- to four-star rating, principal cast, director, producer, and writer, and his critical commentary. The film title index points to editions as early as 1986—which had incarnations under the titles the *Movie Home Companion* and *Video Companion*—as well as to the current edition, and includes not only title, but release year, rating, number of stars, and edition. Current editions also include their own general index. Unlike his competitors, Ebert cumulates films one year at a time. Like his competitors, the value of his reviews will depend somewhat on how much the reader agrees with his opinions. All of Ebert's reviews going back to 1967 are available on the *Chicago Sun-Times* Web site <http://rogerebert. suntimes.com>.

147.   *Film Review Annual.* Englewood, N.J.: J. S. Ozer.

Published briefly in 1976 and 1977 as *Film Review Digest Annual,* this annual cumulation of movie reviews resumed publication in 1981. Each annual reprints reviews from over 20 magazines and newspapers published in the prior year, including such publications as the *Los Angeles Times, Time Magazine, Cineaste,* and *Sight and Sound.* In addition to several complete reviews, each film also lists cast and crew credits. Academy of Motion Picture Arts and Sciences, National Society of Film Critics, New York Film Critics Circle, Golden Globes, National Board of Review, and Cannes Film Festival awards are listed in an appendix. Separate indexes list film critics, publications, cast, producers, directors, cinematographers, editors, music, and production crew. Gathering reviews together in one place makes the *Film Review Annual* a convenient and essential resource for students researching how a film was originally received.

148.   Magill, Frank Northen. 1982. *Magill's Cinema Annual.* Englewood Cliffs, N.J.: Salem Press.

Magill's Cinema Annual serves as an annual supplement to *Magill's Survey of Cinema* (see entries 161 and 162). Published each year for significant domestic and foreign films released in the Unites States the prior year, each entry includes the film title, above-the-line crew, running time, and cast matched to character. Each signed essay delves into the history of the production and provides a detailed plot description followed by the film's popular and critical reception, a critical analysis, and citations to reviews. Appendixes list obituaries and awards. The numerous indexes include title, director, screenwriter, cinematographer, editor, art director, music, performer, and subject. In 1995, Gale purchased Magill and made the *Annual* part of its *VideoHound* collection (see entry 155), and at the same time increased the size of the publication substantially with additional films, credits, and a cumulative title index. Along with the base set, the *Annual* serves as one of the standard reference books for plot summaries.

149.   *Motion Picture Review Digest.* New York: H.W. Wilson.

From 1936 through the beginning of 1940, H.W. Wilson published excerpts from movie reviews. Each entry names the movie, release date, and actors. Modeled on their *Book Review Digest,* they excerpt reviews in newspapers, magazines, and trade papers that include "audience suitability ratings" and summarize and evaluate each film. The *Motion Picture Review Digest* was published weekly, with quarterly cumulations.

COLLECTIONS AND CUMULATIONS

Collections gather lists of films, plot summaries, reviews and criticism, and production information from many years into one or more volumes.

150. Bleiler, David, and TLA Video (Firm). 2004. *TLA Video & DVD Guide: The Discerning Film Lover's Guide, 2004.* New York: St. Martin's Griffin.

Bleiler, the buyer for TLA Video, led a team of writers in creating this guide to films available on video or DVD. Updated annually, the latest edition contains over 10,000 films. Each entry includes title, year, length, country, director, cast, a capsule review, a one- to four-star rating, and cost to purchase on video or DVD (the 2005 edition is the last year that will offer video prices). Although it includes fewer films than its competitors, its larger physical format leaves room for a scattering of black-and-white stills. Indexes list TLA favorites, country of origin, directors, actors, and themes. Appendixes list TLA and other awards as well as box office champion stars and films. Unlike competing guides, TLA excludes many of the films that it would have given one or two stars, so readers interested in the full range of film might not find every film they seek. As with all such guides, whether readers will want to use it to choose films will depend on how much they agree with the reviewers. The TLA Web site offers the same information plus the lesser-rated videos and DVDs in its freely searchable database at <http://www.tlavideo.com>.

151. Brown, Gene. 1984. *The New York Times Encyclopedia of Film.* New York: Times Books.

The *New York Times* has reprinted reviews of films from articles that appeared in its pages between 1896 and 1979. Facsimiles of each review are printed in chronological order over 12 volumes. Volume 13 is a cumulative index of film titles and "significant people, places, things, and themes." The *New York Times* is known for its excellent reviews, so it is useful to have them gathered in one place.

152. CineBooks Inc. 2004. *TV Guide Film & Video Companion.* New York: Friedman/Fairfax.

The *TV Guide* editors selected 3,500 films from their *TV Guide Movie Database,* which in turn were selected from the 40,000 entries in the *Motion Picture Guide* (see entry 169), to include in their new *Film & Video Companion.* Each entry includes title, a one- to five-star rating, production data, cast and crew credits, and a review condensed from the original database. Indexes provide complete lists of actors and directors and a list of all movies by star rating. The editors don't say so, but the *TV Guide Film & Video Companion* is an updated version of *The Movie Guide* produced by CineBooks in the 1990s.

153. *Cinemania 97.* 1997. [CD-ROM]. Microsoft 1996. [Accessed 1997].

Each year from 1993 to 1997, *Cinemania* combined Katz's *Film Encyclopedia* (see entry 108), Maltin's *Movie and Video Guide* (see entry 163), Ebert's *Video Companion* (see entry 146), Kael's *5001 Nights at the Movies* (see entry 160), and *The Movie Guide* (see entry 152) into one CD-ROM.

154.   Clamen, Stewart M. *Movie Review Query Engine (MRQE)* [World Wide Web Resource]. 144574 Canada Inc. Address: http://www.mrqe.com/lookup. [Accessed: March 2005].

MRQE is the premier site for finding the full range of movie reviews available on the Internet. Over 430,000 articles from online newspapers, magazines, and movie sites review over 43,000 films. Users search by words in the film title to pull up a list of films and the numbers of reviews for each. Results may be sorted alphabetically or by popularity, rating, or ranking algorithm. Selecting a film provides a list with links to reviews. Users may also use one of the "precomputed" searches by recent releases, most popular based on searches, AFI best film lists, or select film festivals.

155.   Craddock, Jim, and Videohound. 2004. *VideoHound's Golden Movie Retriever 2005.* Detroit; London: Gale.

A subset of the *Video Source Book* (see entry 156) intended for the general public, the latest edition of *VideoHound's Golden Movie Retriever* lists 26,000 videos available on video or DVD. Each entry includes title, a one- to four-bone rating (with a woof for the real dogs), year released, production data, MPAA rating, and a synopsis with commentary. Additional fields, each with their own index, include category, cast, director, writer, cinematographer, composer, and "kibbles"—a miscellaneous index covering adaptations, series, director/actor pairings, and prominent producers and special effects artists. Categories cover genres, themes, and scenes. There is also a distributor's index and guide. *VideoHound's* oversized video and DVD guide is one of the best is its class.

156.   Craddock, James M. 2004. *Video Source Book: A Guide to Programs Currently Available on Video.* 32nd ed. Detroit: Thompson/Gale.

This annual compilation is the most complete guide to videos "in print"— videos, DVDs, and laserdiscs that are available for purchase, rent, lease, loan, or duplication. Most of the two volumes consist of an alphabetical list of programs. Each entry includes the title, year of release, and a description. Additional information includes the intended audience and purpose, language, credits, and who can use the item. The distributor is listed, but it is necessary to turn to a separate program distributors section to get contact information. Other sections include indexes to alternate titles, subjects, credits, awards, and special formats. Although this is the best guide for video availability, the best guide to programming rights is the *Television Programming Source Books* (see entry 1197).

157.   Gathje, Curtis, and Larry Cohn, 2004. *2005 Movie Guide.* New York: Zagat Survey.

Bringing new meaning to "dinner and a movie," the Zagat Guides best known for surveying diners to find the best restaurants have now come up with a similar system for evaluating films. Rated on a scale from 1 to 30 in the categories of acting, story, production values, and overall, each film includes release year, director, principal cast, length, MPAA rating, and brief review cobbled together from comments made by the voters. At the beginning, the survey lists the most popular overall films and then breaks them down by genre, decade, director, actor, production value, and foreign language. Indexes list genres, decades, and categories.

158.   Halliwell, Leslie, and John Walker. 2004. *Halliwell's Film, Video & DVD Guide 2005.* 20th ed. London: HarperCollinsEntertainment.

Halliwell published his biennial guide to movies from 1977 through his death in 1989. In 1991, Walker began publishing *Halliwell's Film and Video Guide* as an annual. In 2004, he renamed it *Halliwell's Film, Video & DVD Guide* to reflect the fact that DVD had surpassed video in homes. The constant throughout the years has been Halliwell's name, reflecting his stature as a film reviewer and the personal stamp he placed on his synopses. The latest edition includes over 23,000 films in alphabetical order that include a zero- to four-star rating, standard technical data, a synopsis, a pithy and usually highly opinionated assessment (favoring films from the Golden Era), principal crew and cast, symbols indicating suitability for family viewing, whether the film has ever been released on video or DVD, and awards. Appendixes list Academy Award winners and four- and three-star films by title and by year. This is the longest running, although not the largest, guide for movie fans deciding whether to watch a movie on cable or satellite or to rent a movie. Preference will depend primarily on how much the fan agrees with Halliwell and Walker's opinions.

159.   Harrison, P. S., and D. Richard Baer. 1991. *Harrison's Reports and Film Reviews.* Reprint ed. Hollywood, Calif.: Hollywood Film Archive.

Harrison was an independent movie reviewer from 1919 to 1962, publishing a service called *Harrison's Reports.* Each of his weekly reports includes news from the industry, Harrison's editorials, and movie reviews. Fourteen volumes chronologically reprint his reports and include approximately 17,000 reviews in all. Annual film title indexes appear in each volume, and volume 15 cumulates all titles. The reviews are idiosyncratic and unusual in that Harrison accepted no advertising, meaning he felt no compunction in tearing a movie to shreds.

160.   Kael, Pauline. 1991. *5001 Nights at the Movies.* New York: H. Holt.

Kael was the influential film reviewer for *The New Yorker.* This book represents a large selection of the reviews she wrote for the "Goings On About Town" section of the magazine and has been updated from the original edition with approximately 800 reviews from the 1980s taking her through her retirement in 1991. While her reviews are designed to answer the standard question of whether a movie is worth watching, she answers the question with a flair and depth not always found in other reviews. Includes a name index. *The New Yorker* brief film reviews written since her retirement are available on the Web at <http://www.newyorker.com/online/filmfile>.

161.   Magill, Frank Northen, Patricia King Hanson, and Stephen L. Hanson. 1980. *Magill's Survey of Cinema—English Language Films, First Series.* Englewood Cliffs, N.J.: Salem Press.

162.   Magill, Frank Northen, Stephen L. Hanson, and Patricia King Hanson. 1981. *Magill's Survey of Cinema—English Language Films, Second Series.* Englewood Cliffs, N.J.: Salem Press.

Brought to you by the same people who created *Masterplots,* this set is one of several that provides the same kind of plot summaries for film. Over 100 contributors have written summaries for more than 1,200 English-language films. Each entry includes the film title, release date, above-the-line crew, running time, and cast matched to character. Each signed essay delves into the history of the production and provides a detailed plot description followed by the film's popular and critical reception. Most entries provide critical analysis. The numerous indexes include director, screenwriter, cinematographer, editor, and performer. There is also a chronological list of titles covered in the set. Combined with *Magill's Survey of Cinema—Silent Films* (see entry 740) and *Foreign Films* (see entry 254), and supplemented by *Magill's Cinema Annual* (see entry 148), this set is one of the standard reference books for plot summaries.

163.   Maltin, Leonard. 2004. *Leonard Maltin's 2005 Movie Guide.* New York; London: Plume.

Since 1969, Maltin has been cumulating his capsule movie reviews into one volume. For several years now, he has had to top the reviews out at just over 18,000 films in order to keep the one-volume paperback format. This has meant removing approximately 300 reviews each year. Beginning in 2005, a separate volume is published for classic movies made before 1960, and the annual volume includes only movies made later. Each entry in the current volume includes title, year and country of release, director, principal cast, a capsule review written by Maltin or one of his team, MPAA rating, and video/DVD availability. A selective index lists stars (earlier editions also had indexes to directors). As with all such guides, whether readers will want to use it to choose films will depend on how much they agree with the reviewers.

164.   Martin, Mick, and Marsha Porter. 2004. *DVD & Video Guide 2005.* Rev. ed. New York: Ballantine Books.

Now in its 19th edition, Martin and Porter provide capsule reviews of over 18,000 films and television shows available on either video or DVD. Each entry includes title, release year, a turkey to five-star rating, a critical capsule review, director, cast, parental guidance, and availability (select video/DVD sources are listed after the foreword). Indexes list cast, directors, Academy Award winners, and alternate titles. As with all such guides, whether readers will want to use it to choose films will depend on how much they agree with the reviewers.

165.   *Metacritic* [World Wide Web Resource]. Metacritic Inc. Address: http://www.metacritic.com. [Accessed: March 2005].

Since 1999, *Metacritic* has gathered movie reviews written by critics from up to 41 newspapers and combined them into one score. It does so by assigning a point value to each critic's review and then assigning each review a weight factor based on the stature and quality of the critics and their newspapers. The product is a "metascore" ranging from 1 to 100, which is then color-coded green for favorable, yellow for mixed, or red for unfavorable reviews. A typical film includes title, metascore, MPAA rating, stars, genre, writer, director, release dates, running time, and country of origin, with a brief description. Excerpts from each review are used along with links to the original reviews. The archive contains mostly films and DVDs released since 1999 with a smattering of older films from the eighties and nineties. *Metacritic* gives the same treatment to music, games, and books, because its mission is "to help you make an informed decision about how to spend your money on entertainment." If the theory that two heads are better than one is true, then the *Metacritic* site succeeds.

166.   Moses, Robert, and American Movie Classics Company. 1999. *Classic Movie Companion.* 1st ed. New York: Hyperion.

Moses, editor of the American Movie Classics Magazine, has compiled a list of more than 5,000 classic American films made between 1929 and 1979. Each entry includes title, release year, distributor, a review, awards, and cast and production credits. Supplementary materials include actor and director filmographies, Academy Award and box office winners through 1980, and several "greatest film" lists. Moses has put together a nice selection for all movie lovers, especially those who prefer the classics.

167.   *Movie Pooper* [World Wide Web Resource]. Address: http://www.moviepooper. com. [Accessed: January 2005].

On the *Movie Pooper* Web site, fans have described the endings of over 1,400 movies. Because the rest of the plot is not summarized, the out-of-context endings can be confusing. The site primarily complements the majority of summaries and reviews that are very careful not to give away plot twists or endings.

168.   *The Movie Spoiler.com* [World Wide Web Resource]. Address: http:// themoviespoiler.com. [Accessed: January 2005].

On *The Movie Spoiler* Web site, fans have sent in plot summaries for over 500 movies that are usually quite detailed and that always give away the ending. The site primarily complements the majority of summaries and reviews that are very careful not to give away plot twists or endings.

169.   Nash, Jay Robert, and Stanley Ralph Ross. 1985. *The Motion Picture Guide.* Chicago: CineBooks.

With over 50,000 films, this landmark publication was the first attempt at a comprehensive guide to English-language films. Over 25 years in the making, Nash and Ross succeeded admirably, providing a 10-volume set that covers not only the English language, but also covers several thousand foreign-language films and, in a volume written by Connelly, 3,500 silent films as well. *The Motion Picture Guide* excludes X-rated films. The films are arranged in alphabetical order by title, and entries include a one- to five-star rating, year of release, running time, production and distribution companies, cast, credits, genre, parental recommendations and MPAA ratings, and a synopsis. The two-volume index serves as a complete filmography for the actors, producers, directors, writers, cinematographers, composers, editors, art directors, stunts, makeup, and others as merited. *The Motion Picture Guide* was updated annually through 1999 with the same basic content but more in-depth synopses for films released in U.S. theaters or on video during the prior year. Unique to the updates are obituaries for prominent filmmakers who died during the year and separate indexes for country, distributor, genre, MPAA rating, parental recommendation, names, and reviewers. *The Motion Picture Guide* is a core resource for libraries that serve patrons interested in film. With free registration, *The Motion Picture Guide* is available on the Web as TV Guide's *Movie Database* at <http://www.tvguide.com>.

170. *The New York Times Film Reviews.* 2002. New York: Times Books.

From 1931 to 2000, the *New York Times* reprinted its well-known movie reviews in this collection. Cumulating anywhere from seven years to two years in one volume, the books resemble the newspaper itself, with four columns in the same font with many black-and-white photographs. Articles are in chronological order, with awards and lists of the year's best films appearing at the end of each year. Volume 6, published in 1971, is a title and personal name index to films reviewed between 1913 and 1968—additional sections correct errors in the first five volumes, list awards, and include a portrait gallery of almost 2,000 actors. An alternative version of the index volume was revised and published the same year under the title *The New York Times Directory of the Film* by updating the 10 best and award winning lists and including the reviews for those films. Subsequent years include their own indexes. Reviews of films released since 1983 are available on the *New York Times* Web site to registered users at <http://movies.nytimes.com/ref/movies/reviews>. In 1971, George Amberg selected films from the original seven-volume set to publish *The New York Times Film Reviews; a One-Volume Selection, 1913–1970.*

171. Pym, John. 2004. *Time Out Film Guide.* Rev. and enl. 13th ed. London: Time Out.

Time Out Magazine compiled its weekly reviews and wrote new reviews for the time period before it began publication to create an annual cumulated compilation of film reviews. The 2005 edition has over 15,500 films listed alphabetically by title. Each entry includes principal cast and crew and a brief critical synopsis. An appendix lists obituaries for the year. Indexes cover films by genre, country, actor, director, and subject. Like its competitors, the readers of this guide will be fans deciding what movie to watch on a Saturday night. Unlike its competitors, *Time Out* covers foreign films very well. *Time Out* is affiliated with <www.filmsite.org> (see entry 206).

172. *Rotten Tomatoes* [World Wide Web Resource]. Rotten Tomatoes. Address: http://www.rottentomatoes.com. [Accessed: March 2005].

Rotten Tomatoes combines movie reviews written by critics from accredited media outlets or online film societies to give each film an overall good or bad rating. They do so by assigning either a fresh tomato (good) or a rotten tomato (bad) to each critic's review. 60 percent or more positive ratings lead to an overall fresh tomato for the film. The *Rotten Tomatoes* movie database contains over 87,000 titles and is searchable by title, actor or filmmaker, or keyword and is browsable by current release, genre, decade, or a "Tomatometer" that includes the percentage of fresh reviews and a score on a 1-to-10 scale. A typical entry includes title, cast and crew credits, genre, a synopsis, MPAA rating, length, release date, and a "Tomatometer" rating. Excerpts from each review are used along with links to the original reviews. Records for actors and filmmakers include a filmography and the average "Tomatometer" of all of their films. The site also provides news, previews, box office figures, trailers, show times, tickets sales, and comparison prices for DVDs. *Rotten Tomatoes* is good for getting a quick look at the overall critical reception of a movie.

173. Ryan, Desmond. 1985. *Video Capsule Reviews.* New York: Simon & Schuster.

Ryan has compiled one of the many guides to movies available for rent. The book includes the standard major cast and crew information along with a better-than-average summary and evaluation crammed into two or three sentences. He rates the films on a one- to five-star scale and includes MPAA ratings plus additional commentary on sex and violence to guide parents selecting videos. Unlike many video guides, this book has not been updated since its publication in 1985, so it has lost much of its value as a rental guide.

174. Sadoul, Georges, and Peter Morris. 1972. *Dictionary of Films.* Berkeley: University of California Press.

In 1965, Sadoul wrote one of the first film dictionaries as a companion to his *Dictionary of Film Makers* (see entry 965). Listing 1,200 films, each entry includes above-the-line credits for cast and crew and includes a brief synopsis and evaluation. Sadoul viewed 95 percent of the films in the dictionary and relied on secondhand information for the 5 percent he did not see. The book was updated by Morris as he translated from French into English. The dictionary would have benefited from a name index, although the companion filmmaker volume does include an asterisk in the filmographies to indicate that the film is described here.

175. Salem, James M. 1971. *A Guide to Critical Reviews, Part IV: The Screenplay, from the Jazz Singer to Dr. Strangelove.* Metuchen, N.J.: Scarecrow Press.

176. Salem, James M. 1982. *A Guide to Critical Reviews, Part IV: The Screenplay, Supplement One, 1963 to 1980.* Metuchen, N.J.: Scarecrow Press.

A Guide to Critical Reviews cites reviews of films and videos published in popular magazines. The vast majority of the 6,500 works included are reviewed by several sources, citing magazine title, volume, page numbers, and date. An appendix lists Academy Award and New York Film Critics award winners. Similar to the *Film Review Index* (see entry 35), Salem doesn't cover as many years.

177. Scarecrow Video. 2004. *The Scarecrow Video Movie Guide.* Seattle: Sasquatch Books.

Scarecrow Video claims to be "the biggest little video store in America, carrying more than 72,000 titles" in its Seattle store. In this guide, the store's staff review close to 4,000 films they would recommend to their customers. Organized into genres, each film includes title, subgenre, release year, length, director, cast, and a critical plot summary. Indexes list stars, directors, and films. The store's complete video catalog is searchable on its Web site at <http://www.scarecrow.com>, but it contains only capsule summaries instead of full reviews.

178. Slide, Anthony. 1982. *Selected Film Criticism.* Metuchen, N.J.: Scarecrow Press.

Film researcher Slide has compiled the complete text of critical reviews for films made between 1896 and 1960. Each of the seven volumes in the series draws from a dozen or so publications and features one or more contemporary reviews of 100 to 200 films selected for each decade, with a total of 1,146 films covered in the set. Films were selected "based on the production's importance in terms of its director or its performers, its historical value and its contemporary relevance." Reviews were included only if they offered critical commentary—a plot synopsis was not enough. Volume 6 features criticism of 160 foreign films (including those made in English) released in the United States between 1930 and 1950 and includes indexes by country and by director. Volume 7 offers cumulative indexes to critics and reviewers and to film titles, but not to directors. Reviews from the earliest days of cinema can be difficult to find, so Slide's cumulation is an essential source for criticism from this era.

179.   Variety *and* Daily Variety *Television Reviews.* 1992. New York: Garland.

   Variety <http://www.variety.com> has reprinted reviews of television shows from Hollywood's *Daily Variety* and New York's *Variety.* The first two volumes of the set contain *Daily Variety* reviews from 1946 through 1960. The next 12 volumes contain *Variety* reviews from 1923 through 1988. In chronological order, the reviews are facsimiles of the reviews found in the entertainment industry newspaper. Volume 15 consists of cumulative title, subject, name, and program indexes. *Variety* published three more biennial indexes before ceasing publication in 1994.

180.   *Variety Film Reviews.* 1983. New York: Garland.

   Variety has reprinted film reviews from its pages published between 1907 and 1996. In chronological order, the reviews are facsimiles of the reviews found in the entertainment industry newspaper. Volume 34 is a cumulative title index. *Variety* published eight more biennial indexes before ceasing publication in 1996. Subscribers may search the complete archives back to 1914 on the *Variety* Web site.

BEST AND WORST

   Selecting the best and worst in film and television is a purely subjective exercise. Awards are one indication, as is popular appeal. The most common method for determining the best and worst is for one or more critics or reviewers to compile lists. Publishing lists of the best and worst films became commonplace as film celebrated its centennial in the late 1990s.

AWARDS (SEE ALSO FILM FESTIVALS)

181.   Franks, Don. 1996. *Entertainment Awards: A Music, Cinema, Theatre and Broadcasting Reference, 1928 through 1993.* Jefferson, N.C.: McFarland.

   Franks has compiled a list of award winning entertainment. For television, he includes the Emmy Awards, the Peabody Awards, and the Golden Globe Awards. For film, he includes the Academy Awards, the Golden Globe Awards, and the New York Film Critics Circle Award. Franks lists only award winners—he does not include nominees. Also included are music and theater awards. Indexes list personal and corporate names and titles.

182.   Hammer, Tad Bentley. 1991. *International Film Prizes: An Encyclopedia,* Garland Reference Library of the Humanities; Vol. 1333. New York: Garland.

   Hammer has compiled the most complete guide to international film awards available—at least through 1989. Listed alphabetically by 42 countries, he includes prizes awarded on an annual basis to feature films. He does not include awards given by festivals, because festival films tend to be invited. For each country, he gives an overview of the film industry and the history of awards followed by a chronological listing of award winners. Title and biographical indexes list awards won by films and the people who made and starred in them.

183. Kaplan, Mike. 1989. *Variety's Directory of Major U.S. Show Business Awards.* New York: R.R. Bowker.

Variety has compiled a list of Oscar, Emmy, Tony, and Grammy Award winners and Pulitzer Prize plays through 1988. The index lists titles and names of award winners and nominees.

184. Lyon, Richard Sean. 1990. *The Complete Book of Film Awards.* West Los Angeles, Calif.: LyonHeart Publishers.

Lyon compiles a list of all major U.S. film awards from the earliest awarded through 1989. The book is organized in reverse chronological order; each year lists the nominees and winners of each award along with a brief commentary. The "Record-Breakers" section lists the most nominated and most award winning individuals and films. He offers one index to the Oscars and a second to the rest of the awards.

185. Mowrey, Peter C. 1994. *Award Winning Films: A Viewer's Reference to 2700 Acclaimed Motion Pictures.* Jefferson, N.C.: McFarland.

Mowrey has compiled a dictionary of award winning films, listing in alphabetical order any film that has won at least one award from among 29 major film awards from the days of silent film through 1990. For each of 2,688 films, he includes technical information, credits for director, writer, and cast, a one-sentence synopsis, and the awards won. An appendix lists the "204 most award-winning movies of all time," although the ranking is somewhat misleading, because there were fewer awards in the early days of cinema. Indexes list studios and countries, names, and subjects. Mowrey's book is similar to the much smaller book by Pickard (see entry 187), which includes fewer awards and lists only 318 films.

186. O'Neil, Thomas. 2003. *Movie Awards: The Ultimate, Unofficial Guide to the Oscars, Golden Globes, Critics, Guild & Indie Honors.* 1st ed. New York: Perigee Books.

Awards expert O'Neil has compiled a chronological list of all of the nominees and award winners for 13 American film awards from their inceptions through 2002: the Oscars, the Golden Globes, *New York Times* Film Critics, the Los Angeles Film Critics, the National Society of Film Critics, the Broadcast Film Critics, the Screen Actors Guild, the Directors Guild, the Writers Guild, the Producers Guild, the Independent Spirit, the Sundance, and the National Board of Review. Appendixes list best pictures and rank films by numbers of nominations and victories. Includes an index.

187. Pickard, Roy. 1981. *The Award Movies: A Complete Guide from A to Z.* New York: Schocken Books.

Pickard takes an unusual approach by listing award winning films in alphabetical order. He includes all films that won best picture awards before 1980 from the "American and British Film Academies; the New York Film Critics Circle; the National Board of

Review; and the prizes presented at the Cannes, Venice, Berlin, Moscow and Karlovy Vary Festivals." For each of the 318 films made before 1980, he lists the awards won, writes a plot synopsis with commentary, and credits the principal cast and crew. The second half of the book takes the more traditional approach of listing each of the awards in chronological order. In a postscript, he lists the directors, actors, and actresses who have won the most awards, but not the top films. He does list the largest box office hits among the award winners. Includes illustrations and an index.

188. *Screen Actors Guild Awards* [World Wide Web Resource]. Screen Actors Guild. Address: http://www.sagawards.com. [Accessed: March 2005].

The Screen Actors Guild lists current and past Screen Actors Guild Awards nominees and recipients for outstanding film and television performances. The lists are browsable by year and category and list the actor, character, and film as well as transcriptions of the winners' speeches.

189. Sheward, David. 1997. *The Big Book of Show Business Awards.* New York: Billboard Books.

Sheward, an editor and reviewer, has compiled a list of show business award winners and nominees. For film, he includes a year-by-year listing of Academy Awards, National Board of Review, New York Film Critics Circle, National Society of Film Critics, Los Angeles Film Critics Association, Golden Globe Awards, and Cannes Film Festival prizes. For television, he includes a year-by-year listing of Emmy Awards, Peabody Awards, Golden Globe Awards, and Cable Ace Awards. Also included are music and theater awards. The index lists titles and personal names.

Academy Awards

Hollywood Sings! An Inside Look at Sixty Years of Academy Award-Nominated Songs (see entry 599)

190. Kinn, Gail, and Jim Piazza. 2005. *The Academy Awards: The Complete Unofficial History.* 3rd rev. and updated ed. New York: Black Dog & Leventhal.

Popular culture writers Kinn and Piazza have written a lavishly illustrated unofficial guide to the Academy Awards from their inception in 1927 through 2003. Organized chronologically, each year begins with an introduction followed by a list all of the nominees and winners. Paragraphs are devoted to the most important awards while the rest are merely listed as nominees and winners. The reason the book is trumpeted as unofficial is because of the attention to the politics and gossip surrounding the awards. Includes another chronological list of the winners in the five key categories and an index.

191. Matthews, Charles E. 1995. *Oscar A to Z: A Complete Guide to More Than 2,400 Movies Nominated for Academy Awards.* 1st ed. New York: Doubleday.

Matthews's unofficial encyclopedia of the Oscars is a nice complement to Osborne's glossy official guide (see entry 192). Arranged alphabetically by film title, each entry lists the production company and release date, the category for which the film was nominated, and a synopsis and discussion of the movie, its cast, and the effect the nomination had on their careers. Winners are listed in the text if the nominee did not win. Cross-references point to other films for which an individual was nominated. The index lists Academy Award nominees and is followed by a chronological list of nominees and winners in each category.

192.   Osborne, Robert A. 1999. *70 Years of the Oscar: The Official History of the Academy Awards*. Expanded and updated. ed. New York: Abbeville Press.

Osborne is the official historian for the Academy of Motion Picture Arts and Sciences awards, better known as the Oscars. He wrote books celebrating 50, 60, and 65 years before publishing this volume covering the first 70 years. Osborne writes historical overviews of the movie industry for each 10-year period and individual introductions to each year covering the major nominations and the highlights of each Oscar show. The book lists complete nominations and winners and includes quotes from nominees and award winners. It is illustrated with captioned photos of nominated stars and films. The index lists names, movie and song titles, and award categories. Lists of Academy Award winners are easy to come by, including on the Academy of Motion Picture Arts and Sciences Web site (<http://www.oscars.org>), but Osborne's lively text, plentiful photographs with captions, and index add value to his coffee table book.

193.   *Oscar.com* [World Wide Web Resource]. Academy of Motion Picture Arts and Sciences. Address: http://www.oscar.com. [Accessed: March 2005].

Oscar.com presents information about the awards given each year by the Academy of Motion Picture Arts and Sciences "recognizing excellence in cinema achievement." The front page features the most recent awards, while the Legacy section provides a database <http://www.oscars.org/awardsdatabase> of past winners and nominees in every category. Records for films include title, year, production and distribution company, and nominees. Records for names include year nominated, film, and role. Winners are indicated by asterisks. Every element in the results is a hyperlink, leading to titles, names, and categories. Users may also browse statistics on the most nominated and winning films, filmmakers, and actors.

194.   Pickard, Roy. 1994. *The Oscar Movies*. 4th ed. New York: Facts on File.

Pickard lists films that have won an Academy Award in any category. For each film, he lists the awards won followed by a synopsis and credits for production company, director, and principal cast. Multiple award winners stand out, because he includes a bold star for each award won. Appendixes list film, actor, actress, and director winners by year, nominees by year, Oscar record holders, documentary and short subject winners, Oscar winner box office performance, directors who worked with winning actors, nominated films that failed to garner a single win, a list of 200 films Pickard believes were great but that were not nominated in any category, honorary awards, and hosts of the Award ceremony. Includes a name and title index.

195.   Pickard, Roy. 1996. *The Oscar Stars from A–Z*. London: Headline.

Pickard takes the same approach to actors in *Oscar Stars* as he does to films in his book *Oscar Movies* (see entry 194) by profiling every actor and actress to have been nominated for an Academy Award. In alphabetical order by actor, each entry includes place and date of birth and year of death, lists of Oscars and nominations, and an essay describing the actor and the circumstances and the film that warranted the nomination and perhaps the victory. Added materials include a sparse collection of black-and-white stills, a chronological list of awards (for film and director as well as actors), and a film title index.

196. Shale, Richard. 1993. *The Academy Awards Index: The Complete Categorical and Chronological Record.* Westport, Conn.: Greenwood Press.

Shale has compiled a list of Academy Award nominees and victors from their inception in 1927 through 1992. The first half of the book lists first by category and then by year, while the second half of the book lists first by year and then by category. Unlike many other books listing awards, Shale also includes the technical awards. Appendixes list Academy of Motion Picture Arts and Sciences founders and presidents, directors of best pictures, and a selected bibliography. Includes a name and title index.

American Film Institute Awards

197. *AFI Awards* [World Wide Web Resource]. American Film Institute. Address: http://www.afi.com/tvevents/afiawards. [Accessed: March 2005].

Each year since 2000, the American Film Institute names the 10 best movies and 10 best television shows. Each entry lists principal cast, director, producer, writer, composer, cinematographer, editor, and production designer and includes a rationale on why the work was included on the list. AFI also names up to 10 "moments of significance" that "may include accomplishments of considerable merit; influences with either a positive or negative impression; trends, either new or re-emerging; anniversaries or memorials of special note; and/or movements in new technologies, education, preservation, government or other areas that impact the art of the moving image." With the inclusion of this last category, the AFI Awards are a nice addition to other twenty-first-century awards.

British Academy Film Awards

198. *British Academy of Film and Television Arts* [World Wide Web Resource]. British Academy of Film and Television Arts. Address: http://www.bafta.org. [Accessed: March 2005].

Each year, the British Academy of Film and Television Arts (BAFTA) gives awards in film, television, crafts, and children's television and film. Award winners and nominees are all listed on BAFTA's Web site. Archives list film awards and nominees back to 1947. The other awards are newer, with television beginning in 1998 and the crafts and children's awards in 2000.

Emmy Awards

199. *Emmy Online* [World Wide Web Resource]. Academy of Television Arts & Sciences. Address: http://www.emmys.org/awards/awardsearch.php. [Accessed: March 2005].

The Academy of Television Arts & Sciences encourages excellence by giving awards for U.S. television shows. Its Web site offers a search box for all prime-time Emmy

Awards since 1949 searchable by program, person, year, network, and category. Results list the show, the network, and the winners and nominees. The Academy of Television Arts & Sciences is known as the Television Academy for short. Under that name, it maintains a separate site at <http://www.emmyonline.org/emmy/awards.html> describing and listing the national awards for daytime television, news and documentaries, business and financial reporting, sports, public and community service, technology and engineering, management, and students. It also links to 20 regional chapters that give and list their own awards.

200.   O'Neil, Thomas. 2000. *The Emmys: The Ultimate, Unofficial Guide to the Battle of TV's Best Shows and Greatest Stars.* 3rd rev. and updated ed. New York: Perigee.

Awards expert O'Neil has compiled a chronological list of all Emmy Award winners and nominees from their inception through 1999. Appendixes list prime-time winners and rank programs and performers by numbers of nominations and victories. Includes an index.

BEST

201.   *AFI's 100 Years 100 Lists* [World Wide Web Resource]. Address: http://www.afi. com/tvevents/100years/100yearslist.aspx. [Accessed: February 2005].

Each year beginning in 1998, the American Film Institute (AFI) has created lists of the 100 best films in various categories. It began with a list of the 100 best American movies and since that time has covered stars, laughs, thrills, passions, heroes and villains, songs, and quotes. Experts at AFI come up with a list of 400 worthy films based on box office success and critical acclaim. They then send the list to voters who whittle the list down to the best 100. The Web site offers both the 400 nominated films as well as the 100 best in each category.

202.   Ash, Russell. 2003. *The Top 10 of Film.* New York: Dorling Kindersley.

Ash, compiler of the *Top 10 of Everything,* has compiled list after list of top 10 films from studios, stars, directors, and genres. Most of the lists are based on box office performance, but there is a section devoted to awards. Lavishly illustrated, the lists are of interest to fans as well as researchers.

203.   Berardinelli, James. 2003. *ReelViews: The Ultimate Guide to the Best 1,000 Modern Movies on DVD and Video.* 1st U.S. ed. Boston; Lanham, Md.: Justin Charless; Distributed by National Book Network.

Berardinelli, one of the better film reviewers to get his start on the Internet, has compiled his full-length reviews of approximately 1,000 of the best films made beginning in the 1990s. Organized by category, each entry includes cast and production credits, technical date, MPAA rating, and an engaging review. Each entry also includes a recommendation of either "recommended," "highly recommended," or "must see." Nearly 3,000 of his reviews are available on the ReelViews Web site at <http://movie-reviews.colossus.net>.

204.   Crouse, Richard. 2003. *The 100 Best Movies You've Never Seen.* Toronto: ECW Press.

Crouse, host of the Reel to Real movie review show, has written a guide to 100 films he feels were underrated. These are his personal favorites, and they range from the truly great to the plain bad. Crouse writes an engaging review of each film explaining why he included it on the list. For fans seeking movies they first overlooked.

205.   Crowther, Bosley. 1967. *The Great Films; Fifty Golden Years of Motion Pictures.* New York: Putnam.

Crowther names 50 great films from the first 50 years of cinema. Listed in chronological order, he includes illustrations, production and cast credits, and an essay describing the groundbreaking, original, and significant content and technique that make the film great. Supplementary materials include a list of 100 more great films, a bibliography, and an index.

206.   Dirks, Tim. *The Greatest Films* [World Wide Web Resource]. Tim Dirks. Address: http://www.greatestfilms.org. [Accessed: March 2005].

Greatest Films lists the best English-language films ever made. The core of the site consists of the three top 100 lists as selected and reviewed by Dirks. He chooses films from all time periods across all genres that have received critical and popular acclaim and writes substantial reviews. Each list is in alphabetical order and is not ranked from 1 to 100. He also lists the most influential directors and biggest stars with a sample of their films, including *The Film 100* (see entry 967), a ranking of the most influential filmmakers, actors, and inventors. Other sections provide the top 100 box office hits of all time with and without adjustments for inflation, lists of the greatest film quotes and the greatest scenes, commentary on each of the *AFI 100* lists (see entry 201) and the Oscars winners, chronologies of milestones in film history and in visual and special effects, and a glossary of film terms and lists and discussions of film genres. Also known as *Filmsite.org, Greatest Films* is a labor of love that is not only informative, but fun to read as well.

207.   Ebert, Roger. 2003. *The Great Movies.* 1st. ed. New York: Broadway Books.

208.   Ebert, Roger, and Mary Corliss. 2005. *The Great Movies II.* 1st ed. New York: Broadway Books.

In addition to his reviews for the *Chicago Sun-Times* and his "thumbs up" and "thumbs down" for television, Ebert has been writing a series of critical essays on "Great Movies." In each of these books, he cumulates 100 of the essays that focus on mostly older classics. The essays assume knowledge of the film. Instead of providing the standard plot synopsis with critical commentary, he instead argues a thesis on what made the film great. While not strictly "best of" lists, Ebert's compilations qualify due to their focus on great films. Note that all of Ebert's reviews going back to 1967, including his *Great Movies* articles, are available on the *Chicago Sun Times* Web site <http://rogerebert.suntimes.com>.

209.   Engelmeier, Peter W., and Michael Althen. 2000. *Icons of Film: The 20th Century.* Munich; New York: Prestel.

Engelmeier led a team of film critics and writers in selecting 84 films that have reached iconic stature and that represent the best, most popular, and the most visually interesting films made around the world during the twentieth century. A two-page spread is devoted to each film. The first page describes the making of the film, its plot, and the elements that make it an icon. A sidebar lists the technical data, the principal cast and crew, and includes the director's career highlights and a filmography. The second page is usually completely devoted to stills from the film. Although a few of the choices for inclusion can be argued (*The Fearless Vampire Killers*), the overall result is an engaging portrait of film in the twentieth century.

210. *ForeignFilms.com* [World Wide Web Resource]. ForeignFilms.com. 1999 Address: http://www.foreignfilms.com. [Accessed: March 2005].

ForeignFilms.com features "the best in world cinema." The site begins with a list of the top 100 foreign films and provides links to the best Chinese-, French-, German-, Italian-, Japanese-, and Spanish-language films available on DVD. There is no indication how the films were selected, but since they are partners with *Amazon.com* (see entry 87), it seems likely that the ratings are drawn from the *IMDb* (see entry 66). *ForeignFilms.com* offers the DVDs for sale via Amazon.

211. Garbicz, Adam, and Jacek Klinowski. 1975. *Cinema, the Magic Vehicle: A Guide to Its Achievement.* Metuchen, N.J.: Scarecrow Press.

Garbicz and Klinowski have compiled a chronological film-by-film guide to "all films which anyone seriously interested in the cinema would consider worth seeing." The list reflects the authors' primary concern with the aesthetics of film. Volume 1 covers films made around the world between 1913 and 1949, while Volume 2 covers the 1950s. Each film entry includes principal cast and crew, technical data, a plot synopsis, and a critical analysis. Indexes list directors and films.

212. Kinn, Gail, and Jim Piazza. 2003. *Four-Star Movies: The 101 Greatest Films of All Time.* New York: Black Dog & Leventhal.

Popular culture writers Kinn and Piazza have compiled a lavishly illustrated list of the 101 films they consider the best. They selected films that "break cinematic ground;" that were prototypical in their genre, inspiring countless more films; or that contain great performances. In ranked order, each entry includes an introduction describing the qualities that rank the film on the list, a plot summary, cast credits, commentary on directors and actors, critical reception, awards won, and scads of stills. Includes an index.

213. Levine, Sanford. 1992. *The 247 Best Movie Scenes in Film History.* Jefferson, N.C.: McFarland.

Levine has written a peculiar little book of the best movie scenes in 42 categories such as "best laughing scenes" and "best mirror scenes." Each category lists a selection of movies and what made the scene unique or interesting. While not systematic and in fact quite idiosyncratic, the book is fun to read and potentially useful to film scholars. An index is included.

214. Leydon, Joe. 2004. *Joe Leydon's Guide to Essential Movies You Must See If You Read, Write About, or Make Movies.* Studio City, Calif.: Michael Wiese Productions.

Film critic Leydon has compiled a list of 100 films he considers essential to view in order to speak intelligently about film. These are the films that movie lovers often allude to, whether they are masterpieces or examples of schlock or overpriced hubris. Divided into 13 genres, each film is treated to a critical analysis, major credits, similar films, and "lessons for filmmakers"—a commentary on what aspect of the film makes it critical viewing. Leydon's guide will be of most interest to film students and teachers.

215.   Meyer, David N. 1997. *The 100 Best Films to Rent You've Never Heard Of: Hidden Treasures, Neglected Classics, and Hits from Bygone Eras.* 1st St. Martin's Griffin ed. New York: St. Martin's Griffin.

Meyer, a film critic, scholar, and programmer, has compiled a list of 100 underappreciated films. For each film, he describes the attitude of the film and the mood necessary to view it, followed by an engaging review. He also lists cast, director, and a list of other films by the director. Includes indexes for director, cast, and genre. Although few of the films on the list are obscure, the book will still be appreciated by fans seeking movies they may have overlooked.

216.   *National Film Registry* [World Wide Web Resource]. National Film Preservation Board (U.S.). Address: http://lcweb.loc.gov/film. [Accessed: March 2005].

Each year since 1989, the National Film Preservation Board (NFPB) has named 25 "culturally, historically or aesthetically significant films" to the National Film Registry. Browsers may view the films by title, year released, filmmaker and performer, or year named to the registry. Only the year-by-year listings include credits, so the NFPB provides a link to the list of *National Film Registry* films hosted by *IMDb* (see entry 66).

217.   Nichols, Peter M. 2004. *The New York Times Guide to the Best 1,000 Movies Ever Made.* Updated and rev. ed. New York: St. Martin's Griffin.

Nichols has compiled reviews from the *New York Times* of the 1,000 best movies. Most of the films are drawn from the end-of-year lists of "10 Best Films," although some were removed to be replaced by films overlooked by critics at the time. Each film includes the crew and cast and the original high-quality review published in the *Times*. Appendixes contain the top 10 lists for each year beginning in 1931, films by genre, and foreign films by country of origin. There is no name index. The book is most useful as a one-volume compilation of reviews, especially for readers without access to the *New York Times* or to the compilation of *New York Times Film Reviews* (see entry 170).

218.   Peary, Danny. 1986. *Guide for the Film Fanatic.* New York: Simon & Schuster.

Peary, a film critic and self-described film fanatic, has compiled a list of 4,200 "must see" films for people who wish to expand their film horizons. For 1,650 of these, he lists technical information, major cast and crew credits, and an engaging summary and evaluation. As the author of four books on cult films (see entries 523 to 526), he includes quite a few cult, class, and trash movies neglected by other books that recommend best movies. At the end of the book, he lists the remainder of the movies he recommends for viewing.

219.   Pickard, R.A.E. 1971. *Dictionary of 1,000 Best Films.* New York: Association Press.

In 1970, Pickard selected what he considered the 1,000 best films ever made. He includes critical masterpieces, popular entertainment, and his personal favorite "minor" films from all over the world, although most come from the United States. Organized by title, each film includes a summary with commentary and extensive cast and crew credits. Lightly illustrated.

220.   Robertson, Sandy. 1999. *Top 1000 Videos To Rent or Buy.* 2nd ed. London: Foulsham.

Film critic Robertson has compiled a list of 1,000 films available on video that he recommends watching. Divided into genres, each film lists cast and director and includes a brief review. Indexes list film titles, stars, and directors. Yet another guide to what movie to watch on a Saturday night.

221.   Schneider, Steven Jay. 2004. *1001 Movies You Must See before You Die.* Revised ed. London: Cassell Illustrated.

Schneider led a team of film critics and scholars in coming up with a list of 1,001 films from all over the world that are essential viewing for movie lovers. Beginning with various top 100 lists that had been compiled by other critics, they winnowed the list down by using their own expertise while trying to maintain representation from all eras, regions, and genres. The result is a chronological guide to some of the best films made from 1902 through 2003. Each film includes technical information, lists director, producer, writer, and cinematographer, and offers a critical plot summary. Most entries are illustrated. Indexes list films by genre and title. With most "best" lists, one might quibble with films that were left off. With this guide, one is more likely to argue with what was included. Still, Schneider has produced an excellent guide to some of the best international films ever made.

222.   *The Sight & Sound Top Ten Poll* [World Wide Web Resource]. British Film Institute. Address: http://www.bfi.org.uk/sightandsound/topten. [Accessed: March 2005].

Every 10 years beginning in 1952, *Sight & Sound* has polled film critics from around the world to compile lists of the 10 best films. In 1992, they began polling directors, and in 2002, they began listing more than 10 films and ranking the best directors as well. The entry for each film includes a still, a synopsis, and a list of voters. The entry for each director lists nominated films. The results of all six polls are listed, making it possible to see which films have stood the test of time.

223.   Sinyard, Neil. 1985. *Classic Movies.* Salem, N.H.: Salem House.

Sinyard has compiled a lavishly illustrated guide to 71 of the best movies of all time. Unfortunately, the book doesn't explain the selection criteria. Instead, 14 chapters list the four to eight best movies in genres such as westerns, musicals, social realism, and a category called the "art of the cinema," where directors "express a profound and personal view of life." Chapter introductions consist of one sentence describing the genre. The films are international in scope and range from 1916 to 1977. The strengths of the book are the evaluative film descriptions and numerous stills. The index lists filmmakers and films.

224.   Turan, Kenneth. 2004. *Never Coming to a Theater near You: A Celebration of a Certain Kind of Movie.* 1st ed. New York: PublicAffairs.

Film critic Turan compiles reviews of worthwhile films that failed to reach blockbuster status. Intended to help movie fans discover 150 films they might have overlooked, he divides the films into the categories of English language, foreign language, documentaries, classics, and retrospectives on directors and Chinese martial arts, pre-code Hollywood, and Yiddish films. His reviews are typical of what he writes for the *Los Angeles Times,* discoursing on what he liked about the film. Includes indexes by country, film, and name.

225.   *The Ultimate Film* [World Wide Web Resource]. Address: http://www.bfi.org. uk/features/ultimatefilm. [Accessed: January 2005].

The British Film Institute estimated the number of people in the United Kingdom who watched movies in the theater during the first 100 years of cinema. The result is a list of the top 100 most viewed films, from *Gone with the Wind* in first place to the *Magnificent Seven* hanging on at number 100. Each film includes a synopsis and excerpts from a review written at the time the film was released. Films are also sorted alphabetically and by decade.

WORST

Film

226.   *Mr. Cranky* [World Wide Web Resource]. Address: http://www.mrcranky.com. [Accessed: January 2005].

Mr. Cranky's often humorous gimmick is to hate each and every of the nearly 2,000 movies he has seen. No movie is safe from his skewering, from classics to current releases. He provides a review focusing on the aspects of the movie that annoy him. He then ranks it on a scale of one (barely tolerable) to four (a poke in the eye) with dynamite sticks and atomic clouds reserved for the worst of the worst.

227.   Wilson, John. 2005. *The Official Razzie Movie Guide: Enjoying the Best of Hollywood's Worst.* New York: Warner Books.

Wilson, creator of the Razzie Award <http://razzies.com> given to the worst movies and actors each year since 1980, has compiled a guide to some of the worst all-time movies and performances. Divided into a dozen categories, the entry for each film includes cast and crew, excerpts from reviews, and a detailed discussion of the qualities that make the movie awful. An appendix lists the nominees and winners year-by-year—which are also available on the IMDb Web site at <http://us.imdb.com/Sections/Awards/Razzie_Awards>. Includes an index.

Television

228.   Andrews, Bart, and Brad Dunning. 1980. *The Worst TV Shows—Ever: Those TV Turkeys We Will Never Forget. (No Matter How Hard We Try).* 1st ed. New York: Dutton.

TV addicts Andrews and Dunning have compiled their personal list of the worst shows ever to air in prime time before 1980. They save most of their disdain for sitcoms, with over two dozen shows listed in alphabetical order and given royal treatment with technical, production, and cast credits, a lengthy review citing particularly memorable moments, and plenty of illustrations. Includes an index.

229.   Nelson, Craig. 1995. *Bad TV: The Very Best of the Very Worst.* New York: Delta.

Nelson led a team of critics and writers in selecting the worst television shows ever aired in the United States. The first half of the book lists the all-time worst shows, highlights bad moments in good shows, and discusses the elements that lead to bad television. The second half of the book lists the Tammi awards, given to the worst shows each year. Organized by genre, Nelson describes the elements that make each show so bad. Includes illustrations and an index.

ERRORS

230.   Givens, Bill. 1996. *Roman Soldiers Don't Wear Watches: 333 Film Flubs—Memorable Movie Mistakes.* Secaucus, N.J.: Carol.

Givens gathers "goofs, gaffes, and glitches" in movies. This volume adds new movies to the best from his earlier three volumes. Arranged into categories such as costume flubs and geography lessons, Givens shares film flubs that have been brought to his attention by legions of movie fans. Without an index or systematic organization beyond the broad categories, this one is purely for fans.

231.   Johnson, Brendan B. *The Nitpickers Site* [World Wide Web Resource]. Address: http://www.nitpickers.com. [Accessed: January 2005].

Johnson hosts a site that features continuity errors and bloopers or "nitpicks" in movies and television shows. Fans and critics have submitted nearly 75,000 nitpicks to date, with some movies and television shows receiving hundreds of entries each. The site is a bit busy and can be difficult to navigate (the best bet is browsing by title), but the sheer number of entries makes it worth pursuing for those who like to nitpick at movies.

232.   Molinari, Matteo, and Jim Kamm. 2002. *Oops! Movie Mistakes That Made the Cut.* New York: Citadel Press.

233.   Molinari, Matteo, and Jim Kamm. 2002. *Oops! They Did It Again! More Movie Mistakes That Made the Cut.* New York: Citadel Press.

Molinari and Kamm have scoured countless films to come up with lists of continuity errors and bloopers in mostly newer mostly popular movies. In alphabetical order by film title, each entry lists the number of bloopers, director, cast, a synopsis brief enough to barely identify the plot, and a list of bloopers. Each blooper describes the error, gives the time it appears in the film, and, for the most egregious or picky errors, a descriptive icon.

234.   Sandys, Jon. *Movie Mistakes* [World Wide Web Resource]. Address: http://www.moviemistakes.com. [Accessed: March 2005].

Sandys hosts a Web site dedicated to mistakes made in movies. Volunteers submit continuity problems, factual errors, plot holes, visible crew/equipment, and audio problems.

Searchable by film, TV show, person, or year, films are also browsable by updates, most mistakes, best mistakes, popular titles, and "perfect films." In 2004, Sandys published a third edition of the print version featuring some of the more interesting errors entitled *Movie Mistakes: Take 3.*

LISTS

235.   Essoe, Gabe. 1981. *The Book of Movie Lists.* Westport, Conn.: Arlington House.

Obviously inspired by the *Book of Lists,* Essoe has compiled a series of movie lists. He includes the standard best and worst compilations plus lists of films, stars, and genres. The tone is chatty and idiosyncratic, so the book is of limited reference value, but fun to read.

236.   Foley, Catherine, Milos Stehlik, and Facets Multi-Media. *Facets Movie Lovers Video Guide.* Chicago: Facets Multi-Media.

Facets, better known as a video distributor (see entry 88), has collected lists of movies that include best and worst and award winning foreign, classic, and independent movies, genres, and lists of characters. Sidebars add more peculiar and idiosyncratic lists such as the worst weather films, best dance videos, and "some like it gothic." The categories and sidebars are included in the table of contents but can be hard to find, because the index lists only film titles.

237.   McBride, Joseph. 1998. *The Book of Movie Lists: An Offbeat, Provocative Collection of the Best and Worst of Everything in Movies.* Lincolnwood, Ill.: Contemporary Books.

McBride, a film critic and writer, has compiled a series of quirky lists such as the "12 best mental hospital movies" and "movies stars would like to leave off of their resumes." Mostly fun for film buffs, some of the lists could promote discussions or programming ideas.

238.   Robertson, Patrick. 2001. *Film Facts.* London: Aurum.

Robertson has compiled lists of the best and worse, the biggest and smallest, the shortest and longest, and the first and last in the movies. The book is organized into 17 broad categories that include chapters on the industry, stories, themes, and performers. Interspersed with lists of largest and smallest casts, the most successful sports movie, and the first trailer are the more unusual lists of stars putting each other down or non-actors playing themselves or other people in films. Fun, the book also supplies the answers to many difficult reference questions. Robertson published earlier editions under the title *Guinness Movie Facts and Feats.*

239.   Steinberg, Cobbett. 1980. *Film Facts.* New York: Facts on File.

Steinberg has compiled lists and numbers about film and the film industry. Divided into seven sections, the book is a compendium of just about any numerical bit of information. The section on marketplace lists top money-makers, numbers of films made, and most expensive movies. The section on stars lists annual top 10 box office actors and the top salaries. The section on studios includes a brief history of each along with the profits and top earning films. The sections on festivals and awards lists prizes. The section on "ten best" lists covers films, eras, and filmmakers. The last section lists censorship codes and regulations. Includes an index. Although dated, especially for the all-time lists, the book contains information that is still useful to researchers.

240. Steinberg, Cobbett. 1985. *TV Facts.* Rev. and updated. ed. New York: Facts on File.

Steinberg has compiled lists and numbers about television from 1950 to 1985. Divided into six sections, the book is a cornucopia of information. The section on programs includes prime-time schedules, longest running shows, and cost of programs. The section on viewers lists number of households with television and cable and viewing habits. The section on ratings lists top-rated series and movies. The section on advertising publishes revenue figures and lists top markets. The section on awards includes not only Emmys, but eight other awards and *Film Comment*'s list of the most memorable moments on television. The section on networks includes a brief history and then lists stations on the air, profits, and owners. Although dated, especially for the all-time lists, the book provides information that is still useful to researchers.

MISCELLANEOUS

241. Cairella, Giancarlo. *The Movie Cliches List* [World Wide Web Resource]. Address: http://www.moviecliches.com. [Accessed: March 2005].

Cairella has compiled a "list of the most annoying and common logic flaws and stereotypes found in movies." Organized into more than 70 categories such as answering machines, music, or radio, each entry includes one or more clichés. In radio, for example: "A character turns on the radio just in time to hear a special announcement or some important news item. Then turns the radio off." A fun site for film buffs.

242. *Film Affinity* [World Wide Web Resource]. Address: http://www.filmaffinity. com. [Accessed: January 2005].

Film Affinity works on the theory that people who enjoy the same movies will want to consult each other's lists when deciding on what movies to watch. Users register and rate well-known movies on a scale of one to ten. The system will then provide a ranked list of other users who share the same tastes. Once users select a "soulmate," they can view that person's favorite movies and see how they rated new releases.

5
National Cinema

Filmographies of national cinema list films produced internationally, by region, or by country. Due to my decision to include only English-language titles, some of the best international and country filmographies have been excluded due solely to the fact that they are not in English. The *Bibliography of National Filmographies,* written by Gebauer and Harrison in 1985, lists many of the most important. For more recent publications, searching union catalogs such as *WorldCat* (see entry 64) and *RedLightGreen* (see entry 63) or checking the introductions of the English-language filmographies for citations to the key national filmographies are the two best options.

INTERNATIONAL CINEMA

243. Allan, Elkan, and National Film Theatre (London). 1985. *A Guide to World Cinema: Covering 7,200 Films of 1950–84 Including Capsule Reviews and Stills from the Programmes of the National Film Theatre, London.* London; Detroit: Whittet Books in association with the British Film Institute.

Allan compiled the notes from the monthly programs presented at the National Film Theatre. Over 7,200 films are presented in alphabetical order and include the director, lead actors, and a small black-and-white still from the movie. One-sentence synopses and one-sentence comments sum up the films nicely. There is an index to directors.

244. Bergan, Ronald, and Robyn Karney. 1992. *The Faber Companion to Foreign Films.* Boston: Faber and Faber.

Bergan and Karney have compiled a list of over 2,000 artistically significant or successful films from over 50 countries that have been released or broadcast in the United States or Great Britain. In alphabetical order by original title, each entry includes country of origin and language, original date of release, technical data, director, writer, cinematographer, music, cast credits, a critical plot summary, and awards won. In 1988, Bergan and Karney also wrote *The Holt Foreign Film Guide,* which in Britain was entitled the *Bloomsbury Foreign Film Guide.*

245. British Film Institute. 1975. *Film Title Index.* London: World Microfilms Publications.

I was not able to view *Film Title Index,* because it is owned by only a handful of libraries across the globe. One hundred twenty microfilm reels list over 200,000 films made around the world from 1908 through 1974. Each title includes a plot summary and references to reviews. Twenty-nine additional reels update the set every two years through 1982.

246.   Cowie, Peter. 1977. *Eighty Years of Cinema.* South Brunswick, N.J.: A.S. Barnes.

Cowie has written a chronological guide to the first 80 years of filmmaking, covering 1885 through 1975. He reviews 280 international films that offer "signposts to the significant developments in film art and entertainment." The reviews include principal crew and cast, a plot summary, and a brief criticism. Each year also includes a checklist of other important films, a list of shorts and documentaries, and facts of interest such as deaths, technical achievements, and important events in film history. Includes only a title index.

247.   Cowie, Peter. 1977. *World Filmography, 1967.* London; South Brunswick, N.J.: Tantivy Press; A.S. Barnes.

248.   Cowie, Peter. 1977. *World Filmography, 1968.* London; South Brunswick, N.J.: Tantivy Press; A.S. Barnes.

Cowie, at the time editor of the annual *International Film Guide* (see entry 145), made an ambitious attempt to expand the scope of that publication by documenting all of the films made around the world each year. He succeeded for only two years, covering films made in 1967 and 1968. The filmography relied on correspondents for each country, and he was able to cover 45 countries in 1967 and 49 in 1968. Arranged first by country and then alphabetically by film, correspondents list principal crew and cast and write an English-language capsule summary for each. Illustrated and with indexes by title and director, this publication is still of use to students researching international films made in the late 1960s.

249.   *Film History* [World Wide Web Resource]. Address: http://www.filmsite.org/filmh.html. [Accessed: January 2005].

Filmsite (see entry 206), best known for its lists ranking the top films of all time, also offers a chronological survey of film history. Organized by decade, each page provides a historical, social, and technological overview and highlights key filmmakers and turning points from the era. The greatest films and award winners are also listed year by year. In order to search the history pages, it is necessary to go back to the main page and use the search box for the entire site.

250.   Gebauer, Dorothea, Harriet Harrison, and FIAF Cataloguing Commission. 1985. *Bibliography of National Filmographies.* Bruxelles: FIAF.

FIAF has compiled a list of national filmographies for 59 countries. Intended as a tool for catalogers, it is also very useful as a research tool, because it includes books, periodicals, and unpublished filmographies that compile lists of films made in one country.

251.   Gray, John. 1990. *Blacks in Film and Television: A Pan-African Bibliography of Films, Filmmakers, and Performers, Bibliographies and Indexes in Afro-American and African Studies, No. 27.* New York: Greenwood Press.

A historian and director of the Black Arts Research Center, Gray spent five years compiling this international bibliography of black filmmakers and films. Chapters cover cultural history and film made in Africa, Europe, the Caribbean, Latin America, and the United States. The bibliography covers the full range of formats in most Western languages. Although Gray did examine every book and most journal articles, he unfortunately did not write abstracts. Instead, it is necessary to browse sections or use indexes to artists, film title, subject, or author. Gray's book is most useful in its comprehensiveness and in its coverage of black filmmakers outside the United States.

252.   Hecht, Hermann, Ann Hecht, and British Film Institute. 1993. *Pre-Cinema History: An Encyclopaedia and Annotated Bibliography of the Moving Image before 1896.* London: Bowker Saur.

The authors have compiled an annotated bibliography that doubles as an encyclopedia of the history of projection before the advent of cinema, including such technologies as the camera obscura and the magic lantern. The entries are in chronological order, beginning with a publication from 1321 and continuing through 1985, when Hermann Hecht died. As a bibliography, the work is excellent, exhibiting careful scholarship and detailed annotations. As an encyclopedia, the work is difficult to use. To find information on a topic, it is necessary to use the subject index and cobble together the various entries to come up with an overview. Mirror projection, for example, lists dozens of entries. Despite the difficulties, it is still worthwhile, because little exists on early projection technologies. Includes a name index.

253.   Karney, Robyn, Joel W. Finler, and Ronald Bergan. 2004. *Cinema: Year by Year, 1894–2004.* London; New York: Dorling Kindersley.

Beginning in 1894 and ending with 2004, the authors take a chronological news magazine approach to the cinema. Essays introduce each decade, followed by year-by-year chronologies of events and feature stories describing the most important films and developments during the year. Although international in scope, the primary focus is on American film. The book is lavishly illustrated with both black-and-white and color stills, publicity and news photos, and movie posters. The index is comprehensive and highlights the information on each page. The book is great fun for movie fans while also serving as a solid chronology. Earlier editions were entitled *Chronicle of the Cinema.*

254.   Magill, Frank Northen. 1985. *Magill's Survey of Cinema, Foreign Language Films.* Englewood Cliffs, N.J.: Salem Press.

Completing *Magill's Survey of Cinema* that began with *English Language Films* (see entries 161 and 162) and *Silent Films* (see entry 740), the guide to foreign films covers 515 films. Each entry includes the film title, release date, above-the-line crew, running time, and cast matched to character. Over 100 contributors wrote the essays, which cover the history of the production and provide a detailed plot description followed by the film's popular and critical reception. Most films also include critical analysis. As in each set, indexes include director, screenwriter, cinematographer, editor, and performer. There is also a chronological list of titles covered in the set. Supplemented by *Magill's Cinema Annual* (see entry 148).

255.   Nowell-Smith, Geoffrey. 1997. *The Oxford History of World Cinema.* Oxford; New York: Oxford University Press.

Nowell-Smith and a team of expert contributors have succeeded in the daunting task of writing a historical overview of international cinema. Divided into three broad periods—the silent cinema through 1930, the sound cinema through 1960, and the modern cinema through 1995—the history is chock-full of essays on national cinemas, genres, and movements mixed with briefer articles on filmmakers, actors, and technology. The history is nicely illustrated in black and white, with one color section featuring the use of color in film. Includes an index. For researchers as well as fans, this book belongs in most libraries.

256. Paris, James Reid. 1993. *Classic Foreign Films: From 1960 to Today.* New York: Carol.

Paris lists the 70 best foreign-language films distributed in the United States between 1960 and 1991. Although based on awards won, critical reputation, and lasting influence, the author's choices are ultimately personal. Arranged chronologically, each film includes credits, cast, background information, a synopsis, and a commentary. The book is lavishly illustrated in black and white and provides an excellent overview of foreign films.

257. Shipman, David. 1982. *The Story of Cinema: A Complete Narrative History, from the Beginnings to the Present.* 1st U.S. ed. New York: St. Martin's Press.

Film historian Shipman spent more than 10 years watching or rewatching films to write this international historical survey of cinema as art, business, and a reflection of its times. Volume 1 covers film "from the beginnings to Gone with the Wind," and Volume 2 continues "from Citizen Kane to the present day," meaning 1983. The books take a roughly chronological approach mixed with chapters on national cinema, directors, and topics. The essays explore the times by analyzing individual films. Interesting to read for its opinionated look at film, the extensive index makes this a good reference source as well.

258. Sigoloff, Marc. 1984. *The Films of the Seventies: A Filmography of American, British, and Canadian Films, 1970–1979.* Jefferson, N.C.: McFarland.

Sigoloff has written a guide to the mainstream films of the 1970s made in the United States, Great Britain, and Canada. Organized alphabetically by title, each entry includes a one- to five-star rating, release date, crew and cast credits, and a summary with opinionated commentary. Includes a name index.

259. Slide, Anthony. 1989. *The International Film Industry: A Historical Dictionary.* New York: Greenwood Press.

Slide, a film historian, has written a "what's what" guide to the international film industry. Entries cover studios, production companies, distributors, organizations, technical innovations, and historical essays on the history of cinema in most countries that produce films. Although films and filmmakers are mentioned in the context of the discussion and definitions, they do not warrant their own entries. Slide cites sources for most of his descriptions along with a separate bibliography and index. Slide wrote a companion volume entitled *The New Historical Dictionary of the American Film Industry* (see entry 418). Together, the two guides to the film industry are useful companions for film history researchers.

260. Wiener, Tom. 2002. *The Off-Hollywood Film Guide: The Definitive Guide to Independent and Foreign Films on Video and DVD.* 1st trade pbk. ed. New York: Random House Trade Paperbacks.

Wiener, a popular culture writer, has written a guide to more than 650 foreign and independent films for movie lovers deciding which video or DVD to watch. In alphabetical order by title, each entry includes country of origin, year of release, technical data, rating, genre, director, principal cast, a suggestion for double feature viewing, and a critical summary. Supplementary materials include a list of "essential movies," lists of genres and subgenres, and indexes by director, actor, and country.

261.   Wilhelm, Elliot. 1999. *VideoHound's World Cinema: The Adventurer's Guide to Movie Watching.* Detroit: Visible Ink Press.

Wilhelm, movie critic and director of the Detroit Film Theater series, has compiled a list of over 800 films produced outside of the United States. Films are listed in alphabetical order by original title. Wilhelm writes engaging capsule reviews for each, followed by principal cast and crew. "Next stop" suggests films with either the same cast or director or with similar themes. The book contains over 100 illustrations, and occasional sidebars salute prominent foreign filmmakers and actors. The indexes are superb and include title, country of origin, cast, director, writer, cinematographer, composer, and category. Sources for videos and distributors are listed separately.

AFRICA AND THE MIDDLE EAST

AFRICA SOUTH OF THE SAHARA

Blacks in Film and Television: A Pan-African Bibliography of Films, Filmmakers, and Performers (see entry 251)

262.   Pfaff, Françoise. 1988. *Twenty-Five Black African Filmmakers: A Critical Study, with Filmography and Bio-Bibliography.* New York: Greenwood Press.

Professor Pfaff "highlights a selected group of representative cineastes whose works have both significantly enriched African filmmaking and received substantial international exposure." For each filmmaker, she includes name, birth place and date, a rich biography, an exploration of themes in the films, a survey of criticism, a filmography, and a bibliography. Includes a bibliography and a detailed index. The depth of coverage makes Pfaff's book an excellent place to begin research on prominent African filmmakers.

263.   Russell, Sharon A. 1998. *Guide to African Cinema, Reference Guides to the World's Cinema.* Westport, Conn.: Greenwood Press.

Professor of Communication and Women's Studies Russell has compiled a dictionary of African feature films, directors, and actors. Her criteria for selection are practical (she was able to watch the film) and political (the film has a European perspective or is stereotypical). Her goal is to "include films and directors who are trying to define a uniquely African perspective." For films, she summarizes and critically analyzes the plot and its themes. For filmmakers, she follows a brief biography with a discussion of their work, a filmography, and a bibliography. In addition to films and filmmakers, the index also lists countries with the films produced there. While not comprehensive, the book is well worth consulting for its in-depth examinations of African films and filmmakers.

264.   Schmidt, Nancy J. 1988. *Sub-Saharan African Films and Filmmakers: An Annotated Bibliography = Films Et Cinéastes Africains De La Région Subsaharienne: Une Bibliographie Commentée.* London; New York: Hans Zell.

265.   Schmidt, Nancy J. 1994. *Sub-Saharan African Films and Filmmakers, 1987– 1992: An Annotated Bibliography.* London; New Providence, N.J.: Hans Zell.

Schmidt, an African studies librarian, has compiled bibliographies of literature about Sub-Saharan African film and filmmakers. The first edition contains nearly 4,000 references to books and journal, magazine, and newspaper articles and the second adds 3,200 more. The majority of the entries are briefly annotated for content. The bibliographies are in order by author, so the indexes list coauthors, film festivals, film titles, filmmakers, other film personnel, countries, and subjects.

266.   Shiri, Keith. 1992. *Directory of African Film-Makers and Films.* Westport, Conn.: Greenwood Press.

Shiri "attempts to provide a single comprehensive reference guide to the most important and active directors who have been involved in feature, documentary and animation film production in 29 countries and states from the whole of the African continent over the last 60 years." He sent questionnaires and received a very high response rate of 75 percent. After an index at the beginning of the book that categorizes directors by country, the rest of the book is organized by director, with each entry including career highlights followed by as complete a filmography as possible. A title index lists approximately 3,000 films, and a general index lists organizations, companies, literary titles, and names other than the directors.

SOUTH AFRICA

267.   Blignaut, Johan, and Martin Botha. 1992. *Movies, Moguls, Mavericks: South African Cinema 1979–1991.* Cape Town: Showdata.

Blignaut and Botha, South African film and media experts, have written a survey of South African films made between 1979 and 1991. Just over half of the book consists of 18 chapters on South African film history, filmmakers, Apartheid, and Afrikaans cinema. The rest of the book consists of separate filmographies for 944 feature films, numerous television programs, and 998 documentaries. Entries include title, release year, language, genre, technical and production data, principal crew and cast, and a synopsis. There are no indexes, but there are cross-references from alternate and non-English language titles at the front of each filmography.

MIDDLE EAST

268.   Armes, Roy. 1996. *Dictionary of North African Film Makers = Dictionnaire Des Cinéastes Du Maghreb.* Bilingual ed., Collection Caméra Des Trois Mondes; Vol. 2. Paris: Editions ATM.

Film professor Armes has compiled a list of North African filmmakers and the films they have made. Chapters on Algeria, Morocco, Tunisia, and émigré cinema (filmmakers from these countries making films elsewhere) each begin with a filmographic history and a chronology before listing individual filmmakers. Each entry describes the filmmaker's career and lists his or her feature films. Indexes list films and filmmakers. The book is bilingual—turn it over and the same text appears in French as translated by Valerie Beunardeau. Armes has produced a very useful book for national cinemas that can be difficult to research.

269. Leaman, Oliver. 2001. *Companion Encyclopedia of Middle Eastern and North African Film.* London; New York: Routledge.

Leaman led a team of film scholars in compiling a guide to the cinema of the Middle East, North Africa, and Central Asia. Organized by region and by country, each entry includes a history, a filmography, a list of filmmakers, and a bibliography. The histories cover filmmaking, filmmakers, and key films in depth. The filmographies list prominent films in alphabetical order, providing year, length, lead production crew and cast, and a plot summary. The filmmakers include career biographies of directors, with some country overviews also adding actors and other filmmakers. Includes general, name, and title indexes. The encyclopedia does an excellent job of covering a region that has been neglected in the film literature.

Orient: A Survey of Films Produced in Countries of Arab and Asian Culture (see entry 273)

IRAN

270. Maghsoudlou, Bahman. 1987. *Iranian Cinema.* New York: Hagop Kevorkian Center for Near Eastern Studies, New York University.

Maghsoudlou has written the most complete filmography of Iranian cinema. The book begins with a chronological and cultural history of filmmaking in Iran. Most of the book is a chronological filmography of over 1,200 films made in Iran between 1930 and 1985. Each entry includes the original title with an English translation, genre, principal crew and cast, awards, and, for select films, a plot summary. Appendixes list numbers of films produced by year, theaters and seating capacity in Iran, and Iranian directors and actors. The index lists film titles in the original language.

271. Naficy, Hamid. 1984. *Iran Media Index, Bibliographies and Indexes in World History, No. 1.* Westport, Conn.: Greenwood Press.

A producer and director of educational films, Naficy has compiled an index to 3,539 film and television documentaries produced in English–speaking countries on the topic of Iran. He begins with the earliest days of motion pictures in the 1880s and ends in 1982. The index is organized under 125 topics such as Ancient Persia, the Pahlavis, or U.S. Hostages in Iran. Entries are minimal; they include title, format, dates, producer, and a one-sentence synopsis. Many of the documentaries are difficult to find, so Naficy also includes the archives that hold the documentary. He includes a title index and an index of producers, holders, and distributors. The book will be most useful for researchers seeking visuals of Iran. Bring a magnifying glass, because the type is extremely small.

ISRAEL

272.   Kronish, Amy, and Costel Safirman. 2003. *Israeli Film: A Reference Guide, Reference Guides to the World's Cinema.* Westport, Conn.: Praeger.

As with all books in the Greenwood series *Reference Guides to the World's Cinema,* an introduction to the national cinema is followed by selections of the most prominent filmmakers and films of that country. Kronish and Safirman, both film archivists, select films and filmmakers based on their historical and social impact. The first section lists films in alphabetical order, with each entry including principal crew and cast, awards, and a summary discussing themes, history, and reception. The second section lists filmmakers; each entry includes a brief biography followed by an extensive filmography. Supplementary materials include an appendix listing international awards won by Israeli films, a bibliography, and indexes to film titles, personalities, and subjects. As with all books in the series, this is a good place to go for an overview of Israeli cinema.

ASIA

Companion Encyclopedia of Middle Eastern and North African Film (see entry 269)

273.   Holmes, Winifred, and British Film Institute. 1959. *Orient: A Survey of Films Produced in Countries of Arab and Asian Culture.* London: British Film Institute.

UNESCO asked the British Film Institute to produce a survey of feature films and documentaries produced in Asia and the Middle East. The result is a guide that is still useful for identifying films made in the first half of the twentieth century. Part I lists feature films that have been shown at international film festivals or were financially successful or important to the development of film in their own country. Arranged first by country and second by title, each entry includes production and distribution information, principal crew and cast, awards, and a detailed plot summary. Part II lists short films examining family life, arts, performing arts, work, play, and society in each country. Entries begin with a brief discussion and summary followed by names of principal crew, technical details, and distribution. Includes only a name index. Although ancient by film standards, the survey is still useful, particularly for finding earlier films made in some of the countries that are not well covered by other national films guides.

274.   Thomas, Brian, Cynthia Rothrock, and Visible Ink Press. 2003. *VideoHound's Dragon: Asian Action & Cult Flicks.* Detroit: Visible Ink Press.

Thomas led a team of film experts in compiling a list of 1,150 action and cult films made in Asia and available on video. The majority of films are from Hong Kong, but all of Asia except Russia is represented—there is even a selection of anime films from Japan. Films are listed in alphabetical order by title and include summaries and reviews for each followed by principal cast and crew and the typical VideoHound rating of one to four bones. The book is moderately well illustrated, and occasional sidebars salute countries and prominent filmmakers, actors, and topics. The indexes are superb and include alternative titles (critical in a world where films receive multiple titles and translations), cast, director, writer, cinematographer, composer, and category. Sources for videos and distributors are listed separately.

275. Weisser, Thomas. 1994. *Asian Trash Cinema: The Book.* Houston: Asian Trash Cinema/European Trash Cinema Publications.

276. Weisser, Thomas. 1996. *Asian Trash Cinema: The Book (Part 2).* 2nd ed. Miami: Vital Sounds Group, Asian Trash Cinema Publications.

Drawn from the reviews published in the 'zine *Asian Trash Cinema,* these two volumes list films made in Asia. The films represent the full range of releases, but tend to cover mostly action, horror, fantasy, and sexploitation films. Many of the films fall into Hong Kong's Category 3, movies for adults only that feature extreme violence or explicit sex. Because so many of the films are indeed trash, Weisser's rating of one to four stars can be quite useful. Although the titles claim all of Asia, the vast majority of the films, especially in Volume 1, come from Hong Kong. Volume 1 includes director and genre indexes, while Volume 2 also includes a performer index. A nice complement to *The Hong Kong Filmography* (see entry 277).

CHINA

277. Charles, John. 2000. *The Hong Kong Filmography, 1977–1997: A Complete Reference to 1,100 Films Produced by British Hong Kong Studios.* Jefferson, N.C.: McFarland.

Charles covers the heyday of Hong Kong new wave cinema from its early days until Hong Kong's return to China in 1997. While Hong Kong is best known in the West for its action films, the book includes all genres. The films are organized alphabetically by title. Each entry includes English and Chinese titles, release date, production company, and a 1 to 10 rating. Cast and crew are listed in a combination of English and Chinese names. Reflecting the author's love for the genre, the descriptions of each film are lively and interesting. Charles's knowledge of Cantonese and Mandarin enables him to point out poorly subtitled films. The book concludes with a glossary, a bibliography, and—because Hong Kong films can be difficult to obtain—a list of video resources. The index lists names and films. For films from Mainland China, see *The Chinese Filmography* (see entry 280).

278. Dannen, Fredric, and Barry Long. 1997. *Hong Kong Babylon: An Insider's Guide to the Hollywood of the East.* 1st ed. New York: Hyperion.

Hong Kong Babylon is designed to introduce readers to the Hong Kong film world. Like the other Hong Kong filmographies, it lists films made in Hong Kong, including the English and Chinese titles, the director, and a plot summary. Far less complete than *The Hong Kong Filmography* (see entry 277) in both quantity of films and depth of description, the advantage of *Hong Kong Babylon* is the added materials, which include an excellent introduction to Cantonese cinema, interviews with filmmakers, and recommended viewing from 12 film critics.

279.   Hammond, Stefan, and Mike Wilkins. 1996. *Sex and Zen & a Bullet in the Head.* New York: Simon & Schuster.

To introduce Westerners to their favorite cinema, Hong Kong movie fans Hammond and Wilkins have written a guide to approximately 150 new wave Hong Kong films made beginning in the early eighties. The book is divided into 14 chapters such as "ten that rip" and "nail polished fists" and contains features on individual filmmakers and stars. The book is chock-full of stills from the films and sidebars featuring less prominent films and actors as well as factoids. Individual films are described in great detail and include a list of the principal cast and the director. The final chapter lists means of renting or purchasing the films. A glossary lists terms, an appendix provides the Chinese characters for each film title listed in the book, and an index points to names and titles. Fans of Hong Kong movies will enjoy this book.

280.   Marion, Donald J. 1997. *The Chinese Filmography: The 2444 Feature Films Produced by Studios in the People's Republic of China from 1949 through 1995.* Jefferson, N.C.: McFarland.

After a useful historical overview of Chinese filmmaking, Marion lists the films in alphabetical order by English title. He includes the Romanized Chinese title, date of release, name of studio, technical information, literary source, cast and credits, and a plot summary. He also mentions if the film won either of China's major awards. Included are a bibliography of sources and a name index. Marion has produced an essential guide to Chinese film and an excellent complement to *The Hong Kong Filmography* (see entry 277). Because of the political nature of Chinese film, this resource will be as useful to students of politics as it is to students of film.

281.   Zhang, Yingjin, and Zhiwei Xiao. 1998. *Encyclopedia of Chinese Film.* London; New York: Routledge.

Zhang led a team of film scholars in compiling a guide to "Chinese film in its historical, cultural, geopolitical, generic, thematic and textual aspects." The encyclopedia begins with six essays on the history of cinema in China, Taiwan, and Hong Kong. The encyclopedia covers films, filmmakers, genres, and subjects. Entries for films include English and Pinyin title, director, writer, actors, production company, and a plot summary. Entries for filmmakers include date and place of birth and date of death, specialty, and a career biography featuring the most prominent works. Entries for genres and subjects provide clear definitions and discuss relevant films. Supplementary materials include a classified guide to the encyclopedia, an extensive bibliography, a name index cross-referencing Pinyin and Chinese characters, and indexes by title, name, and studio. The *Encyclopedia* is an excellent resource for researchers and fans interested in the full range of Chinese film.

INDIA

282.   Banerjee, Shampa, and Anil Srivastava. 1988. *One Hundred Indian Feature Films: An Annotated Filmography, Garland Reference Library of the Humanities; Vol. 915.* New York: Garland.

Banerjee and Srivastava introduce readers to the best in Indian film by bringing "together a representative selection from the first talkies to the present day." They selected the 100 films by consulting with almost 90 film critics and scholars and then adjusted the list based on availability of information about each film. The films are listed in alphabetical order by original title and include the title in English, technical details, production, and crew and cast. A detailed plot summary is followed by an in-depth discussion. In addition to a general index, there is a chronological index and an index to English-language titles.

283. Chabria, Suresh, Paolo Cherchi Usai, Virchand Dharamsey, and National Film Archive of India. 1994. *Light of Asia: Indian Silent Cinema, 1912–1934.* New Delhi: Wiley Eastern.

With most of the silent film era films lost to the ravages of time, Chabria, who works for the National Film Archive of India, proposed an Indian Silent Cinema Retrospective. This volume reflects the outcome of the work that went into the screening. Part one offers two perspectives on the history of Indian silent film plus the notes for the Retrospective. Part two is the filmography. Listed in chronological order, each film includes the production company, director, cinematographer, screenwriter, and leading players. With most films lost, there are no plot summaries except in the section devoted to the Retrospective.

284. Gulzar, Govind Nihalani, and Saibal Chatterjee. 2003. *Encyclopaedia of Hindi Cinema.* New Delhi; Maidstone, England: Encyclopaedia Britannica; Amalgamated Book Services.

Gulzar, Nihalani, and Chatterjee led a team of scholars in producing this lavishly illustrated guide to Hindi-language cinema. Critical scholarly essays are gathered under sections on history, business, narrative forms, and genres and movements. After a section with interviews, prominent filmmakers and stars are featured in career biographies that include filmographies. It is to these biographies that readers must turn to see whether the films listed in the film title index are described, because it includes only the title, director, and year of release. This excellent resource also includes a general index. See the *Encyclopaedia of Indian Cinema* (see entry 287) for coverage of Indian films in languages other than Hindi.

285. Narwekar, Sanjit. 1994. *Directory of Indian Film-Makers and Films.* Westport, Conn.: Greenwood Press.

Narwekar has compiled a biographical dictionary of "all prominent film directors working in all Indian languages between 1899 and the end of 1993." He includes biographies for 383 filmmakers' lives and careers and complete filmographies. The filmographies include language, year released, and original and English-language titles. The film title index includes cross-references to English-language titles. A general index lists names, organizations, and literary sources.

286. Raheja, Dinesh, and Jitendra Kothari. 1996. *The Hundred Luminaries of Hindi Cinema.* Bombay: India Book House.

Raheja profiles 100 of the most prominent filmmakers and performers from Hindi cinema. Organized chronologically by birthday, each entry includes several photographs and an essay on life and career highlighting key films. With no index, it can be difficult to locate an individual, so the book works best as a browsing collection.

287.   Rajadhyaksha, Ashish, and Paul Willemen. 1999. *Encyclopaedia of Indian Cinema.* New rev. ed. New Delhi; New York: Oxford University Press.

A short five years after producing the most authoritative and complete guide to Indian cinema, the British Film Institute produced a new and revised edition in response to an outpouring of feedback on names left out of the first edition. Both editions have a strong historical focus and make an effort to represent all six major language industries. The newer edition updates the films and makes corrections, and also fills gaps recommended by Indian film enthusiasts in response to the first edition. The book is divided into two main parts. The first part is a dictionary of people, institutions, and subject entries. The entries for people include biographies and complete filmographies. The entries for institutions provide a history and discussion of their impact. The subject entries focus on themes and genres. The second part of the book is a chronological list of films produced in India from 1912 to 1995. Each entry includes the title in its original language and translated to English, technical information, crew, cast, and a plot summary. The name and title indexes are excellent, as is the bibliography. This reference book is the first place to look when researching Indian film.

288.   Roy, Rajata. 1983. *Filmography of Sixty Eminent Indian Movie-Makers, Along with Their Short Biographical Notes.* Mosaboni Mines, Singhbhum, Bihar, India; Calcutta: Cine Society Mosaboni; Exclusive distributor K.P. Bagchi.

One of the earliest English-language filmographies of Indian cinema is still useful for its coverage of 60 directors and the almost 800 films they made. The title describes the book nicely—for each director there is a portrait and a short biography followed by a filmography. For each film, there is the standard listing of titles in both the original language and English, language, cast and crew, release date, and awards. There are no plot summaries. The index lists only the original title, making it necessary for readers who are working with an English title to browse the director's section to find the film.

JAPAN (SEE ALSO ANIME)

289.   Bock, Audie. 1985. *Japanese Film Directors.* Tokyo; New York: Kodansha International.

Bock, a lecturer and filmmaker, has written in-depth studies of 10 of the most prominent Japanese directors. Her essays are based on both published materials and, in most cases, personal interviews with the directors. Each essay thoroughly covers life and career and is followed by a complete filmography that includes credits for principal crew and cast and a plot summary—note that the filmography is updated from 1977 to 1985 in an appendix. Glossy black-and-white stills are bound in separate sections. Includes a bibliography and an index to the text (but not to the filmographies).

290.   Buehrer, Beverley Bare. 1990. *Japanese Films: A Filmography and Commentary, 1921–1989.* Jefferson, N.C.: McFarland.

Buehrer has selected the 80 films that she feels will best reveal Japanese cinema to readers. She chose films that represent a period in filmmaking or a director, that received popular or critical attention, and that were distributed in the West. The films are presented in chronological order. Each entry includes the English title and the Romanized Japanese title along with the standard technical information plus crew and cast. The strength of the book lies in its detailed plot summaries and in-depth discussions and analyses of the films and directors. Buehrer also includes a chronology of Japanese history and a glossary of Japanese terms used in the filmography. An extensive bibliography, a directory of video sources, and an index round out the book. Buehrer succeeds in her goal of creating an interesting introduction to Japanese film.

291. Galbraith, Stuart. 1996. *The Japanese Filmography: A Complete Reference to 209 Filmmakers and the Over 1250 Films Released in the United States, 1900 through 1994.* Jefferson, N.C.: McFarland.

As indicated in the title, Galbraith has created a detailed reference guide to Japanese films released in the United States. The book is divided into three parts. Personnel entries list birth date (and death date if deceased), education, a brief biography, and a filmography. The studio section is extremely short, listing six major studios. By far the largest section of the book is the list of feature films. These include the standard technical information, cast and crew, plus U.S. release information. The cast and crew information is invaluable, because subtitles often give only the most prominent names. Unfortunately, Galbraith does not provide synopses or evaluations of the films. Other sections include a chronology, statistics, awards, animated features, a selected bibliography, and a title index.

292. Svensson, Arne. 1971. *Japan.* London; New York: A. Zwemmer Ltd.; A.S. Barnes.

Japan is informally subtitled "an illustrated guide to the work of the major directors, players, technicians and other key figures in the Japanese Cinema, with an index to 2,000 titles." One hundred thirty-two entries intersperse prominent filmmakers and actors with prominent films. Biographical entries include name, year of birth and death, a brief biography, and a filmography—complete for directors, but select for others. Film entries list principal crew and cast and provide a plot outline and a commentary. Well illustrated with a glossary of Japanese terms and an index to 2,000 titles in both Romanized Japanese and English. *Japan* is a part of Screen Series editor Peter Cowie's books on national cinema.

293. Weisser, Thomas, and Yuko Mihara Weisser. 2003. *Japanese Cinema: The Essential Handbook.* 5th ed. Miami: Vital Books; Asian Cult Cinema Publications.

Weisser is a well-known aficionado of Asian cult films. He is editor of *Asian Cult Cinema* (formerly *Asian Trash Cinema*) and has written several reference guides on the subject. *Japanese Cinema: The Essential Handbook* is the most complete guide to Japanese cult films made since 1955, a category that refers to an entire range of genres, from Samurai to Yakuza, from monster to superhero, from comedy to pink movies. Working with his wife, who speaks Japanese, he has completely updated previous editions and has corrected many long-standing errors from earlier Japanese film guides. Films are in alphabetical order by English title with the Romanized Japanese title in parentheses. Each film lists director and main actors along with a rating of one to four stars. The authors' love of Japanese cinema is evident in their entertaining plot summaries. One appendix translates the original Japanese titles to English while a second provides a filmography by director.

AUSTRALIA, NEW ZEALAND, AND THE SOUTH PACIFIC

294. Verhoeven, Deb. 1999. *Twin Peeks: Australian and New Zealand Feature Films.* Melbourne, VIC: Damned Pub.

The first half of *Twin Peeks* consists of a dozen essays on the history and state of film in Australia and New Zealand. The articles were written by professors and graduate students and reflect the sensibilities of academia. The second half of *Twin Peeks* is what makes this useful as a reference. Verhoeven lists films made in Australia and New Zealand since the earliest days of cinema. Each entry includes the title, director, producer and production company, major crew, cast, genre, and a synopsis. Although the Australian films are well covered elsewhere (see the other books in this section), the book is useful for its coverage of the New Zealand cinema.

AUSTRALIA

Get the Picture: Essential Data on Australian Film, Television, Video, and Interactive Media (see entry 1173)

295. Hall, Sandra. 1992. *Australian Film Index: A Guide to Australian Feature Films since 1900.* Port Melbourne, Vic.: Thorpe.

Film critic Hall has compiled a list of 1,400 films produced in Australia. In alphabetical order by title, she lists date, length, and credits for production, direction, screenwriting, cinematography, editing, music, and principal cast, with separate indexes for each. Appendixes include sources consulted and Australian Film Institute Awards from 1976 to 1992. The best use of Hall's index is as a filmography for Australian filmmakers and actors.

296. Halliwell, William K. 1985. *The Filmgoer's Guide to Australian Films.* North Ryde, NSW: Angus & Robertson.

Halliwell has written an engaging little guide to Australian film. While not comprehensive, he does cover most mainstream films released during the first 50 years after the silent era. For each film, he includes the title, director, running time, production crew, and cast. Brief synopses are followed by critiques based on the entertainment value and quality of the script, the film, and the direction and acting. For entries on filmmakers and actors, he includes the name, a very brief biography, and a list of film credits.

297. Harrison, Tony. 1994. *The Australian Film and Television Companion: Over 2400 Alphabetical Entries.* East Roseville, NSW: Simon & Schuster Australia.

Harrison took over 10 years to compile this guide to Australian film and television. Three sections list most films, the majority of nationally televised television programs, and 400 prominent people who helped make them. Entries for films and television programs include production and cast credits, year, length, and a capsule review. Entries for individuals include career specialty and film and television credits.

298. McFarlane, Brian, Geoff Mayer, and Ina Bertrand. 1999. *The Oxford Companion to Australian Film.* Melbourne; New York: Oxford University Press.

This book lives up to the high quality expected of an Oxford Companion. Its broad scope encompasses the films, people, and issues that make Australian film distinct. The companion is selective. Films were included if they were commercially or critically popular or influential or "quintessentially 'Australian.'" People were selected if they had a significant body of Australian work. Most of these articles were written by the editors, who also sought over 80 contributors to write issue-oriented articles on the history, art, and critical analysis of film and the motion picture industry. Appendices list Australian Film Institute Award winners. The subject index is ineffective, because it is too broad.

299. Murray, Scott, Raffaele Caputo, and Alissa Tanskaya. 1995. *Australian Film, 1978–1994: A Survey of Theatrical Features.* 2nd ed. Melbourne: Oxford University Press.

Presented chronologically by year, Murray and colleagues have continued the work began in *Australian Film, 1900–1977* (see entry 301). Each year lists the films made, including the title, director, production company, technical data, crew, cast, and a still. Each film receives a brief synopsis, a critical analysis, and a list of references consulted. Includes appendixes on Super 8 and video theatrical features, recently completed features, a bibliography, and a comprehensive index.

300. Murray, Scott. 1996. *Australia on the Small Screen: Film and Mini-Series on Television and Video, 1970–1995.* Melbourne: Oxford University Press.

This companion volume to *Australian Films 1978–1994: A Survey of Theatrical Features* lists TV and direct-to-video movies, miniseries, and films intended for theatrical release that were never shown in theaters. All movies produced or directed by Australians or made in Australia are included. Each entry lists the director, the crew and cast, and a brief synopsis. Because of the nature of the product, the author was able to view only 200 of the 570 films and miniseries listed, but since no reviews are included, this has not affected the quality of the book. The book includes an index to directors, but unfortunately does not include a name index for crew or cast.

301. Pike, Andrew, and Ross Cooper. 1998. *Australian Film, 1900–1977: A Guide to Feature Film Production.* Rev. ed. Melbourne; New York: Oxford University Press.

Presented chronologically, the authors have divided Australian cinema into seven distinct time periods. For each era, they provide an overview of the film industry, the major films, and their impact on society. Each entry includes the title, director, production company and crew, and cast. Each film receives a brief synopsis and a critical analysis written by the authors. The index is comprehensive. The Australian Film Commission updated this book with *Australian Film, 1978–1994* (see entry 299).

302. Reis, Brian. 1997. *Australian Film: A Bibliography.* London; Washington, D.C.: Mansell.

With nearly 15,000 entries, Reis has compiled the most complete bibliography of the literature about Australian film. The subject section covers topics such as reference works, periodicals, and book reviews and criticism, the film industry, and society and film. Subsequent sections cover works about people and individual films. Includes author and film title indexes.

303.   Stewart, John. 1984. *An Encyclopaedia of Australian Film.* Frenchs Forest, NSW: Reed Books.

Although not stated explicitly, Stewart most likely wrote this reference guide to Australian filmmakers to complement the fine Australian filmography in *Australian Film, 1900–1977* (see entry 301). Most entries are for directors or actors, but also include "more recent producers, directors of photography, editors, composers, writers, and soundmen." For each filmmaker, Stewart lists name, year of birth, specialty with a very brief career biography, and a complete list of film and television credits. Illustrated throughout with black-and-white stills, supplementary materials include a chronological list of films with year, director, and principal cast, novels filmed, title changes, and a complete index.

NEW ZEALAND

304.   Martin, Helen, and Sam Edwards. 1997. *New Zealand Film, 1912–1996.* Auckland; New York: Oxford.

Writer and film teacher Martin and film researcher Edwards have compiled a "reference book which aims to chronicle all New Zealand's feature films" with the exception of adult movies. Arranged chronologically, the book devotes an entire page to each film. Entries include production and cast credits, a plot synopsis with critical review, and a black-and-white still from the film. The book includes an appendix that lists "international films associated with New Zealand," a bibliography, and an index. New Zealand film is the most comprehensive look at New Zealand feature films available.

SOUTH PACIFIC

Made in Paradise: Hollywood's Films of Hawai'i and the South Seas (see entry 1234)

Return to Paradise: A Guide to South Sea Island Films (see entry 1233)

EUROPE

305.   Vincendeau, Ginette. 1995. *Encyclopedia of European Cinema.* New York: Facts on File.

This encyclopedia was produced under the auspices of the British Film Institute in celebration of 100 years of European cinema. The best place to begin most research is in one of the 26 national essays, because they provide an overview of each country's cinematic history and refer to other entries that include filmmakers, institutions, and critical articles on themes and genres. The book does not have separate entries for individual films. Appendixes include statistics on number of films produced by country each year with audience figures and a bibliography. There is no index, and illustrations are limited to four blocks scattered throughout the book. The *Encyclopedia* is a good place to begin research, especially for countries not as well covered by other publications. The BFI published a series of companions to cinema for individual European countries with exactly the same text.

WESTERN EUROPE
Belgium

306.   Thys, Marianne, René Michelems, and Cinémathèque Royale de Belgique. 1999. *Belgian Cinema = Le Cinéma Belge = De Belgische Film.* Brussels; Ghent; Paris: Royal Belgian Film Archive; Ludion; Flammarion.

With the goal of bringing international attention to Belgian cinema, the Royal Belgian Film Archive compiled this comprehensive catalog of 1,647 full-length films produced in Belgium. Because its definition included films financed by Belgian production companies, the catalog also includes films created in the Congo, Rwanda, and Burundi prior to their independence from Belgium. The catalog is divided into the silent and sound eras, and films are listed in chronological order. Each entry includes the title, director, screenwriter, year of production, cast and crew, and language. A brief bibliography lists the books, magazines, newspapers, annuals, and festival catalogs that were consulted to supplement the holdings of the archive. Separate indexes contain film titles and names. Each part of the catalog is in English, French, and Flemish. This catalog is the premier guide to Belgian cinema.

France

307.   Biggs, Melissa E. 1996. *French Films, 1945–1993: A Critical Filmography of the 400 Most Important Releases.* Jefferson, N.C.: McFarland.

Francophile Biggs has compiled a list of the 400 films she felt were most representative of French cinema. In alphabetical order by the film's French title, she includes English title, technical data, principal crew and cast, and a critical synopsis. Includes a complete index. Although not comprehensive, the filmography is nevertheless a useful resource for people interested in French film.

French-Speaking Women Film Directors: A Guide (see entry 944)

308.   Martin, Marcel. 1971. *France.* London; New York: Zwemmer; A.S. Barnes.

France is informally subtitled An Illustrated Guide to 400 Key Figures in French Cinema. Martin writes career biographies of the most prominent contemporary and historical French filmmakers and actors. Each entry includes name, year and place of birth, a brief biography, and a select filmography. Lavishly illustrated with an index to French-language titles. *France* is a part of Screen Series editor Peter Cowie's books on national cinema.

309. Paris, James Reid. 1983. *The Great French Films.* 1st ed. Secaucus, N.J.: Citadel Press.

Paris has produced an excellent introduction to 50 years of French feature films. Although his selection criteria are not explicitly stated, he does "stress the work of those directors whose reputations have extended far beyond France." The introduction by François Truffaut shares his perspective on the history of French cinema in counterpoint to American film. The rest of the book gives detailed information on 100 French films that includes credits, cast, background information, a synopsis, and a commentary. The book is lavishly illustrated in black and white. Although dated, the book still is an excellent introduction to French cinema.

310. Vincendeau, Ginette. 1996. *The Companion to French Cinema.* London: Cassell: British Film Institute.

Vincendeau's excellent introduction to French cinema begins with a historical overview for those unfamiliar with the country's oeuvre. Most of the book consists of articles on filmmakers, institutions, and "critical entries" such as themes and genres. The introduction and the entries are identical to those found in the *Encyclopedia of European Cinema* (see entry 305), which Vincendeau also edited for the British Film Institute and for which she provided the information on France.

Germany

311. Bucher, Felix, and Leonhard H. Gmür. 1970. *Germany.* London; New York: A. Zwemmer; A.S. Barnes.

Germany is informally subtitled "an illustrated guide to the work of over 400 directors, players, technicians and other leading figures in the German cinema." Bucher writes career biographies of the most prominent contemporary and historical German filmmakers and actors. Each entry includes name, year and place of birth, a brief biography, and a select filmography. Includes an index to 6,000 German-language titles. *Germany* is a part of Screen Series editor Peter Cowie's books on national cinema.

312. Elsaesser, Thomas, and Michael Wedel. 1999. *The BFI Companion to German Cinema.* London: British Film Institute.

Elsaesser led a team of specialists in writing a concise dictionary of German, Austrian, and Swiss cinema. Entries for personnel include name, job specialty, date and place of birth and death, and a bibliography. The career biography discusses career and works, listing the most important films in the body and reserving the rest for a section called "other films." Entries for theory, movements, genres, and institutions provide a well-written overview. There is no index, but extensive cross-references do a good job of guiding readers.

313. Helt, Richard C., and Marie E. Helt. 1987. *West German Cinema since 1945: A Reference Handbook.* Metuchen, N.J.: Scarecrow Press.

314. Helt, Richard C., and Marie E. Helt. 1992. *West German Cinema, 1985–1990: A Reference Handbook.* Metuchen, N.J.: Scarecrow Press.

These compilations are most useful as a complete list of films produced in West Germany from 1945 to 1990. The information on each film is minimal, including date, English title, a brief synopsis, and top cast and crew. The authors also provide introductory essays on the history of German cinema and an interview with a filmmaker about how he financed his film. The books provide brief biographies of the film directors whose movies are featured. There are separate indexes for directors, actors, and English film titles.

315.   Inter Nationes. 1986. *Films from the Federal Republic of Germany.* Bonn: Press and Information Office of the Federal Government; Inter Nationes.

This work lists documentaries, experimental films, and cartoons available for distribution by Inter Nationes and the Press and Information Office of the Federal Government. The productions are intended "for cultural and political public relations work abroad," but despite these educational and propaganda purposes, the list is useful because it provides unique access. The documentaries are organized by broad subject areas. Each documentary lists the length and date of release, rights, and a brief synopsis. The index is an alphabetical list of titles.

316.   Ott, Frederick W. 1986. *The Great German Films.* Secaucus, N.J.: Citadel Press.

Ott profiles 45 of the most significant West German films made from the earliest years of cinema through 1981. Organized chronologically, each film includes German and English title, credits for principal cast and crew, a synopsis with production notes and critical commentary, and black-and-white stills. Intended primarily as an introduction to German film, the book lacks an index that would have improved its reference value.

Great Britain

317.   Allon, Yoram, Del Cullen, and Hannah Patterson. 2001. *Contemporary British and Irish Film Directors: A Wallflower Critical Guide.* London; New York: Wallflower.

The *Wallflower Critical Guides* feature biographies of "well-established and emerging directors." In this volume, the focus is on directors currently working in Great Britain or Ireland. The articles are written by film critics and scholars and discuss the director's life, career, and films. Films are listed in the margin with year of release. No cast or crew is included, as the Guides are intended to be biographies rather than filmographies. The "filmography" is actually the film title index.

318.   *The British Film Institute* [World Wide Web Resource]. British Film Institute. Address: http://www.bfi.org.uk. [Accessed: March 2005].

The mission at the British Film Institute (BFI) is to "develop greater understanding and appreciation of film, television and the moving image." As such, the BFI serves as a portal to just about anything dealing with film and television in Great Britain. Sections are devoted to films in current release, books, videos, and DVDs available for purchase, *Sight & Sound* film journal, listings for film courses, and links to Web resources. With over 42,000 books, the British Film Institute National Library holds one of the "world's largest collections of books on cinema and television"—the collection is searchable using the OLIB Webview catalogue. BFI also publishes the annual industry directory *BFI Film and*

Television Handbook (see entry 1174) and *The Ultimate Film,* a list of the top 100 films of all time (see entry 225).

> *Broadcasting It: An Encyclopaedia of Homosexuality in Film, Radio and TV in the UK, 1923–1993* (see entry 930)

319.   Butler, Ivan. 1973. *Cinema in Britain: An Illustrated Survey.* South Brunswick: A.S. Barnes.

Butler surveys "important" British films made between 1895 and 1971. His definition of important is undefined, but he has seen virtually all of the films listed. The films are in chronological order and include scriptwriter, director, photographer, art director, players, and production company. Butler writes a synopsis with commentary and includes numerous stills, many from his own collection. Includes a film title index, but no name index.

320.   Caughie, John, and Kevin Rockett. 1996. *The Companion to British and Irish Cinema.* London: Cassell: British Film Institute.

Caughie and Rockett write excellent introductions to British and Irish cinema. As with all volumes of the *Encyclopedia of European Cinema* (see entry 305), the book begins with a historical overview for those unfamiliar with the country's oeuvre. Most of the dictionary consists of articles on filmmakers, institutions, and "critical entries" such as themes and genres. The introduction and the entries are identical to those found in the *Encyclopedia of European Cinema,* for which Caughie and Rockett provided the information on Britain and Ireland.

321.   Gifford, Denis. 2000. *The British Film Catalogue. Vol. 1, Fiction Film, 1895–1994.* 3rd ed. London: Fitzroy Dearborn.

322.   Gifford, Denis. 2000. *The British Film Catalogue. Vol. 2, Non-Fiction Film, 1888–1994.* 3rd ed. London: Fitzroy Dearborn.

This catalog represents a complete list of films "produced for public entertainment" by British movie companies from 1895 to 1994. Volume 1 presents fiction films of all genres, and volume 2, which was not available in the first two editions, presents documentaries. For each film, Gifford includes title, date, technical information, production and distribution companies, credits, cast and characters, story source, genre, and awards. Beginning in 1971, he also includes editors and music composers and directors. The catalog has title indexes for each volume, but unfortunately does not include a name index. For names, refer to the *Complete Index to British Sound Film* (see entry 324).

323.   Gifford, Denis. 1978. *The Illustrated Who's Who in British Films.* London: Batsford.

Gifford has compiled a list of 1,000 "stars, character actors, and directors" featured in British films from 1895 through 1977. Alphabetical by last name, entries include real name, main profession within the industry with a capsule on the career, place and date of birth, dates of death and career highlights, and biographies. The filmographies are chronological lists of films produced by British film companies; they do not include Hollywood films. The biographical bibliography "includes personalities whose work in films lies beyond the scope" of the book, and thus Gifford claims it is the "most complete British Film Bibliography yet published." Over 250 illustrations put faces to names. There is no index.

324.   Goble, Alan. 1999. *The Complete Index to British Sound Film since 1928.* London; New Providence, N.J.: Bowker Saur.

With 12,862 sound films, this is the most complete catalog of British films produced between 1928 and 1998. The information for each film is of necessity brief, including title, director, actors, cinematographer, production company, composer, and author. In addition, the book contains indexes "for 3561 directors, 25675 actors, 1135 cinematographers, 1243 composers, 4252 production and releasing companies and 2043 authors." Additional indexes list films in chronological order and actors' birthdays and places of birth. The book is aptly named an index, as there are no plot summaries or reviews.

325.   Mayer, Geoff. 2003. *Guide to British Cinema, Reference Guides to the World's Cinema.* Westport, Conn.: Greenwood Press.

As with all books in the Greenwood series *Reference Guides to the World's Cinema,* an introduction to the national cinema is followed by selections of the most prominent filmmakers and films of that country. Professor Mayer selected films and filmmakers that are considered "best," that were considered significant at the time, or that were representative of various genres. The guide is organized as a dictionary, with entries for films and filmmakers interfiled. Entries for film list principal crew and cast, awards, and a critical summary discussing plot and themes. The entries for filmmakers include a career biography followed by an extensive filmography. Includes a bibliography and an index. Although the introduction to the national cinema is not as extensive as other books in the series, this is still a good overview of British cinema.

326.   McFarlane, Brian, and Anthony Slide. 2003. *The Encyclopedia of British Film.* London: Methuen.

McFarlane led a team of scholars in compiling a guide to British cinema. The encyclopedia covers filmmakers, actors, institutions, genres, and subjects, but there are no entries for individual films. The 4,500 entries for filmmakers—by far the largest category—include year and place of birth and death, specialty, a career biography, and a filmography listing British films. Entries for institutions provide substantial histories. Entries for genres and subjects provide clear definitions and discuss relevant films. The *Encyclopedia* is an excellent resource for researchers and fans interested in the people and organizations behind British cinema.

327.   Palmer, Scott. 1981. *A Who's Who of British Film Actors.* Metuchen, N.J.: Scarecrow Press.

Palmer lists the film credits for approximately 1,400 British actors, either because they made their careers in British films or because they were born someplace in the Commonwealth before making films elsewhere. Organized by name, each actor is briefly described with years of birth and death along with complete credits for films made through 1979. Silent films are included for actors who were active in the sound era, but players who made their entire careers during the silent era are excluded. There is no index, so use is limited to finding credits.

328. Palmer, Scott. 1988. *British Film Actors' Credits, 1895–1987.* Jefferson, N.C.: McFarland.

Palmer "attempted to list virtually every British actor or actress who could be considered to have worked in films, with complete filmographies through December 1987." He includes nearly 5,000 performers who appeared in at least three films and who hailed from anywhere in the Commonwealth. In separate sections for the sound and silent eras, each entry lists actor, dates of birth and death if available, a character description, and a list of films in chronological order. Added materials include lists of actors with honorary titles who have appeared in at least 100 films, and who have won British Film Academy or MPAA Academy Awards.

329. Quinlan, David. 1984. *British Sound Films: The Studio Years 1928–1959.* London: Batsford.

Quinlan has compiled a list of films made by British studios in Britain from 1928 through 1959. Each chapter covers a decade and begins with a survey and sections naming the film and star of the decade before listing the films alphabetically by title and ending with a list of shorts. Quinlan has made every effort to be as comprehensive and accurate as possible, listing title, release date, principal cast and crew, a plot summary, and a personal rating on a scale of one to six. Unfortunately, the book does not include indexes, making it difficult to find films and impossible to find filmmakers. Includes a brief bibliography and is illustrated throughout with small black-and-white stills.

330. Slide, Anthony. 1996. *Some Joe You Don't Know: An American Biographical Guide to 100 British Television Personalities.* Westport, Conn.: Greenwood Press.

A prolific writer of film and television reference books, Slide has written a bio-graphical dictionary of 100 British actors featured on British television shows broadcast in the United States through the mid-1990s. The biographies are lengthy career entries based on the books and articles listed in each entry's bibliography. The index contains shows and names mentioned in articles. About one quarter of the entries are accompanied by portraits.

331. Vahimagi, Tise, Michael Ian Grade, and British Film Institute. 1996. *British Tele-vision: An Illustrated Guide.* 2nd ed. Oxford; New York: Oxford University Press.

This year-by-year examination of British television shows and specials begins in 1936 and ends in 1995. Compiler Vahimagi, a researcher at the British Film Institute, felt it "impossible to include every single programme" due to space considerations, but does not explain the criteria for which shows were included and which were left out, except to share his goal of providing a "perspective on the totality of British Television." He did indeed succeed in that goal. Each decade is introduced with an overview followed by a list of shows that began broadcasting each year. Each program entry includes the title, dates aired, a description with names of cast members, and at least one photograph. The book includes name and title indexes. Despite the fact that it is not comprehensive, this is the place to go for information about British television programs.

Greece

332.   Koliodimos, Dimitris. 1999. *The Greek Filmography, 1914 through 1996.* Jefferson, N.C.: McFarland.

Koliodimos has compiled a catalog of the over 2,300 films produced, but not necessarily released, in Greece between 1914 and 1996. He excludes pornographic and religious proselytizing movies. The films are in order by Romanized Greek title, followed by Greek and English titles. Each entry lists the above-the-line cast and crew and contains a two- or three-paragraph synopsis. Appendixes list the winners of the two major Greek film awards. There are English and Greek indexes to names and a Greek index to titles. Easily the most complete guide to Greek films.

Ireland

The Companion to British and Irish Cinema (see entry 320)

334.   Gray, Michael. 1999. *Stills, Reels, and Rushes: Ireland and the Irish in 20th Century Cinema.* Dublin: Ashfield Press.

Gray examines "one hundred of the most important fiction films of Ireland's people, places and Diaspora" from the first film in 1910 through 1999. Unlike most national filmographies, this book is not limited to films produced in Ireland, but also includes films produced elsewhere that either feature Ireland as a place or feature Irish people no matter where they live. For each film, Gray lists the title, release date, the production team, and the cast and provides his own rating. Each film is illustrated by at least one black-and-white still. Most useful to readers are the lengthy and engaging plot summaries and discussions on each film.

335.   Monks, Robert, and National Library of Ireland. 1996. *Cinema Ireland: A Database of Irish Films and Filmakers, 1896–1986.* Dublin: National Library of Ireland.

I was not able to view this CD-ROM. Publicity from the National Library of Ireland describes a browsable and searchable database of more than 1,600 Irish films.

336.   Rockett, Kevin. 1996. *The Irish Filmography: Fiction Films, 1896–1996.* Dublin: Red Mountain Media.

In this mammoth undertaking, Rockett has set out to "document as completely as possible all fiction films made in Ireland and about Ireland and the Irish produced worldwide since the beginnings of cinema." With nearly 2,000 titles, he has apparently succeeded beyond expectations. The first chapter chronologically lists films made in Ireland, and subsequent chapters list films made about Ireland and the Irish in Australia, Belgium, Canada, France, Germany, Great Britain, Holland, Israel, Russia, Spain, and the United States (by far the largest section). Entries are comprehensive, listing technical data, production and cast credits, a synopsis, production notes, a list of contemporary reviews, and, when available, later criticism and reviews. Indexes list personal names, corporate names, composers, literary sources, and film titles. Rockett has produced the premier source for Irish films.

337.   Stevens, Matthew. 1989. *Directory of Irish and Irish-Related Films.* Trowbridge, England: Flicks Books.

Stevens made the first attempt to comprehensively document Irish film and films made by Irish filmmakers, including "films made abroad by Irish directors, films with an Irish theme or contents, and films based on Irish literary works." The book is divided into sections on Irish Films and Irish-related films. Each entry lists the title, principal crew and cast, and a brief description, along with country of origin in the second section. While nowhere near as comprehensive as *The Irish Filmography: Fiction Films, 1896–1996* (see entry 336), the inclusion of documentaries makes this work a nice complement.

Italy

338.   Buss, Robin. 1989. *Italian Films.* New York: Holmes & Meier.

Buss has written a critical analysis of how Italian cinema has "depicted Italy and Italian society." Of most interest for reference purposes are the filmographies that comprise the second half of the book. Divided into 12 sections such as Fascism and War, Politics and Religion, and Women and the Family, the 206 films are listed chronologically and include title, year of release, principal crew and cast, and a critical summary. A title (along with a general index) makes it possible to look up individual films.

339.   Nowell-Smith, Geoffrey, James Hay, and Gianni Volpi. 1996. *The Companion to Italian Cinema.* London: Cassell: British Film Institute.

Nowell-Smith and colleagues write an excellent introduction to Italian cinema. As with all volumes in the *Encyclopedia of European Cinema* (see entry 305), the book begins with a historical overview for those unfamiliar with the country's oeuvre. Most of the dictionary consists of articles on filmmakers, institutions, and "critical entries" such as themes and genres. The introduction and the entries are identical to those found in the *Encyclopedia of European Cinema,* for which Nowell-Smith, Hay, and Volpi provided the information on Italy.

340.   Stewart, John. 1994. *Italian Film: A Who's Who.* Jefferson, N.C.: McFarland.

Stewart has compiled filmographies for almost 5,000 filmmakers and actors appearing in films from the first 100 years of Italian cinema. For each person, he lists occupation and a brief biography followed by a complete filmography. Includes a bibliography and film title index.

341.   Vermilye, Jerry. 1994. *Great Italian Films.* Secaucus, N.J.: Carol.

Film writer Vermilye has written a chronological guide to 100 Italian films made between 1934 and 1992. Each film is listed by Italian title with English translation and includes production company, Italian and U.S. year of release, crew and cast credits, a critical summary, and stills. Without an index or bibliography, Vermilye's book is most useful as a guide to the best Italian films.

With Fire and Sword: Italian Spectacles on American Screens, 1958–1968 (see entry 548)

Netherlands

Of Joy and Sorrow: A Filmography of Dutch Silent Fiction (see entry 725)

342. Stevens, Matthew. 1990. *Directory of Contemporary Dutch Films and Film-Makers.* Trowbridge, England: Flicks Books.

Stevens has attempted to write a complete guide to the new Dutch cinema by including all feature films and documentaries made by Dutch directors on Dutch topics from 1965 through 1990. The book is arranged alphabetically by English title with cross-references to the Dutch title. Information is minimal, including basic crew and cast and a no more than one-sentence description. There are indexes to filmmaker, production company, and selected subjects.

Portugal

343. España, Rafael de. 1994. *Directory of Spanish and Portuguese Film-Makers and Films.* Westport, Conn.: Greenwood Press.

Film researcher de España has compiled a guide designed to "provide reference information on Spanish and Portuguese film-makers who worked in these countries between 1896 and 1994." Designed to be representative rather than comprehensive, the 215 filmmakers are included based on whether they were born or raised in Spain or Portugal or, if foreign-born, whether they made their careers there, as well as the quality or the quantity or the financial success of their films. Entries include a career biography and a complete feature film filmography with selective listings of shorts. With so few Spanish and especially Portuguese films released in English-language countries, the author often translated titles. Includes film title and general indexes. Overall, de España has produced an excellent guide for researchers interested in filmmakers from the Iberian Peninsula.

Spain

Directory of Spanish and Portuguese Film-Makers and Films (see entry 343)

344. D'Lugo, Marvin. 1997. *Guide to the Cinema of Spain, Reference Guides to the World's Cinema.* Westport, Conn.: Greenwood Press.

Professor D'Lugo has written a guide to the "major movements, trends, and the careers of individual artists" of Spanish cinema. After a lengthy historical overview of cinema in Spain, the book is divided into sections. First, the author describes 80 films "most frequently commented upon by film historians." For each film, he includes original and English-language title, a plot summary with critical commentary, and a bibliography. Second, career biographies for directors, producers, cinematographers, and critics include narrative filmographies and a bibliography. Third, D'Lugo gives the same treatment to actors. An appendix lists international awards won by Spanish films through 1994, and an index lists names, titles, and subjects. The guide is of most interest to students of Spanish film.

345. Schwartz, Ronald. 1991. *The Great Spanish Films, 1950–1990.* Metuchen, N.J.: Scarecrow Press.

Film professor and scholar Schwartz has written the first English-language guide to what he terms significant Spanish films, films that "reflect in some way the mentality of Spanish society." He begins with 1950 because he considers that the year that authentic Spanish cinema emerged. The book starts with a chronology of major film events and then presents the films in chronological order. Entries for films include title, director, credits, and cast followed by background, plot, and a valuable commentary. Each entry includes a large black-and-white still from the film. The fifties and sixties are represented by only 12 films; most of the book covers the post-Franco filmmaking explosion of the seventies and eighties. An appendix gives similar treatment for other "noteworthy" films, combining a plot summary with a brief commentary. Includes a selected bibliography and index.

346. Schwartz, Ronald. 1986. *Spanish Film Directors (1950–1985): 21 Profiles.* Metuchen, N.J.: Scarecrow Press.

Film professor and scholar Schwartz has written a guide to 21 prominent Spanish film directors who began their careers after 1950. Each entry includes a portrait, a filmography, an in-depth exploration of the director as an auteur, a bibliography, and black-and-white illustrations. Supplementary materials include brief biographies on up-and-coming directors, an essay on Luis Buñuel (who began his career well before 1950), a bibliography, and indexes by film title and director.

347. Torres, Augusto M., Roger Mortimer, and E. Nelson Modlin III. 1986. *Spanish Cinema 1896–1983.* Madrid: Ministerio de Cultura Instituto de Cine.

Torres has written an excellent guide to Spanish cinema. Organized by time period, each chapter contains a filmographic essay on the films in the context of the time. Other chapters list directors and actors, with each including a brief career biography and credits. Additional materials include chapters on the avant-garde and animation, a chronology, and title and name indexes. Unlike most guides to Spanish film, Torres covers films made throughout history from the earliest days of cinema through publication in the mid-eighties. Translated from the Spanish by E. Nelson Modlin III.

EASTERN EUROPE, RUSSIA, AND SCANDINAVIA

348. Balski, Grzegorz. 1992. *Directory of Eastern European Film-Makers and Films, 1945–1991.* Westport, Conn.: Greenwood Press.

Balski has compiled a comprehensive list of "directors active in Eastern European film-making during the period 1945–1991" who made a least three films released in theaters. Countries include Albania, Bulgaria, Czechoslovakia, East Germany, Hungary, Poland, Romania, the Soviet Union, and Yugoslavia. For each director, he includes the country where he or she worked, a brief biography, and a filmography divided into shorts and features. Indexes list film titles and a general index listing organizations, source materials, and names of non-directors. The useful bibliography lists film books by country.

349. Hibbin, Nina. 1969. *Eastern Europe; An Illustrated Guide.* London; New York: A. Zwemmer; A.S. Barnes.

Eastern Europe is informally subtitled "an illustrated guide to the postwar work of film directors, players and technicians in Albania, Bulgaria, Czechoslovakia, East Germany Hungary, Poland, Romania, the Soviet Union and Yugoslavia." Hibbin writes career biographies of the most prominent contemporary and historical Eastern European filmmakers and actors. Each entry includes name, year of birth and death, a brief biography, and a select filmography. The book is lavishly illustrated and includes an index to 2,500 English-language titles. *Eastern Europe* is a part of Screen Series editor Peter Cowie's books on national cinema.

350.   Slater, Thomas J. 1992. *Handbook of Soviet and East European Films and Filmmakers.* New York: Greenwood Press.

Slater and a small team of fellow film professors have compiled a handy guide to the cinema of the Soviet Union, Poland, Czechoslovakia, Yugoslavia, Hungary, East Germany, Romania, and Bulgaria. For each country, he includes a lengthy essay describing the historical, cultural, political, and artistic aspects of the national cinema, supported by an extensive bibliography. Following each essay are biographical sketches of prominent filmmakers and a selective chronological filmography. The appendix is a chronology of "major historical, cultural and film events in the Soviet Union and Eastern Europe" through 1990. Although slightly dated, the fact that the publication of the book coincided with the fall of the Soviet Union means that this is still an excellent reference to Eastern European cinema. Includes a film index.

351.   Taylor, Richard. 2000. *The BFI Companion to Eastern European and Russian Cinema.* London: British Film Institute.

A dozen British film and area studies professors have contributed to this concise guide to Eastern European and Russian film and filmmakers. The dictionary covers "important figures and landmarks," national cinemas, film genres, and organizations. The longest entries are for countries and include an in-depth history with a discussion of major figures and films. The genre entries are also broken down by country. Most entries are for individual filmmakers, which include a brief biography, a career overview, and a filmography. There are no entries for individual films. Rife with cross-references, the dictionary still would have benefited from an index, if only to look up discussions of individual films within larger discussions. Nevertheless, the writing is clear and authoritative, making it a good place to begin research on Eastern European and Russian Cinema. Includes a bibliography of sources consulted.

Armenia

352.   Gulyan, Svetlana, and Hayastani Kinogetneri ev Kinolragroghneri Asotsìatsìa. 2001. *Armenian Cinema Catalogue, 1924–1999: Features & Shorts, Documentaries, Animation.* Yerevan: Armenian Association of Film Critics and Cinema Journalists: Artagers.

Gulyan led a team from the Armenian Association of Film Critics and Cinema Journalists as they compiled a catalog of Armenian film. Arranged first into chapters on feature and short films, animation, and documentaries, and then chronologically, each film entry includes technical information, production and cast credits, and a synopsis. With film title and name indexes, this is the most comprehensive guide to Armenian cinema available in English. Translated by Shushan Harutyunyan and Hasmik Khachikian.

353. Pilikian, Hovhanness I. 1981. *Armenian Cinema: A Source Book.* London: Counter-Point.

Sampling only color films of the 1970s, Pilikian compiled this slim guide to Armenian cinema. Each film is treated to one or two pages and includes the title in English and Armenian , black-and-white stills, credits for writer, director, cinematographer, art director, sound, and a critical analysis rife with Soviet agit-prop. Separate sections list other films (including many older films), a television program, documentaries, and cartoons. Appendixes cover the Armenian holocaust and the subsequent Communist condemnation. Indexes list Armenian titles and directors.

Bulgaria

354. Holloway, Ronald. 1986. *The Bulgarian Cinema.* Rutherford, N.J.; London: Fairleigh Dickinson University Press; Associated Presses.

Holloway has written a well-illustrated guide to Socialist Bulgarian cinema. Part 1 devotes chapters to the art, culture, history, and trends in Bulgarian cinema. Part 2 provides career biographies of a dozen of the most prominent directors. Part 3 is a chronological filmography of films made between 1915 and 1985, listing Romanized and English-language title, principal crew and cast, release date, and a plot synopsis. Includes a title index. Holloway's guide is a welcome addition to a cinema that is not well covered.

Czechoslovakia, Czech Republic, and Slovakia

355. Dewey, Langdon. 1971. *Outline of Czechoslovakian Cinema.* London: Informatics.

The first English-language biographical dictionary of Czechoslovakian film is now dated, but is still interesting for its coverage of early Czech filmmakers. Dewey organized the dictionary chronologically, which makes it simple to introduce the state of filmmaking in each time period; however, because all of the entries are biographical and introduce filmmakers and actors by the year they first came to prominence, it is necessary to use the index to find names. The biographical entries describe career accomplishments and list the most prominent works.

356. Šmatláková, Renáta. 1999. *Katalóg Slovenských Celovečerných Filmov, 1921–1999 = The Catalogue of Slovak Full-Length Feature Films, 1921–1999.* Bratislave: Slovenský Filmový Ústav.

Šmatláková has compiled a bilingual guide to Slovak feature films made between 1921 and 1999. In alphabetical order by original Slovak title, each entry includes English title, release year, a synopsis, awards, credits for principal crew and cast, distributor, locations, and a black-and-white still. All information for films is listed in both Slovak and English, but the biographical profiles later in the book are in Slovak only. Indexes list locations, literary authors, names, and films by year. The Slovak Film Institute maintains an archive at <http://www.sfu.sk/english/articles.php?category_id = 6> that offers a Slovak-language only database of the films listed in the guide and updates them regularly.

Estonia

357.   Sokmann, Reet. 2000. *Eesti Film = Estonian Film: 1991–1999.* Tallinn: F-Seitse OÜ.

The catalog presents films produced in the first decade of Estonia's independence. Two essays introduce readers to the history of Estonian film and the current financial situation for filmmakers. The book is then divided into sections on feature films, shorts, cartoons and puppet films, documentaries, and even includes student films. Reflecting the massive changes brought on by independence, by far the largest section is on documentaries. The entry for each film lists title, date of release, technical details, and cast and crew. The book also includes motion picture industry statistics and a directory. Indexes are to film titles and to directors. All information is written in both Estonian and English. All in all, a useful guide to a little-known national cinema.

Hungary

358.   Somogyi, Lia. 1984. *Hungarian Film Directors, 1948–1983.* Budapest: Interpress.

A special issue of the Hungarofilm Bulletin, this directory is a compendium of Hungarian film directors who made films from the nationalization of the film industry in 1948 through compilation of the directory in 1983. For each director, there is a date of birth (and death if deceased), a biography, and a filmography. An appendix describes the Hungarian film industry. Title indexes are in both Hungarian and English. With limited publications on Hungarian film, this source is quite valuable.

Lithuania

359.   Tapinas, Laimonas, and Dialita Didziulyte. 1988. *Lithuanian Film Makers.* Vilnius: Vilnius Mintis Publishers.

Tapinas has compiled a list of Soviet Lithuanian filmmakers active from 1940 to 1988. Organized by filmmaker, each entry includes specialty, date and place of birth and death, where educated, career highlights, a complete filmography, and a bibliography. Lightly illustrated. The book was translated from Lithuanian by Dalija Tekoriené, and film titles, including those in the index, are in English.

Poland

360.   Grzelecki, Stanislaw, and Alicja Helman. 1969. *Twenty Years of Polish Cinema; Film 1947–1967.* Warsaw: Art and Film Publishers.

This book is nothing more than a series of black-and-white stills selected from the 300 films made in the years after World War II. Each is captioned with the title and a brief overview. A chronology at the end of the book lists each film during that time period with credits for screenwriter, director, cinematographer, and composer.

361.   Sobański, Oskar. 1987. *Polish Feature Films: A Reference Guide 1945–1985.* West Cornwall, Conn.: Locust Hill Press.

Sobański has compiled a list of feature filmmakers and actors working in postwar Poland. For each person, he includes occupation, date and place of birth, and a brief biography focusing on education and career. The filmography lists dates, Polish and English film title, and source material. Appendixes list the number of films made by year, the top box office hits, and the government film units. Indexes list films by Polish and English title and names.

Russia

362. Birkos, Alexander S. 1976. *Soviet Cinema: Directors and Films.* Hamden, Conn.: Archon Books.

Birkos has compiled a guide to Soviet directors and films. The first part of the book takes a critical look at the lives and works of Soviet directors and contains filmographies and bibliographies. The second part briefly describes Soviet films these directors made between 1918 and 1975. Added materials include a list of Soviet film studios and a bibliography, but no index. *Soviet Cinema* is a part of Screen Series editor Peter Cowie's books on national cinema.

363. Leyda, Jay. 1973. *Kino: A History of the Russian and Soviet Film.* London: Allen and Unwin.

Leyda has written 17 chapters as "an account of the artistic development" of Russian and Soviet cinema. The book is included here for its appendix, which chronologically lists Russian and Soviet films made from 1907 to 1982, with each entry including English-language title, length, and credits for lead crew and principal cast.

Scandinavia

364. Cowie, Peter, and Arne Svensson. 1970. *Sweden.* London; New York: A. Zwemmer; A.S. Barnes.

Sweden is informally subtitled "an illustrated guide to the work of the leading directors, players, technicians, and other key figures in Swedish cinema." Cowie and Svensson write career biographies of the most prominent contemporary and historical Swedish filmmakers and actors. Each entry includes name, year of birth and death, a brief biography, and a select filmography. They also write plot summaries and list credits for "more than seventy important films." The book is lavishly illustrated and includes an index to 1,000 Swedish and English-language titles. *Sweden* is a part of Screen Series editor Peter Cowie's books on national cinema.

365. Cowie, Peter, and Scandinavian Films. 1992. *Scandinavian Cinema: A Survey of the Films and Film-Makers of Denmark, Finland, Iceland, Norway, and Sweden.* London; Hollywood: Tantivy Press on behalf of Scandinavian Films.

Cowie, an editor, author, and lecturer on Scandinavian film, has created a guide and filmography of films made in Denmark, Finland, Iceland, Norway, and Sweden. The book begins with a chronology that parallels political and cultural events with important milestones in cinema. Half of the book is devoted to surveys for each of the five Scandinavian countries as well as the Nordic Film Institutes, which are the governmental funding agencies for film. The remainder of the book is a filmography organized by country. Entries are arranged chronologically and include English-language and original title, dates, director, screenwriter, cinematographer, and players followed by a brief synopsis. The book is well illustrated with black-and-white stills. The book includes a dictionary of directors, a bibliography, and a film title index. As the most comprehensive guide to films of the region, *Scandinavian Cinema* is of interest to both film scholars and movie fans.

366.   Qvist, Per Olov, and Peter von Bagh. 2000. *Guide to the Cinema of Sweden and Finland, Reference Guides to the World's Cinema.* Westport, Conn.: Greenwood Press.

As with all books in the Greenwood series *Reference Guides to the World's Cinema,* an introduction to the national cinema is followed by selections of the most prominent filmmakers and films of that country. Qvist writes on Swedish cinema, and von Bagh writes about Finnish cinema. Both write informative histories and overviews and then select films and filmmakers based on their social impact or popularity. For filmmakers, they provide brief biographies followed by extensive filmographies. For films, they include a summary and discussion followed by crew, cast, and premier date, plus any awards won. Both authors point to bibliographies where they obtained much of the information. The book has one combined index. As with all books in the series, this is a good place to go for an overview of Swedish and Finnish cinema.

SOUTH AMERICA, LATIN AMERICA, AND THE CARIBBEAN

367.   Barnard, Tim, and Peter Rist. 1996. *South American Cinema: A Critical Filmography, 1915–1994, Garland Reference Library of the Humanities; Vol. 1077.* New York: Garland.

Barnard and Rist led a team of 20 film scholars as they developed this excellent guide to over 140 films made in Argentina, Bolivia, Brazil, Chile, Colombia, Ecuador, Paraguay, Peru, Uruguay, and Venezuela (excluding Guyana, Surinam, and French Guiana). For each country, films are listed chronologically and include original and English-language title, credits, a critical analysis of the film placing it in its historical and political context, and any awards won. Indexes include original language titles, English titles, film directors, names and titles mentioned in the main text of an entry, and subject indexes for South American cinema and society. Includes a glossary of Brazilian and English-language film terms and a bibliography of works consulted. Intended primarily for film educators and students, the filmography is of interest to all South American film buffs.

368.   Burton, Julianne. 1983. *The New Latin American Cinema: An Annotated Bibliography of Sources in English, Spanish, and Portuguese, 1960–1980.* New York: Smyrna Press.

Burton compiled her bibliography as "a research guide to historical, theoretical, and critical works on Latin American cinema." Including English, Spanish, and Portuguese books and articles written between 1960 and 1980, chapters cover nine countries as well as Hispanic cinema in the United States. Entries include standard bibliographic data and an annotation. There is no index.

369.   Ranucci, Karen, and Julie Feldman. 1998. *A Guide to Latin American, Caribbean, and U.S. Latino Made Film and Video.* Lanham, Md.: Scarecrow Press.

On behalf of the International Media Resource Exchange—an organization dedicated to bringing previously inaccessible films to the United States—Ranucci and Feldman and a team of film experts have compiled a list of 445 feature films and documentaries made in Latin America and the Caribbean that are available for distribution in the United States. Organized by country, each film includes original and English-language title, genre, director, producer, and distributor. Intended for teachers, added material includes a summary, strengths and weaknesses, and how instructors can introduce and use the video in their classes. Includes an extensive bibliography, subject and title indexes, and a distributors directory. With close to 4,000 titles, the much larger *Latin American Video Archives* (*LAVA*) database from which this guide was drawn, is now available at <http://lavavideo. org>. Unfortunately, the online records include substantially less added information about each film (just a summary), so it is still worth purchasing the book for instructors.

370. Schwartz, Ronald. 1997. *Latin American Films, 1932–1994: A Critical Filmography.* Jefferson, N.C.: McFarland.

Film professor and scholar Schwartz has compiled a guide to 301 "significant Latin American films from 1932 through 1994." The book starts with an introduction to Latin American cinema and a chronology of major film events and then presents the films in alphabetical order. Entries for films include original and English-language title, director, country of origin, and a critical commentary. Includes a selected bibliography and index. The filmography will be useful to teachers and students of Latin American cinema in both its selection of films and in its critical commentary.

371. Siegmund, Marianne. *Film in Latin America: A Selective Bibliography* [World Wide Web Resource]. SALALM. 1999. Address: http://www.libs.uga.edu/lais/laisno7. html. [Accessed: March 2005].

Siegmund has compiled a nice list of reference books and historical and national monographs covering the cinema of Latin America and the countries of Argentina, Bolivia, Brazil, Chile, Colombia, Costa Rica, Cuba, Ecuador, Haiti, Mexico, Peru, Uruguay, and Venezuela. Entries include standard bibliographic data without annotations.

372. Trelles Plazaola, Luis. 1989. *South American Cinema: Dictionary of Film Makers.* 1st ed. Río Piedras: Editorial de la Universidad de Puerto Rico.

Trelles Plazaola has written a biographical dictionary of "film directors who are either native to South America or foreigners who, during certain periods, made their contributions to those countries' film production." In alphabetical order by name, entries include dates of birth and death, a brief biographical and career essay, a filmography of South American films, and a bibliography. Originally in Spanish, the dictionary was translated by Yudit de Ferdinandy. The dictionary includes no film index, so it is necessary to consult other works such as *South American Cinema: A Critical Filmography, 1915–1994* (see entry 367). An intended companion volume on directors of Mexico, Central America, and the Antilles has not yet materialized.

MEXICO

373.   Wilt, David E. 2004. *The Mexican Filmography: 1916 through 2001*. Jefferson, N.C.: McFarland.

Wilt, a Mexican film scholar, has compiled the most comprehensive English-language list of feature-length fictional films made in Mexico from 1916 to 2001. Organized chronologically by year production began, films include title, an English translation, production company, genre, director, principal cast, and a synopsis. Notes cover general production and location information, Ariel Award winners, films named to the *Somos* "100 Best Films of Mexican Cinema," literary sources, and remakes, sequels, and series. Supplementary materials include an appendix listing direct-to-video and made-for-television movies, a selective bibliography, and a comprehensive name and title index. The book is lightly illustrated with stills and posters, but the primary value lies in its scholarly collection of film titles.

UNITED STATES AND CANADA
CANADA

374.   Beattie, Eleanor. 1977. *The Handbook of Canadian Film*. 2d ed. Toronto: P. Martin Associates.

Beattie, an employee of Canada's National Film Board, created this one-stop guide to Canadian filmmakers and filmmaking. Twenty-seven chapters cover everything from music in films to film festivals to educational material. Of most use today are the entries on filmmakers, which include a biography, a filmography, and a bibliography. The rest of the handbook is too dated to be of much use. Includes an index of films, but no name index.

375.   Easterbrook, Ian K., and Susan Waterman MacLean. 1996. *Canada and Canadians in Feature Films: A Filmography, 1928–1990*. Guelph, Ont.: Canadian Film Project University of Guelph.

Easterbook and Waterman MacLean have compiled a list of 1,341 feature films from all over the world "which clearly identify Canada as a location or which feature Canadians as Characters." The filmography is chronological, with each entry including title, country where produced, year released, credits, a plot summary listing film locations, and technical data. Appendix A lists 11 serials, complete with episode titles. Appendix B identifies 633 films that were filmed in Canada, but that are not located there in the script. Appendix C includes 291 films for which information is incomplete. Indexes list actors, authors, characters, directors, literary sources, locations, producers, subjects, and titles. This massive undertaking will be most useful to film scholars interested in Canada.

376.   Morris, Peter. 1984. *The Film Companion*. Toronto: Irwin.

Morris wrote one of the first dictionaries of Canadian films and filmmakers. Not intended to be comprehensive, it includes works that are significant "for artistic, historic or even commercial reasons" and filmmakers with substantial bodies of work. He does not include actors. Film entries list significant cast and crew followed by a brief synopsis and discussion and a list of references. Filmmaker entries include a brief biography followed by a complete list of credits and references. The book does not include an index.

377.   Pratley, Gerald. 2003. *A Century of Canadian Cinema: Gerald Pratley's Feature Film Guide, 1900 to the Present.* Toronto: Lynx Images.

Pratley, a Canadian film critic and founder of the Ontario Film Institute, has written a guide to the first century of Canadian cinema. Just over half of the book lists feature films and made-for-television movies, including year of release, length, director, writer, principal cast, and a synopsis with brief commentary. The second half of the book serves as both an index and as filmographies for directors, writers, and actors.

378.   Rist, Peter. 2001. *Guide to the Cinema(s) of Canada, Reference Guides to the World's Cinema.* Westport, Conn.: Greenwood Press.

Rist led a group of film faculty at Concordia University in compiling this dictionary of 125 English, French, and native Canadian filmmakers and 175 films. Rist selected filmmakers who work primarily in Canada and films based on a poll of the best Canadian films "conducted by the Canadian film magazine, *Take One*, in 1993" as well as films that won awards or attained international prominence (both lists are included in appendixes). The entries for filmmakers include a brief biography and discussion of their work followed by a list of film credits and a bibliography. The entries for films include a synopsis and discussion of the film's style and impact followed by a bibliography. Extras include a chronology of films, a list of 100 prominent Canadian filmmakers and actors who work outside of Canada, a bibliography, and a good index. Not as comprehensive as Peter Morris's older *Film Companion* (see entry 376), the engaging style, the more up-to-date entries, and the inclusion of actors make this worthwhile to anyone studying Canadian film.

379.   Turner, D.J., and Micheline Morisset. 1987. *Canadian Feature Film Index, 1913–1985.* Ottawa: Public Archives Canada National Film Television and Sound Archives = Archives Publiques Canada Archives Nationales du Film de la Télévision et de l'Enregistrement Sonore.

Turner, an archivist for Canada's National Film, Television and Sound Archives, has compiled a comprehensive survey of the 1,222 feature films produced in Canada between 1913 and 1985. The chronological directory has the impressive goal of listing the "principal credits of every Canadian feature film." For each film, all principal crew and above-the-line cast are listed, along with the shooting dates, format, location, and language. As with all official Canadian publications, the filmography is bilingual, although the information for French-language films is in French and in English for all others. Indexes list films by title, title by year, name, production company, and by government finance companies CFDC/Telefilm and IQC/SGC. This is the most complete, accurate, and significant guide to Canadian feature films available.

380.   *Who's Who in Canadian Film and Television = Qui Est Qui au Cinéma et à La Télévision au Canada.* 1985. Toronto: Academy of Canadian Cinema & Television = Académie Canadienne du Cinéma et de la Télévision.

Who's Who in Canadian Film and Television is the official directory of the Academy of Canadian Cinema & Television. Organized by job specialty, each entry contains address, specialty, a career biography, and a filmography. Whether the entry is in English or French depends on how the individual submitted the information. An awards section lists all Genie, Gemini, and Gémeaux winners. Includes a name index and a separate directory of e-mail addresses and Web sites.

381. Wise, Wyndham. 2001. *Take One's Essential Guide to Canadian Film.* Toronto; Buffalo, N.Y.: University of Toronto Press.

This dictionary's origin was a special issue of *Take One* published in 1996 to celebrate 100 years of film in Canada. Over 700 entries "identify Canadians who have made a contribution to the world of cinema and important, award-winning Canadian films." Similar to the *Guide to the Cinema(s) of Canada* (see entry 378), but with many more films, entries for films provide basic cast and crew credits and a brief critical synopsis; entries for people provide a brief biography with a list of credits. Appendixes include a chronology and a list of award winning films.

UNITED STATES
Copyright

382. Hurst, Walter E. 1973. *Film Superlist: 20,000 Motion Pictures in the Public Domain.* Hollywood, Calif.: 7 Arts Press.

383. Hurst, Walter E. 1979. *Film Superlist for 1940–49: Motion Pictures in the U.S. Public Domain.* Hollywood, Calif.: 7 Arts Press.

384. Hurst, Walter E. 1989. *Film Superlist: Motion Pictures in the U.S. Public Domain, 1950–1959.* Hollywood, Calif.: 7 Arts Press.

Hurst came up with a list of 20,000 films in the public domain by comparing the original *Catalog of Copyright Entries* (see entries 388 to 390) from the Library of Congress against requests for copyright renewals. The first part of the book lists films made from 1894 through 1912, all of which are in the public domain. The second part lists films from 1912 through 1939. A copy of the *Catalog of Copyright Entries* is annotated by hand with registration numbers to indicate renewal, which can be used to see who owns current copyright. Hurst published later volumes for the next two decades with the *Film Superlist for 1940–49 Motion Pictures in the U.S. Public Domain* and the *Film Superlist: Motion Pictures in the U.S. Public Domain, 1950–1959.* The first book was also published under the title *Films: 1st–10th Book[s] of Over 1000 Public Domain Films.* The books are most useful for those seeking to use footage without cost, but should not be relied upon as 100 percent accurate.

385. *Openflix* [World Wide Web Resource]. Address: http://www.openflix.com. [Accessed: January 2005].

OpenFlix "provides a directory of movies commonly thought to be in the public domain and works their owners are willing to let be distributed." Searchable by title and browsable by genre, director, and actor, each title lists language, country and year of release, director, stars, genre, and a synopsis. Links to *Amazon.com* (see entry 87) offer the option of purchasing the film, while a handful of films may be downloaded from Web sites such as the *Movie Archive* (see entry 93) and *MovieFlix.com* (see entry 94). With fewer than 200 films, the site is not reliable for seeing all films in the public domain.

386.   Pierce, David, and Library of Congress. Copyright Office. 1989. *Motion Picture Copyrights & Renewals, 1950–1959.* Laurel, Md.: Milestone.

By listing copyrights for films made in the 1950s that were renewed in the 1980s, Pierce makes it possible to determine which films were not renewed and therefore might have fallen into the public domain. A facsimile of the original *Catalog of Copyright Entries* (see entries 388 to 390) is annotated by hand with registration numbers to indicate renewal. The registrations indicate who renewed the item and are good indications of who owns the current copyright. The book is most useful for those seeking to use footage without paying royalties, but the information should not be considered 100 percent reliable. Most feature films are renewed, and those that are not tend to be corporate and educational shorts.

387.   Walls, Howard Lamarr, and Library of Congress. Copyright Office. 1953. *Motion Pictures, 1894–1912, Identified from the Records of the United States Copyright Office.* Washington, D.C.: Copyright Office, Library of Congress.

388.   Library of Congress. Copyright Office. *Catalog of Copyright Entries.* 1951. *Motion Pictures, 1912–1939.* Washington, D.C.: Copyright Office, Library of Congress.

389.   Library of Congress. Copyright Office. *Catalog of Copyright Entries.* 1953. *Motion Pictures, 1940–1949.* Washington, D.C.: Copyright Office, Library of Congress.

390.   Library of Congress. Copyright Office. *Catalog of Copyright Entries.* Washington, D.C.: U.S. Government Printing Office.

Walls searched the records of the Copyright Office for items registered between 1893 and 1913 as photographs so he could identify those that were films. The result is a list of 8,506 films made between 1894 and 1912. Combined with cumulated lists of motion pictures made from 1912 to 1939 and from 1940 to 1949 from the *Catalog of Copyright Entries*—which are the official record of copyright registration in the United States—these sources "comprise an unbroken record of the copyright registration of motion pictures." As such, they also make a very good guide to films made in the United States during the period. The *Catalog of Copyright Entries, Third Series, Parts 12–13, Motion Pictures and Filmstrips* was regularly published until 1982.

Film

391.   American Film Institute, and Patricia King Hanson. 1988. *The American Film Institute Catalog of Motion Pictures Produced in the United States.* Berkeley; London: University of California Press.

392.   American Film Institute, and Chadwyck-Healey Inc. *AFI Catalog.* Chadwyck-Healey. 2002. Address: http://afi.chadwyck.com. [Accessed: March 2005].

393.   American Film Institute. *American Film Institute Catalog on CD-ROM* [Text Bibliographic database]. Alexandria, Va.: Chadwyck-Healey.

The American Film Institute is compiling the most authoritative catalog of feature films produced in the United States. Late in 2004, the film scholars responsible for viewing and analyzing each film had almost completed the 1950s set, which would make the catalog complete from 1893 through 1970. They will begin indexing 1970s films as soon as they complete the 1950s. Each decade (with the first set covering 1893–1910) devotes two or three volumes to listing complete production facts, crew and cast credits, and a plot summary that includes genre, source, and notes on such details as working and alternate titles, conflicts in credit information, and locations. Volumes that were produced later also note newsworthy stories and include citations to reviews. An extremely useful feature is the multiple subjects assigned to each film that cover ethnic, racial, and national group, occupation, themes, holidays and seasons, cinematic devices, animals, and historical events, places, and people. The subjects are listed in the index volume for each decade, making it possible for film scholars to locate films by content and to make connections between disparate films. The earliest produced volumes include only the credit and subject index; subsequent volumes also include a chronological list of films and indexes for personal and corporate names, genres, series, geography, foreign languages, songwriters and composers, and literary and dramatic credits. Chadwyck-Healey also makes a CD-ROM version available under the name *American Film Institute Catalog,* which offers keyword searching across all fields and years as well as browsing by film title, character name, cast and crew, literary source, release date, subject, genre, and songs. With ProQuest, the Web version is available under the name *AFI Catalog* <http://afi.chadwyck.com>, which also offers browsing by director and country, offers hyperlinks for just about every element in a record, and includes top 10 lists for each year. The CD-ROM is updated as new years are produced, while the Web database is constantly updated; both online versions correct errors and add information to earlier entries. With over 45,000 films, the AFI catalog may not be as large as the *IMDb* (see entry 66) or the *All-Movie Guide* (see entry 65), but it is certainly the most authoritative national filmography available and definitely the most useful for subject coverage. The *AFI Catalog* belongs in every library with patrons interested in film.

394.   Baxter, John. 1973. *Sixty Years of Hollywood.* South Brunswick, N.J.: A.S. Barnes.

This year-by-year survey of Hollywood looks at filmmaking in "the context of the times, choosing films for their importance to the industry and its image rather than because of outstanding merit." Paragraphs describe the major news of each year and films with principal crew and cast, illustrations, and a synopsis with commentary. Includes title and illustration indexes, but no name or subject indexes, so *Sixty Years* is best used as a chronology.

395.   Beaver, Frank Eugene. 1999. *100 Years of American Film.* New York: Macmillan Library Reference.

Intended primarily for movie buffs, this dictionary covers the movies, stars, filmmakers, genres, history, and business of American cinema. Scattered throughout the in-depth main entries are quotes, statistics, factoids, and photographs. End materials include Academy Award winning films, more factoids, a glossary, a suggested reading list, and a name and title index. Beaver has produced a one-stop reference book for movie fans that is engaging and fun.

396.   Brode, Douglas. 1976. *The Films of the Fifties: Sunset Boulevard to On the Beach.* 1st ed. Secaucus, N.J.: Citadel Press.

397.   Brode, Douglas. 1980. *The Films of the Sixties.* 1st ed. Secaucus, N.J.: Citadel Press.

398.   Brode, Douglas. 1991. *The Films of the Eighties.* 1st Carol Publishing Group ed. New York: Carol.

In each of his guides, Brode selected films "that most clearly caught the spirit" of the decade. Arranged chronologically, he includes plenty of illustrations, production and cast credits, and a critical essay on the film and its times. There are no indexes. For a guide to the seventies, see Marc Sigoloff's *The Films of the Seventies* (see entry 258).

399.   Brown, Gene. 1995. *Movie Time: A Chronology of Hollywood and the Movie Industry from Its Beginnings to the Present.* New York: Macmillan.

Brown has compiled a very useful and quite interesting year-by-year chronology of American movies from 1910 to 1994. The book begins with an overview that includes a list of the top stars, top box office, and top awards. Each year is divided into four categories: Personalities deals with celebrities in the news; Movies chronicles the release of major English language films; Business and Society covers major news stories about the movie industry and Births, Deaths, Marriages and Divorces is self-explanatory, listing major life events for Hollywood celebrities. An additional chronology covers 1830 to 1909, and a bibliography lists the resources used to compile the book. While the book is fun to browse, Brown provides an excellent index as well.

400.   Coursodon, Jean Pierre, and Pierre Sauvage. 1983. *American Directors.* New York: McGraw-Hill.

Film scholar and teacher Coursodon leads a team of film scholars writing about 117 directors of "recognized (and, in quite a few instances, under recognized) stature." The book excludes directors who were dead or inactive by 1940 and only includes contemporary directors (to the early 1980s) who had created substantial bodies of work. Each entry includes a filmography and a critical essay. Each volume includes separate general and title indexes. Students and scholars interested in an auteur approach will find this biographical guide of interest.

401.   Curran, Daniel. 1998. *Guide to American Cinema, 1965–1995, Reference Guides to the World's Cinema.* Westport, Conn.: Greenwood Press.

As with all books in the Greenwood series *Reference Guides to the World's Cinema,* an introduction to the national cinema is followed by selections of the most prominent filmmakers and films of that country. Curran selects American films and filmmakers in an "attempt to give a representation of the times" based on his favorites. For filmmakers, he provides brief biographies followed by an extensive filmography and a selective bibliography. For films, he includes above-the-line cast and crew followed by a summary and discussion of the film, and awards won. Appendixes provide chronologies of film and studio releases, lists of notable producers and screenwriters, Academy Award winners, and films in the Library of Congress *National Film Registry,* plus a name and film title index. As with all books in the series, this is a good place to go for an overview of American cinema from 1930 through 1965. For coverage from 1930 to 1965, consult the companion volume from the series by Thomas Whissen (see entry 420).

402.   Fetrow, Alan G. 1992. *Sound Films, 1927–1939: A United States Filmography.* Jefferson, N.C.: McFarland.

Fetrow has compiled a comprehensive list of films produced in the United States during the beginning of the talkie era in 1927 through the thirties. Each film entry includes the production company, year of release, credits for cast and crew, a one- or two-sentence synopsis, and awards. An appendix lists award winning and nominated films; a bibliography lists sources consulted; and a very extensive name index adds great value to the book. Fetrow wrote similar books covering the forties (see entry 403) and the fifties (see entry 404).

403.   Fetrow, Alan G. 1994. *Feature Films, 1940–1949: A United States Filmography.* Jefferson, N.C.: McFarland.

Fetrow has compiled a comprehensive list of 4,296 films produced in the United States during the forties. Each film entry includes the production company, year of release, credits for cast and crew, a one-sentence synopsis, and awards. An appendix lists award winning and nominated films; a bibliography lists sources consulted; and a very extensive name index adds great value to the book. Fetrow wrote similar books covering 1927–1239 (see entry 402) and the fifties (see entry 404).

404.   Fetrow, Alan G. 1999. *Feature Films, 1950–1959: A United States Filmography.* Jefferson, N.C.: McFarland.

Fetrow has compiled a comprehensive list of films produced in the United States during the fifties. Each film entry includes the production company, year of release, credits for cast and crew, a one- or two-sentence synopsis, and awards. An appendix lists award winning and nominated films; a bibliography lists sources consulted; and a very extensive name index adds great value to the book. Fetrow wrote similar books covering 1927–1239 (see entry 402) and the forties (see entry 403).

405.   Harpole, Charles Henry. 1990. *History of the American Cinema.* New York: Charles Scribner's Sons.

Over 20 years in the making, this massive 10-volume encyclopedia covers the history of movies and movie making in the United States. Each volume covers approximately one decade and is edited by a film scholar specializing in the era. Each volume begins with an overview of the film industry; devotes several articles to issues and trends important to the time period; and concludes with discussions of filmmakers, genres, and the films of the era, plus a chapter on avant-garde or experimental films. Appendixes cover box office, awards, and, in later volumes, films added to the National Film Registry. The encyclopedia is a work of scholarship, so extensive notes and a bibliography accompany each volume. A general index and a separate film title index add to the value. *History of the American Cinema* is essential to students and scholars studying the history of moviemaking in the United States. CONTENTS: v.1 The Emergence of Cinema: The American Screen to 1907 by Charles Musser; v.2 The Transformation of Cinema: 1907–1915 by

Eileen Bowser; v.3 An Evening's Entertainment: The Age of the Silent Feature Picture, 1915–1928 by Richard Koszarski; v.4 The Talkies: American Cinema's Transition to Sound, 1926–1931 by Donald Crafton; v.5 Grand Design: Hollywood as a Modern Business Enterprise, 1930–1939 by Tino Balio; v.6 Boom and Bust: The American Cinema in the 1940s by Thomas Schatz; v.7: Transforming the Screen, 1950–1959 by Peter Lev; v.8 The Sixties: 1960–1969 by Paul Monaco; v.9 Lost Illusions: American Cinema in the Shadow of Watergate and Vietnam, 1970–1979 by David A. Cook; v.10 A New Pot of Gold: Hollywood Under the Electronic Rainbow, 1980–1989 by Stephen Prince.

406.   Hochman, Stanley. 1974. *American Film Directors. With Filmographies and Index of Critics and Films.* New York: Ungar.

Hochman has compiled excerpts from criticism and reviews of the films of "65 American directors whose reputations had been established by the mid-1960s." Each director's works are critiqued in chronological order, giving readers a sense of not only how individual films were received but how the director's career was viewed. Filmographies are listed in a separate section. Includes an index of critics and film titles. Readers interested in criticism will especially benefit from Hochman's work. Originally intended as the first in a series that would also cover European and Asian directors, this was the only volume published.

407.   Langman, Larry. 1981. *A Guide to American Film Directors: The Sound Era, 1929–1979.* Metuchen, N.J.: Scarecrow Press.

Langman has compiled a simple two-volume filmography of American sound films by director. The first volume lists directors in alphabetical order, with the year and title of each film they made. Volume 2 is a film title index. Because most other guides are either more up-to-date or offer additional information on the directors or the films, this book is now of secondary value.

408.   Lentz, Harris M. 2001. *Feature Films, 1960–1969: A Filmography of English-Language and Major Foreign-Language United States Releases.* Jefferson, N.C.: McFarland.

Lentz has compiled a comprehensive list of more than 4,300 feature films released theatrically in the United States in the 1960s. Each film entry lists the standard technical information, genre, principal crew, and speaking cast followed by a brief synopsis. The index lists personal names.

409.   Magill, Frank Northen, Stephen L. Hanson, and Patricia King Hanson. 1983. *Magill's American Film Guide.* Englewood Cliffs, N.J.: Salem Press.

Magill's American Film Guide reprints 1,000 reviews from *Magill's Survey of Cinema* series (see entries 161, 162, and 740).

410.   Nowlan, Robert A., and Gwendolyn Wright Nowlan. 1991. *The Films of the Eighties: A Complete, Qualitative Filmography to Over 3400 Feature-Length English Language Films, Theatrical and Video-Only, Released between January 1, 1980, and December 31, 1989.* Jefferson, N.C.: McFarland.

The Nowlans' list of over 3,400 English-language films released in the United States during the 1980s includes basic crew and cast and a summary for each film. They use cross-references for films and reserve the index for personal names.

411.   Nowlan, Robert A., and Gwendolyn Wright Nowlan. 2001. *The Films of the Nineties: A Complete, Qualitative Filmography of Over 3000 Feature-Length English Language Films, Theatrical and Video-Only, Released between January 1, 1990, and December 31, 1999.* Jefferson, N.C.: McFarland.

The Nowlans' list of almost 3,300 English-language films released in United States theaters during the 1990s includes basic crew and cast and a summary for each film. They use cross-references for films and reserve the index for personal names.

412.   Parish, James Robert, and Michael R. Pitts. 1974. *Film Directors: A Guide to Their American Films.* Metuchen, N.J.: Scarecrow Press.

The prolific duo of Parish and Pitts have compiled lists of credits for "domestic and international motion picture directors who have contributed feature-length productions to the American cinema." In alphabetical order by director, each entry lists name, real name, date and place of birth and death, and a filmography listing films with production company and year of production.

413.   Quigley, Martin, and Richard Gertner. 1970. *Films in America, 1929–1969.* New York: Golden Press.

Quigley and Gertner created one of the earliest compilations focusing on films rather than individuals or institutions. Organized chronologically beginning with the first sound films, the book includes nearly 400 films that are significant because of box office, artistic merit, censorship, or advancement of an individual's career. For each year, the authors provide a historical overview of significant developments in the film industry followed by a random list of the films. For each film, they provide a small black-and-white still; discuss the film's significance; evaluate the film; and list producer, director, scriptwriter, and principal cast. To find a particular film, it is necessary to use the index, which also lists filmmakers. Although dated—the last year covered is 1969—the book is still valuable for its historical assessment of each year and the engaging evaluations of each film.

414.   *Rediscovering American Cinema. Films Incorporated.* 1977. New York: Northeast Office & National Theatrical Rentals.

In response to a resurgence of interest in American films in the sixties and seventies, Films Incorporated compiled a list of the best genre films produced in the United States. The book is divided into 17 genres, presenting one or two dozen films chronologically in each. The entertaining and informative introductions to each genre are written by renowned film critics. Each film entry includes the standard technical information plus cast and crew along with a synopsis and excerpts of critical commentary. Each film is illustrated with one or more sepia-toned photographs. Additional films are listed at the end of each section. The book is most useful for readers seeking lists of the best genre films.

415.   Sackett, Susan. 1996. *The Hollywood Reporter Book of Box Office Hits.* Rev. and enl. ed. New York: Billboard Books.

Sackett compiled a list of the top five movies for each year since 1939 and then wrote a detailed synopsis and discussion of each. She determined the top movies based on rental figures—the amount paid to the film's distributors. Although her descriptions of the films are well written and entertaining, the most valuable information is the rankings for each year. She provides a standard general index plus indexes that list films by year (again), title, and studio. A final index entitled "But what About?" lists other popular or critically acclaimed films from each year. Unfortunately, the book does not contain a combined list by rentals earned, nor are box office figures converted into current dollars to make comparison possible from year to year.

416. Sarris, Andrew. 1968. *The American Cinema; Directors and Directions, 1929–1968.* 1st ed. New York: Dutton.

Sarris, a strong and early proponent of the auteur theory, criticizes the work of some 200 American directors. Categorized by quality, each entry lists the director's works (the best are italicized) and offers a substantial essay. Added materials include a chronology of important films made between 1915 and 1967 and an index to all 6,000 works mentioned in the book.

417. Siegel, Scott, Barbara Siegel, Thomas L. Erskine, and James Michael Welsh. 2004. *The Encyclopedia of Hollywood.* New York: Facts on File.

The authors of this one-volume encyclopedia have covered every aspect of American cinema: films, film history, filmmakers, actors, genres, events, studios, jargon, and job descriptions. With the exception of short technical definitions, most entries devote several paragraphs to a person or topic. The book is lightly illustrated and includes a selective bibliography and an index. The encyclopedia is of most interest to movie fans.

418. Slide, Anthony. 1998. *The New Historical Dictionary of the American Film Industry.* Lanham, Md.: Scarecrow Press.

Film historian Slide has updated his first edition (*The American Film Industry: A Historical Dictionary*) with over 200 additional entries. Designed as a "what's what" rather than a who's who, the dictionary is an alphabetical arrangement of companies, studios, organizations, and film technology and business terms. Entries cover each subject succinctly and completely, are extensively cross-referenced, and most include a brief bibliography. Includes an index. With Slide's companion volume entitled *The International Film Industry: A Historical Dictionary* (see entry 259), these two guides to the film industry are good sources for film history researchers.

419. Slifkin, Irv. 2004. *VideoHound's Groovy Movies: Far-out Films of the Psychedelic Era.* Detroit: Visible Ink.

Slifkin led a team of film experts in compiling a list of over 200 films that show the spirit of the 1960s. The majority of the films were made between 1965 and 1975, but films made later that show that same spirit are also included. Films are organized into 20 categories such as "silly secret agents," "far out, man," and "do they make you horny, baby?" Within each category, films are listed in alphabetical order by title and include the typical VideoHound rating of one to four bones, summaries and reviews, and a list of principal cast and crew. The book is well illustrated (although in black and white), and occasional sidebars salute prominent filmmakers, actors, and topics. The indexes are superb and include alternative titles, cast, director, writer, cinematographer, and composer. Unlike other VideoHound titles, there is no category index, perhaps assuming the chapters are enough. Sources for videos and distributors are listed separately.

420. Whissen, Thomas R. 1998. *Guide to American Cinema, 1930–1965, Reference Guides to the World's Cinema.* Westport, Conn.: Greenwood Press.

As with all books in the Greenwood series *Reference Guides to the World's Cinema,* an introduction to the national cinema is followed by selections of the most prominent filmmakers and films of that country. Whissen selects American films and filmmakers based on seven criteria: quantity and availability of written materials, number of awards, notoriety, test of time, critical acclaim, cult favorites, and his personal favorites. For filmmakers, he provides brief biographies followed by a selective filmography and bibliography. For films, he includes director, screenwriter, and above-the-line cast followed by a summary and discussion of the film, awards won, and a selective bibliography. He provides a bibliography of sources of much of his information, appendixes to film festivals, film archives and museums, and an index. As with all books in the series, this is a good place to go for an overview of American cinema from 1930 through 1965. For coverage from 1965 to 1995, consult the companion volume from the series by Daniel Curran (see entry 401).

Television

421. Brooks, Tim, and Earle Marsh. 2003. *The Complete Directory to Prime Time Network and Cable TV Shows, 1946–Present.* 8th ed. New York: Ballantine Books.

Television executives Brooks and Marsh have produced the most complete guide to American television shows available. The eighth edition lists more than 6,000 network, cable, and syndicated series broadcast on commercial networks between 6:00 P.M. and 3:00 A.M. through 2002. In addition to series, there are generic listings for news, movies, and types of sports. The entry for each show includes dates of first and last telecast, broadcast history, and regular cast, as well as a description of the show and its cast. The first appendix lists the prime-time schedules (7:00 P.M.–11:30 P.M.) for each year from 1946 to 1998. Additional appendixes lists Emmy Award winners, top-rated programs by season, longest running series, reunion telecasts, spin-offs, series based on movies, series that first began airing on radio, and hit theme songs. Includes a proper name index. The latest edition adds a guide to TV-related Web sites. Brooks and Marsh have indeed produced a "complete" guide that will serve the needs of both researchers and people in the television industry.

422. Castleman, Harry, and Walter J. Podrazik. 2003. *Watching TV: Six Decades of American Television.* 2nd ed, *Television Series.* Syracuse, N.Y.: Syracuse University Press.

Popular culture writers Castleman and Podrazik have written a season-by-season survey of American television. The first three chapters cover the development of television. Subsequent chapters, beginning with 1944–1945, chronicle each season through 2002–2003 with a critical essay highlighting everything from key events to production trivia. Also included are the prime-time schedules and numerous illustrations. The chronological arrangement makes it difficult to follow a theme over time such as reality television or sports, but it is somewhat possible using the index, which includes topics as well as proper names and titles. The book is of equal interest to researchers and nostalgic television fans.

423. Erickson, Hal. 1989. *Syndicated Television: The First Forty Years, 1947–1987.* Jefferson, N.C.: McFarland.

Erickson has compiled a selective list of first-run syndicated television programs aired in the United States from 1947 to 1987. Each decade is subdivided into 14 genres. Shows are in alphabetical order by title and include dates aired and a description of the show, its characters, and how it was received. Erickson includes an excellent annotated bibliography and an index. The book is a useful complement to the many publications that focus exclusively on network programming.

424. Gianakos, Larry James. 1978. *Television Drama Series Programming: A Comprehensive Chronicle.* Metuchen, N.J.: Scarecrow Press.

Gianakos has compiled a series-by-series and show-by-show guide to dramatic television programs aired during prime time in the United States between 1947 and 1986. Each volume begins with a season overview and listings of days and times programs were broadcast. The bulk of each book is a chronology of shows. Drawn from the *New York Times, Cue, TV Guide* and the author's own viewing, the entries include series title with cast regulars followed by episode titles, adaptation when applicable, date aired, and guest cast. Later volumes cover series missed in earlier volumes. Coverage is as follows: Book 1 1947–1959, Book 2 1959–1975, Book 3 1975–1980, Book 4 1980–1982, Book 5 1982–1984, Book 6 1984–1986. The final volume provides a cumulative series title index, but no name index.

425. Goldstein, Fred P., and Stan Goldstein. 1983. *Prime-Time Television: A Pictorial History from Milton Berle to "Falcon Crest."* 1st ed. New York: Crown.

Presented in two-year segments from 1948–1949 to 1981–1982, the brief overviews of the seasons are mere excuses to share hundreds of black-and-white photographs from the programs. Each photograph is captioned with the name of the television show, air dates, and the names of the actors appearing in the photos. An index also refers to television shows and actors. An excellent resource to find pictures of the stars.

426. Hyatt, Wesley. 1997. *The Encyclopedia of Daytime Television.* New York: Billboard Books.

Hyatt lists series aired on U.S. network television before 6:00 P.M. from the earliest days through 1996. Shows include not only soaps, kid's shows, talk shows, and game shows, but news, sports, cartoons, and selected syndicated shows. Each entry includes genre, viewing format, air dates, cast regulars, and brief synopses. Appendixes list nighttime shows rerun in daytime, the longest running daytime shows, and a bibliography. The index includes shows and actors. The longest and most detailed descriptions are reserved for soap operas, but all the synopses are well written and will prove useful to people interested in daytime television.

427. Hyatt, Wesley. 2003. *Short-Lived Television Series, 1948–1978: Thirty Years of More Than 1,000 Flops.* Jefferson, N.C.: McFarland.

Hyatt has compiled a guide to more than 1,000 American network "series that were cancelled within one year after their premieres" between 1948 and 1978. Organized by season, each entry includes title, genre, network, air dates, principal cast and crew, and, for a good number of the shows, an in-depth profile and production history based on print sources and interviews with the people who made them. Hyatt's book fills a niche, because most guides gloss over shows that lasted less than one season. Includes an index.

428. Lackmann, Ronald W. 2003. *The Encyclopedia of American Television: Broadcast Programming Post World War II to 2000.* New York: Facts on File.

Popular culture writer Lackmann has written a "reference to the programs, personalities, and practices of network television" in the United States. Entries for programs list air dates and a review of the show's premise, plot, characters, and actors. Entries for personalities offer a career biography focusing on key programs. Despite the advertising claim, entries for genres and history are few and far between. Appendixes list top-rated programs and Emmy Awards. In addition to extensive cross-references, there is also a fine index. The best use for this book is as a companion for television watchers. Checkmark Books released an identical work under the name *The Encyclopedia of 20th-Century American Television.*

429. Library of Congress, Motion Picture Broadcasting and Recorded Sound Division, Sarah Rouse, and Katharine Loughney. 1989. *3 Decades of Television: A Catalog of Television Programs Acquired by the Library of Congress, 1949–1979.* Washington, D.C.: Library of Congress.

The Library of Congress began collecting television programs in 1949, building a collection that held 14,000 programs by 1979. Archivists Rouse and Loughney compiled a list of each of these programs with the exception of news broadcasts, which they thought were well covered by the *Vanderbilt Television News Archive.* Arranged by title, entries for programs include production data, air dates, genre, and a brief synopsis. Entries for series also list individual episode titles with air dates. The index organizes the programs by content, dividing them into 41 genres and subject descriptors. Coverage in the early years is sparse, because few producers registered their programs with the Copyright Office and the Library of Congress collected only selectively; despite that fact, *3 Decades of Television* remains a useful source for early American television programming.

430. McNeil, Alex. 1996. *Total Television: The Comprehensive Guide to Programming from 1948 to the Present.* 4th ed. New York: Penguin Books.

McNeil competes with *The Complete Directory to Prime Time Network and Cable TV Shows* (see entry 421) to provide the most comprehensive guide to U.S. television programs. *Total Television* includes 5,400 series aired between 1948 and 1995. The book is intended for TV fans, but will serve the needs of researchers as well. Most of the book describes the shows. Those that ran the longest or had the most impact have the longest entries, but even the short entries are well written and informative. The cast are listed as part of the narrative. Part II lists noteworthy specials as selected by the author. Part III charts prime-time fall schedules. Part IV lists Emmy and Peabody Award winners. Part V lists the top-rated series by season. The name index gives page numbers, which means readers must browse the description of each television show listed on that page to determine which show featured the actor. The CD-ROM covers over 7,000 shows and also includes sound bites and video clips.

431.   National Endowment for the Arts. 1991. *The Arts on Television, 1976–1990: Fifteen Years of Cultural Programming.* Washington, D.C.: Media Arts: Film/Radio/Television Program National Endowment for the Arts.

Between 1976 and 1990, the National Endowment for the Arts supported "over 1,000 television programs in 31 series" that feature the arts on public television. Every show is listed here, in chapters covering series and specials on dance, theatre, music, and art. Each chapter introduces a series and describes the individual episodes with air dates, production credits, and awards won. Appendixes list corporate co-sponsors, awards, and distributors, while indexes list programs, directors and producers, and topics. Today's PBS programs may be searched and browsed online at <http://www.shoppbs.org>, but the older programs listed in this book are not generally available on the Web site.

432.   Sackett, Susan. 1993. *Prime-Time Hits: Television's Most Popular Network Programs, 1950 to the Present.* New York: Billboard Books.

Sackett compiled a list of the top 10 television shows for each year from 1950 through the 1991–1992 season and then wrote a detailed synopsis and discussion of each. She determined the top shows based on Nielsen ratings. Her descriptions are well written and entertaining and include credits and Emmys won. Equally valuable are the rankings for each year that are listed in an appendix. Appendixes also list shows by length of time in the top ten, shows that were one-year wonders, shows that began on radio, shows that were spin-offs, and reunion specials. Includes an index.

433.   Shapiro, Mitchell E. 1990. *Television Network Daytime and Late-Night Programming, 1959–1989.* Jefferson, N.C.: McFarland.

Communication professor Shapiro has compiled a comprehensive chronicle of U.S. daytime and late-night programming through 1989. Divided into early morning, daytime, and late-night programming and then divided by network (ABC, CBS, NBC, Fox), Shapiro shows the schedules on monthly grids followed by columns that list programming moves such as premier, time change, or cancellation by network, date, time, title, length, and genre. The index lists programs and select individuals. With *Television Network Prime-Time Programming* and *Television Network Weekend Programming* (see entries 434 and 435), Shapiro has created a useful and comprehensive guide for anyone needing to pinpoint the exact dates and times programs were aired.

434.   Shapiro, Mitchell E. 1989. *Television Network Prime-Time Programming, 1948–1988.* Jefferson, N.C.: McFarland.

Communication professor Shapiro has compiled a comprehensive chronicle of U.S. prime-time network programming through 1988. Organized first by day of the week and then by network (ABC, CBS, NBC, DuMont, and Fox), Shapiro shows the schedules on monthly grids followed by columns that list programming moves such as premier, time change, or cancellation by network, date, time, title, length, and genre. The index lists programs. With *Television Network Daytime and Late-Night Programming* and *Television Network Weekend*

Programming (see entries 433 and 435), Shapiro has created a useful and comprehensive guide for anyone needing to pinpoint the exact dates and times programs were aired.

435. Shapiro, Mitchell E. 1992. *Television Network Weekend Programming, 1959–1990.* Jefferson, N.C.: McFarland.

Communication professor Shapiro has compiled a comprehensive chronicle of U.S. daytime weekend network programming through 1990. Divided into Saturday and Sunday morning, early afternoon, and late afternoon and then divided by network (ABC, CBS, NBC), Shapiro shows the schedules on monthly grids followed by columns that list programming moves such as premier, time change, or cancellation by network, date, time, title, length, and genre. The index lists programs and select individuals. With *Television Network Daytime and Late-Night Programming* and *Television Network Prime-Time Programming* (see entries 433 and 434), Shapiro has created a useful and comprehensive guide for anyone needing to pinpoint the exact dates and times programs were aired.

436. Slide, Anthony. 1991. *The Television Industry: A Historical Dictionary.* New York: Greenwood Press.

Best known for his prolific writing of high-quality reference books about film, Slide wrote this historical dictionary of the American television industry as a complement to his historical dictionaries of the American and international film industries (see entries 259 and 418). This is a dictionary not of people or shows, but of "more than 1,000 entries on production companies, distributors, organizations, genres, technical terms, and much, much more"—the "more" tending toward subjects. Entries provide well-written histories and include cross-references and bibliographies. Includes separate name and program indexes.

437. Terrace, Vincent. 1986. *Encyclopedia of Television: Series, Pilots and Specials, A Baseline Production.* New York: New York Zoetrope.

Terrace has compiled a list of "almost 5,000 series, pilots, specials, and experimental programs" broadcast by American networks between 1937 and 1984. Volume 1 covers 1937–1973, and volume 2 covers 1974–1984. In order by title, each program includes the genre, a synopsis, principal cast and crew, network, length, and date aired. Volume 3, "The Index: Who's Who in Television 1937–1984," provides separate indexes to "over 18,000 performers, 5000 producers, 5000 writers, and 3500 directors." Terrace's encyclopedia was certainly the most comprehensive reference on American television when published and remains one of the more useful today.

438. TV Guide. 2004. *TV Guide Guide to TV: The Most Definitive Encyclopedia of Television.* New York: Barnes & Noble Books.

TV Guide lists more than 7,100 TV shows and miniseries that aired on U.S. prime-time, daytime, and late-night television. Each entry includes show title, network or syndicator, air dates, cast, and a synopsis. Additional materials include network histories, prime-time and Saturday morning programming grids for 1953 through 2005, and a complete cast index. The *TV Guide Guide to TV* is now the largest of the three regularly published U.S. television program catalogs.

6
Genres

With nearly 150 genre terms, *The Moving Image Genre-Form Guide* lists the full range of possible genres in film and television, but reference sources tend to cover genres in general or the 30 genres included in this section. One of the best guides to films by genre is the index of the *AFI Catalog* (see entries 391 to 393), which is in the National Cinema chapter in the United States section. See also the Lists section in the chapter on General Film and Television Filmographies.

439. Taves, Brian, Judi Hoffman, and Karen C. Lund. *The Moving Image Genre-Form Guide* [World Wide Web Resource]. Library of Congress. Motion Picture Broadcasting and Recorded Sound Division. 1998 Address: http://lcweb.loc.gov/rr/mopic/migintro.html. [Accessed: March 2005].

After a thorough review of the literature, a committee from the Library of Congress Motion Picture Broadcasting and Recorded Sound Division compiled a list of nearly 150 genre terms used in film and television. For each genre, they provide "a definition, describing conventions of story construction, character types, and setting" along with examples. In addition, they define the standard form subheading terms of feature, short, serial, animation, and television as well as numerous other forms. The terms are not hierarchical, making the terms most useful in indexing and catalogs rather than in classification systems. See *Appendix B* for the complete list.

FILM

440. Arany, Lynne, Tom Dyja, and Gary Goldsmith. 1995. *The Reel List: A Categorical Companion to Over 2,000 Memorable Films.* New York: Delta.

The authors categorize over 2,000 movies. Most categories are straightforward, including lists of occupations, sports, or movies about movies. Others are more unusual or fun, such as uncredited remakes, nymphets, or the Algonquin Round Table. A film title index makes it possible to begin with a film and find others that share a similar theme.

441. Armstrong, Richard B., and Mary Willems Armstrong. 2001. *Encyclopedia of Film Themes, Settings and Series.* Jefferson, N.C.: McFarland.

The Armstrongs have completely revised their earlier *Movie List Book* to create lists of films on topics "ranging from film themes and series to settings, occupations, animals and happenstances." For over 670 categories, they write an introduction about the most important films followed by a filmography listing film titles and release dates. Cross-references point readers to appropriate entries. Film title and personal name indexes would have added reference value to the book, but the lists are useful in their own right.

442.   Case, Christopher. 1996. *The Ultimate Movie Thesaurus.* 1st ed, *A Henry Holt Reference Book.* New York: Henry Holt.

Case, a filmmaker, film professor, and movie buff, has compiled this very useful guide to 5,639 films by theme, category, and genre. Arranged alphabetically by film, entries include year of release, length, a one- to four-star rating, a one- to six-dollar-sign box office reputation, a synopsis, writer, director, adaptation, and principal cast, along with any Oscar Award nominations and winners. What makes the book useful are the listings for genre, subjects, and similar films. Similar films generally include two to four films that are similar enough that a fan of one film might like the others. The indexes list films by nearly 1,600 categories that make it possible for fans to locate films that they like and for scholars to locate films with similar themes or content. Only the *AFI Catalog* (see entries 391 to 393) gives better access by subject, and it has only films made through 1970. *The Ultimate Movie Thesaurus* is substantially less costly and belongs in every film reference collection.

443.   Gehring, Wes D. 1988. *Handbook of American Film Genres.* New York: Greenwood Press.

For 18 genres, the *Handbook* gives "a historical/analytical overview, a bibliographical overview of the genre's key literature, a checklist of these texts, and a filmography of the genre's pivotal movies." Gehring and his team have compiled a nice, well-indexed set of literature reviews and filmographies.

444.   López, Daniel. 1993. *Films by Genre: 775 Categories, Styles, Trends, and Movements Defined, with a Filmography for Each.* Jefferson, N.C.: McFarland.

López created this guide with the intention of providing "a quick referral to the numerous film genres, movements, styles, categories, and trends into which films may be readily classified." Genres are listed in alphabetical order, with numerous cross-references. Each genre is defined and followed by a list of films or of defined subgenres with their own lists of films. Many entries include only a definition, because it would be impossible or ridiculous to list films (examples include A-picture, foreign version, and trailer). López provides no information on how he developed the list of genres or of how he selected films, but the guide is still useful for anyone tracking down films by genre, especially for the many subgenres covered.

445.   Wiener, Tom. 1993. *The Book of Video Lists.* 5th ed. Kansas City, Mo.: Andrews and McMeel.

Intended to guide movie lovers in renting videos, Wiener categorizes more than 4,000 films available for rental. The book is divided into 12 chapters that reflect the genres commonly found in video stores. Each chapter is then further subdivided into selective subject lists and complete filmmaker checklists. In the Action/Adventure chapter, for example, 3 of the 26 subject lists are war movies, racing movies, and sword and sorcery fantasies. Checklists include individual action stars—in addition to the star checklists, other chapters might also include checklists of filmmakers, directors, or authors. The second half of the book is an index to movies by title. Each title entry includes the year released, length, MPAA rating, and a brief description. A code points readers to the genre section of the book. A useful quick guide to genres.

TELEVISION

446.   Miller, Toby, John Tulloch, Glen Creeber, and British Film Institute. 2001. *The Television Genre Book*. London: British Film Institute.

Television professor and researcher Creeber and his colleagues have edited a collection designed to introduce students to television genres. After an introduction to genre in television are sections on drama, soap opera, comedy, popular entertainment (a catch-all for quiz shows, talk shows, sports, and music), children's television, news, and documentary. Each section includes several chapters written by mostly British media experts, although the book does include both British and U.S. programs. There is minimal coverage of programs from other countries. The focus of each chapter is not only on describing the genres, but also on how they are studied. Sidebars and boxes feature case studies. Each chapter recommends further reading. The index lists people and programs but, strangely enough, omits the genres themselves. This interesting book will be of most use to students of television.

447.   Rose, Brian Geoffrey, and Robert S. Alley. 1985. *TV Genres: A Handbook and Reference Guide*. Westport, Conn.: Greenwood Press.

Rose, a professor of media studies, and Alley have edited a guide to 19 television genres ranging from detective shows to sitcoms and talk shows to commercials. Each chapter is written by an expert and includes an overview of the genre, a lengthy history of its development, and a discussion of themes and issues. Each chapter concludes with a bibliography and a videography that lists the most important programs in the genre. Although dated (any new edition would have to include new genres such as reality shows and update the examples), the book is still valuable as a social history of television and its genres. Includes an index to names, programs, subjects, and, of course, genres.

TV ACRES (see entry 780)

ACTION AND ADVENTURE

Black Action Films: Plots, Critiques, Casts, and Credits for 235 Theatrical and Made-for-Television Releases (see entry 906)

448.   Broderick, Mick. 1991. *Nuclear Movies: A Critical Analysis and Filmography of International Feature Length Films Dealing with Experimentation, Aliens, Terrorism, Holocaust, and Other Disaster Scenarios, 1914–1989*. Jefferson, N.C.: McFarland.

Broderick attempts "to list all the feature-length films, serials, made-for-television movies, and miniseries that deal in one way or another with nuclear themes" produced worldwide from the early days of nuclear power through the 1980s. He includes not only nuclear holocaust films, but also films that deal with cold war paranoia, monster mutations, and even beneficial technologies. Broderick begins with a 50-page essay placing nuclear films into a historical context. The rest of the book lists films in chronological order; entries include title, year, production and distribution companies, running time, and names of director, producer, scriptwriter, cinematographer, and leading and support players. The plot summary focuses on the nuclear content. Appendixes list the top nuclear film rentals and the most viewed nuclear movies on U.S. television. Includes an impressive select bibliography and an index.

449.   Frank, Alan. 1997. *Frank's 500: The Thriller Film Guide.* London: Batsford.

Film critic Frank has written an illustrated guide to 500 international thrillers, defined as movies "that make the pulse race a little faster." Each entry includes above-the-line production crew, cast, a well-written critical plot summary, and a quote from a contemporaneous review. *Frank's 500* will be of most interest to fans of the thriller genre.

450.   Julius, Marshall. 1996. *Action! The Action Movie A–Z.* Bloomington: Indiana University Press.

Julius, a fan of action films, has compiled a list of 250 of the best action films from all over the world. Each entry includes title, place and year of release, a one- to five-"gun" rating, and a humorous and informative review followed by production and cast credits. Sidebars feature action stars and lists of films. There is no index, so the guide is primarily of interest to fans of the genre.

451.   Mann, Dave, and Ron Main. 1994. *Races, Chases & Crashes.* Osceola, Wis.: Motorbooks International.

Mann and Main have written a book for "motorheads" listing movies that "feature hot rods, race cars, sports cars, motorcycles, trucks, racing, outstanding chase scenes, crashes, and anything directly related to the automobile industry." The mostly "B" movies are listed in alphabetical order with brief synopses that highlight the cars or chases. The illustrations capture the feel of the book, featuring black-and-white movie posters and stills from the films. The index adds no value, because it merely lists the same movies in the same order as they appear in the book.

452.   Muir, John Kenneth. 2004. *The Encyclopedia of Superheroes on Film and Television.* Jefferson, N.C.: McFarland.

Muir, a popular culture reference book writer, has compiled a guide to film and television superheroes. After a history of the genre, he gives a detailed history of over 60 superheroes, discussing origins, powers, villains, and the quality of the films or shows in which they appear. Entries also include excerpts from reviews, production data, cast and crew credits, and a film synopsis or episode guide. Appendixes list conventions and clichés, multiple incarnations, ad-lines, and the best, worst, and most influential productions. Includes a bibliography and an index.

454.   Parish, James Robert. 1995. *Pirates and Seafaring Swashbucklers on the Hollywood Screen: Plots, Critiques, Casts and Credits for 137 Theatrical and Made-for-Television Releases.* Jefferson, N.C.: McFarland.

Parish, a prolific filmographer, has compiled a list of 137 pirate movies. As in his other filmographies, he lists the major cast and crew followed by an engaging plot summary and discussion informed by reviews written upon the film's release. The index lists movies and personal names.

Southern Mountaineers in Silent Films: Plot Synopses of Movies about Moonshining, Feuding, and Other Mountain Topics, 1904–1929 (see entry 751)

455. Stacy, Jan, and Ryder Syvertsen. 1984. *The Great Book of Movie Villains: A Guide to the Screen's Meanies, Tough Guys, and Bullies.* Chicago: Contemporary Books.

Stacy and Syvertsen have compiled a list of villains in the movies. Villains are arranged alphabetically by character name, from Aguirre to Zampano. Each entry lists the movie and includes a physical description, the reason for the villainy, strengths and weaknesses, friends and enemies, evil deeds, and what to do if you run into them. Separate indexes list actors, movies, directors, and studios. Like Stacy and Syvertsen's other book, *The Great Book of Movie Monsters* (see entry 676), the book is fun to read and most useful for people seeking "biographies" of movie villains.

456. Thomas, Tony. 1988. *The Cinema of the Sea: A Critical Survey and Filmography, 1925–1986.* Jefferson, N.C.: McFarland.

A lifelong fascination with the sea and with movies led Thomas to compile this highly specialized list of films that deal "with the sea, with sailors and with ships," films that "comment directly on the character of nautical life." Divided into 10 chapters on such topics as pirates, mutiny, war on the water, and disaster, each is a filmographic essay on the most prominent films discussing plots and themes. The book is not intended to be a complete listing, as the filmography at the end of the book includes only about 140 films, complete with production data, release date, and principal cast and crew. With no page numbers in the filmography, it is necessary to consult the index to see where each film is discussed.

457. Thomas, Tony. 1976. *The Great Adventure Films.* 1st ed. Secaucus, N.J.: Citadel Press.

Thomas selected 50 of the best American and British adventure films made through 1975. He roughly defines adventure films as films that feature adventurers—Errol Flynn is the exemplar. He excludes science fiction, fantasy, and disaster pictures, but includes selected westerns and war films. The films are organized chronologically, each featuring a multipage essay and lavish black-and-white stills. Includes a film title and name index.

VideoHound's Dragon: Asian Action & Cult Flicks (see entry 274)

MARTIAL ARTS

458. Lott, M. Ray. 2004. *The American Martial Arts Film.* Jefferson, N.C.: McFarland.

Lott's historical guide to American martial arts films is organized as a series of filmographic essays each covering a decade. The reference value of the book lies in the filmography of some 300 films listed in alphabetical order at the end of the book. Each entry lists title, year of release, genre, director, writer, stars, a one-sentence synopsis, releasing company, and length. Includes a bibliography and index.

459.   Palmer, Bill, Karen Palmer, and Richard Meyers. 1995. *The Encyclopedia of Martial Arts Movies.* Metuchen, N.J.: Scarecrow Press.

The authors, martial arts film reviewers and writers, have compiled a comprehensive list of films from all over the world that feature Asian martial arts. Films are listed in alphabetical order by title of American release. Each includes title and alternate titles, dates of release, technical information, and principal cast. The crew is not always listed, but when available, includes the martial arts instructor. The plot summaries feature the fighting, and the authors rate the films on a scale of one to four stars based on the quality of martial arts. The name index is excellent and can serve as a filmography, although, because it points to entry numbers, it is quite a bit of work to compile.

ANIMALS

460.   Paietta, Ann Catherine, and Jean L. Kauppila. 1994. *Animals on Screen and Radio: An Annotated Sourcebook.* Metuchen, N.J.: Scarecrow Press.

Paietta and Kauppila have compiled a list of films, television series, and radio series that feature real or animated animals. With one chapter for each category, films and series are listed in alphabetical order by title and include technical information, director, writer, and cast, and a plot synopsis that features the animal. Includes subject and name indexes.

ANIMATION

AIDB: Animation Industry Database (see entry 1199)

461.   *The Big Cartoon Database* [World Wide Web Resource]. Address: http://www. bcdb.com. [Accessed: March 2005].

Dave Koch and friends began the *Big Cartoon DataBase* (BCDB) as a labor of love. Thinking that *IMDb* (see entry 66) lacked sufficient coverage of cartoons, they began compiling their own online database and asking people to add to it. The result is a database approaching 60,000 cartoons and 4,000 series with episodes. Fans may browse by studio with subcategories for characters, commercials, feature films and featurettes, shorts, and television series and specials. The database is also browsable by the cartoons that are rated the highest or received the most hits. It is possible to conduct a simple search by title, character, voice, director, or writer or a detailed search by the added fields of animator, producer, other crew, and the cartoon's description and notes. Each record includes complete voice and production credits, a synopsis, production notes, and, for approximately 4,000 cartoons, user reviews. The site also offers a calendar of events (mostly animator and character birthdays), videos, DVDs, and books available for sale, and discussion forums for fans. As with any database whose content is provided by the public, BCDB is only as complete and as accurate as its contributors make it, but keeping that caveat in mind, it remains the premier Web-based database for cartoons.

462.   Grant, John. 2001. *Masters of Animation.* New York: Watson-Guptill.

Grant, a popular culture writer, has written a guide to 37 of the most prominent animators from all over the world. The biographies devote several pages to the lives and careers of the animators and their contributions to animation. Their most important features and shorts are described in both the body of the essays and in sidebars. Includes an index.

463.   Mangels, Andy. 2003. *Animation on DVD: The Ultimate Guide.* Berkeley, Calif.: Stone Bridge Press.

Entertainment writer and cartoon fan Mangels has compiled a list of over 1,600 animated films and shows available on DVD in North America. He personally viewed over 1,000 DVDs; over 300 more entries were written by other writers; and the rest were not made available for review by the publishers. In alphabetical order by title, each entry includes director and writer credits, source material, technical data, genre, rating, and a review that includes a synopsis and commentary. A separate section lists adult films. Additional features include a listing of Easter eggs (hidden features AKA Omake), a list of animated feature length films made in the United States, a Web directory of animation companies, a bibliography, and a complete index. Mangels' massive guide is of interest to both researchers and fans of animation and anime.

FILM

464.   Beck, Jerry. 1994. *The 50 Greatest Cartoons: As Selected by 1,000 Animation Professionals.* 1st ed. Atlanta; Kansas City, Mo.: Turner; Distributed by Andrews and McMeel.

Beck, an animator and writer, polled over 1,000 cartoon historians to assemble a list of the 50 greatest cartoons of all time. In order from 1st to 50th, each cartoon includes color stills, a plot summary, the production history, and an exploration of the qualities that merited inclusion as one of the best. Sidebars include commentary by some of the cartoon historians who were polled as well as features on individual animators, characters, and studios. An additional 57 cartoons "that received a substantial number of votes" are listed separately. An appendix directs readers to places to watch or obtain each cartoon, and an index pulls the book together. Beck has provided an excellent resource for both cartoon fans and scholars.

465.   Borowiec, Piotr. 1998. *Animated Short Films: A Critical Index to Theatrical Cartoons.* Lanham, Md.: Scarecrow Press.

Film critic Borowiec has compiled a guide to American animated shorts originally released in theaters that are available on video. He includes all types of animation from major studios and independent producers. Arranged by title, each entry includes year released, animator, and studio followed by a summary and a one- to five-star rating. Added materials include a history of animation, a director index, a chronology, and a list of the four- and five-star cartoons.

466.   Edera, Bruno, and John Halas. 1977. *Full Length Animated Feature Films.* London; New York: Focal Press.

The authors spent five years compiling this illustrated international guide to over 300 feature-length animated films that had been made by the mid-1970s. After chapters on the history of animation and regional surveys of films and animators, a catalog lists the features. Organized chronologically, each entry includes original and English language titles, release year, medium, production and animation credits, and a synopsis. Also listed are productions that were announced but never made, works in progress, and live-action features that contain some animation. Most surveys focus on one country, so this work is useful for its international coverage.

467.   Friedwald, Will, and Jerry Beck. 1981. *The Warner Brothers Cartoons*. Metuchen, N.J.: Scarecrow Press.

Friedwald and Beck have listed all 850 of the seven-minute cartoons made by Warner Bros. for theatrical release between 1930 and 1969. After describing the featured Warner Bros. characters, the cartoons are listed in chronological order. Each entry contains characters, producer and director, animators, and a story summary. The appendix lists government propaganda films, and the index lists titles.

Gardner's Computer Graphics & Animation Dictionary (see entry 125)

468.   Gifford, Denis. 1990. *American Animated Films: The Silent Era, 1897–1929*. Jefferson, N.C.: McFarland.

Gifford's catalog of silent cartoons made in the United States between 1897 and 1925 lists 140 series in chronological order and lists every cartoon from each series. For series, he includes title, production company, producer, and distributor. For cartoons in the series, he lists release date, title, and director. The indexes point to names and titles. Gifford wrote a companion volume entitled *British Animated Films* (see entry 469) covering 1895 to 1985.

469.   Gifford, Denis. 1987. *British Animated Films, 1895–1985: A Filmography*. Jefferson, N.C.: McFarland.

Gifford has compiled the most complete catalog of cartoons made in Great Britain between 1895 and 1985. He includes 1,284 entertainment and educational, advertising and propaganda, and experimental and art cartoons. Arranged in chronological order, each entry contains the production company and distributor, the animators, a description, and a quote from a review when available. The index points to cartoon titles and their makers. Gifford wrote a companion volume entitled *American Animated Films* (see entry 468) covering just the silent era.

470.   Lawson, Tim, and Alisa Persons. 2004. *The Magic behind the Voices: A Who's Who of Cartoon Voice Actors*. Jackson: University Press of Mississippi.

Lawson and Persons, writers and filmmakers both, have written an excellent biographical guide to the voice actors who bring life to the cartoons. After a portrait, each in-depth biography details the career with particular attention to the skills behind voice work, which in many cases the authors drew from interviews with the voice artists themselves. Each essay ends with a list of cartoons each artist voiced, which are as complete as possible considering that early voice actors were not given credit. Includes a bibliography and index.

471. Llewellyn, Richard. *Chronology of Animation* [World Wide Web Resource]. R. Llewellyn. Address: http://www.public.iastate.edu/%7Erllew/chronst.html. [Accessed: March 2005].

Llewellyn has produced a chronological arrangement of significant films, people, and events in animation history. Arranged into tables with columns for the United States, the rest of the Americas, Japan, Australasia, Europe, the Middle East, and Africa, the earliest entry is dated 1824 and the latest is current. Entries for animated works include title, type of production and animation, artists, and studio. Entries for biographies tend to scatter birth and death dates and significant events throughout the tables. Other entries describe animation techniques and studio histories. Designed for browsing, the chronology may be searched by using the Iowa State University search engine.

472. Madsen, Roy P. 1969. *Animated Film; Concepts, Methods, Uses.* New York: Interland; distributed by Pitman.

Although predating computers, Madsen's guide is of use to prospective animators because it provides grounding in traditional animation techniques using cels, models, and puppets. Chapters cover the history, concepts, various techniques and processes, and the production sequence. A glossary defines terms. Includes a comprehensive index.

473. Markstein, Don. *Don Markstein's Toonopedia: A Vast Repository of Toonological Knowledge* [World Wide Web Resource]. Address: http://www.toonopedia.com. [Accessed: March 2005].

Markstein's "encyclopedia of toons" features characters from animated films and television shows as well as comic books and newspaper and magazine strips. Organized by work rather than character, each of the nearly 1,000 records includes medium, distributor or publisher, first appearance, and creator along with an essay describing the cartoon and its characters and commenting on its quality. Additional sections cover the "Companies That Produce the Toons" and the still very small "People behind the Toons."

474. Pettigrew, Neil. 1999. *The Stop-Motion Filmography: A Critical Guide to 297 Features Using Puppet Animation.* Jefferson, N.C.: McFarland.

Since the late 1960s, Pettigrew has taken notes on the stop-motion sequences in films, whether they last just a few seconds or are featured for minutes at a time. From this lifelong interest, he has compiled "an alphabetical survey of full-length films that have featured stop-motion photography combined with live action." For each film, he includes credits, with particular attention to the animators and special effects crews. After ranking both the film and the quality of stop-motion on a four-star scale, he describes the film and examines the animation sequences shot-by-shot for realism, direction and editing, the quality of the models, and integration with live-action and the film itself. Black-and-white stills are scattered throughout the book along with 51 color plates featuring the most important films. Appendixes include artist's filmographies, Academy Award nominations, and lists of favorite stop-motion sequences shared by effects artists. A glossary defines terms, a bibliography lists books and magazines, and an index points to the films, artists, and photographs. Pettigrew's book is a must for animation collections.

475.   Webb, Graham. 2000. *The Animated Film Encyclopedia: A Complete Guide to American Shorts, Features, and Sequences, 1900–1979.* Jefferson, N.C.: McFarland.

Webb spent 30 years compiling this guide to every animated short and feature shown in an American theater between 1900 and 1979. The body of the work lists 6,900 cartoons by title with credits and a brief synopsis. Some entries feature all of the titles produced by a company by year, which—along with the appendix that lists series and the index that lists names—can be used to look up individual titles. Webb has created a magnificent piece of scholarship that is essential for those seeking the most complete lists and credits for American cartoons of all types.

TELEVISION

476.   Erickson, Hal. 1995. *Television Cartoon Shows: An Illustrated Encyclopedia, 1949 through 1993.* Jefferson City, N.C.: McFarland.

Erickson has produced one of the first guides devoted exclusively to the television cartoon. The book begins with a lengthy history of the format followed by an alphabetical listing of shows aired from 1949 through 1993 on network television or major cable channels or that were widely syndicated. Entries are as comprehensive as possible, listing all of the production crew included in the credits. Erickson describes the premise and plot of each cartoon, production history and reception, and gives his own evaluation. Closing materials include a discussion of cartoon voices, a brief bibliography, and an index. The book is of interest to both researchers and fans of cartoons.

477.   Woolery, George W. 1989. *Animated TV Specials: The Complete Directory to the First Twenty-Five Years, 1962–1987.* Metuchen, N.J.: Scarecrow Press.

Woolery has compiled a list of American animated television specials to complement his *Children's Television: The First Thirty-Five Years, 1946–1981. Part I: Animated Cartoon Series* (see entry 478). The introductory essay describes the history of the animated special, highlighting trends and important "series" of specials. The book is arranged alphabetically by title and includes broadcast history, production credits, principal characters with who voiced them, and a description of the special. Appendixes include the most aired and longest running specials, stop-motion specials, holiday specials, and special series. Woolery provides separate indexes for producers/directors/filmmakers, writers, musicians/lyricists, and voices, plus subject indexes to studios/production companies and distributors.

478.   Woolery, George W. 1985. *Children's Television: The First Thirty-Five Years, 1946–1981. Part I: Animated Cartoon Series.* Metuchen, N.J.: Scarecrow Press.

Woolery has compiled a list of over 300 cartoons aired on commercial networks, public television, or "syndicated extensively to local stations in the United States." Each cartoon entry contains where and when aired or syndicated, principle characters and their voices, and an essay describing the show and discussing its characters and themes. Appendixes list other series that used animation, network shows that were later syndicated, foreign cartoons syndicated in the United States, longest running series, prime-time series, cartoons based on comic books, newspaper comics, literary sources, TV programs, and award winners. Indexes point to filmmakers, voice artists, production and distribution companies, and series made originally for the movie theater. With its companion volume *Children's Television: The First Thirty-Five Years, 1946–1981—Part II: Live, Film, and Tape Series* (see entry 499), Woolery has produced an excellent, if dated, look at children's television.

ANIME

479. Ledoux, Trish, Doug Ranney, and Fred Patten. 1997. *The Complete Anime Guide: Japanese Animation Film Directory & Resource Guide.* 2nd ed. Issaquah, Wash.: Tiger Mountain Press.

Ledoux and Ranney compiled the first comprehensive English-language guide to anime. One chapter covers animated "television series made in Japan and broadcast in America," while another lists videos available for purchase in the United States. Each entry includes an illustration, credits, and a description of the show and its broadcast or release history. Serials are described episode by episode. Additional chapters cover genres, fan clubs, and video suppliers. Appendixes include a glossary and a list of creative credits—this last is useful because the index excludes the video list. Although no longer the largest or most updated anime guide (that honor goes to Mangels's *Animation on DVD*—see entry 463), the excellent descriptions make this book a good resource for anime fans.

480. McCarthy, Helen. 1996. *The Anime! Movie Guide: [Movie-by-Movie Guide to Japanese Animation since 1983].* London: Titan Books.

Anime expert McCarthy has produced a chronological guide to anime films made in Japan from 1983 through 1995. In alphabetical order by English-language title each year, entries include Japanese and English titles, Japanese and Western credits and release dates, trivia, genre, a plot summary, and a one- to four-star rating. Includes illustrations, a bibliography, and a film title index. McCarthy also co-wrote the complementary title *The Erotic Anime Movie Guide* (see entry 481).

481. McCarthy, Helen, and Jonathan Clements. 1999. *The Erotic Anime Movie Guide.* Woodstock, N.Y.: Overlook Press.

Anime experts McCarthy and Clements wrote this guide to erotic anime as a companion to McCarthy's book *The Anime! Movie Guide* (see entry 480). The first two-thirds of the book consist of filmographic essays on history, themes, and genres. The last third of the book is a selective title list of pornographic anime films that includes English and Japanese titles, Japanese and Western credits and release dates, source material, spin-offs, a plot summary, and a rating that indicates the amount of sex. Includes illustrations, a glossary, a bibliography, and a Japanese and alternate film title index.

482. Nagatomi, Akio, and Jane Nagatomi. *The Anime Cafe* [World Wide Web Resource]. Address: http://www.abcb.com. [Accessed: March 2005].

Although the Web site is not up-to-date, there is enough of interest to anime fans to continue consulting it for the over 150 reviews and the encyclopedia of terms. Reviews include genre, a plot summary, comments for parents, and episode reviews for series. Often, there are links to encyclopedia articles, which can also be entered independently, which include entries for films, companies, and terms describing anime and its viewers as well as slang used in the movies. *The Anime Cafe* shows signs of being only occasionally updated by the Nagatomis in the years since they launched it in 1997. Their latest update was the middle of 2004, although the fan forums seem to be active.

"B" FILMS

483.   Dixon, Wheeler W. 1985. *The "B" Directors: A Biographical Directory.* Metuchen, N.J.: Scarecrow Press.

Teacher, critic, and filmmaker Dixon has created a "guide to the work of more than 350 American film directors." Dixon goes beyond the limited definition of the "B" movie as the cheaper feature in a double feature and instead encompasses "talented" directors who made movies on a small budget in a short amount of time. Organized by director, each entry includes a filmography and a critical career biography. An appendix lists major films cited in the volume. The directory is most useful in its coverage of some of the more obscure directors.

CHILDREN AND YOUNG ADULTS

484.   Kohn, Martin F. 1995. *VideoHound's Family Video Guide.* 2nd ed. Detroit: Visible Ink Press.

Kohn led a team of film experts in compiling a list of over 4,000 videos appropriate for children or teenagers. Films are listed in alphabetical order by title and include the typical VideoHound rating of one to four bones, age level, a summary, parental warnings (for films that may not be appropriate for all children), and a list of principal cast and crew. The book is sparsely illustrated, and occasional sidebars salute prominent filmmakers or offer lists of similar films called "if you liked." The indexes are superb and include alternate titles, MPAA rating, cast and director, and category. Sources for videos and distributors are listed separately.

485.   Moss, Joyce, and George Wilson. 1992. *From Page to Screen: Children's and Young Adult Books on Film and Video.* Detroit: Gale Research.

Moss and Wilson evaluate more than 1,400 videos that have been adapted from over 750 works of literature intended for children and young adults. They selected the titles based on recommendations from state education associations, teachers, and librarians. Organized by literary work, each entry includes a description of the work and one or more films. Each film is also described and rated on a three-point scale on how closely the film follows the book and on overall quality of the film. Entries also contain basic production and cast credits, indicate appropriate age, and cite reviews. Appendixes list films for the hearing impaired, film and video distributors, age level, awards, subjects, and author and title. Although Moss and Wilson rarely criticize the films (these are, after all, recommended titles), their book will serve the needs of teachers, librarians, programmers, and parents quite well.

486.   Trojan, Judith. 1981. *American Family Life Films.* Metuchen, N.J.: Scarecrow Press.

Trojan has compiled a list of more than 2,000 "16mm films that cover the broad spectrum of family dynamics in America" made through 1978. The largest portion of the book covers shorts and documentaries with a smaller section devoted to feature films. Each entry includes title, production data, producer, distributor, and a synopsis. Additional materials include a subject index, an annotated bibliography, a now ancient distributor directory, and a title index.

CHILDREN

487.   Association for Library Service to Children. 1987. *Notable Children's Films and Videos Filmstrips and Recordings, 1973–1986.* Chicago: American Library Association.

Each year, the American Library Association's Association for Library Service to Children identifies the best videos for children. Video lists are available on the ALA Web site back to 1996 (see <http://www.ala.org/ala/alsc/awardsscholarships/childrensnotable>), but the lists have been compiled since 1973. This guide gathers these lists of "high quality, noteworthy films, filmstrips, and recordings for children" from 1973 to 1986 into one volume. Arranged first by format and then alphabetically by title, each entry includes date of release, producer, running time, format, sales and rental prices, distributor, a summary, and grade level. Indexes by subject and author make it possible for teachers to select appropriate videos for their students. Although the availability and cost information is hopelessly out-of-date, the guide is still useful for identifying high-quality videos.

Film

488.   *Cinema Review* [World Wide Web Resource]. Address: http://www.cinemareview.com. [Accessed: January 2005].

Cinema Review evaluates films in theatres, on video and DVD, and on television for quality and appropriateness for children. It does so by citing prominent critics and polling approximately 100 viewers for each film to find out what age and gender enjoyed the movie. Browsers may look at all or recent films alphabetically or by genre or see them by MPAA rating, fan rating, teen favorites, or movies suitable for children. Records for individual films summarize the story and the genre, list cast and crew credits, explicitly describe the film's content in terms of profanity, violence, sex, drugs and alcohol, and offer reviews from leading critics with links to the full article. Cast and crew names link to detailed biographies. Of interest not only to parents, but to fans deciding what movie to watch.

489.   *Dove Family Approved Videos* [World Wide Web Resource]. Address: http://www.dove.org. [Accessed: January 2005].

The Dove Foundation was "established to encourage and promote the creation, production and distribution of wholesome family entertainment." Each film in the database is stamped as approved or not approved and contains a brief synopsis from the perspective of the Dove Foundation; a description of the sex, language, violence, drugs, nudity, and the occult; and rates each category on a scale from zero to five. To date the foundation has given the Dove Family-Approved Seal to over 3,000 films of the nearly 4,500 in the database.

490. *Grading the Movies* [World Wide Web Resource]. Address: http://www. gradingthemovies.com. [Accessed: January 2005].

The tagline at *Grading the Movies* is "helping families find entertainment with values." Each film in the database contains U.S. and Canadian ratings and an A to F grade on overall family value as well as on violence, sexual content, language, and drugs/alcohol. The summary focuses on content that might concern parents as well talking points families can use when discussing the movie. The site also offers alternative films with similar themes that might be more family friendly. *Grading the Movies* began as a weekly newspaper column in 1993 and moved to the Internet in 2000, so the coverage is selective for the 1990s and a little more comprehensive for the first part of the twenty-first century.

491. Hack, Richard. 1995. *Richard Hack's Complete Home Video Companion for Parents: Over 300 Reviews of the Best Videos for Children.* Beverly Hills, Calif.: Dove Books.

Hack, a film critic and popular culture writer, has compiled a list of 300 films that he recommends for children or teenagers. Each review describes the film with particular attention to content that might require parental guidance. Includes an age guide and an index.

492. Minow, Nell. *Movie Mom* [World Wide Web Resource]. Address: http://movies. yahoo.com/mv/moviemom. [Accessed: January 2005].

Minow is the *Movie Mom,* providing "parents with the information they need to decide which movies, DVDs and videos are best for kids from ages 2 through 18" since 1995. Now hosted on *Yahoo! Movies* (see entry 84), *Movie Mom* reviews movies and recommends them by age: preschool, kindergarten to grade 3, grades 4 to 8, high school, and mature high school. In addition to age appropriateness, each movie also includes MPAA rating and describes any profanity, nudity or sex, alcohol or drugs, violence or scariness, and diversity issues. The reviews summarize the plot and focus on content that may concern parents and grade the movie A to F. Minow also has cumulated select reviews into her book: *Movie Mom's Guide to Family Movies.*

493. Nichols, Peter M. 2003. *Children's Movies: A Critic's Guide to the Best Films Available on Video and DVD.* 1st ed, *New York Times Essential Library.* New York: Times Books.

As part of the cultural series from the *New York Times* entitled the Essential Library, film critic Nichols has compiled a guide to the 100 best children's movies available on video or DVD. As with any list, readers might quibble with the selection, especially because not all are movies that were intended for children. In any case, each entry includes a plot summary with behind-the-scene stories and cautionary notes to parents. Nichols has produced a useful guide for parents hoping to expand their children's movie horizons.

494.   *Screen It!* [World Wide Web resource]. Screen It Inc. Address: http://www. screenit.com. [Accessed: March 2005].

Since 1996, a husband-and-wife team who are "not affiliated with any political, social or religious group" have provided a guide for parents deciding whether a movie is appropriate for their children. They rate movies on a scale of none to extreme in 15 categories, from the usual sex, nudity, language, alcohol/drugs, and violence to more unusual categories such as disrespect, imitative behavior, and tense family scenes. For each film, they summarize the plot, discuss whether kids will want to see the film and what kind of role models the characters provide, give the MPAA rating, and rate the film's quality on a scale of one to ten. They then write detailed and comprehensive lists of the potentially offensive scenes in each of the 15 categories. *Screen It!* is more detailed than its competitors, making it a good place for worried parents to preview a movie.

495.   Simpson, Paul. 2004. *The Rough Guide to Kids' Movies.* London: Rough Guides.

Best known for its travel and music guides, Rough also offers a couple of guides to film. In this guide, the editors review more than 400 films made for children as well as adult films that should appeal to older kids. Divided into 20 categories, entries for each film include a critical review with special attention to content and suitability for children. Includes an index.

Television

496.   Davis, Jeffery. 1995. *Children's Television, 1947–1990: Over 200 Series, Game and Variety Shows, Cartoons, Educational Programs, and Specials.* Jefferson, N.C.: McFarland.

Davis, fascinated with children's television since his childhood, has written a guide to over 200 children's television shows made between 1947 and 1990. Organized by genre, Davis writes a lively description of each show describing its content, characters, and history. Appendixes include award winners, a chronology of landmark events, an alphabetical list of prime time shows, and shows that got their starts in radio or movies. Includes an index.

497.   McGown, Alistair D., and Mark J. Docherty. 2003. *The Hill and Beyond: Children's Television Drama: An Encyclopedia.* London: British Film Institute.

BFI researchers McGown and Docherty have compiled a survey of "every British-made live action children's drama shown on television" between 1950 and 2000. Programs made elsewhere and aired on British television are excluded. Included are shows that express "emotional realism" with content aimed at children. Coverage is selective for the 1950s and 1960s due to lack of video availability. The amount of coverage given to individual shows is based on "popularity, longevity and quality." Series are listed in chronological order by date first aired and include a plot overview, number of episodes, dates broadcast, and regular cast and top crew. Each decade is treated to an in-depth look at the decade's shows. The index covers cast and crew names and show and episode titles.

498. TV Now. *G-Rated Movies* [World Wide Web Resource]. VisionSoft Corp. Address: http://www.tv-now.com/stars/grated.htm. [Accessed: March 2005].

TV Now lists and describes all the G-rated movies that will be televised on cable TV each month. Each movie includes director, stars, a brief description, and a schedule.

499. Woolery, George W. 1985. *Children's Television: The First Thirty-Five Years, 1946–1981. Part II: Live, Film, and Tape Series.* Metuchen, N.J.: Scarecrow Press.

Woolery has compiled a list of 610 live-action television series for children "programmed on the various networks and syndicated extensively in the United States since the start of regular networking in 1946." For each series, he provides where and when aired or syndicated, cast, and an essay describing the show and discussing its characters and themes. Appendixes include a chronology, Emmy and Peabody Awards, longest-running series, imported series, animated series with live components, and series that began on radio, film, in other television programs, literary sources, or comic characters. Indexes point to proper names, subjects, and public, network, and syndicated series. With its companion volume *Children's Television: The First Thirty-Five Years, 1946–1981—Part I: Animated Cartoon Series* (see entry 478), Woolery has produced an excellent, if dated, look at children's television.

YOUNG ADULTS

From Page to Screen: Children's and Young Adult Books on Film and Video (see entry 485)

500. Lekich, John. 2002. *Reel Adventures: The Savvy Teens' Guide to Great Movies.* Toronto; Willowdale, Ont.: Annick Press; Distributed by Firefly Books.

Film critic Lekich has written a guide to 250 of the best films for teenagers and young adults. Divided into five categories that teens might like—such as coming-of-age or horror or pure escape—each entry includes director, principal cast, a plot synopsis, a memorable scene, and the message behind the film. The films tend to be contemporary, but each chapter does list 10 classics worth viewing. Includes film title and actor indexes.

501. Lort, Don. 1997. *Coming of Age: Movie & Video Guide.* Laguna Hills, Calif.: Companion Press.

Lort has compiled a list of over 200 films that dramatize the maturation of a child or teenager, most often through a loss of innocence. Most likely reflecting the actual number of films that are made, the vast majority focus on the coming-of-age of boys rather than girls. He gives each film a one- to five-star rating and lists director, screenwriter, cast, awards, and genre. The plot summaries include very little analysis. The ratings section discusses the elements that might make the film unsuitable for children. Indexes list actors, directors, genre, and category of sexuality. An appendix lists over 300 additional coming-of-age films.

502. Perritt, Patsy H., Jean T. Kreamer, and American Library Association. Young Adult Services Division. 1986. *Selected Videos and Films for Young Adults, 1975–1985.* Chicago: American Library Association.

Each year, the American Library Association's Young Adult Services Division identifies the best DVDs and videos for young adults. Lists are available on the ALA Web site back to 1997 (see <http://www.ala.org/ala/yalsa/booklistsawards/selecteddvds/selecteddvdsvideos.htm>), but the lists have been compiled since 1975. This guide contains 198 films from 1975 to 1985 into one volume that are suitable "for young adult programming" and "aimed at the young adult audience." Arranged alphabetically by title, each entry includes date of release, producer, running time, format, sales and rental prices, distributor, a summary, and grade level. An appendix makes it possible for teachers to select appropriate literary videos for their students, but lack of a subject index weakens this guide substantially. Although the availability and cost information is hopelessly out-of-date, the guide is still somewhat useful for identifying high-quality videos.

COMEDY

FILM

A–Z of Silent Film Comedy (see entry 744)

American Silent Film Comedies: An Illustrated Encyclopedia of Persons, Studios, and Terminology (see entry 743)

503. Byrge, Duane, and Robert Milton Miller. 1991. *The Screwball Comedy Films: A History and Filmography, 1934–1942.* Jefferson, N.C.: McFarland.

Film critic Byrge and communication studies professor Miller have compiled a list of over 50 screwball comedies and the people who made them. The chapters on major performers, directors, and writers are nicely researched well-written essays rather than collections of individual entries. The largest part of the book lists the films in chronological order and includes the date, length, director, producer, writers, cinematographer, and cast followed by a plot synopsis and discussion of the film's merits. The book illustrates select films with black-and-white stills. The essays in the early chapters and the chronological order of the films make the index essential for reference use. The book is of interest to fans and students of film.

The Columbia Comedy Shorts: Two-Reel Hollywood Film Comedies, 1933–1958 (see entry 860)

Comedy Quotes from the Movies: Over 4,000 Bits of Humorous Dialogue from All Film Genres, Topically Arranged and Indexed (see entry 1106)

504. Langman, Larry. 1987. *Encyclopedia of American Film Comedy, Garland Reference Library of the Humanities; Vol. 744.* New York: Garland.

Langman's dictionary includes the comedians and filmmakers, fictional characters, films and series, and genres and topics of American film comedies. For people in comedy, the dictionary includes a description of the career and films plus a selective filmography. Langman created separate entries for landmark films that were critically or popularly acclaimed. The topical articles are the best part of the dictionary, giving excellent overviews of types of humor or genres.

505. Maltin, Leonard. 1982. *The Great Movie Comedians: From Charlie Chaplin to Woody Allen.* Updated ed. New York: Bell.

Maltin explores the lives, careers, and works of 22 of the greatest film comedians of all time. His essays focus on the substance and style of the humor and the reasons for their lasting appeal and lists their shorts and feature films. Includes a name and title index.

506. Neibaur, James L. 1986. *Movie Comedians: The Complete Guide.* Jefferson, N.C.: McFarland.

In a highly opinionated look at screen comedians and their films, Neibaur devotes 16 chapters to the giants of comedy and 5 more to the less prominent comedians in each era. The chapters devoted to one comedian or team begin with an in-depth filmographic essay followed by a complete filmography that includes film title, year or release, actor and director credits, technical data, and a zero- to five-star rating. The chapters on eras explore the careers of a handful of "significant minor" comedians, listing films only in the context of a brief essay. An appendix lists "supporting players and secondary clowns," and an index points to names and titles. Neibaur is partial to earlier comedians, dismissing most comedy from the seventies forward, making his guide most useful for the periods he enjoys.

507. Parish, James Robert, and William T. Leonard. 1979. *The Funsters.* New Rochelle, N.Y.: Arlington House.

Parish, a prolific writer of film reference books, and Leonard, a librarian and film researcher, have written 62 chapters about "the comics, the clowns, and the jesters of the Silver Screen." Each chapter provides a comprehensive career biography chock-full of quotes from interviews and reviews, numerous black-and-white photographs, and a complete list of film credits. Unlike Parish's books on movies, *Funsters* includes an index to both filmmakers and films. *Funsters* is for those interested in in-depth biographies of the biggest names in film comedy.

508. Parish, James Robert. 1973. *The Slapstick Queens.* South Brunswick, N.J.: A.S. Barnes.

Parish writes a biographical homage to five leading female slapstick comedy stars: Marjorie Main, Martha Raye, Joan Davis, Judy Canova, and Phyllis Diller. Each entry is a lavishly illustrated biography of life and career complete with filmography. The filmography, incidentally, lists cast and crew credits. The book will be of interest to anyone investigating these five leading stars. There is no index.

509. Sennett, Ted. 1999. *Comedy on Tape: A Guide to Over 800 Movies That Made America Laugh.* New York: Billboard Books.

Sennett lists and rates over 800 comedies for prospective viewers. The book is divided into movies made by comedy icons, by comedy filmmakers, and by 11 comedy genres. The films included in each category include the standard technical details, the director, the screenwriter, and the principal cast, plus a rating on a scale of one to four stars. The film descriptions are clear and the commentary pithy. The index lists movies by title.

510.   Siegel, Scott, and Barbara Siegel. 1994. *American Film Comedy.* 1st ed. New York: Prentice Hall General Reference.

The Siegels, popular culture critics and writers, have written a dictionary of Hollywood comedians and filmmakers, comic terms and genres, and histories. Most of the entries are about people. The biographies meander between the life and movies and are followed by a selective filmography. The entries for terms, genres, and histories are all well written. The book is illustrated with 75 stills. A bibliography points to the resources used by the authors. The index can be misleading, because it does not include the main entries from the dictionary, pointing only to people and films that fall under another entry. While not comprehensive, the dictionary is an excellent resource on film comedy.

511.   Slide, Anthony. 1998. *Eccentrics of Comedy.* Lanham, Md.: Scarecrow Press.

Slide, a film historian, has written a biographical guide to 13 of the most eccentric film comedians. These unique individuals achieved high comedic stature because they didn't neatly fit into any standard comedy subgenre or mold. The biographical essays are based on interviews with the comedians or people who knew them. The essays cover life, career, and works. Includes an index.

TELEVISION

512.   Adir, Karin. 1988. *The Great Clowns of American Television.* Jefferson, N.C.: McFarland.

Adir, a professional clown, has written biographies of 17 television comedians. Her in-depth biographies cover life, career, works, and comedic style. Their "TV-ographies" are listed separately at the end, along with a bibliography and index.

513.   Eisner, Joel, and David Krinsky. 1984. *Television Comedy Series: An Episode Guide to 153 TV Sitcoms in Syndication.* Jefferson, N.C.: McFarland.

Eisner and Krinsky have compiled an episode-by-episode guide to American sitcoms available in syndication. Although it is the most complete guide for its time, it excludes series such as live shows from the 1950s of which no record exists, series that didn't last long enough to be offered in syndication, series unavailable because they were banned, and recent series (meaning that shows are only covered selectively after the 1979–1980 season). In all, the guide contains over 11,000 episodes from 153 series. Series are listed in alphabetical order and include dates originally aired, number of episodes, producers, distributors, cast, and a description of the show's premise. Episodes are listed in the order they were produced and include title, writer, director, guest stars, and a one-sentence synopsis. A separate section gives the same treatment to animated comedy series. Includes a name index as well as an interesting addendum to the introduction that describes standard comedy plots.

514.   Javna, John. 1988. *The Best of TV Sitcoms: Burns and Allen to The Cosby Show, The Munsters to Mary Tyler Moore.* 1st ed. New York: Harmony Books.

Javna polled over 75 television critics to derive a list of the 10 best and 5 worst U.S. television series for each decade from the 1950s through the 1980s. The result is an entertaining guide to sitcoms. The best get treated to four pages of information, beginning with an introductory overview followed by a description of the show and its characters, representative quotes from an episode, miscellaneous tidbits and statistics about the show and its characters, and comments from the critics polled. The worst shows receive a similar treatment, but only in two pages. Scattered throughout the book is the sitcom hall of fame, featuring such categories as animals, precocious kids, and jobs. The book is interesting to both fans of the shows and people interested in seeing the results of the polls.

515.   Koseluk, Gregory. 2000. *Great Brit-Coms: British Television Situation Comedy.* Jefferson, N.C.: McFarland.

Koseluk provides an exhaustive portrayal of 13 British situation comedies that have achieved some level of popularity in the United States. For each series, there is a multipage description and analysis. Each episode includes title, production and cast credits, a one- to four-star rating, and a one-page description. The appendix lists an additional 18 shows with much briefer summaries and no episodic information. Useful for the shows covered.

516.   Mitz, Rick. 1988. *The Great TV Sitcom Book.* Expanded ed. New York: Perigee Books.

Mitz has compiled a comprehensive season-by-season guide to U.S. television sitcoms aired from 1949 to 1987. Each season begins with a couple of photographs and a calendar of contemporary world events. For significant shows—termed "front runners"—Mitz includes a cast list, several pages of narrative describing the show, and illustrative quotes from individual episodes. For shows he terms "also rans," Mitz provides much briefer descriptions. Included is an amusing and informative introduction to types of sitcoms, stock characters, and other bits of miscellaneous information. An appendix lists every sitcom not already covered under "front runners" and "also rans." The index points to people and sitcoms by name. The book is well illustrated.

517.   Pegg, Robert. 2002. *Comical Co-Stars of Television: From Ed Norton to Kramer.* Jefferson, N.C.: McFarland.

Pegg, a writer on television and popular culture, has paid biographical homage to the second banana in television comedies—usually the "wacky neighbor, goofy co-worker or dorky best friend." Pegg was able to interview 20 of the 29 second bananas, adding depth to his already substantial critical analysis. Essays are followed by endnotes, film and television credits, and notable TV guest appearances. Includes an index.

518.   Terrace, Vincent. 2002. *Sitcom Factfinder, 1948–1984: Over 9,700 Details from 168 Television Shows.* Jefferson, N.C.: McFarland.

519.   Terrace, Vincent. 2000. *Television Sitcom Factbook: Over 8,700 Details from 130 Shows, 1985–2000.* Jefferson, N.C.: McFarland.

In these companion volumes, prolific television writer Terrace has gathered in once place a massive compendium of facts about the characters from nearly 300 sitcoms. Organized alphabetically by title, each entry includes network and air dates and a synopsis of the show complete with names, dates, numbers, and biographies for each character. Also included are production history tidbits and facts about alternate pilots and missing or lost episodes. The book serves fans of television, people devising and answering trivia questions, and researchers seeking patterns in popular culture. Includes a name index.

520. Waldron, Vince. 1997. *Classic Sitcoms: A Celebration of the Best Prime-Time Comedy.* 2nd ed. Los Angeles: Silman-James Press.

Waldron has written a guide to 10 classic American sitcoms. The comedies were selected based on a 1985 poll of 45 television critics—appendixes list the top sitcoms and how each critic voted. Each sitcom is introduced with a history of how it came to be and a summary of the basic premise. A list of regular cast, supporting cast, and stock players is followed by a description of the pilot, an overview of each season, and every episode in the series. Additional appendixes include a selective who's who, a short list for further research, and a bibliography. The episode guide index connects cast and crew to the sitcoms with which they were associated. As in Koseluk's *Great Brit-Coms* (see entry 515), the book is useful for the shows covered.

CULT AND CAMP

FILM

521. French, Karl, and Philip French. 2000. *Cult Movies.* New York: Billboard Books.

French and French have compiled a list of 150 cult movies—movies that have attracted intense and devoted interest of a small group of people. Films are listed in alphabetical order; each entry includes a still photograph, principal cast and crew credits, a story synopsis, a discussion of the film and its reception, and the odd facts, memorable moments, and key lines that contribute to the film's cult status.

522. McCarthy, Soren. 2003. *Cult Movies in Sixty Seconds: The Best Films in the World in Less Than a Minute.* London: Fusion.

McCarthy, a performer and writer, has written reviews of 61 cult films made over the past 50 years. He defines cult as an original film that resonates with viewers and inspires enduring affection. He writes a critical essay on each film describing the plot and defining the characteristics that qualify it as cult.

523. Peary, Danny. 1991. *Cult Movie Stars.* New York: Simon & Schuster.

Peary, a film and television critic, has compiled a list of more than 750 actors who have fanatical fan followings or who were featured in cult films. Each entry describes the actors and contains an interesting biography that expounds on the roles that made them fan favorites. Stills illustrate many of the features actors. The filmography is divided into cult favorites and other key films. Includes a film title index.

524. Peary, Danny. 1981. *Cult Movies: The Classics, the Sleepers, the Weird, and the Wonderful.* New York: Dell.

525. Peary, Danny. 1983. *Cult Movies 2: 50 More of the Classics, the Sleepers, the Weird, and the Wonderful.* New York: Dell.

526. Peary, Danny. 1988. *Cult Movies 3: 50 More of the Classics, the Sleepers, the Weird, and the Wonderful.* New York: Simon & Schuster.

Peary defines cult movies as "special films that elicit a fiery passion in moviegoers long after their initial releases," but were not otherwise widely popular. The original volume and its two sequels cover 200 cult films. Each film entry includes stills from the film, production data, principal cast and crew, a detailed synopsis, and an extensive critical analysis discussing the film's themes, characters, production history, and critical and popular reception. Although dated, Peary's commentary makes this book one of the better cult film guides.

527. Roen, Paul. 1994. *High Camp: A Gay Guide to Camp and Cult Films.* 1st ed. San Francisco: Leyland.

Roen defines camp as the "triumph of style over substance" in a movie that is ironic and funny, that is often "so bad that it's good." The author gathers films that have gay themes or undercurrents or appeal to the gay community. His descriptions summarize the plots and focus on the elements that make the movies campy in the first place. The index lists principal performers.

528. Schwartz, Carol A., and Jim Olenski. 2002. *VideoHound's Cult Flicks & Trash Pics.* 2nd ed. Detroit: Visible Ink Press.

For its second edition, Schwartz and Olenski took recommendations from viewers and added 250 titles to come up with reviews of 1,313 cult films. In alphabetical order by title, each entry includes a review of the film's cultish elements followed by cast and production credits and a one- to four-"bone" rating. Illustrated throughout with black-and-white stills, there are also numerous sidebars mostly featuring cult filmmakers. Indexes list alternate titles, cast, director, writer, cinematographer, composer, and category.

529. Simpson, Paul, Helen Rodiss, and Michaela Bushell. 2004. *The Rough Guide to Cult Movies.* 2nd ed. London: Rough Guides.

Best known for its travel and music guides, Rough also offers a couple of guides to film. The editors define cult as "any cause, person or object admired by a minority"—in other words, any underappreciated film that wasn't a hit or a movie "so bad it's a hoot." Divided into over 80 genres, each chapter introduces the genre and lists cult films. Each entry lists director and principal cast followed by a plot summary. Additional materials include numerous sidebars and a miscellany section that includes sundry odd lists, guilty pleasures that the editors like without being able to defend, and an index. Although physically a pocket book, the *Rough Guide* packs in a large number of cult films.

TELEVISION

530. Javna, John, Ron Addad, and Roland Addad. 1985. *Cult TV: A Viewer's Guide to the Shows America Can't Live Without.* 1st ed. New York: St. Martin's Press.

Javna researched shows and contacted fans to come up with 75 television programs with very dedicated followings. Each show is treated to a magazine-style layout that includes an essay describing the show and its appeal and sidebars on broadcast history, miscellaneous tidbits and statistics about the show and its characters, and classic quotes and episodes. Separate sections address lost, underground, and prime-time cults, while appendixes list fan clubs (out-of-date), recommended readings, and shows available on video (even more out-of-date). There is no index, which is unfortunate, because there is no logical arrangement of the shows. Readers must rely on scanning the table of contents or the admittedly fun task of paging through the book.

531. Lewis, Jon E., and Penny Stempel. 1993. *Cult TV: The Essential Critical Guide.* London: Pavilion Books.

Lewis has compiled a list of over 300 shows that have attracted "special devotion" by viewers in the United States or Great Britain. Arranged first by genre and then by show, each entry includes where and when broadcast, production and cast credits, and an essay describing the qualities that endeared the show to its viewers. Includes an index.

DOCUMENTARIES

532. International Documentary Association. *IDA Survival Guide & Membership Directory.* Los Angeles: The Association.

The International Documentary Association exists to "promote nonfiction film and video, to support the efforts of documentary film and video makers around the world, and to increase public appreciation and demand for the documentary." In addition to the list of members, the directory lists resources for documentary filmmakers, archives and stock footage libraries, broadcasters, distributors, and festivals. Indexes list members by profession and by geography.

533. International Documentary Association. *Bureau's International Documentary Source Book* [CD-ROM]. North American Pub. Co. 1998. [Accessed: July 2002].

The International Documentary Association has compiled the most complete guide to film and television documentaries available. The book begins with title and format indexes. The main part of the book is a topical arrangement of documentaries in broad categories such as animals, careers, or social issues. Each entry lists the title, technical information, director, a brief synopsis, and current distributor. Other indexes include language, narrator/host, director, distributor, and a list of documentaries that do not at the time of publication have distributors. Intended for programmers, this book is useful to anyone seeking documentaries. The *Source Book* is also a subscriber feature on the BiBnet Web site at <http://www.bibnet.com/docszone>.

Reel Change: A Guide to Social Issue Films (see entry 756)

Special Edition: A Guide to Network Television Documentary Series and Special News Reports, 1955–1979 (see entry 791)

Special Edition: A Guide to Network Television Documentary Series and Special News Reports, 1980–1989 (see entry 792)

EXPLOITATION

534.   Meyers, Richard. 1983. *For One Week Only: The World of Exploitation Films.* Piscataway, N.J.: New Century.

Meyers highlights lesser-known independently made and distributed exploitation films that "tap the basest desires within people." Divided into chapters on "sex, drugs, and rock 'n' roll," violence, and horror, each film includes production and cast credits and a critical analysis that describes the film in all its Mondo glory. Lavish illustrations give a feel for the genre, and an index guides readers to their favorite films and stars.

535.   Weldon, Michael. 1983. *The Psychotronic Encyclopedia of Film.* 1st ed. New York: Ballantine Books.

Weldon briefly produced a 'zine (before there were 'zines) called *Psychotronic* that recommended which bad movies to watch on television. Psychotronic refers to not only horror or science fiction, but to "exploitation films of any sort." The filmography includes more than 3,000 of the exploitation movies deemed unfit for inclusion by most other movie guides of the time. For each movie, the author lists producer, director, and screenwriter and provides a brief synopsis interspersed with commentary and cast names. Black-and-white photos nicely complement this fun reference book. Includes a name index.

FILM NOIR (SEE ALSO *MYSTERY, CRIME,* AND *ESPIONAGE*)

536.   Hannsberry, Karen Burroughs. 2003. *Bad Boys: The Actors of Film Noir.* Jefferson, N.C.: McFarland.

Hannsberry has written a biographical guide to 95 actors who were featured in at least four film noirs and the 240 films in which they appeared. Each star receives several illustrated pages describing his life and career followed by a film noir filmography and references. Appendixes list supporting actors and quotable lines. Includes a bibliography and index. Hannsberry earlier published a complementary guide to the women in film noir entitled *Femme Noir: Bad Girls of Film* (see entry 537).

537.   Hannsberry, Karen Burroughs. 1998. *Femme Noir: Bad Girls of Film.* Jefferson, N.C.: McFarland.

Hannsberry has written a biographical guide to "49 actresses who were most frequently featured in the movies of the film noir era." Each star receives several illustrated pages describing her life and career followed by a film noir filmography and references. Includes a complete index to the stars, the 149 films in which they appeared, and other names and films mentioned in the biographies. Hannsberry later published a complementary guide to the men in film noir entitled *Bad Boys: The Actors of Film Noir* (see entry 536).

538.   Keaney, Michael F. 2003. *Film Noir Guide: 745 Films of the Classic Era, 1940–1959.* Jefferson, N.C.: McFarland.

Keaney has written a guide to 745 noir films made during the heyday of film noir in the 1940s and 1950s. Keaney defines film noir as a style, so he includes films from many genres. For each film, he lists cast, director, and writer, identifies noir type and themes, provides a one- to five-star rating, and writes a critical summary followed by a bulleted list of memorable noir moments. Appendixes list films by director, by type, and by year of release. Includes an annotated bibliography and an index.

539.   Meyer, David N. 1998. *A Girl and a Gun: The Complete Guide to Film Noir on Video.* New York: Avon Books.

Despite an excellent introduction to and definition of film noir involving theme, motif, style, character, and mood, Meyer's "know it when he sees it" definition leads to the inclusion of some unexpected films in this otherwise fine guide to the genre. He begins the entry for each film with a terse phrase that describes the overall tone of the film followed by the standard crew and cast information and a brief plot summary. The value of the book lies in the lengthy discussions of each film describing the elements that make it noir. For most of the films, Meyer recommends more films by the same director and in his introduction includes a "canon" of 17 must-see noir films. Added materials include a purchasing and rental guide, suggested readings, and a chronological list of films. Indexes list actors, cinematographers, directors, and screenwriters.

540.   Ottoson, Robert. 1981. *A Reference Guide to the American Film Noir, 1940–1958.* Metuchen, N.J.: Scarecrow Press.

Film scholar Ottoson has compiled a descriptive filmography and bibliography of the American film noir. Each film entry lists title, principal cast and crew, and a summary with critical commentary and quotes and endnotes. Separate from the endnotes is the selected bibliography, which is not annotated. Includes an index.

541.   Silver, Alain, and Elizabeth Ward. 1992. *Film Noir: An Encyclopedic Reference to the American Style.* 3rd ed. Woodstock, N.Y.: Overlook Press.

A team of film scholars compiled this filmography of the uniquely American film noir. Alphabetical by title, entries include principal crew and complete cast credits, location, dates completed and released, running time, and a plot summary and critical analysis. The first appendix lists films from other genres such as gangster films and westerns that share some characteristics of noir films. Additional sections include a chronology (through 1976), filmmakers and actors associated with film noir, a selected bibliography, and an index. Although now dated, the guide was published after the heyday of film noir and so is still useful to researchers interested in the genre.

542.   Stephens, Michael L. 1995. *Film Noir: A Comprehensive, Illustrated Reference to Movies, Terms, and Persons.* Jefferson, N.C.: McFarland.

Stephens defines film noir as movies with corruptible characters with a feel of fatalism and a style that builds on these themes. This fine dictionary contains a list of films that meet his criteria and the actors who played leading roles in them. For films, he lists the principal crew and cast and writes an evaluative summary. For people, he names their profession, their accomplishments in film noir, and a filmography of noir films. As stated in the title, the book is illustrated, but only sparsely. The bibliography is extensive and the index comprehensive.

GAME SHOWS

543.   Schwartz, David, Steve Ryan, and Fred Wostbrock. 1999. *The Encyclopedia of TV Game Shows.* 3rd ed. New York: Facts on File.

This most complete guide to American game shows is now in its third edition. Each entry includes premiere date, packager, broadcast history, host and announcer, producer, director, set designer, and select crew. Debut guests are listed if they were celebrities. Show descriptions might include background on how the show was developed or the hosts, but always include the premise of the game and how it was played. Interesting features include the photographs scattered throughout and trivia in the categories "did you know" and "were you watching when." Appendixes include a list of networks and game shows by network, a chronology of game shows, lists of the longest running and most popular game shows, game show award winners, and game show personalities. The index lists the shows and the people involved in making them.

HISTORICAL FILMS AND BIOPICS
BIOPICS

544.   Emmens, Carol A. 1977. *Famous People on Film.* Metuchen, N.J.: Scarecrow Press.

Emmens has compiled an index of biographical 16mm films available for rental by educators. She excludes biopics, sales films, and films that mention an individual only in passing. Arranged by last name, entries include the film title, running time, release date, producer and distributor, appropriate grade level, and an annotation. No longer useful as a source for renting biographies, the index is still useful to students for seeing what biographies were made and to historians because of the interviews. Includes a selected list of feature films and title and subject indexes.

545.   Karsten, Eileen, and Dorothy-Ellen Gross. 1993. *From Real Life to Reel Life: A Filmography of Biographical Films.* Metuchen, N.J.: Scarecrow Press.

Karsten has compiled a list of biopics, featuring English-language films that deal with the life of a real person. Listed alphabetically by last name, each entry includes birth and death dates, claim to fame, and a list of movies. The movies list date of release, length, distributor, director, and leading actors. Cross-references point to real people secondary to the character featured in a movie. Separate indexes list performers, film titles, subjects, and dates of release.

546.   Stevens, Michael G., and Rita M. Thompson. 2003. *Reel Portrayals: The Lives of 640 Historical Persons on Film, 1929 through 2001.* Jefferson, N.C.: McFarland.

Stevens lists 569 real people and 71 categories of people portrayed in at least two films made between 1929 and 2001. For each individual, the authors provide a brief biography and then list the films complete with actor, film, director, and principal cast. Categories such as U.S. presidents, British monarchs, French monarchs, Russian Czars and Czarinas, and Kaiser Wilhelm II are listed in appendixes, as are Western series. The index points to real and fictional names and film titles.

HISTORICAL FILMS
(*SEE ALSO* WAR FILMS)

547. Roquemore, Joseph H. 1999. *History Goes to the Movies: A Viewer's Guide to Some of the Best (and Some of the Worst) Historical Films Ever Made.* 1st ed. New York: Main Street Books/Doubleday.

Roquemore compares historical feature films with the history they presume to represent. The book is organized by historical time periods, with a chapter at the end on biopics. For each film, the author includes "an essay on the history covered in one or more movies, a brief plot summary, an assessment of each film's historical accuracy and enter-tainment value, and a list of books for readers interested in learning more." He also recom-mends further viewing. Ratings on a one- to five-star scale are based on the film's historical accuracy. Unfortunately, there is no index, so it is necessary to locate the time period or event in the table of contents in order to find a particular film.

Classical Era

548. Lucanio, Patrick. 1994. *With Fire and Sword: Italian Spectacles on American Screens, 1958–1968.* Metuchen, N.J.: Scarecrow Press.

Luciano has compiled a list of approximately 350 Italian spectacle movies, "large-scale works depicting in either a historical or mythological sense life in the ancient world" screened in the United States or the United Kingdom. Organized by English-language title, the filmography includes technical information, key crew and cast, and a plot summary. Appendixes list foreign films, precursors to the genre, Samuel Bronston films, English-language films, and additional films that might fit the genre but were unavailable. Includes a bibliography and index.

549. Smith, Gary A. 2004. *Epic Films: Casts, Credits, and Commentary on Over 350 Historical Spectacle Movies.* 2nd ed. Jefferson, N.C.: McFarland.

Smith has compiled a list of sword and sandal movies, films "concerned with monumental events and larger than life characters" that "take place during the period of time from the Creation to the thirteenth century." In alphabetical order, the entries for each historical, religious, or mythological epic include English-language and original title, the advertising catch phrase, principal crew and cast, and a historical and critical analysis. An appendix lists additional films that don't quite fit the epic definition. Includes a bibliogra-phy and a name and title index.

Middle Ages

550. Harty, Kevin J. *Arthurian Film* [World Wide Web Resource]. Camelot Project, University of Rochester. 1997. Address: http://www.lib.rochester.edu/camelot/acpbibs/harty.htm. [Accessed: March 2005].

Harty uses this Web site to update and supercede his list of films based on the Arthurian legend that originally appeared in his book *Cinema Arthuriana, Essays on Arthurian Film.* The entire filmography is on one Web page, with an alphabetical title list that has internal links to fuller records that include release date, country of origin, director, production company, and principal cast, followed by a brief summary with commentary and citations to reviews and discussions of each film.

551.   Harty, Kevin J. 1999. *The Reel Middle Ages: American, Western and Eastern European, Middle Eastern, and Asian Films about Medieval Europe.* Jefferson, N.C.: McFarland.

Harty, a professor of English and a medievalist, has compiled a comprehensive list of over 600 films that depict the Middle Ages. Although his definition of the medieval time period is very generous, his geography of the Middle Ages is limited to include only the Occident and its incursions into the Middle East and the East. He includes films from all over the world released through 1996. Because they are covered so well elsewhere (see entry 1085), he excludes films based on Shakespeare's plays. Arranged in alphabetical order by film title, each entry includes the film's country of origin, director, distribution company, and cast. Harty writes a synopsis and brief evaluation of each film. If the film portrays historical events, the author often includes comments on the accuracy of the portrayal. He cites film reviews and "additional discussions" for each film with general sources listed in a separate bibliography. The book is sparsely illustrated with black-and-white stills and includes a name and title index. Harty's bibliography is most useful for the list of medieval films and the bibliography included for each.

The Modern Era

552.   Klossner, Michael. 2002. *The Europe of 1500–1815 on Film and Television: A Worldwide Filmography of Over 2550 Works, 1895 through 2000.* Jefferson, N.C.: McFarland.

Designed to complement Smith's *Epic Films* (see entry 549) and Harty's *The Reel Middle Ages* (see entry 551), librarian and film reviewer Klossner has written a guide to "more than 2,500 features, shorts, television series, and miniseries" that portray European history from the Renaissance through Napoleon's reign. Like Harty, Klossner excludes films based on Shakespeare's works, because they are well covered in other publications (see entry 1085). Coverage extends from 1895 through the end of 2000. In alphabetical order by title, each entry includes the film's title, year of release, country of origin, director, cast, and a brief plot synopsis. Supplementary materials include a bibliography, a name index, and a subject index that includes the names of real people, places, and events.

American History

553.   Österberg, Bertil O. 2000. *Colonial America on Film and Television: A Filmography.* Jefferson, N.C.: McFarland.

Österberg, a film historian, has compiled a list of over 160 films that take place during the American colonial period. He begins with an excellent overview of films and how they reflect the period. The films are listed in alphabetical order and include principal cast and crew, a summary of the story, and notes about the film or excerpts from reviews. The index lists film titles, personal names, and sources of review excerpts.

554.   Pitts, Michael R. 1984. *Hollywood and American History: A Filmography of Over 250 Motion Pictures Depicting U.S. History.* Jefferson, N.C.: McFarland.

Pitts has compiled a list of over 250 feature films that illustrate American history, either by portraying real people or using fictional characters to depict actual events or time periods. In alphabetical order by title, each entry lists technical data, above-the-line crew, cast with character names, and critical commentary. A general index lists people and events as well as film titles, but the book would have benefited from an additional chronological listing. Lightly illustrated.

555.   Tracey, Grant Annis George. 2002. *Filmography of American History.* Westport, Conn.: Greenwood Press.

Tracey explores "the relationship between American history and American film," analyzing how films reflect their times. The book is organized by events in American history. For each time period, he writes detailed plot summaries of films representative of the time period and provides lists of books and articles for further reading and films for further viewing. Appendixes list multicultural films and woman-centered films. The general index is to people and events, while the title index lists individual films. Tracey doesn't always live up to his promise to connect films to history, but the book is still quite interesting.

Holocaust Films

556.   Gellert, Charles Lawrence, and U.S. National Archives and Records Administration. 1989. *The Holocaust, Israel, and the Jews: Motion Pictures in the National Archives.* Washington, D.C.: National Archives Trust Fund Board, for the National Archives and Records Administration.

Gellert has compiled a list of films and newsreels in the U.S. National Archives relating to Jews in the United States, Europe, Palestine, and Israel. The films were either made by U.S. government agencies or were given to the Archives. Most entries were drawn from donated newsreels, but also include the liberation of the Nazi concentration camps and the Nuremberg war crimes trials. Fully a quarter of the book is devoted to the Holocaust, making the catalog a good supplement to *The Holocaust Film Sourcebook* (see entry 558). Includes a film title appendix and an index.

557.   Muff, Judith Herschlag, Dennis B. Klein, and International Center for Holocaust Studies (U.S.). 1986. *The Holocaust in Books and Films: A Selected, Annotated List.* 3rd ed. New York: Hippocrene Books.

On behalf of the Anti-defamation League of B'nai B'rith's International Center for Holocaust Studies, Muff and Klein compiled a list of books and films about the Holocaust. The book is "designed primarily as a guide for teachers and librarians in the junior and senior high schools." Divided into chapters such as the European Jewry Before the Holocaust, The Third Reich, and Survivors and the Generation After, the majority of works cited are books, with a briefer section devoted to audiovisual materials. Audiovisual entries include title, length, technical data, and a summary. Teachers will benefit most from this guide. Now called the Braun Holocaust Institute, there is no indication that the guide has been updated or made available on its Web site: <http://www.adl.org/focus_sheets/focus_braun.html>.

558.   Picart, Caroline Joan. 2004. *The Holocaust Film Sourcebook.* Westport, Conn.: Praeger.

Professor Picart has produced the most comprehensive international guide to films and documentaries made about the Holocaust. Volume 1 includes fictional works that "touch upon the Holocaust through the format of a narrative story—drama, action, crime, thriller, love story, and so forth." Volume 2 lists documentaries and propaganda films—the propaganda films are listed separately and include many fictional films. Each entry includes original and English-language title, technical information, credits for screenplay, direction, cinematography, editing, music, and cast, source material, and a story summary. Many of the entries also include lists of primary and secondary sources commenting on the work. Each volume contains its own subject index, but there are no cumulative indexes, meaning it is necessary to consult all three sections to locate a film. There are no name indexes. Picart has produced an excellent sourcebook on Holocaust films.

559.   Skirball, Sheba F., and Steven Spielberg Jewish Film Archive. 1990. *Films of the Holocaust: An Annotated Filmography of Collections in Israel, Garland Filmographies; 2.* New York: Garland.

Skirball, director of the Israel Filmography Database Project, has compiled a list of films and television programs relating to all aspects of the Jewish Holocaust, from the rise of Nazism to the persecution and deportation of Jews to the concentration camps and mass murders. The catalog is drawn from the collections of 11 holding institutions. The core of the filmography comes from two institutions—the Ghetto Fighters' Museum and the Holocaust Martyrs and Heroes Remembrance Authority—that actively seek films and television programs about the Holocaust from around the world. Most of the book is the alphabetical list of titles in the original language with an English translation. Each entry includes the film's country of origin, language, release date, distributor, and a synopsis. Other sections include newsreels, television clips, and testimonies. A language and a detailed subject and name index complete the book.

INDEPENDENT FILMS

560.   *Film Threat* [World Wide Web Resource]. Gore Group Publications. Address: http://www.filmthreat.com. [Accessed: March 2005].

Begun as a now defunct magazine, *Film Threat*'s mission is "to champion the increasingly popular explosion of independent and underground films." It does so by interviewing filmmakers, featuring festivals, and writing reviews of independent and underground cinema and alternative reviews of mainstream movies. Unfortunately, the *Film Threat Video Guide* no longer exists, but there is an alphabetical archive of over 6,000 film and DVD reviews that can take its place. A typical entry includes the film's title, release year, rating, length, a one- to five-star rating, and a quality review.

Independent Jewish Film: A Resource Guide (see entry 920)

561.   *IndieWIRE.com* [World Wide Web Resource]. IndieWIRE. Address: http://www.indiewire.com. [Accessed: March 2005].

IndieWIRE.com features independent film and filmmaking with industry news, reviews and previews of films and coverage of events and festivals. The site is primarily a current awareness tool, because the archives only go back to 1998.

562.   LoBrutto, Vincent. 2002. *The Encyclopedia of American Independent Filmmaking.* Westport, Conn.: Greenwood Press.

LoBrutto's aim is to "provide information, perspective, and insight into historical, technical, aesthetic, practical, fiscal, and critical aspects of independent filmmaking." He does so by writing critical reviews of significant independent films, definitions of genres with examples, and career biographies of filmmakers, with most entries including a bibliography. The encyclopedia is lightly illustrated with black-and-white stills and posters and includes a substantial index.

The Off-Hollywood Film Guide: The Definitive Guide to Independent and Foreign Films on Video and DVD (see entry 260)

563.   Skorman, Richard. 1989. *Off-Hollywood Movies: A Film Lover's Guide.* 1st ed. New York: Harmony Books.

Skorman, a film festival programmer and movie reviewer, has created a guide to films that were not made by major U.S. studios. Other guides cover independent and foreign films, but Skorman's reviews are more in-depth, making this a nice complement for video renters. The beginning lists the movies, directors, actors, cinematographers, and countries. Unfortunately, the book has not been updated with new films since its publication in 1989.

564.   Sullivan, Monica. 1999. *VideoHound's Independent Film Guide.* 2nd ed. Detroit: Visible Ink Press.

Sullivan, a public radio movie critic, has compiled a list of over 1,000 independent feature films. The films are listed in alphabetical order and include a brief and idiosyncratic review followed by VideoHound's standard one- to four-bone rating. Credits include the director, writer, cinematographer, composer, and principal cast. Sidebars featuring independent filmmakers and illustrations from the films add life to this interesting guide. An appendix lists independent filmmaker organizations. Indexes list alternate titles, cast, directors, and a category section of genres, themes, settings, events, occupations, and country of origin.

565.   Wood, Jason. 2004. *100 American Independent Films, BFI Screen Guides.* London: British Film Institute.

Wood has compiled a pocket guide to 100 of the best American films made with "economic independence and aesthetic independence." Each film entry contains a critical analysis and a list of production and cast credits. Lightly illustrated, the book also includes a bibliography and index. Of interest to fans seeking alternatives to mainstream fare.

MOVIES ABOUT MAKING MOVIES

566.   Parish, James Robert, Michael R. Pitts, and Gregory W. Mank. 1978. *Hollywood on Hollywood.* Metuchen, N.J.: Scarecrow Press.

Screenwriter DeWitt Bodeen writes the introduction to this list of movies about movie-making. As in all of Parish and Pitts's genre guides, they list principal crew and cast for each film followed by a synopsis and discussion based on the film's critical reception. The book shares the same weakness of the rest of the series by not including an index.

567.   Slide, Anthony. 1979. *Films on Film History.* Metuchen, N.J.: Scarecrow Press.

Prolific film historian Slide has compiled a list of films about film history and the people who made them. He includes feature films, shorts, documentaries, and compilations but excludes films about filmmaking, films about the making of an individual film, and productions made exclusively for television. For each film, he lists title, length, format, credits, and a plot summary. A subject index guides readers to people, genres, countries, and time periods.

MUSIC AND DANCE

DANCE

568.   Billman, Larry. 1997. *Film Choreographers and Dance Directors: An Illustrated Biographical Encyclopedia, with a History and Filmographies, 1893 through 1995.* Jefferson, N.C.: McFarland.

Billman, a writer, director, and producer of plays, has written a comprehensive biographical dictionary of "970 choreographers and dance directors who worked in nearly 3,500 films." Part I takes a decade-by-decade look at dance in film. Part II consists of career biographies of individual choreographers that focus on dance style and list films, stage productions, and night club acts that they choreographed. The book is lightly illustrated, with an appendix listing films and their choreographers and an index to names and titles.

569.   Parker, David L., and Esther Siegel. 1978. *Guide to Dance in Film: A Catalog of U.S. Productions Including Dance Sequences, with Names of Dancers, Choreographers, Directors, and Other Details.* Detroit: Gale Research.

Parker and Siegel have compiled a guide to 1,750 35mm films and documentaries that feature dance performances. Each entry includes production data and credits and lists choreographer, composer, and dancers. When the dance appears in a non-dance film, the authors include a brief note such as "includes a ballet sequence." This is a careful scholarly compilation, but the lack of annotation does the work a disservice.

570.   Spain, Louise. 1998. *Dance on Camera: A Guide to Dance Films and Videos.* Lanham, Md.; New York: Scarecrow Press; Neal-Schuman.

Spain scoured catalogs to compile a list of over 1,400 films and videos that feature dance. She includes feature films as well as filmed dance performances. The main part of the book consists of an alphabetical list of works with credits for producer, director, choreographer, dancers, dance companies, and composers. Indexes by category, choreographer, composer, dancer, dance company, and director guide dance fans and scholars seeking filmed dance performances. A distributor directory lists places where videos and DVDs could be purchased at the time the book was published in 1998.

MUSIC

571.   Anderson, Gillian B. 1988. *Music for Silent Films, 1894–1929: A Guide.* Washington, D.C.: Library of Congress (for sale by the Supt. of Docs. U.S. Government Printing Office).

Music for Silent Films is "a guide for locating scores and musical cue sheets made for films of the silent era, 1894–1929." Organized alphabetically, each entry contains film title, literary source, adaptor and author, production credits, composer or compiler, music publisher, instrumentation, and copyright registration and renewal information. Records point to sets of microfilm taken from the music collections of the Library of Congress and the Museum of Modern Arts (on permanent loan to the Library of Congress). Appendixes list the contents of the microfilm collection by reel as well as items found in four other major collections. Includes a bibliography and an index.

572.   Limbacher, James L. 1974. *Film Music: From Violins to Video.* Metuchen, N.J.: Scarecrow Press.

573.   Limbacher, James L. 1981. *Keeping Score: Film Music 1972–1979.* Metuchen, N.J.: Scarecrow Press.

574.   Limbacher, James L., and H. Stephen Wright. 1991. *Keeping Score: Film and Television Music, 1980–1988: With Additional Coverage of 1921–1979.* Metuchen, N.J.: Scarecrow Press.

575.   Marill, Alvin H., and James L. Limbacher. 1998. *Keeping Score: Film and Television Music, 1988–1997.* Lanham, Md.: Scarecrow Press.

Originally started by Limbacher and now continued by Marill, this four-book set covers over 7,300 films, videos, and made-for-television movies and the composers who scored them. One section of each book lists works and their composers by year. Another section lists composers and their films. Supplementary materials include a film title index, soundtracks and scores, and film and television music awards. Massive in scope, the coverage of television as well as films makes this an excellent resource for tracking down film composers.

576.   *SoundtrackNet* [World Wide Web Resource]. SoundtrackNet. Address: http://www.soundtrack.net. [Accessed: March 2005].

SoundtrackNet, which absorbed *Filmmusic.com* in 1997, is devoted to the "art of film and television music." In operation since 1996, the site contains feature articles, news, reviews, interviews of composers, a database, and a directory. The database lists album title, a one- to five-star rating by both SoundtrackNet and viewers, a list of songs, a review, and links to reviews on other Web sites. A typical record includes album title, composer, manufacturer, year released, catalog number, and estimated value. The directory lists composers, agents, managers, and publicists, and a typical record includes name, address, links to interviews, and a filmography. Additional pages include lists of scores isolated on DVD, a marketplace section of retailers and publishers, and links to trailers and teaser music, studios, and other resources for film music. The best way to find soundtracks and composers is to use the search function, because the browser feature is simply a series of alphabetical lists.

Jazz

577. Meeker, David. 1977. *Jazz in the Movies: A Guide to Jazz Musicians 1917–1977.* New Rochelle, N.Y.: Arlington House.

A jazz fan, Meeker has compiled a list of 2,239 films made between 1917 and 1977 that either feature a jazz performance or have jazz music on the soundtrack. Each entry includes country, release year, length, director, and a plot summary highlighting the role jazz plays in the film and describing the music and its performers. The index lists musicians.

Musicals

578. Baxter, Joan. 1997. *Television Musicals: Plots, Critiques, Casts, and Credits for 222 Shows Written for and Presented on Television, 1944–1996.* Jefferson, N.C.: McFarland.

Baxter has compiled a guide to 222 "original musicals written for and presented on television." She includes not only specials and made-for-television movies, but musical episodes from nonmusical series as well. She does not include variety shows, reviews, animated shorts, or Broadway musicals adapted for television. Each entry includes title, length, genre, broadcast date, cast and crew credits, a song list, and a summary with production notes. Supplementary materials include a chronology, a bibliography, and song and name indexes. Much has been written about stage and movie musicals, but less so about television, so Baxter's guide is welcome.

579. Bradley, Edwin M. 1996. *The First Hollywood Musicals: A Critical Filmography of 171 Features, 1927 through 1932.* Jefferson, N.C.: McFarland.

Bradley has compiled a list of 171 of the earliest feature film musicals, coinciding with the birth of the sound era. His definition of musical is broad, because the genre was being invented even as the films were being produced. The films are listed chronologically in 12 chapters on various themes. Each chapter has an introduction and many endnotes. Each film entry contains the cast, crew, songs sung, a plot summary, and a discussion. Appendixes list silent feature films inspired by Broadway musicals and short subjects. The index to film titles and personal names, strangely, only points to songs if they are mentioned in the synopsis, but not if they are mentioned only in the songs section.

580. Green, Stanley. 1988. *Encyclopaedia of the Musical Film.* New York: Oxford University Press.

Green's excellent companion for fans of feature film musicals "contains succinct information regarding the musical screen's most prominent individuals, productions, and songs." Entries for musicals include year of release, composer and lyricist, screenwriter, principal crew, complete speaking and singing cast, a list of songs, and a plot summary with commentary. Entries for individuals include career specialty, a career biography, and a musical filmography. Entries for songs list composer and lyricist, describe the theme, and indicate in which musicals it was featured. Appendixes list Academy Award nominees and winners, biographical films, title changes between the United States and England, and a discography.

581. Green, Stanley, and Elaine Schmidt. 2001. *Hollywood Musicals: Year by Year.* 2nd ed. New York; Northam, England: Hal Leonard; Roundhouse.

Green, a prolific writer on Broadway and movie musicals, has compiled a chronological list of approximately 300 musicals made in Hollywood beginning in 1927 with *The Jazz Singer* and ending in 1989 with *The Little Mermaid.* For each musical, the title, principal crew and cast, date released, and songs are listed. The authors summarize the plot, provide background on the making of the film, and offer a critical appraisal (Green admittedly prefers the older more wholesome musicals). When the film was adapted from Broadway, the differences are delineated. Separate indexes list movies, composers and lyricists, screenwriters, directors, choreographers, producers, cinematographers, cast, and studios. The book is illustrated throughout with black-and-white stills. Schmidt updated this second edition to include the nineties.

582. Hischak, Thomas S. 2000. *Film It with Music: An Encyclopedic Guide to the American Movie Musical.* Westport, Conn.: Greenwood Press.

Hischak's encyclopedia "identifies and describes the cinematic musicals and the artists who made them." The guide lists 383 musicals plus prominent "performers, songwriters, directors, choreographers, producers, studios, and designers." Film entries contain distributor, year of release, and a plot summary. Name entries provide brief career profiles. All entries are extensively cross-referenced. Appendixes include a chronological list of musicals, Academy Award winning musicals, and a bibliography. The index is exhaustive, pointing to movies, people, and songs. Hischak wrote *Film It with Music* as a companion to *The American Musical Film Song Encyclopedia* (see entry 597).

583. Hirschhorn, Clive. 1991. *The Hollywood Musical.* 2nd ed. New York: Portland House.

At the time it was first published, film writer Hirschhorn had compiled the most complete guide to movie musicals made by American production companies. Arranged chronologically, each musical is described in a narrative that weaves together the story behind the making of the film, the plot, and Hirschhorn's pithy commentary followed by a list of principal cast and crew and the songs. The musicals begin with *The Jazz Singer* in 1927 and take readers through the eighties. Each year is introduced by a list of award nominees and winners. Appendixes include "fringe" musicals, movies that include music but don't quite reach the definition of a musical, pop musicals, and documentaries. The extensive indexes (title, song, performer, composer and lyricist, and "other creative personnel") and comprehensive coverage make this an excellent reference book; the large format and black-and-white illustrations from every movie included also make this a nice coffee table book.

584. Kenrick, John. *Musicals101.com: The Cyber Encyclopedia of Musical Theatre, TV and Film* [World Wide Web Resource]. John Kenrick. Address: http://www.Musicals101.com. [Accessed: March 2005].

Kenrick, a theatrical producer and manager, has written a historical encyclopedia of musicals, providing chronological histories of stage, film, and television musicals. For each decade, he discusses a handful of the most prominent musicals of the era. The film section provides no credits, but the television section lists network, air date, composer, lyricist, writer, director, and principal cast. Most of the feature articles discuss stage musicals, but one article discusses dance in both stage and film musicals. One nice feature is the listing of rights to more than 500 musicals available for nonprofessional performances in the United States.

585. Parish, James Robert, and Michael R. Pitts. 1992. *The Great Hollywood Musical Pictures.* Metuchen, N.J.: Scarecrow Press.

The prolific duo of Parish and Pitts has compiled a list of nearly 350 feature-length musical films. As with all books in the series, each film entry includes extensive cast and crew information, a detailed plot summary, and a brief discussion of the film. The appendix is a film chronology. Unfortunately, there are no actor or character name indexes, reducing the book's usefulness somewhat.

586. Taylor, John Russell, and Arthur Jackson. 1971. *The Hollywood Musical.* New York: McGraw-Hill.

The first third of *The Hollywood Musical* takes a critical look at the genre, examining the history, the music, the performers, the filmmakers, and the films. The middle third is a select filmography of musical films, complete with cast, crew, and songs. The final third consists of indexes for names, songs, and titles. The name index offers complete filmographies; musicals mentioned in the book are in bold type. The title index lists 1,437 films, but only a fraction are in bold type, indicating that the filmography is nowhere near complete. The book is illustrated, mostly with black-and-white stills, but with a selection of color plates as well.

587. Vallance, Tom. 1970. *The American Musical.* London; New York: A. Zwemmer; A.S. Barnes.

Vallance has compiled a biographical dictionary of the directors, performers, composers, lyricists, conductors, dancers, and other filmmakers who have made film musicals. Each entry includes career specialty, a brief biographical sketch, and a musical filmography with select songs highlighted. Includes a film title index. Although dated, the dictionary covers the golden era of movie musicals and is worth consulting.

Opera

588. Wlaschin, Ken. 2004. *Encyclopedia of Opera on Screen: A Guide to More Than 100 Years of Opera Films, Videos, and DVDs.* New Haven, Conn.: Yale University Press.

Wlaschin, a film writer and film festival organizer, has compiled a guide to the "thousands of films and videos featuring operas and opera singers made in the last one hundred years." The entries include "operas, operettas, zarzuelas, singers, composers, writers, conductors, and subjects" such as Animated Opera, Operas as Movies, and Silent Films about Opera, as well as several best and worst lists. Entries for operas include composer, a plot synopsis, and a list of the films and videos. Entries for individuals include a biography and a complete filmography. Entries for subjects include a definition or explanation followed by a list of exemplars. Although there is no index, the extensive cross-references are adequate for guiding researchers between films, individuals, and subjects.

Rock

589.   Crenshaw, Marshall, and Ted Mico. 1994. *Hollywood Rock.* 1st ed. New York: HarperPerennial.

Crenshaw led a team of film and music experts in reviewing films and documentaries that feature rock and roll music. Arranged by film, the writers offer their opinions and highlight the best scenes and lines before listing songs. Entries also include production and cast credits, a one- to five-star rating in the categories of music, attitude, and fun, and a list of cameo appearances. Appendixes list more rock films, primarily those in which the music is on the soundtrack rather than performed on screen, straight-to-video titles, filmed concerts, and background performers in club scenes. Other appendixes list rock actors' filmographies and give brief bios for those who made cameo appearance in film (this last is not particularly useful, because it doesn't refer back to the films). Includes a performer index. With the supplementary materials, this is probably the most complete guide to rock music in film.

590.   McGee, Mark Thomas. 1990. *The Rock and Roll Movie Encyclopedia of the 1950s.* Jefferson, N.C.: McFarland.

In the early days of rock and roll, there were no music videos, so many of the only recorded performances were on film. McGee has compiled a list of movies made in the 1950s that feature performances by rock and roll musicians. For each movie, he includes a plot summary, background information on the filmmakers and musicians, a list of the songs performed, how the film was received, cast and crew credits, and sources of information. Appendixes list the movies in which songs were performed and which songs performers sang. The index lists performers' names and movie titles.

591.   Sandahl, Linda J. 1987. *Rock Films: A Viewer's Guide to Three Decades of Musicals, Concerts, Documentaries and Soundtracks 1955–1986.* New York: Facts on File.

Sandahl's filmography of films featuring rock music is categorized into musicals, concerts and documentaries, and soundtracks. The author lists principal crew and cast, performers, and songs for each movie. Her brief synopses typically end with a quip about the movie. Indexes list film titles, names, and song titles. Illustrated with stills and posters.

592.   Stacy, Jan, and Ryder Syvertsen. 1984. *Rockin' Reels: An Illustrated History of Rock & Roll Movies.* Chicago: Contemporary Books.

Stacy and Syvertsen have compiled a list of movies featuring rock music and rock stars. Organized by decade, the book begins in the 1950s with *Blackboard Jungle* and ends in the early 1980s. Each decade includes an introduction and an alphabetical list of the movies. For each movie, they list cast and crew, write a plot summary, list the songs, describe the dance and outfits, and comment on the movie's social significance. Indexes list movies and filmmakers, including composers and performers, but strangely omit the songs.

COMPOSERS

593.   Craggs, Stewart R. 1998. *Soundtracks: An International Dictionary of Composers for Film.* Aldershot, Hants, England; Brookfield, Vt.: Ashgate.

Craggs has compiled a dictionary of composers who have written film scores. Organized by composer, each entry includes a brief career biography, a filmography (usually select), and a list of available soundtracks. Supplementary materials include a list of films using classical music and an index of film titles.

594. McCarty, Clifford. 2000. *Film Composers in America: A Filmography, 1911–1970.* 2nd ed. New York: Oxford University Press.

McCarty has compiled a list of scores written expressly to serve as background music for films made from 1911 to 1970—he describes a score as "the only element of a film's soundtrack that cannot be heard by the film's characters but only by the audience." In addition to feature films, McCarty includes documentaries and trailers that had new music expressly written for them. The first two-thirds of the book is organized by composer, listing the films they composed by year. The last third of the book is an index to film titles, listing the composer for each. In between is a supplementary list of composers who collaborated only once on a score, who worked on music other than scores, or who were falsely credited with composing a score. Although McCarty's guide is a great work of scholarship, it is useful only to correctly credit composers, because it offers no other information on the music or the composers.

SONGS AND SINGERS

595. Benjamin, Ruth, and Arthur Rosenblatt. 1993. *Movie Song Catalog: Performers and Supporting Crew for the Songs Sung in 1460 Musical and Nonmusical Films, 1928–1988.* Jefferson, N.C.: McFarland.

Benjamin and Rosenblatt, a husband-and-wife team who love movies, have compiled a list of the songs from the soundtracks of 1,460 films made between 1928 and 1988. Each film entry lists the songs, performers, composers and lyricists. Some entries include comments or excerpts from reviews. Indexes list performers, songwriters, and songs.

596. Bloom, Ken. 1995. *Hollywood Song: The Complete Film & Musical Companion.* New York: Facts on File.

Bloom examined cue sheets from virtually every major studio to compile a list of songs from 7,039 films. Included are American films, foreign films released in the United States, and even unproduced films that had songs composed for them. The first two volumes list the films and include the composer, lyricist, choreographer, songs, and the standard production and cast credits—including an indication that an actor was dubbed by a singer. Unfortunately, songs are not linked to performers. The third volume contains a film chronology and indexes for personnel and songs. Easily the most complete guide to songs in film, Bloom's book is well worth consulting.

597. Hischak, Thomas S. 1999. *The American Musical Film Song Encyclopedia.* Westport, Conn.: Greenwood Press.

Professor Hischak has compiled a dictionary of 1,760 songs written for and originally performed in 500 American movie musicals. Organized by song, each entry includes an analysis of the song placing it in the context of the story and citing performer, composer, and lyricist. Appendixes list alternate titles, songs performed in musicals that came from other sources, best song Oscars, musicals nominated for Oscars, and musicals with their songs. The index lists performers, composers, lyricists, and musicals. Because Hischak excludes songs originally written for stage musicals, it is useful to consult his companion volume on the theater entitled *The American Musical Theatre Song Encyclopedia* (Greenwood, 1995) to read about songs in movie musicals first performed in another venue.

598.   Parish, James Robert, and Michael R. Pitts. 2003. *Hollywood Songsters: Singers Who Act and Actors Who Sing: A Biographical Dictionary*. 2nd ed. New York: Routledge.

Film writers Parish and Pitts have written biographies of over 100 "performers who have had success both as singers and as film stars" in films made since the beginning of the sound era. Each chapter provides a comprehensive career biography chock-full of quotes from interviews and reviews and a complete list of credits for film, Broadway, radio, television, and albums. Includes an index.

599.   Sackett, Susan, and Marcia Rovins. 1995. *Hollywood Sings! An Inside Look at Sixty Years of Academy Award–Nominated Songs; Researched by Marcia Rovins*. New York: Billboard Books.

Sackett has written a dictionary of every song nominated for an Academy Award from 1934 to 1993. Organized by year, each song receives its own entry that contains the composer and lyricist and an essay that describes the film, the history of its production, and the context in which the song was performed or used in the soundtrack. Appendixes list songs used as titles of films, films that had songs nominated, most Oscar nominations by lyricist and by composer, and songs that made it to number one on the music charts. Includes a bibliography and a name and title index.

600.   Warner, Alan. 1984. *Who Sang What on the Screen*. North Ryde; London: Angus & Robertson.

Warner, a music executive, has accumulated thematic lists of songs used in the movies. In 19 chapters are such categories as "songs based on the classics," "television theme songs," and "movie musical songs." Indexes list song titles, artists, and movies and television programs.

601.   Woll, Allen L. 1976. *Songs from Hollywood Musical Comedies, 1927 to the Present: A Dictionary*. New York: Garland.

Woll's list of 1,187 musical comedies made from 1927 through the mid-1970s lists each film's title, year, stars, and directors. All musicals made after 1950 and those made before 1950 that had soundtrack recordings available at the time of publication list songs and composers as well. The over 8,000 songs that fit these categories are listed separately by title. Additional sections include a chronological list of musicals and an index to composers and lyricists.

MYSTERY, CRIME, AND ESPIONAGE
(SEE ALSO *FILM NOIR*)

602. Cocchiarelli, Joseph J. 1992. *Screen Sleuths: A Filmography, Garland Filmographies; 3.* New York: Garland.

The first half of this book lists 200 films "in which the sleuthing process plays a critical role in the overall plot and structure of the mystery." In alphabetical order by film title, each entry includes production and technical information, writer, director, principal cast, a critical summary, and memorable quotes or scenes. The second half of the book highlights a dozen films for in-depth critical analysis. Cocchiarelli includes a chronological list of some 500 films, a bibliography, and a subject index.

603. Mulay, James J., Daniel Curran, and Jeffrey H. Wallenfeldt. 1988. *Spies and Sleuths: Mystery, Spy, and Suspense Films on Videocassette.* 1st ed, *CineBooks Home Library Series; No. 1.* Evanston, Ill.: CineBooks.

Spies and Sleuths is a guide for movie fans who like to watch mystery, spy, and suspense films. More than 400 films are listed in alphabetical order by title; each entry contains a plot synopsis, star rating (zero to five), critical appraisal, anecdotal material, actors and roles played, production credits, and now-dated cassette availability notes. Lists at the beginning of the book sort the films by rating (from masterpiece to without merit), by parental recommendation, and by year of release. Indexes list principal actors, cinematographers, directors, editors, composers, producers, screenwriters, and source authors. Although designed for movie fans, *Spies and Sleuths* also is a good starting point for researchers of the genre.

604. Penzler, Otto. 2000. *101 Greatest Films of Mystery & Suspense.* New York: Ibooks: Distributed by Simon & Schuster.

Penzler, owner of a mystery bookstore and press, ranks the best mystery and suspense films from 101 to 1. Each entry lists genre, studio, producer, director, writer, source, running time, and principal cast followed by an essay that offers trivia, a plot summary, commentary, and the best line from the film. There is no index.

605. Sennett, Ted. 1997. *Murder on Tape: A Comprehensive Guide to Murder and Mystery on Video.* New York: Billboard Books.

Sennett, a film writer and editor, has compiled a guide to films featuring murder and its consequences. In alphabetical order by title, each film includes a one to four star rating, technical data, director and writer, principal cast, and a critical plot summary. A handful of sidebars entertain and black and white stills illustrate, but there is no index, so this is primarily for the fan.

CRIME AND CRIMINALS

606. Baxter, John. 1970. *The Gangster Film.* New York: A.S. Barnes.

Baxter has compiled a list of films that deal (sometimes loosely) with organized crime. Entries are well written, particularly the longer discussions about types of gangster films or gangsters who had at least two films made about them. Entries for individuals include a brief career biography and gangster film credits. A title index provides easy access by pointing directly to citation numbers. Baxter's book is of most use for the golden era of gangster movies made in the 1930s, having been published before the revival brought about by the Godfather films. Illustrated throughout with black-and-white stills.

A Guide to American Silent Crime Films (see entry 733)

607.   Hardy, Phil, and British Film Institute. 1997. *The BFI Companion to Crime*. Berkeley: University of California Press.

Popular culture writer Hardy led a team of 10 writers as they compiled this dictionary of crime in film. Although international in scope, the majority of the entries are of American and British cinema, with Sherlock Holmes, gangster films, film noir, police procedurals, and political crime thrillers all well represented. Excluded are horror films and westerns. Most of the entries are for individual films and include a critical synopsis with credits for principal crew and cast. Other entries cover historical events, places, and people, subgenres, and crime fiction writers. Includes numerous black-and-white stills and a small section in color. Although it lacks an index, *The BFI Companion to Crime* is a nice addition to the literature.

608.   Hardy, Phil, Jeremy Clarke, and Kobal Collection. 1998. *The Overlook Film Encyclopedia. The Gangster Film*. Woodstock, N.Y.: Overlook Press.

Hardy and colleagues have compiled a list of movies featuring "public crime by organized groups of people, to mobsters and G-men, to rogue cops and corrupt city officials, and to capers." In chronological order, each decade is introduced by a filmographic essay placing the movies in the context of the time and is followed by an alphabetical list of films released each year. Each film entry contains a critical analysis, technical data, lead cast and crew, and often a black-and-white illustration. Appendixes list rental champs and gangster Oscars, and an index points to titles. Overlook Press intended to publish a companion guide to the film noir to complete the coverage of crime movies, but there is no indication that it still intends to do so; Overlook instead published *Film Noir: An Encyclopedic Reference to the American Style* (see entry 541). The British edition is entitled the *Aurum Film Encyclopedia*. Hardy later went on to write *The BFI Companion to Crime* (see entry 607).

609.   Langman, Larry, and Daniel Finn. 1995. *A Guide to American Crime Films of the Thirties, Bibliographies and Indexes in the Performing Arts, No. 18*. Westport, Conn.: Greenwood Press.

Langman and Finn list "the screen credits of more than 1,100 features released from 1928 through 1939." The introduction defines crime films as those that deal with "basic questions of 'right' and 'wrong' in human behavior." Each film lists the title, distributor, director, screenwriter, and principal cast and is followed by a brief synopsis. Appendixes list film serials and series, a bibliography lists sources, and the index points to names. This guide is a companion to *A Guide to American Silent Crime Films* (see entry 733) and *A Guide to American Crime Films of the Forties and Fifties* (see entry 610).

610.   Langman, Larry, and Daniel Finn. 1995. *A Guide to American Crime Films of the Forties and Fifties, Bibliographies and Indexes in the Performing Arts, No. 19.* Westport, Conn.: Greenwood Press.

Langman and Finn list the screen credits of "more than 1,200 films released from 1940 through 1959." The introduction defines crime films as those "whose plots chiefly revolve around a crime or criminal intent." Each film lists the title, distributor, director, screenwriter, and principal cast and is followed by a brief synopsis. Appendixes list film serials and series, a bibliography lists sources, and the index points to names. This guide is a companion to *A Guide to American Silent Crime Films* (see entry 733) and *A Guide to American Crime Films of the Thirties* (see entry 609).

611.   Mottram, James. 1998. *Public Enemies: The Gangster Movie A–Z: From Cagney to Tarantino and Beyond.* London: Batsford.

Mottram analyzes 200 of what he considers the most essential gangster films—defined as those portraying organized crime and including such subgenres as "the heist, the prison movie, the hit-man movie, the yakuza, the semi-doc biopic, the lovers-on-the-run, blaxploitation and gangsta rap." Each film includes title, production data, credits for principal crew and cast, a one-sentence synopsis, and an engaging critical review. There is no index, but each entry contains plenty of cross-references and a list of similar movies.

612.   Parish, James Robert, and Michael R. Pitts. 1976. *The Great Gangster Pictures.* Metuchen, N.J.: Scarecrow Press.

613.   Parish, James Robert, and Michael R. Pitts. 1987. *The Great Gangster Pictures II.* Metuchen, N.J.: Scarecrow Press.

Parish and Pitts have produced a list of U.S.-made gangster pictures. Film scholar Edward Connor lays the groundwork with an introduction to the gangster genre and its history. The films are listed alphabetically by title. Each entry includes principal crew and cast followed by a plot summary and a review based on critical reception. An appendix by Vincent Terrace lists radio and television shows. Volume II updates the list of films. Neither book includes an index, reducing their usefulness somewhat.

614.   Parish, James Robert. 1991. *Prison Pictures from Hollywood: Plots, Critiques, Casts, and Credits for 293 Theatrical and Made-for-Television Releases.* Jefferson, N.C.: McFarland.

Parish, a prolific filmographer, has compiled a list of 293 prison movies. As in his other filmographies, he lists the major cast and crew followed by an engaging plot summary and discussion informed by reviews written upon the film's release. A supplement lists seven television shows. The index points to movies and personal names.

615.   Parish, James Robert. 1992. *Prostitution in Hollywood Films: Plots, Critiques, Casts, and Credits for 389 Theatrical and Made-for-Television Releases.* Jefferson, N.C.: McFarland.

Parish, a prolific filmographer, has compiled a list of 389 movies featuring prostitution. As in his other filmographies, he lists the major cast and crew followed by an engaging plot summary and discussion informed by reviews written upon the film's release. An appendix list the films in chronological order. There is an index to movies and personal names.

616.   Stephens, Michael L. 1996. *Gangster Films: A Comprehensive, Illustrated Reference to People, Films, and Terms.* Jefferson, N.C.: McFarland.

Stephens has compiled a list of international (but mostly American) gangster films and filmmakers from the earliest days to the present. For films, he lists the principal crew and cast and writes an evaluative summary. For people, he names their profession, their accomplishments in gangster movies, and a filmography of gangster movies. As stated in the title, the book is illustrated, but only sparsely. An appendix lists "films with peripheral gangster characters," a bibliography includes sources consulted, and the index lists films and names. Complements *Film Noir: A Comprehensive, Illustrated Reference to Movies, Terms, and Persons* (see entry 542).

DETECTIVES AND COPS

Film

617.   Everson, William K. 1980. *The Detective in Film.* Secaucus, N.J.: Citadel Press.

Everson has compiled a list of films featuring detectives. Twelve chapters on such topics as Sherlock Holmes, the silent period, and the FBI consist of lavishly illustrated filmographic essays. Although *The Detective in Film* is designed primarily to read rather than to consult, the name and title index makes the book useful as a reference source.

618.   Parish, James Robert. 1990. *The Great Cop Pictures.* Metuchen, N.J.: Scarecrow Press.

Parish continues his "great" series with a guide to feature films and made-for-television movies featuring American police officers. Alphabetical by title, each film includes featured cast and crew, a plot summary, and comments based on critical reception. An appendix lists cop series on radio and television, a film chronology, and a bibliography of books about the police. Like the rest of the series, the usefulness of the book is lessened by the absence of an index.

619.   Parish, James Robert, and Michael R. Pitts. 1990. *The Great Detective Pictures.* Metuchen, N.J.: Scarecrow Press.

Parish and Pitts have compiled a list of over 350 feature-length detective films. As with all books in the series, each film entry includes extensive cast and crew information, a detailed plot summary, and a brief discussion of the film. Appendixes list the titles of radio and television detective programs, a film chronology, and a bibliography. Unfortunately, there are no actor or character name indexes, reducing the book's usefulness somewhat.

620.   Pitts, Michael R. 1979. *Famous Movie Detectives.* Metuchen, N.J.: Scarecrow Press.

621.   Pitts, Michael R. 1991. *Famous Movie Detectives II.* Metuchen, N.J.: Scarecrow Press.

622.   Pitts, Michael R. 2004. *Famous Movie Detectives III.* Lanham, Md.: Scarecrow Press.

Pitts lists movie detectives and the films that feature them. For each detective, he writes a history of the character and a "biography" of the detective based on the films followed by a complete filmography. Interestingly, two of the most famous detectives were not included until the second book, because other books had already been written on Sherlock Holmes and Raymond Chandler. A bibliography lists the novels about each detective, and the index lists names and movies.

Television

623.   Collins, Max Allan, and John Javna. 1988. *The Best of Crime & Detective TV: Perry Mason to Hill Street Blues, the Rockford Files to Murder She Wrote.* 1st ed. New York: Harmony Books.

Collins and Javna polled more than 75 mystery writers and television critics to derive a list of the best U.S. crime television series: 10 each in the categories of private eyes and police procedurals and five each in the categories of amateur sleuths and comedy crimefighters. Each series is treated to three to five pages that contain an introductory overview and description of the show and its characters, a cast list, quotes from interviews with the cast as well as representative quotes from episodes, and comments from the critics polled. Each section features additional worthy shows and comments on the worst shows. Interspersed among the best and worst are 10 topical lists in such categories as the "ethnic detective" and "television attorneys." The book is interesting to fans of the shows and people interested in seeing the results of the polls.

624.   Martindale, David. 1991. *Television Detective Shows of the 1970s: Credits, Storylines, and Episode Guides for 109 Series.* Jefferson, N.C.: McFarland.

Martindale lists cop, lawyer, sleuth, and private detective series from the 1970s. Excludes espionage, rescue shows, newspaper dramas, sitcoms, and westerns. For each series, Martindale includes an airing history, cast and crew, and an overview of the show followed by thumbnail sketches of each episode.

625.   Terrace, Vincent. 2002. *Crime Fighting Heroes of Television: Over 10,000 Facts from 151 Shows, 1949–2001.* Jefferson, N.C.: McFarland.

Prolific television writer Terrace has written a guide to superheroes and crime fighters featured in 125 regular television series and 26 pilots. Excluded are police and detective shows and cartoons. Organized by television series, each entry includes a complete biography of the featured crime-fighting characters. Biographies might include how a character acquired superpowers, personal information such as addresses, telephone numbers, and hometowns, beliefs and preferences, or just about any bit of trivia revealed during the show. Appendixes list superheroes by name and by mortal name and also list crime-fighting machines such as the Batmobile or the Silver Dart. Includes a performer index. This book is of most interest to fans of the shows and their characters.

626.   Tibballs, Geoff. 1992. *The Boxtree Encyclopedia of TV Detectives.* London: Boxtree.

Tibballs has compiled a guide to nearly 500 "detective series to have been screened on British and American TV since the war." Organized by series title, each entry includes an engaging overview of the show complete with tidbits on its history and descriptions of the detective's style and working methods followed by a list of regular cast and production credits and air dates. For select shows, he lists episode titles. Includes a chronology of premier dates but no index.

ESPIONAGE

627.   Langman, Larry, and David Ebner. 1990. *Encyclopedia of American Spy Films, Garland Reference Library of the Humanities; Vol. 1187.* New York: Garland.

Langman and Ebner made every effort "to bring together in one volume virtu-ally every American-produced film from the early silent period to the late 1980s concern-ing spies, government operatives and undercover agents." More than 1,000 alphabetical film entries include director, writer, principal cast, and a plot summary. An additional 100 topical, historical, and biographical entries place spy films in context—these are outlined separately in an appendix. Other appendixes list serials, awards and nominations, political assassinations, and wars. There is no name index, so it is not possible to track directors or actors who specialized in the genre.

628.   Lisanti, Tom, and Louis Paul. 2002. *Film Fatales: Women in Espionage Films and Television, 1962–1973.* Jefferson, N.C.: McFarland.

Popular culture writers Lisanti and Paul profile 107 women featured in spy films and television shows between 1962 and 1973. After an extensive introduction to the genre, they devote several pages to each actor, discussing their lives and careers with much atten-tion to their appearance—hence the many illustrations. Supplementary materials include links to official and fan Web sites for approximately one-third of the actors, a bibliography, and an index. The book is intended primarily for fans.

629.   Mavis, Paul. 2001. *The Espionage Filmography: United States Releases, 1898 through 1999.* Jefferson, N.C.: McFarland.

Mavis, a film historian and writer, has compiled a filmography of films that "deal with undercover agents of any government." The films are listed in alphabetical order by title and include the standard technical information, principal cast and crew, and a synopsis with commentary. Mavis provides a bibliography and indexes to cast and crew.

630.   Parish, James Robert, and Michael R. Pitts. 1974. *The Great Spy Pictures.* Metuchen, N.J.: Scarecrow Press.

631.   Parish, James Robert, and Michael R. Pitts. 1986. *The Great Spy Pictures II.* Metuchen, N.J.: Scarecrow Press.

Film reference book writers Parish and Pitts have compiled a list of 463 spy films that relate to "national interest and with the interest being in some way threatened by a foreign power." As with all books in the series, each film entry includes extensive cast and crew information, a detailed plot summary, and a brief discussion of the film. Appendixes list the titles of spy shows on radio and television and a select bibliography of spy novels and series. Unfortunately, there are no actor or character name indexes, reducing the book's usefulness somewhat. The sequel updates the filmography with new feature films as well as "TV movies, serials, and even other movie genres which have used the spy motif."

REMAKES AND SEQUELS

632. Drew, Bernard A. 1990. *Motion Picture Series and Sequels: A Reference Guide, Garland Reference Library of the Humanities; Vol. 1186.* New York: Garland.

Drew lists over 900 English-language films that have one or more sequels. Listed in alphabetical order by title, character name, and actor, each series is given a brief overview followed by the movies in the series. The index lists individual film titles.

633. Goldberg, Lee. 1993. *Television Series Revivals: Sequels or Remakes of Cancelled Shows.* Jefferson, N.C.: McFarland.

Goldberg has compiled a list of television shows that were revived as new series or specials after having been cancelled at least one year before. Each entry includes dates aired, describes the show, lists cast members, and gives background information on why the original was cancelled and the revival produced. An appendix lists animated revivals. Mostly of interest to fans, the book is also useful to researchers who need to be sure of the complete run of a show. Includes a name index.

634. Limbacher, James L. 1991. *Haven't I Seen You Somewhere Before? Remakes, Sequels, and Series in Motion Pictures, Videos, and Television, 1896–1990.* Ann Arbor, Mich.: Pierian Press.

Limbacher's title is somewhat misleading. Although he does list remakes, sequels, and series, his goal is to list all films made from the same source material, whether it was originally a book, a play, a biography, another film, or some other type of material. The first and largest part of the book lists remakes. Reader looking up the film will most often get a cross-reference to the original source material where they will find a chronological list of films using that source material. The sequels section lists movies that feature the same characters and a progression from an earlier film. The series section is similar to the sequels section, but lists productions with at least three films. The lack of indexes hurts the last two sections, because they don't have cross-references to sequels or later films in the series. Despite these drawbacks, the remake section alone makes this a valuable reference book.

635. Nowlan, Robert A., and Gwendolyn Wright Nowlan. 1989. *Cinema Sequels and Remakes, 1903–1987.* Jefferson, N.C.: McFarland.

The Nowlans have compiled the largest list of sequels and remakes, listing over 1,000 English-language sequences. For each entry, they describe the source material, list basic cast and crew, and write a summary for each film in the sequence. They use cross-references for films and reserve the index for personal names, song titles, and source materials. To save space, the book is not comprehensive, listing prominent films and excluding some genres. Complements *Science Fiction, Fantasy and Horror Film Sequels, Series and Remakes: An Illustrated Filmography* (see entry 642).

ROMANCE

636.   Halpern, Leslie. 2003. *Reel Romance: The Lovers' Guide to the 100 Best Date Movies.* 1st Taylor Trade Pub. ed. Lanham, Md.: Taylor Trade; Distributed by National Book Network.

Halpern, a popular entertainment writer, has written a guide to the 100 best romance films that both men and women will enjoy. Divided into subgenres, each chapter includes films from the 1980s forward with a single classic thrown in for good measure. Each film entry includes cast, director, intimacy level, "make-out meter," scenes for him and for her, and a plot summary with commentary focusing on the film's romantic aspects. Includes an index.

SCIENCE FICTION, FANTASY, AND HORROR

637.   Lentz, Harris M. 2001. *Science Fiction, Horror & Fantasy Film and Television Credits.* 2nd ed. Jefferson, N.C.: McFarland.

Reference book writer Lentz spent 20 years compiling this index to the people who created films and television shows released in the United States that include elements of science fiction, horror, or fantasy. Volume 1 lists area of specialization and credits for actors, directors, producers, writers, cinematographers, special effects, makeup artists, art directors, and more. Volume 2 lists films with credits. Volume 3 lists television series with general credits for the series as well as credits for individual episodes.

638.   *Science Fiction and Fantasy World* [World Wide Web Resource]. Address: http://www.sffworld.com. [Accessed: January 2005].

SFF World is a science fiction and fantasy Web site featuring not only movies and television, but literature, original stories and poems, and games. The movie section contains reviews of films and television shows written by regular staff volunteers as well as by contributors from the Web. Most reviews include title, director, release year, production company, genre, commentary, and a rating on a one-to-five scale. Any time content is created by the Web community, quality will vary; *SFF World* is no exception, but decent coverage of more recent works make it an acceptable place to find reviews.

Film

639.   Berry, Mark F. 2002. *The Dinosaur Filmography.* Jefferson, N.C.: McFarland.

Berry has compiled a list of movies featuring dinosaurs, which he defines as "prehistoric, reptilian, and nonhumanoid," whether the portrayal is accurate or not. Organized alphabetically by title, each entry includes a one half- to four-star rating, production data, credits for principal crew and cast, and a detailed plot summary with critical commentary. Appendixes provide synopses for films in which dinosaurs are less prominently featured, films that never got made, and films featuring Godzilla-type creatures from Japan. Includes a bibliography and index.

640.   Frank, Alan G. 1982. *The Science Fiction and Fantasy Film Handbook.* Totowa, N.J.: Barnes & Noble Books.

Frank has written a guide to over 100 science fiction and fantasy films and the people who made them. The first and largest section of the book lists films alphabetically by title, including basic crew and cast credits followed by an evaluative synopsis with quotes from reviews. In the people section, the author writes brief career biographies with a genre filmography. The themes section discusses seven themes—such as aliens, apocalypse, and space and time travel—in terms of the elements that define the theme and listing the most significant films and contains a more complete filmography. Indexes list alternative titles and filmmakers by specialty. Intended as a companion to *The Horror Film Handbook* by the same author (see entry 659), who ascribes to the school of thought that science fiction, fantasy, and horror make up the larger genre of the "fantastique."

641. Hogan, David. 1980. *Who's Who of the Horrors and Other Fantasy Films: The International Personality Encyclopedia of the Fantastic Film.* 1st ed. San Diego: A.S. Barnes.

Hogan, a fan of monster and horror films, has written a lavishly illustrated "compendium of information about more than one thousand people who have made significant contributions to the fantastic film." He includes performers and the full range of filmmakers, with entries that contain year of birth and death; a career biography with particular attention to fantastic films; a filmography listing their horror, fantasy, and science fiction films; and, for performers, a physical description. The index lists films chronologically, making it difficult to find a film without knowing the year of release.

642. Holston, Kim R., and Tom Winchester. 1997. *Science Fiction, Fantasy, and Horror Film Sequels, Series, and Remakes: An Illustrated Filmography, with Plot Synopses and Critical Commentary.* Jefferson, N.C.: McFarland.

Holston and Winchester have compiled a list of "more than 400 science fiction, fantasy and supernatural horror films released from 1931 through 1995." They define sequel broadly, including movies that come from the same source materials, whether they were formally considered sequels or not. For each film and its sequels, they list the crew and cast and provide a synopsis, excerpts from reviews, and an analysis of the film. The bibliography is extensive, and there is an index to the films and the filmmakers.

643. Lee, Walt. 1972. *Reference Guide to Fantastic Films; Science Fiction, Fantasy, & Horror.* Los Angeles: Chelsea-Lee Books.

Over a period of 17 years, scientist and film buff Lee scoured trade magazines and viewed movies to compile one of the earliest guides to science fiction, fantasy, and horror films. Lee defines fantastic films as "depicting or strongly implying significant exceptions to man's conception of natural reality." He also includes horror films that don't strictly fit this definition but that are designed to frighten the audience. Films are listed in alphabetical order by title and include technical data, principal crew and cast, a comment on the film's fantastic content, references to critical and literary sources, and cross-references to related films. Color-coded sections in each volume indicate problem films that may not exist or may not actually be fantastic (blue) or excluded films that are definitely not fantastic (yellow). Includes a bibliography, but no index. Although dated, the thorough research and inclusion of some 20,000 films means this guide is still useful to fans and researchers.

644.   Maxford, Howard. 1997. *The A–Z of Science Fiction & Fantasy Films.* London: Batsford.

Maxford's dictionary of science fiction and fantasy films and filmmakers includes for each film a zero- to four-"saucer" rating, a plot synopsis, and a list of the major crew and cast. The biographies cover actors and filmmakers who have contributed to the science fiction and fantasy genres and include vital statistics, a career overview, and a filmography of science fiction and fantasy films they have made. Illustrations enhance many of the entries. Maxford wrote a companion volume entitled *The A–Z of Horror Films* (see entry 665).

Of Gods and Monsters: A Critical Guide to Universal Studios' Science Fiction, Horror, and Mystery Films, 1929–1939 (see entry 881)

645.   O'Neill, James. 1997. *Sci-Fi on Tape: A Complete Guide to Science Fiction and Fantasy on Video.* New York: Billboard Books.

O'Neill lists and rates over 1,250 science fiction and fantasy films for prospective viewers. Organized by film title, each entry contains standard technical details, the director and principal cast, a rating on a scale of one to four stars, and a summary with commentary. An appendix offers episode guides to nine of the most popular science fiction television series. Stills illustrate a handful of the films and shows. There are no indexes.

The Psychotronic Encyclopedia of Film (see entry 535)

646.   Senn, Bryan, and John Johnson. 1992. *Fantastic Cinema Subject Guide: A Topical Index to 2500 Horror, Science Fiction, and Fantasy Films.* Jefferson, N.C.: McFarland.

Senn and Johnson divide horror, science fiction, and fantasy films into 81 categories ranging from aliens and monsters and into subgenres such as mad scientists, sword and sorcery, and time travel. Each category is introduced by a paragraph or two describing the subject, discussing the key films, and recommending similar categories. For each film, they list the title, production credits, principal cast, and a synopsis. Some films include quotes or interesting tidbits of information. The authors have placed their one-to-ten rating scale in the index rather than with the film entry. While this somewhat preserves their goal of objectivity, it does require readers who are choosing which film to see to flip back and forth between the subject section and the index. Appendixes list blaxploitation, 3-D, and westerns.

647.   Stanley, John. 2000. *Creature Features: The Science Fiction, Fantasy, and Horror Movie Guide.* Updated ed. New York: Berkley Boulevard Books.

Stanley, a lifelong horror fan and host of the television show "Creature Features," has compiled a list of science fiction, fantasy, and horror movies. His guide for prospective movie viewers gives the title, date, a one- to five-star rating, and principal cast and crew. His love of the horror genre shines through in his capsule reviews. The 1997 edition removed many "older titles, obscure and/or lost movies" that were available in the fourth edition, the *Creature Features Movie Guide Strikes Again* (1994). Unfortunately, there is no index, because the book is primarily intended for fans deciding whether to view a movie.

648.   Willis, Donald C. 1985. *Variety's Complete Science Fiction Reviews.* New York: Garland.

From *Variety*'s pages, Willis compiled a complete set of reviews of science fiction, fantasy, and horror films made between 1907 and 1984. Listed in chronological order, reviews include the standard evaluation for fans and also a substantial description of the making of the film and its box office potential. Reviews also list production data and principal crew and cast. The book will be of interest to fans and researchers investigating how a film was critically received. Includes the necessary title index.

Television

649.   Morton, Alan. 1997. *The Complete Directory to Science Fiction, Fantasy and Horror Television Series: A Comprehensive Guide to the First 50 Years, 1946 to 1996.* 1st ed. Peoria, Ill.: Other Worlds Books.

Morton has compiled a guide to over 360 American and British live-action science fiction, fantasy, and horror television series and the more than 15,000 episodes made between 1946 and 1996. Morton's definition is broad—including such series as "Get Smart," "The Man from U.N.C.L.E.," and the "Wild Wild West"—and as such it is probably the most comprehensive guide available. Each entry lists series regulars and describes the basic premise of the show and its characters. The episode guides include guest stars, a one-sentence synopsis, original broadcast date, writer, director, and an occasional production note. Morton, unfortunately, does not include his indexing, because he thought it would have made the book too long.

650.   Sherman, Fraser A. 2000. *Cyborgs, Santa Claus, and Satan: Science Fiction, Fantasy, and Horror Films Made for Television.* Jefferson, N.C.: McFarland.

Science fiction fan and editor Sherman has compiled a list of nearly 600 made-for-TV science fiction, fantasy, and horror films and miniseries shown in the United States. His list includes pilots but excludes documentaries, extended episodes of regular series, and movies first shown on foreign television. In alphabetical order by title, entries include cast and production credits, original broadcast station and date, and a synopsis with commentary. One appendix summarizes additional films that only had minimal genre elements, while others list alternative titles and films in chronological order. Includes a name and title index. Sherman's filmography will be of interest to fans and researchers.

FANTASY

Film

651.   Parish, James Robert. 1994. *Ghosts and Angels in Hollywood Films: Plots, Critiques, Casts, and Credits for 264 Theatrical and Made-for-Television Releases.* Jefferson, N.C.: McFarland.

Parish, a prolific filmographer, has compiled a list of 264 movies portraying ghosts or angels. As in his other filmographies, each entry lists the major cast and crew followed by an engaging plot summary and discussion informed by reviews written upon the film's release. Appendixes place the films in chronological order and list television series and pilots. There is an index to movies and personal names.

652. Von Gunden, Kenneth. 1989. *Flights of Fancy: The Great Fantasy Films.* Jefferson, N.C.: McFarland.

Von Gunden selects 15 of the best live-action fantasy feature films to represent 15 subgenres. For each film, he writes an in-depth analysis, including critical reception, production history, and a plot summary with commentary. The filmography at the end of the book lists production data and cast and crew credits. An appendix lists additional worthy films in each subgenre. Includes an index.

653. Young, R. G. 2000. *The Encyclopedia of Fantastic Film: Ali Baba to Zombies.* New York: Applause.

Young took 35 years to compile this international filmography of over 9,000 fantastic films made between 1896 and 1999. Fantastic refers to "horror, fantasy, mystery, science fiction, heavy melodrama, and film noir." Most of the book is the alphabetical list of films, each including release year and country, studio, cast and characters, director, writer, cinematographer, songs, genre, and a one-sentence summary. An index to artists serves as a filmography, while an appendix lists films in chronological order. Lightly illustrated, the book is of interest to fans, but will serve researchers as well due to its vast size.

Television

654. Gerani, Gary, and Paul H. Schulman. 1977. *Fantastic Television.* New York: Harmony Books.

Gerani, a science fiction scholar, has compiled a lavishly illustrated episode-by-episode guide to 13 of the best science fiction and fantasy television series. For each series, he writes an in-depth overview that includes information about the lead actors and a description of the series' merits. For each episode, he provides episode title, writer, director, the guest cast, and a synopsis. The last part of the book lists and describes American and British series, kids shows, and made-for-TV movies, albeit without listing episodes. Includes an index.

HORROR

655. Newman, Kim, and British Film Institute. 1996. *The BFI Companion to Horror.* London: Cassell.

Newman led a team of critics, writers, and scholars in composing this dictionary of the people who make horror films and television shows and the themes they explore. Entries for actors and filmmakers describe their careers and list their films and television shows. Entries for subjects discuss themes, subgenres, recurrent characters, places, and list representative films. Interestingly, the companion does not include separate entries for individual films—although it does for film and television series—nor does the companion include an index, making it necessary to consult other works for capsules. Well illustrated, this guide is of most interest to horror film fans.

656.   Wright, Gene. 1986. *Horrorshows: The A-to-Z of Horror in Film, TV, Radio and Theater.* New York: Facts on File.

Wright has written a guide to the horror genre as presented not only on film and television, but also on radio and in theater. He organizes the works into 12 categories such as mad scientists, vampires, and splatter. With the exception of the chapter on anthologies, the vast majority of the works are films. Each work lists title, technical data, principal cast and crew credits, and a brief plot summary with critical analysis. An additional chapter provides career biographies and horror filmographies for the actors and filmmakers prominent in the genre. The index is divided into sections on films, TV films, TV programs, radio programs, theater, and authors. Plentiful illustrations add the final touch for fans of horror.

Film

657.   Everman, Welch D. 1993. *Cult Horror Films: From Attack of the 50 Foot Woman to Zombies of Mora Tau.* Secaucus, N.J.: Carol.

Everman defines cult horror films as movies that "have minimal budgets, they are poorly written and directed, the production values are nearly zero, and the acting is appalling." The films "are so bad they're good—or at least they're funny." Intended for audiences who love this type of film, he has selected over 80 films representative of the genre. For each film, he lists basic cast and crew, a plot summary, and an analysis of the movie's message. There is no index, minimizing the book's usefulness for those seeking films made by their favorite directors and stars.

658.   Fischer, Dennis. 1991. *Horror Film Directors, 1931–1990.* Jefferson, N.C.: McFarland.

Fischer, a horror movie fan because of the occasional great film rather than the more frequent "execrable" film, has compiled a list of directors most associated with making horror films. His definition of horror is broad, including all films that deal with the supernatural or a monster or that promote fear, so he includes many films not usually associated with horror. His introduction to the genre and its history are both excellent. Fischer divides the books into two parts, featuring prominent directors and the "promising directors, obscurities, and horror hacks." For each director, he provides a filmography followed by lengthy biographies and discussions of their work. An appendix lists "classic horror films by non-horror directors." The annotated bibliography is extensive. There is an index to film titles.

659.   Frank, Alan G. 1982. *The Horror Film Handbook.* Totowa, N.J.: Barnes & Noble Books.

Frank, a film critic and researcher, compiled one of the earliest reference books on horror films. While it comprehensively covers the major actors and filmmakers in the genre, it is selective in the films it presents. The first part lists films alphabetically by title. Each entry lists principal crew and cast and offers a brief synopsis and evaluation with quotes from critics. The second part of the book lists horror film actors and filmmakers; a brief career biography and a filmography of horror films is given for each person. The third section lists themes (AKA monsters) and the films made about them. The index lists filmmakers and production companies.

660.   Hardy, Phil, Tom Milne, and Kobal Collection. 1994. *The Overlook Film Encyclopedia. Horror.* Woodstock, N.Y.: Overlook Press.

Hardy has compiled a prodigious list of 1,300 movies from all over the world "in which fear and terror are central." In chronological order, each decade is introduced by a filmographic essay placing the movies in the context of the time followed by an alphabetical list of films released each year. Each film entry includes a critical analysis and lists technical data, lead cast and crew, and often includes a black-and-white illustration. Appendixes list rental champs and most-filmed horror writers, and an index points to titles. The first edition was a publication entitled *The Encyclopedia of Horror Movies.* The British edition is entitled *The Aurum Film Encyclopedia.*

661.   Kinnard, Roy. 2000. *Horror in Silent Films: A Filmography, 1896–1929.* Jefferson, N.C.; London: McFarland.

Although the genre of horror didn't formally exist until *Frankenstein* was made toward the beginning of the sound era, Kinnard catalogs horror films made during the silent era. He includes films that are thematically "horrific" and that contain standard elements of horror movies. Films are listed alphabetically by title, and entries include cast and credit, evaluative summaries, and excerpts from reviews. There are title and name indexes.

662.   Lukeman, Adam, and Anthony Timpone. 2003. *Fangoria's 101 Best Horror Movies You've Never Seen: A Celebration of the World's Most Unheralded Fright Flicks / Adam Lukeman and Fangoria Magazine;* Edited by Anthony Timpone. 1st ed. New York: Three Rivers Press.

On behalf of *Fangoria* magazine, horror script analyst Lukeman has compiled a list of 101 lesser-known horror films. Each film is treated to a couple of pages that include film title, tag line, subgenre, technical data, director, writer, lead actors, a critical plot summary focusing on the aspects that frighten, and trivia. Most entries are illustrated. Includes an index. Like the magazine that inspired it, this book is for horror fans.

663.   Mank, Gregory W. 1999. *Women in Horror Films, 1930s.* Jefferson, N.C.: McFarland.

664.   Mank, Gregory W. 1999. *Women in Horror Films, 1940s.* Jefferson, N.C.: McFarland.

Mank has written biographies of 21 horror actresses each from the 1930s and 1940s, interviewing them if possible. The biographies of the women who played heroines, monsters, femmes fatales, misfits, or victims are lengthy valentines to their lives and careers. Each entry is illustrated with portraits and stills and contains a filmography. Appendixes list the results of a poll on outstanding performances, and indexes point to names and films.

665.   Maxford, Howard. 1997. *The A–Z of Horror Films.* Bloomington: Indiana University Press.

Maxford has produced a dictionary of horror films and filmmakers. The film entries contain a one- to four-star rating, a plot synopsis, and a list of the major crew and cast. The biographies cover the actors and filmmakers who have contributed to the horror genre and include vital statistics, a career overview, and a filmography of horror films they have made. Illustrations enhance a selection of entries. Maxford wrote a companion volume entitled *The A–Z of Science Fiction & Fantasy Films* (see entry 644).

666.   Mayo, Mike. 1998. *VideoHound's Horror Show: 999 Hair-Raising, Hellish, and Humorous Movies.* Detroit: Visible Ink Press.

Mayo, a film reviewer and horror movie fan, has compiled a list of 999 horror films available on video. Films are listed in alphabetical order by title. Mayo writes engaging capsule reviews for each followed by principal cast and crew and the typical VideoHound rating of one to four bones. The book is generously illustrated and occasional sidebars salute prominent horror filmmakers, actors, and topics. The indexes are superb and include alternative titles, cast, director, and category. Sources for videos and distributors are listed separately.

667.   McCallum, Lawrence. 1998. *Italian Horror Films of the 1960s: A Critical Catalog of 62 Chillers.* Jefferson, N.C.: McFarland.

McCallum has written a guide to all 62 films made during the heyday of Italian horror in the 1960s. In alphabetical order by English-language title, each film includes production and cast credits and a review with plot summary. Supplementary materials include a chronological list of films, a bibliography, and an index.

668.   Mitchell, Charles P. 2002. *The Devil on Screen: Feature Films Worldwide, 1913 through 2000.* Jefferson, N.C.: McFarland.

Mitchell has compiled a list of 95 feature films in which the devil appears as an identifiable character. For each film, he lists the title, technical information, and a one- to five-star rating of the film's quality. Credits for crew and cast are followed by an appraisal and synopsis featuring the performance of the devil and notable quotes. Appendixes list "lost, obscure, and arcane Devil films" and television devils. The index points to films and actor and character names. Mitchell's book is interesting and fills a small niche.

669.   Muir, John Kenneth. 2002. *Horror Films of the 1970s.* Jefferson, N.C.: McFarland.

Muir, an independent filmmaker and writer, has produced a year-by-year guide to 228 mostly American horror films made during the 1970s. Organized chronologically by year and then alphabetically by title, each film entry includes a one- to four-star rating, quotes that illustrate the film's reception, a list of cast and crew, and a synopsis with critical commentary from Muir. Appendixes list horror film clichés of the 1970s, actors who appeared in at least three horror films, memorable ad lines, and recommended viewing. Includes an index. Well conceived, Muir's guide will be of interest to both horror movie fans and film researchers.

670.   O'Neill, James. 1994. *Terror on Tape: A Complete Guide to Over 2,000 Horror Movies on Video.* New York: Billboard Books.

O'Neill lists and rates over 2,000 horror films for prospective viewers. Organized by title, each film includes standard technical details, the director and principal cast, a rating on a scale of one to four stars, and a summary with commentary. Sidebars highlight filmmakers and actors known for horror, and stills illustrate a handful of the films. There is no index.

671.   Pitts, Michael R. 2002. *Horror Film Stars.* 3rd ed. Jefferson, N.C.: McFarland.

Pitts has compiled a list of "the stars most associated with horror, science fiction and fantasy movies." For each actor, he provides a brief biography and then delves into his or her roles in horror films, and, to a lesser extent, science fiction and fantasy. Each entry ends with a filmography. A selective bibliography and index complete the book.

672.   Stine, Scott Aaron. 2001. *The Gorehound's Guide to Splatter Films of the 1960s and 1970s.* Jefferson, N.C.: McFarland.

673.   Stine, Scott Aaron. 2003. *The Gorehound's Guide to Splatter Films of the 1980s.* Jefferson, N.C.: McFarland.

Horror fan Stine has written two guides to splatter films, the first covering the 1960s and 1970s and the second covering the 1980s—he is currently working on a third guide to the 1990s. Splatter films are horror films with strong doses of violence and gore. Arranged by title, each entry includes production credits with an emphasis on special, makeup, and visual effects, cast credits, and a plot summary with commentary. Appendixes discuss snuff films and list sources for purchasing videos, and indexes points to names and film titles.

Television

674.   Muir, John Kenneth. 2001. *Terror Television: American Series, 1970–1999.* Jefferson, N.C.: McFarland.

Film writer Muir, who has written several books on individual horror series and filmmakers, has written a book about 57 horror television series that aired during prime time from 1970 to mid-1999. He begins in 1970 with "Night Gallery" because that was the first series in color devoted exclusively to horror rather than science fiction or fantasy. The main part of the book covers 40 series Muir feels "provoke suspense and horror either visually or through drama." For each series, he quotes critics to show how the series was originally received, discusses the format and history, and writes his own in-depth critical commentary. He lists casts and crew for the series as a whole followed by an episode guide that includes title, writer and director, guest casts and a synopsis. The second part of the book covers 17 additional anthologies and series that showed some elements of horror. Appendix A lists the "fifty most common concepts in modern terror television," which is particularly useful in uncovering motifs (or at least clichés). Additional appendixes include a hall of fame of actors who have appeared on more than one horror series, Muir's 10 best and 5 worst programs, program hosts, partnerships, vampires, and soaps with horror themes. Includes a bibliography and a name and title index. Muir has written the most comprehensive book on horror programs covering the last three decades of the century.

MONSTERS

675.   Jones, Stephen. 2000. *The Essential Monster Movie Guide: A Century of Creature Features on Film, TV, and Video.* New York: Billboard Books.

Jones, author of numerous books on film and popular culture, has compiled an exhaustive dictionary of monster movies and television shows. For each film and show, he lists the country and year of release, the director, the principal cast, and a capsule review. He rates the movies on a scale of one to five diamonds. Entries for individuals—boxed to differentiate them from the film and television entries—include one-sentence profiles of their careers with selective filmographies. An appendix lists famous monsters, including a list of the top 20 monster movies and classic movie books. Indexes list personality profiles and alternate titles.

676.   Stacy, Jan, and Ryder Syvertsen. 1983. *The Great Book of Movie Monsters.* Chicago: Contemporary Books.

Monster movie fans Stacy and Syvertsen have compiled "biographies" of more than 300 "creatures that have graced the silver screen." Intended for a popular audience, the writers devote a page to each monster. After listing aliases, dates of birth and death, and films, each entry includes a black-and-white photograph and vitals such as how the monster was created, a physical description, its powers, its territory, and "what to do if you meet" the creature. Indexes list monsters, movies, directors, and studios. Like Stacy and Syvertsen's other book—*The Great Book of Movie Villains* (see entry 455)—this one is fun to read and is most useful for its biographical approach to movie monsters.

Vampires

677.   Flynn, John L. 1992. *Cinematic Vampires: The Living Dead on Film and Television, from the Devil's Castle (1896) to Bram Stoker's Dracula (1992).* Jefferson, N.C.: McFarland.

Flynn has compiled an illustrated guide to the more than 300 vampire films made between 1896 and 1992. Arranged chronologically into 10 time periods, each chapter consists of an introduction to the era followed by a list of films. Each film entry contains production and cast credits and a plot summary with commentary. Appendixes include a list of vampire films in production in 1993, the 10 best and 10 worst vampire films, and films proposed but never made. Includes an index.

678.   Marrero, Robert. 1994. *Vampire Movies.* 1st ed. Key West, Fla.: Fantasma Books.

Marrero has compiled a well-illustrated guide to films made between 1922 and 1994 featuring vampires. Organized chronologically, each film includes year, country, production credits, and a critical review that discusses the film, its making, and its cast. Without an index (which would make it easier to find specific films or filmmakers), the book is of most interest to fans of horror and of vampires.

679.   Melton, J. Gordon. 1997. *VideoHound's Vampires on Video.* Detroit: Visible Ink Press.

Melton, a religion and vampire scholar, has compiled a list of over 600 films that portray vampires—mostly Dracula. The films are listed in alphabetical order by original title and each entry includes a plot summary and evaluation, a list of alternate titles, and the standard VideoHound rating of one to four bones. Credits list director, writer, composer, and principal cast. Lavish illustrations and interesting sidebars add value and interest to the book. Appendixes list video sources and distributors, and indexes list alternate titles, cast, directors, and category.

680.   Nance, Scott. 1992. *Bloodsuckers: Vampires at the Movies.* Las Vegas, N.V.: Pioneer Books.

Nance has compiled a list of hundreds of vampire films and television shows made between 1897 and 1992. Organized into roughly chronological thematic chapters, Nance reviews 45 vampire films in depth, describing plot, characters, actors, and production history. The filmography is included in the appendix, listing anything from title alone to country, year, director, and cast. For a more systematic look at vampire movies, check out *Cinematic Vampires* (see entry 677).

Zombies

681.   Dendle, Peter. 2001. *The Zombie Movie Encyclopedia.* Jefferson, N.C.: McFarland.

Dendle has written a guide to feature films and made-for-TV movies that feature "revived corpses" (but not mummies). After an overview of the genre, he reviews the films from the perspective of an "objective zombie ethologist" and lists director, producer, writer, and principal cast. Appendixes list movies by year and by country. Includes a bibliography and an index.

SCIENCE FICTION

683.   Meehan, Paul. 1998. *Saucer Movies: A UFOlogical History of the Cinema.* Lanham, Md.: Scarecrow Press.

Meehan's definition of flying saucer movies is broad, including films that explore the theme of "first contact between humankind and alien civilization." The filmography is listed in an appendix and includes the film title, principal crew and cast, and release country and company. The discussion of the films occurs in the chapters, which are organized chronologically by common themes. The indexes list authors, films, journalists, radio and television shows, and UFO sightings, specialists, groups, and personalities.

684.   Naha, Ed. 1980. *The Science Fictionary: An A–Z Guide to the World of SF Authors, Films, & TV Shows.* 1st ed. New York: Seaview Books.

Naha's guide to science fiction literature, cinema, and television is made for fans. The two largest sections provide technical data, a synopsis, and principal crew and cast for 1,000 films and four decades of television series. A third section contains brief career biographies and selective bibliographies and filmographies of science fiction authors. Appendixes list awards, magazines, and themes, but there is no index. Although this book is a fun read for science fiction fans, it is too dated for most serious research.

Film

685.   Benson, Michael. 2000. *Vintage Science Fiction Films, 1896–1949.* Jefferson, N.C.; London: McFarland.

Benson has written three filmographic essays on the silent, sound, and serial science fiction films made from the earliest days of cinema through 1949. Of most interest for reference is the filmography in the second half of the book. The filmography is an alphabetical list of films with technical information, principal crew, and cast. The films are not described, so it is necessary to consult the name and title index to see where the film is mentioned in an essay. Includes a bibliography.

686.   Fischer, Dennis. 2000. *Science Fiction Film Directors, 1895–1998.* Jefferson, N.C.: McFarland.

Fischer, a science fiction movie fan and film writer, has compiled a list of directors who have created a significant body of science fiction films. His introduction to the genre and its history is excellent. For each director, he provides a filmography, a lengthy biography, and a discussion of his or her work. An appendix lists "classic science fiction films from non-genre directors." The annotated bibliography is extensive. An index points to film titles and personal names.

687.   Hardy, Phil, and Kobal Collection. 1994. *The Overlook Film Encyclopedia. Science Fiction.* Updated ed. Woodstock, N.Y.: Overlook Press.

Hardy has compiled a list of 1,550 "films with significant Science Fiction elements" from all over the world. In chronological order, each decade is introduced by a filmographic essay placing the movies in the context of the time, which is followed by an alphabetical list of films released each year. Each film includes a critical analysis, lists technical data and lead cast and crew, and often includes a black-and-white illustration. Appendixes list rental champs, critics' top 10s, Oscars, and a bibliography. There is a title index. The British edition is entitled *The Aurum Film Encyclopedia.*

688.   Henderson, C.J. 2001. *The Encyclopedia of Science Fiction Movies, Facts on File Film Reference Library.* New York: Facts on File.

Film critic Henderson has written a guide to over 1,300 science fiction films made from 1897 through 2000. For each film, the author lists production and cast credits and writes an overview with his evaluation of its quality. Lightly illustrated, other supplementary materials include science fiction literature adapted for the screen, science fiction Oscars, a bibliography, and an index. Oddly, Henderson includes a glossary of the language spoken in the movie *Quest for Fire.*

689.   Kinnard, Roy. 1998. *Science Fiction Serials: A Critical Filmography of the 31 Hard SF Cliffhangers: With an Appendix of the 37 Serials with Slight SF Content.* Jefferson, N.C.: McFarland.

For 31 science fiction serials made from the 1930s through the 1950s Kinnard lists the crew and cast and the chapter titles and summarizes the story. Kinnard comments on the quality and reception of each serial. An appendix lists 37 more serials in which the science fiction is incidental to the story, and an index points to films and filmmakers.

690. Parish, James Robert, and Michael R. Pitts. 1977. *The Great Science Fiction Pictures.* Metuchen, N.J.: Scarecrow Press.

691. Parish, James Robert, and Michael R. Pitts. 1990. *The Great Science Fiction Pictures II.* Metuchen, N.J.: Scarecrow Press.

The prolific duo of Parish and Pitts produced an alphabetical list of science fiction pictures by title. Each entry includes principal crew and cast, a plot summary, and a review based on critical reception. An appendix lists radio and television shows. Volume II updates the list of films, not only with new releases, but also by filling in gaps in the first volume. Neither book includes an index, reducing their usefulness somewhat.

692. Schwartz, Carol A. 1997. *VideoHound's Sci-Fi Experience: Your Quantum Guide to the Video Universe.* Detroit: Visible Ink Press.

Schwartz led a team of film experts in compiling a list of nearly 1,200 science fiction films available on video. Films are listed in alphabetical order by title and include the typical VideoHound rating of one to four bones, a summary with commentary, and a list of principal cast and crew. The book is well illustrated, and occasional sidebars salute prominent science fiction filmmakers, actors, and topics. The indexes are superb and include alternate titles, cast, director, and category. Sources for videos and distributors are listed separately.

693. Strickland, A. W., and Forrest J. Ackerman. 1981. *A Reference Guide to American Science Fiction Films.* Bloomington, Ind.: T.I.S. Publications Division.

Originally intended to be a four-volume set, Strickland and Ackerman produced the first volume of a chronological guide to nearly 200 American science fiction films made between 1897 and 1929. Listed first by decade and then by title, each entry includes technical data, references (which point to a bibliography), a classification by subgenre, credits, cast, and a plot summary with commentary. Indexes list films by subgenre, in chronological order, by releasing company, and by title. Although the entire series was never completed, the first volume is an excellent guide to science fiction films of the silent era.

694. Warren, Bill. 1997. *Keep Watching the Skies! American Science Fiction Movies of the Fifties.* Jefferson, N.C.: McFarland Classics.

Warren, a fan of the genre and time period, has compiled a complete list of science fiction films made in the 1950s, defining science fiction films as having a fantastical element that attempts a rational explanation. Volume I covers 1950 to 1957, and the much larger Volume II covers 1958 to 1962. Arranged first by year and then alphabetically by title, Warren writes very personal evaluative essays discussing each film in great detail, from its story to anecdotes on its making to its technical aspects and special effects. Each volume features an appendix crediting crew and cast, a chronology listing films by year of release, a list of films announced but never produced, and an index. The original volumes were published in 1982 and 1986 and were subsequently reprinted in this one volume in 1997.

695. Weisser, Thomas, and Yuko Mihara Weisser. 1998. *Japanese Cinema Encyclopedia. The Horror, Fantasy, and SciFi Films.* 2nd ed. Miami: Vital Books; Asian Cult Cinema Publications.

The Weissers, Asian film experts, have compiled an illustrated guide to horror, fantasy, and science fiction feature films made in Japan from 1955 to 1998—not including anime. Each entry includes English and Japanese title, director, principal cast, a one- to four-star rating, and a plot synopsis with commentary. Appendixes translate Japanese titles to English and provide filmographies for directors and performers. Intended as the first volume in a series of film reference books, only one other on *Sex Films* (see entry 720) has been published.

696. Willis, Donald C. 1972. *Horror and Science Fiction Films: A Checklist.* Metuchen, N.J.: Scarecrow Press.

697. Willis, Donald C. 1982. *Horror and Science Fiction Films II.* Metuchen, N.J.: Scarecrow Press.

698. Willis, Donald C. 1984. *Horror and Science Fiction Films III.* Metuchen, N.J.: Scarecrow Press.

699. Willis, Donald C. 1997. *Horror and Science Fiction Films IV.* Lanham, Md.: Scarecrow Press.

Willis created a filmography of 4,400 horror and science fiction films from around the world in 1972 and has since written three supplements that more than double the original number. Each book lists films alphabetically by title, giving technical, cast, and crew credits and a brief summary and evaluation. Supplements not only add new films, but also incorporate films overlooked in previous volumes. Volume IV is particularly strong in some of the more obscure films, especially foreign titles. Appendixes cover "peripheral and problem films" that are referenced elsewhere but that the author was not able to view. To find films, it is necessary to look both in the body of the texts and in the index to the first three volumes in volume IV.

700. Wingrove, David. 1985. *The Science Fiction Film Source Book.* Harlow, Essex, England: Longman.

Wingrove led a team of science fiction critics in creating this guide to 1,300 science fiction films and the people who made them from the earliest days of silent cinema through 1984. In alphabetical order by title, each entry lists year of release, a critical summary, and principal cast and crew. Each sound film also receives one to five stars each for plot, technical merit, enjoyment, and artistic merit. The section on filmmakers and actors provides very brief career biographies and a filmography. Other sections include a brief history, a chronology, a list of science fiction novels made into films, a special effects essay, film rentals (as of 1985), and a bibliography. Despite its age, science fiction fans will enjoy this book.

Television

701. Fulton, Roger, and John Gregory Betancourt. 2000. *Encyclopedia of TV Science Fiction.* Rev. ed. London: Boxtree.

Fulton and Betancourt list British and American live-action science fiction, fantasy, and horror television series and one-time productions. Each program is described in a thorough and entertaining fashion. The book lists the regular cast, production credits, and number of episodes followed by the title, description, cast, and director of each episode. There is also a chronology by day and month series began. Earlier editions had a section on animation, but the latest edition has dropped that feature. The earlier edition was entitled *The Sci-Fi Channel Encyclopedia of TV Science Fiction.*

702.   Javna, John. 1987. *The Best of Science Fiction TV: The Critics' Choice: From Captain Video to Star Trek, from "The Jetsons" to Robotech.* 1st ed. New York: Harmony Books.

Javna polled over 100 television and science fiction critics, science fiction writers, and fan organizations to derive a list of the 15 best and 10 worst series of all time. The result is an entertaining guide to science fiction television. The best get treated to four pages of information beginning with an introductory overview followed by a description of the show and its characters, representative quotes from a script, miscellaneous tidbits, and comments from the critics polled. The worst shows get a similar treatment, only in two pages. The rest of the book looks at a hodgepodge of categories: British and Japanese shows, golden age and classics, cartoons and supermarionation, and anthologies. A nice complement to Fulton and Betancourt's *Encyclopedia of TV Science Fiction* (see entry 701), the book is most useful for the results of the polls.

703.   Lucanio, Patrick, and Gary Coville. 1998. *American Science Fiction Television Series of the 1950s: Episode Guides and Casts and Credits for Twenty Shows.* Jefferson, N.C.: McFarland.

This episode-by-episode guide to 20 science fiction television series aired in the United States during the 1950s is the most complete available for its era. Excluded are horror, fantasy, and anthology series. Each show receives a painstaking but lively overview of its production history and contents. Regular production staff and cast members are listed. When possible, the authors viewed each episode before writing descriptions and listing cast members. The bibliography lists books, magazines and newspaper articles, and videos available commercially. The index lists everything except episode titles; a separate index is devoted to episode titles.

704.   Phillips, Mark, and Frank Garcia. 1996. *Science Fiction Television Series: Episode Guides, Histories, and Casts and Credits for 62 Prime Time Shows, 1959 through 1989.* Jefferson, N.C.: McFarland.

Phillips and Garcia cover 62 science fiction series that began airing between 1959 and 1989. Each entry includes the show's basic premise and a list of cast and producers followed by an essay based on viewings, readings, and interviews. The authors viewed each episode to write the description and list the cast. Appendix A lists "honorable mentions"—shows that were not strictly science fiction, but that touched upon elements of the genre. Appendix B lists unsold pilots. Appendix C lists Emmy awards. The index is comprehensive. Because this book includes only one series aired before 1959, *American Science Fiction Television Series of the 1950s* (see entry 703) is a nice complement.

SERIALS

FILM

705. Kinnard, Roy. 1983. *Fifty Years of Serial Thrills.* Metuchen, N.J.: Scarecrow Press.

Kinnard has compiled a complete list of the some 500 serials made during the silent era through the sound era, with the last made in 1956. Each chapter represents a studio, listing the serials it produced in chronological order with title, year of release, number of episodes, alternate titles, director, and principal cast. The most prominent serials are listed first and described in great detail, while the lesser serials are not described at all. Includes a title and name index. Unfortunately, this is not an episode guide, but it is worthy of consultation to see what serials were made.

706. Rainey, Buck. 1998. *Serials and Series: A World Filmography, 1912–1956.* Jefferson, N.C.: McFarland.

Rainey lists over 700 serials from the silent film era until their demise in the 1950s. For each, he lists country, language, production company, and date of release, plus principal crew and cast. In addition to listing the number of chapters, he lists the chapter titles when available. For English-language films, he also provides a brief summary. The "selected" bibliography is actually quite large and indicates a tremendous amount of scholarship. The index includes film titles and personal names

707. Rainey, Buck. 1990. *Those Fabulous Serial Heroines: Their Lives and Films.* Metuchen, N.J.: Scarecrow Press.

Rainey has compiled the complete screen credits for 22 "serial heroines" and 25 "beauties in distress." For each actress, he includes a photograph, a lengthy biography focusing on her career, and a chronological filmography. The filmography lists films as well as serials, and includes the production company and date of release, the cast, the director, and the screen writer. An appendix lists actresses who appeared in serials but who were not given the full biographical treatment. A bibliography lists sources, and an index lists film titles.

708. Schutz, Wayne. 1992. *The Motion Picture Serial: An Annotated Bibliography.* Metuchen, N.J.: Scarecrow Press.

Schutz has compiled a bibliography of works on the movie serial. Chapters cover the silent era and the sound era as well as the filmmakers and actors. Works include books, book chapters, and articles, and also entries from reference books. The index lists personal names, serial and film titles, and production companies.

Science Fiction Serials: A Critical Filmography of the 31 Hard SF Cliffhangers: With an Appendix of the 37 Serials with Slight SF Content (see entry 689)

709. Weiss, Ken, and Edwin Goodgold. 1972. *To Be Continued.* New York: Crown Publishers.

Weiss and Goodgold, both childhood fans of serials, have created a year-by-year guide to them. Beginning in 1929 and continuing through the final serial made in 1956, they highlight their favorites with title, a black-and-white still, number of episodes, director, cast, and a thorough plot summary. There is no episode guide. A filmography gives a complete list of sound serials by year, a list not much larger than the coverage in the book. Includes a name and title index.

TELEVISION

710.   Baskin, Ellen. 1996. *Serials on British Television, 1950–1994.* Aldershot, England; Brookfield, Vt.: Scholar Press; Ashgate.

Baskin has compiled a complete guide to serials aired on British television through 1994. Defining a serial as a "multi-part, self-contained drama," serials might be considered a cross between a miniseries and a regular dramatic series—in other words, a series that tells its story in a fixed number of shows. Entries are arranged chronologically by decade and year. Each entry includes the serial title, broadcast history, producer, director, writer, and cast. A synopsis describes each serial in brief. There are separate indexes to titles, original titles of adaptations, writers, authors, producers, directors, players, and genres.

SEX AND NUDITY

NUDITY

711.   Hosoda, Craig. 2000. *The Bare Facts Video Guide.* New ed. London: Titan.

Hosoda identifies celebrity nude scenes on video. There are separate sections for actresses and actors. Each lists the performer's films, highlighting the type and length of nudity in each film, and tells how much time into the film the scene appears.

712.   Martin, Mart. 1994. *The Voyeur's Guide to Men in the Movies = The Voyeur's Guide to Women in the Movies.* Chicago: Contemporary Books.

Martin compiles lists of the titillating and the nasty in the movies. Appealing to voyeurs, the book features sex, nudity, taboos, swearing, and categories of roles played by actors. Turn the book over to choose men or women. The miscellaneous lists can help answer some hard questions, but cutesy chapter headings in the table of contents and lack of an index limit the usefulness as a reference source.

713.   Mr. Skin. 2005. *Mr. Skin's Skincyclopedia: The A-to-Z Guide to Finding Your Favorite Actress Naked.* 1st U.S. ed. New York: St. Martin's Press.

For fans who can't get enough of a favorite actress, *Mr. Skin* has written a guide to the films in which she appears nude. Each entry includes the actress's birth date and place, a "skin-o-meter" indicating how often she appears nude (including those who have never appeared nude), an essay on nudity in her career, her most representative nude film, and a list of other films noting the body part displayed. Includes a film title index. The *Mr. Skin* Web site <http://www.mrskin.com> offers a database searchable by actress, movie, or TV show. The results provide the beginning of a description and a list of films—it is necessary to pay a subscription fee to see the full description and to see film clips.

SEX

714. Bijou Video Sales. 1993. *Bijou Video: The Complete Reference Guide of Gay Adult Films.* Chicago: Images of the World.

The Bijou catalog is the most comprehensive list of gay male porn videos, featuring over 3,500 available for purchase. The catalog is organized by categories such as directors, actors, studios, and distributors. Entries include the title, item number for ordering, and a plot summary describing the actors and the action. Indexes include actor and director filmographies and lists of film and book titles. The catalog is searchable at the Bijou Web site <http://www.bijouworld.com>.

The Erotic Anime Movie Guide (see entry 481)

715. Limbacher, James L. 1983. *Sexuality in World Cinema.* Metuchen, N.J.: Scarecrow Press.

Limbacher spent four years developing a list of over 13,000 films that include sexuality, featuring just about anything except "plain heterosexual intercourse." After an essay on censorship and glossaries of sex and media terms, the first half of Volume I contains 26 chapters featuring various sex acts. Each is introduced by a filmographic essay discussing the most prominent films and is followed by simple title lists of films. The rest of Volume I and all of Volume II is an alphabetical list of films, most with a brief description and all with a letter code keyed to each chapter. Because Limbacher covers not just porn, but also mainstream cinema and independent films, the book can be useful for curious film buffs as well as students examining how sex is portrayed in society.

716. Riley, Patrick. 1994. *The X-Rated Videotape Star Index.* Amherst, N.Y.: Prometheus Books.

717. Riley, Patrick. 1997. *The X-Rated Videotape Star Index II: A Guide to Your Favorite Adult Film Stars.* Amherst, N.Y.: Prometheus Books.

718. Riley, Patrick. 1999. *The X-Rated Videotape Star Index III.* Amherst, N.Y.: Prometheus Books.

The *Star Index* complements the *X-Rated Videotape Guide* (see entry 719), listing porn stars and the movies in which they have appeared. Performers are listed alphabetically by first name; each entry includes other names, a physical description, and codes indicating type of sex and number of movies. The filmography lists the film title, distributor, and type of sex performed. An appendix cross-references from alternate movie titles. The books are not cumulative, so it is necessary to consult all three.

719. Rimmer, Robert H. 1986. *The X-Rated Videotape Guide: Revised and Updated, Including 1300 Reviews and Ratings, 4000 Supplemental Listings, Photos of the Stars.* 2nd ed. New York: Harmony Books.

Rimmer has produced the most complete guide to pornographic films in these eight volumes. The first covers 1970 to 1985, the second 1986 to 1990, and six subsequent volumes cover two years at a time through 1999. Each film has a capsule of the type of sex and lists producer/director, performers, and a plot summary. Later volumes provide a cumulative index. A companion set, Riley's *X-Rated Videotape Star Index* (see entries 716 to 718), makes it possible to look up films by star.

720. Weisser, Thomas, and Yuko Mihara Weisser. 1998. *Japanese Cinema Encyclopedia. The Sex Films.* 1st ed. Miami: Vital Books: Asian Cult Cinema Publications.

The Weissers, Asian film experts, have compiled an illustrated guide to sex films—known as pinku eiga or pink movies—made by major Japanese studios from 1964 to 1998—not including anime. After an essay on censorship, each entry includes English and Japanese title, director, principal cast, a one- to four-star rating, and a plot synopsis with commentary. Appendixes translate Japanese titles to English and provide filmographies for directors and performers. This is the second volume in an intended series of film reference books, but only one other volume on *Horror, Fantasy, and SciFi Films* (see entry 695) has been published.

SHORTS

721. Maltin, Leonard. 1972. *The Great Movie Shorts.* New York: Crown Publishers.

Maltin is better known today for his film guides and movie reviews, but early in his career he was best known as an expert on the short subject. In this survey, he chronicles the one- and two-reel series of the 1930s and 1940s. He begins with an overview of each studio by describing the style for which it was best known. He then writes an extensive essay on each series before listing all the individual shorts in chronological order, including title, date, cast, and a one-sentence synopsis. In an extra section, Maltin gives lighter coverage to a handful of titles and then describes other types of shorts not covered in the book such as newsreels, travelogues, documentaries, musicals, and sports. Cartoons are not covered at all. Includes an index. While selective, Maltin's guide remains one of the best and most comprehensive guides to short subject films.

SILENT FILMS

AFI Catalog (see entries 391 to 393)

722. Altomara, Rita Ecke. 1983. *Hollywood on the Palisades: A Filmography of Silent Features Made in Fort Lee, New Jersey, 1903–1927, Garland Reference Library of the Humanities; Vol. 368.* New York: Garland.

Before there was Hollywood, there was Fort Lee. Many of the earliest movies and studios made their start in the wilds of New Jersey, and Altomara has compiled a list of them. The first part of the book lists the movies by the stars, and the second part lists the movies by the directors. For both the stars and the directors, she provides a brief biography followed by a list of movies. Movie entries include the featured players and the director, writer, cinematographer, art director, and production company. There are no synopses, so the main purpose of the book is as a filmography. The book is illustrated with portraits of the actors and stills from the movies. Includes title and name indexes.

American Animated Films: The Silent Era, 1897–1929 (see entry 468)

Books and Plays in Films, 1896–1915: Literary, Theatrical, and Artistic Sources of the First Twenty Years of Motion Pictures (see entry 1075)

723. Braff, Richard E. 2002. *The Braff Silent Short Film Working Papers: Over 25,000 Films, 1903–1929, Alphabetized and Indexed.* Jefferson, N.C.: McFarland.

Braff spent 37 years building a card catalog of silent split-reel short films. He had just completed an initial draft of the book when he passed away. Without his guiding knowledge, the editors decided to publish this volume as his working papers. The result is date of release, number of reels, production company, and credits for 25,968 silent films made between 1903 and 1929. Due to Braff's untimely death, this monumental work is not 100 percent reliable but is still an excellent place to look up short silent films.

724. Connelly, Robert B. 1998. *The Silents: Silent Feature Films, 1910–36.* Highland Park, Ill.: December Press.

Connelly compiled this guide to 3,500 silent films with credits for 10,000 directors and actors as part of the *Motion Picture Guide* (see entry 169). *The Silents* is a reprint of the *Silent Film* volume that has been made available for separate purchase.

725. Donaldson, Geoffrey. 1997. *Of Joy and Sorrow: A Filmography of Dutch Silent Fiction.* Amsterdam: Stichting Nederlands Filmmuseum.

Donaldson has compiled an illustrated guide to Dutch silent films made between 1896 and 1933, three quarters of which have been lost to the ravages of time. The book begins with an overview of the industry and its films and continues with a chronological filmography. Entries include the Dutch title with an English translation, production company, release date, a synopsis, and references. Credits are listed when available. Indexes list films, persons, companies, and characters.

726. Doyle, Billy H., and Anthony Slide. 1995. *The Ultimate Directory of the Silent Screen Performers: A Necrology of Births and Deaths and Essays on 50 Lost Players.* Metuchen, N.J.: Scarecrow Press.

Based on extensive research, Doyle records the date and place of birth and death for over 7,000 silent film performers. In addition, he writes obituaries of 50 "lost players" whose deaths eluded the notice of the press.

727. *EarlyCinema.com* [World Wide Web Resource]. J.S. Walters/Handprint Productions. 2001. Address: http://www.earlycinema.com. [Accessed: March 2005].

EarlyCinema.com "aims to provide an introduction to the first decade of motion pictures and the developments which helped shape cinema as we know it today." The site includes biographies of eight moving picture pioneers and overviews of six early technologies as well as a timeline and an alphabetical listing of key events that took place between 1827 and 1905. There is no listing of key works, but a films section is "under development."

A Guide to Silent Westerns (see entry 824)

Edison Motion Pictures, 1890–1900: An Annotated Filmography (see entry 863)

728. Herbert, Stephen, and Luke McKernan. 1996. *Who's Who of Victorian Cinema: A Worldwide Survey, Centenary of Cinema.* London: British Film Institute.

Herbert and McKernan led a team of experts in compiling a biographical guide to over 250 people involved in the earliest days of filmmaking. Listed in alphabetical order by name, entries include years of birth and death (when available), job specialty, and a biography of life and career that describes their involvement in early cinema. Supplementary materials include a glossary of technical terms, a list of moving picture equipment, a bibliography, and an index. The *Who's Who of Victorian Cinema* includes people not covered elsewhere and is a nice complement to biographical guides to the silent era.

Horror in Silent Films: A Filmography, 1896–1929 (see entry 661)

729. Katchmer, George A. 1991. *Eighty Silent Film Stars: Biographies and Filmographies of the Obscure to the Well Known.* Jefferson, N.C.: McFarland.

Silent film historian Katchmer wrote biographies of silent film stars for the magazine *Classic Images.* For *Eighty Silent Film Stars,* he selected lesser known stars and character actors (almost all male) for in-depth biographical treatment. In alphabetical order by the actor's screen name, each entry includes a biography of life and career, a still portrait, and a silent film filmography that includes title, year of release, director, writer, and the rest of the cast. The index lists names and film titles.

730. Klepper, Robert K. 1999. *Silent Films, 1877–1996: A Critical Guide to 646 Movies.* Jefferson, N.C.: McFarland.

Silent film historian Klepper has written an excellent guide to silent movies made from the earliest experimental years through a film made as late as 1996. His goal is to present a history of silent cinema by describing a representative list of silent films. In chronological order by year and then alphabetically, each film entry contains a one- to four-star rating, credits, a synopsis, a discussion of cast, and extensive historical and critical analysis of the film. Includes illustrations, a bibliography, and a name and title index. The birth and death dates for the actors are drawn from *Silent Film Necrology* (see entry 984) and *The Ultimate Directory of the Silent Screen Performers* (see entry 978).

731. Klepper, Robert K. 1996. *Silent Films on Video: A Filmography of Over 700 Silent Features Available on Videocassette, with a Directory of Sources.* Jefferson, N.C.: McFarland.

Although the subtitle claims over 700 silent features, Klepper has chosen to review only 29 of them in depth. He selects representative films that were classics, blockbusters, or had unique features. For these films, he writes lengthy summaries and discussions. For the rest of the silents, he lists the director and cast with a very brief synopsis. The third part of the book lists silent shorts. A directory lists sources for obtaining silent videos, a bibliography lists resources, and an index points to names and movies.

732.   Lahue, Kalton C. 1971. *Ladies in Distress.* South Brunswick, N.J.: A.S. Barnes.

Lahue writes admiring biographies of 40 silent film actresses. Each entry explores the life and career in some detail and is well illustrated with black-and-white publicity photos and stills.

733.   Langman, Larry, and Daniel Finn. 1994. *A Guide to American Silent Crime Films, Bibliographies and Indexes in the Performing Arts, No. 15.* Westport, Conn.: Greenwood Press.

Langman and Finn list "the screen credits of more than 2,000 silent features, documentaries, shorts and serials released from the 1890s through 1930." In their excellent introduction, they define crime films as those that deal with "basic questions of 'right' and 'wrong' in human behavior." Each film lists the title, distributor, director, screenwriter, and principal cast and is followed by a brief synopsis if the silent is still available for viewing. Appendixes list film cycles and series, a bibliography lists sources, and the index points to names. This guide is a companion to *A Guide to American Crime Films of the Thirties* (see entry 609) and *A Guide to American Crime Films of the Forties and Fifties* (see entry 610).

734.   Lauritzen, Einar, and Gunnar Lundquist. 1976. *American Film-Index 1908–1915: Motion Pictures, July 1908–December 1915.* Stockholm: Film-Index: Distributed by Akademibokhandeln University of Stockholm.

735.   Lauritzen, Einar, and Gunnar Lundquist. 1984. *American Film-Index, 1916–1920: Motion Pictures, January 1916–December 1920.* Stockholm; Huddinge, Sweden: Film-Index; Distributed by Tonnheims.

The *American Film-Index* was the first attempt to "fill a gap in the knowledge of the early period of American film" by using the trade paper *Moving Picture World* to compile a filmography with cast and credits. The first volume covers over 23,000 feature films made between 1908 and 1915, excluding shorts, animation, documentaries, and newsreels. The second volume covers 12,000 feature films and shorts made between 1916 and 1920 and includes a section of additions and corrections to the first volume. Individual entries list title, producer, director, screenwriter, cinematographer, and cast. In addition, the entries list the date that the film was mentioned in *Moving Picture World,* which means that this filmography can also be used as an index to that publication. Both volumes include portraits of some of the more prominent actors. Unfortunately, neither volume contains indexes of any kind, until the publication of *American Film Personnel and Company Credits, 1908–1920* (see entry 748). Although this set is monumental in scope and the best of its kind upon publication, the *AFI Catalog* (see entries 391 to 393) is a more comprehensive and indexed source for investigating early American cinema.

736.   Library of Congress. Motion Picture Broadcasting and Recorded Sound Division, Kemp R. Niver, and Bebe Bergsten. 1985. *Early Motion Pictures: The Paper Print Collection in the Library of Congress.* Washington, D.C.: Motion Picture Broadcasting and Recorded Sound Division Library of Congress.

From 1894 to 1912, filmmakers looking to protect their copyrights submitted over 3,000 films to the Library of Congress on paper-positive prints. Finishing in 1965, Niver restored the deteriorating paper prints onto more stable medium. Never intended for viewing, these are in many cases the only surviving versions of the earliest films, making the collection indispensable to film historians. The films are organized according to 12 broad categories. Each entry includes title, cast, production company, copyright number and date of copyright, length, and condition of the film. A synopsis describes the film contents. There are subject and title indexes. The Library of Congress published an earlier edition under the title *Motion Pictures from the Library of Congress Paper Print Collection, 1894–1912.*

737.   Library of Congress. Motion Picture Broadcasting and Recorded Sound Division, Rita Horwitz, Harriet Harrison, and Wendy White-Hensen. 1980. *The George Kleine Collection of Early Motion Pictures in the Library of Congress: A Catalog.* Washington, D.C.: Motion Picture Broadcasting and Recorded Sound Division Library of Congress.

In 1947, the Library of Congress acquired the papers and films of the George Kleine estate. The collection contained 456 films made between 1898 and 1926. This catalog details the entire collection, listing title, production company, technical data, genre, a summary, and Library of Congress subject headings. After a chronological index, a general index lists names, titles, and subjects. Kleine's films filled gaps in the Library of Congress collection, and this book serves the same function.

738.   Liebman, Roy. 1996. *Silent Film Performers: An Annotated Bibliography of Published, Unpublished and Archival Sources for Over 350 Actors and Actresses.* Jefferson, N.C.: McFarland.

Designed for both casual and serious researchers, Liebman's guide tells how to find published and archival materials about more than 350 silent film performers. For each performer, he provides a brief biography, a career description, and lists of resources. Published materials include books by and about performers, including encyclopedia articles, bibliographies, credits, books about their films, catalogs, biographies and autobiographies, pictorial collections, theses, and "factoids." A category called obscure published sources includes mostly ephemera. Media include videos and films about the performer. Drawn from 70 institutions, archival materials include clipping files, correspondence, filmographies, interviews, photographs/stills, oral histories, publicity files and studio biographies, programs, scrapbooks, legal files, and more. A directory lists the archives along with addresses, hours, contact information, and a description of the collections. Includes an extensive annotated bibliography and a personal name index. Although useful to anyone seeking information about individual silent film performers, Liebman's guide will be of most interest to researchers seeking primary source materials.

739.   Lowe, Denise. 2004. *An Encyclopedic Dictionary of Women in Early American Films: 1895–1930.* New York: Haworth Press.

Lowe writes biographies of women who made and starred in silent films. Each entry includes year and city of birth and death, a career biography, and a complete list of credits extending into the sound era—many also include a portrait. A handful of entries list organizations, studios, and subjects. Appendixes list longest careers, WAMPAS Baby Stars, Grauman's Chinese hand- and footprints, Hollywood Walk of Fame locations, and an especially useful list of writers, producers, and directors. Women are neglected in many of the silent film guides, so Lowe's compilation is an important contribution. Includes an extensive bibliography and an index.

740. Magill, Frank Northen, Patricia King Hanson, and Stephen L. Hanson. 1982. *Magill's Survey of Cinema—Silent Films.* Englewood Cliffs, N.J.: Salem Press.

Providing the same treatment for silent films as *Magill's Survey of Cinema for English Language Films* (see entries 161 and 162) and *Foreign Language Films* (see entry 254), over 40 contributors have written summaries for more than 375 silent films. Each entry includes the film title, release date, above-the-line crew, length in reels, and cast matched to character. Each signed essay delves into the history of the production and provides a detailed plot description followed by the film's popular and critical reception. Most films also include critical analysis. As in the other *Surveys,* indexes include director, screenwriter, cinematographer, editor, and performer. There is also a chronological list of titles covered in the set. Unique to this set are 17 introductory essays on the history and people that influenced silent film. Although other guides to silent films have since been published, this set remains a standard.

741. Magliozzi, Ronald S., and International Federation of Film Archives. 1988. *Treasures from the Film Archives: A Catalog of Short Silent Fiction Films Held by FIAF Archives.* Metuchen, N.J.: Scarecrow Press.

The Federation Internationale des Archives du Film (FIAF) collects and preserves motion pictures. This catalog lists the short silent fiction films available from participating FIAF archives. The catalog is organized by country where the short was released. Entries include title, year of first exhibition, production company, director, and actor. The holding archive is listed by codes that need to be looked up in the second appendix. Separate indexes provide access by series name, animated shorts, performers, directors, production company, and title. An excellent resource for researchers attempting to locate viewable copies of silent shorts. The *Catalog* is part of the *FIAF International FilmArchive Database* (see entry 33).

742. McCaffrey, Donald W., and Christopher P. Jacobs. 1999. *Guide to the Silent Years of American Cinema, Reference Guides to the World's Cinema.* Westport, Conn.: Greenwood Press.

As with all books in the Greenwood series *Reference Guides to the World's Cinema,* an introduction to the national cinema is followed by selections of the most prominent filmmakers and films of that country. Professors McCaffrey and Jacobs select "key films, actors, directors, and screenwriters" from the silent era based on their favorites. For filmmakers, they provide career biographies followed by an extensive filmography and a selective bibliography. For films, they include release date, genre, above-the-line cast and crew, a summary and discussion of the film, and awards won. Appendixes contain an essay on the legacy of the silent cinema, a list of 160 additional films of note from the silent era, a bibliography, and a name and film title index. As with all books in the series, this is a good place to go for an overview of American cinema in the silent era. For coverage from 1930 through 1965, consult the companion volume by Whissen (see entry 420) and for coverage from 1965 to 1995, consult the companion volume by Curran (see entry 401).

743. Miller, Blair. 1995. *American Silent Film Comedies: An Illustrated Encyclopedia of Persons, Studios, and Terminology.* Jefferson, N.C.: McFarland.

Miller has written an illustrated dictionary of the people, companies, publications, and—to a lesser extent—the vocabulary of silent film comedy. Entries are well written, whether covering a career biography or a company history. Includes a bibliography of sources consulted and an index.

744. Mitchell, Glenn. 1998. *A–Z of Silent Film Comedy.* London: Batsford.

Mitchell's companion to silent film comedy covers prominent films, filmmakers, and topics. The majority of entries cover filmmakers and performers, describing their careers and most important films. Entries for films tend to be longer, including a detailed plot summary, production history, and critical reception. Topical entries include in-depth articles on national cinemas, genres, characters, props, and anything else found in silent films. All entries include cross-references, which prove useful because there is no index. With its lengthy in-depth essays, Mitchell has written an excellent guide to silent film.

Music for Silent Films, 1894–1929: A Guide (see entry 571)

746. Musser, Charles. *A Guide to Motion Picture Catalogs by American Producers and Distributors, 1894–1908: A Microfilm Edition* [World Wide Web Resource]. Rutgers University. 1997. Address: http://edison.rutgers.edu/mopix/mopix.htm. [Accessed: March 2005].

The earliest moving picture companies printed catalogs for exhibitors to describe and promote their films. Rutgers University, which holds the Edison papers, has reprinted these catalogs on six microfilm reels. The "Reel Notes" on these Web pages are a guide to the microfilm set. Unfortunately, most of the listings don't go into great detail, giving instead a general feel for the contents. I was not able to view the microfilm, but I have seen examples of these catalogs. They generally list a title, a price, a still, and a plot summary for each of the films the company is attempting to sell. The catalogs are very useful for studying the earliest days of cinema.

Silent Film Necrology (see entry 984)

747. Slide, Anthony. 2002. *Silent Players: A Biographical and Autobiographical Study of 100 Silent Film Actors and Actresses.* Lexington: University Press of Kentucky.

Each of film historian Slide's biographies of 100 of the most prominent silent film actors contains a portrait and two or more pages of a biography of life and film career based on both research as well as interviews with the majority of the players, most of whom he knew. Slide includes a bibliography but chooses not to include filmographies, leaving that instead to the *AFI Catalog* (see entries 391 to 393). Includes an index.

748. Spehr, Paul C., Gunnar Lundquist, and Einar Lauritzen. 1996. *American Film Personnel and Company Credits, 1908–1920: Filmographies Reordered by Authoritative Organizational and Personal Names from Lauritzen and Lundquist's American Film-Index.* Jefferson, N.C.: McFarland.

This index is a filmography of the filmmakers, production/distribution companies, and source materials of films made between 1908 and 1920 in the United States. Although the index can stand alone, it works much better (as it was designed to do) as an index to the films listed in the two *American Film Index* volumes published by Lauritzen and Lundquist (see entries 734 and 735).

The Universal Silents: A Filmography of the Universal Motion Picture Manufacturing Company, 1912–1929 (see entry 878)

749. Waldman, Harry. 2000. *Missing Reels: Lost Films of American and European Cinema.* Jefferson, N.C.: McFarland.

In his introduction, Waldman estimates that 80 percent of all films made before World War I and two-thirds of all films made between the World Wars in the United States and Europe have been permanently lost. *Missing Reels* describes over 1,000 films that no longer exist from 15 countries. For each country, he writes a brief history of filmmaking and the types of films made and lost followed by descriptions of the films. Descriptions are taken from studio publicity and reviews and include a plot summary, director and cast, and critical reception. Photographic stills are included when available. This unique source fills a niche on the reference shelf.

750. Weaver, John T. 1971. *Twenty Years of Silents, 1908–1928.* Metuchen, N.J.: Scarecrow Press.

Weaver lists credits for approximately 1,200 silent film actors and animal stars. After cast lists for the Keystone Kops, the Sennett Bathing Beauties, the original Our Gang kids, and the WAMPAS Babies, individual entries list years of birth and death followed by year-by-year film credits. Supplementary materials list where producers were born and years of birth and death, the height, weight, and hair and eye color of directors, and silent film studio companies. Weaver died before completion of the book and it was finished by editors, but the result seems to be as reliable as his companion volume *Forty Years of Screen Credits* (see entry 1027).

751. Williamson, J. W. 1994. *Southern Mountaineers in Silent Films: Plot Synopses of Movies about Moonshining, Feuding, and Other Mountain Topics, 1904–1929.* Jefferson, N.C.: McFarland.

Williamson has compiled a list of 476 silent movies made about Southern mountain people. The films are listed by year and include title, company and date of release, and the original company-written synopsis. The appendix is a place and subject guide, while the index lists film titles and names of filmmakers, actors, and companies.

Winners of the West: The Sagebrush Heroes of the Silent Screen (see entry 823)

SOAP OPERAS

752. Groves, Seli. 1995. *The Ultimate Soap Opera Guide.* Detroit: Visible Ink Press.

Soap opera journalist Groves has written a guide to 10 prominent daytime soap operas. For each program, she chronicles its broadcast history, lists original cast and characters (complete with family tree), covers the series story, and then highlights villains, love affairs, breakthroughs (first soap to portray an event or issue), and biographies of characters and current cast. Appendixes include cast lists, fan clubs, and Daytime Emmy and Soap Opera Digest awards. Includes a list of common plot elements, a history of soap operas, and an index. *The Ultimate Soap Opera Guide* is of most interest to fans of the 10 shows included.

753. Morris, Bruce B. 1997. *Prime Time Network Serials: Episode Guides, Casts, and Credits for 37 Continuing Television Dramas, 1964–1993.* Jefferson, N.C.: McFarland.

Morris has compiled an episode-by-episode list of the 37 prime time serials (AKA soaps) aired on American networks between 1964 and 1993. For each series, he describes the premise, discusses the cast, and recounts the production history. For each season, he provides a complete list of regular cast and crew. For each episode, he gives the broadcast date, the writer, the director, the Nielsen rating, guest stars, and a plot synopsis. Includes an index.

754. Schemering, Christopher. 1988. *The Soap Opera Encyclopedia.* Newly updated and expanded ed. New York: Ballantine Books.

Soap opera fan, collector, and writer Schemering has compiled a list of every soap opera that had been broadcast on the three major U.S. networks through the 1985 season. Listed alphabetically by program title, entries for major soaps include premier and cancellation dates, an overview of major story lines, critical analysis, and complete lists of major cast for the entire run of the series. The major shows also have an appendix listing production credits. Lesser-known shows and syndicated, cable, or foreign soaps receive less coverage. A separate section profiles two dozen of the most prominent stars and writers. Appendixes list Emmy award nominees and winners, Nielsen ratings, stars who made their start in soaps, famous guest stars, blacks in daytime drama, longest-running soaps and performers, and a chronology. Includes two sections of black-and-white stills and a name index.

755. *The Soap Opera Book: Who's Who in Daytime Drama.* 1992. West Nyack, N.Y.: Todd.

Fans of soap opera stars will enjoy the *Soap Opera Book.* It consists of biographies that focus on the careers and personal lives of soap opera actors. Each entry includes a portrait, date of birth, marital status, education, interests, awards, and a list of soap operas in which they have appeared. Supplementary materials include directories of the networks and fan clubs and an actor index.

SOCIAL ISSUES
(SEE ALSO *ETHNIC GROUPS*)

756. Peyton, Patricia, and Film Fund. 1979. *Reel Change: A Guide to Social Issue Films.* San Francisco: Film Fund.

Peyton has edited a list of films and documentaries that promote social action. Compiled from distributors' catalogs and a survey of "groups and individuals who use social issue media on a regular basis," the films and documentaries are sorted into

10 broad categories covering contemporary social issues ranging from the environment to ethnic issues to corporate responsibility. A separate section lists classic films that portray social issues from the past. Each entry includes the film's title, the director, technical data, fees to rent, and a summary that focuses on the social issue. Appendixes include a distributor directory, lists of film guides and magazines, and hints on how to screen films. The index lists titles alphabetically. Because *Reel Change* is now over 35 years old, most of the films were only available in 16mm format. Still, the guide is useful for the short list of classic films as well as the contemporaneous films if they can be found on video or DVD.

LABOR

757.   Galerstein, Carolyn L. 1989. *Working Women on the Hollywood Screen: A Filmography, Garland Reference Library of the Humanities; Vol. 469.* New York: Garland.

Professor Galerstein produced a list of "approximately 4500 American feature films released between 1930 and 1975, in which the leading female role is that of a working woman." She categorizes the films by 42 different occupations, beginning each chapter with a discussion of the role and image of women who portray the job followed by a chronological list of films. Most of the films list only the title, actress, distributor, and director, but select films also include a summary that pays particular attention to the job. Lightly illustrated, the book includes actress and movie title indexes. Galerstein's look at working women on film will be of use to researchers interested in how they were portrayed in media.

758.   Zaniello, Tom. 2003. *Working Stiffs, Union Maids, Reds, and Riffraff: An Expanded Guide to Films about Labor.* Ithaca, N.Y.: ILR Press.

Zaniello, a film scholar specializing in labor films, has compiled a list of 350 feature films about unions, labor history, political labor movements, management struggles with labor, or working-class life where economics plays a role in the plot. Each film entry lists the technical information, the director, the screenwriter, and the principal cast. The author's summaries contain great detail about the plot and the labor issues. Zaniello recommends films with similar themes, further reading, and cites *New York Times* and *Variety* film reviews. Appendixes list films in chronological order and by cinematic movement. The thematic index is a catchall of categories from labor themes to various ethnic groups to selected industries.

POLITICS

759.   Booker, M. Keith. 1999. *Film and the American Left: A Research Guide.* Westport, Conn.: Greenwood Press.

Professor Booker has compiled a guide to "more than 260 films that have either addressed ideas and issues of concern to the American Left or at least included central contributions from writers, directors, and actors with leftist inclinations or associations." Films are listed in chronological order. Essays discuss each film's engagement with Leftist ideas and points to books for further reading. Interestingly, Booker provides credits solely for the screenwriter. Only in the appendix is there a list of films by director along with an alphabetical list of all films. Includes a list of works cited and an index.

760.   Combs, James E. 1990. *American Political Movies: An Annotated Filmography of Feature Films, Garland Filmographies; Vol. 1.* New York: Garland.

Combs has written a series of essays on films that feature "political communication," whether consciously or not. Organized by decade from the twenties through the eighties, each chapter takes a look at the times as reflected in its political films. The filmography at the end of the book lists films in alphabetical order by title with release year, length, director, and principal cast. Includes a bibliography and a subject index.

RELIGION

761.   Campbell, Richard H., and Michael R. Pitts. 1981. *The Bible on Film: A Checklist, 1897–1980.* Metuchen, N.J.: Scarecrow Press.

Writers and Christians Campbell and Pitts have attempted to list all feature films derived from the Bible produced internationally between 1897 and 1980. The book is divided into three sections: the Old Testament, the New Testament, and a selective list of television programs. Each film includes the standard technical information along with the director, the screenwriter, the producer, and the cast. The authors write a brief synopsis, discuss the context of the film's release, and add their own commentary. Includes a title index.

762.   Erickson, Hal. 1992. *Religious Radio and Television in the United States, 1921–1991: The Programs and Personalities.* Jefferson, N.C.: McFarland.

Erickson has compiled a guide to religious television and radio programs and the people who make them. Entries for shows contain a synopsis and production history. Entries for people offer career biographies focusing on their ministry and their shows. Includes a bibliography and an index.

SPORTS

763.   Erickson, Hal. 2002. *The Baseball Filmography, 1915 through 2001.* 2nd ed. Jefferson, N.C.: McFarland.

Erickson, a baseball fan and film historian, compiled a comprehensive list of American feature films about baseball. He begins the book with a historical overview of baseball in the movies. For each film, he lists complete above-the-line crew credits and a complete cast list. His plot summaries go into great detail and discuss the baseball in depth. Separate chapters feature baseball short subjects and baseball in non-baseball films. The bibliography of sources used is extensive. The index points to the films, names, and photographs in the text.

764.   Zucker, Harvey Marc, and Lawrence J. Babich. 1987. *Sports Films: A Complete Reference.* Jefferson, N.C.: McFarland.

Zucker and Babich have compiled a filmography of 2,042 theatrical films where spectator sports play an integral role in the plot. International in scope, the 14 chapters feature not only baseball, basketball, and football, but also soccer, winter sports, and the Olympics. Additional sections feature athletes who appeared in films complete with bios and lists of actors who portrayed real athletes. Each chapter begins with a filmographic essay featuring the themes and clichés inherent in the sport and a discussion of some of the better films. Entries include date of release, length, principal crew and cast, and a synopsis. A general index lists names and titles of publications, and a separate index lists film titles. Lightly illustrated, the book is of interest to anyone interested in the portrayal of sports in film.

TELEVISION

765.   Bianculli, David. 1996. *Dictionary of Teleliteracy: Television's 500 Biggest Hits, Misses, and Events.* New York: Continuum.

Television journalist Bianculli first wrote a book entitled *Teleliteracy: Taking Television Seriously* to make the case that "awareness and appreciation" of television was important to cultural literacy. In this dictionary, he fills in the gap left by books such as the *Dictionary of Cultural Literacy,* which virtually ignores the medium, by describing and analyzing the 500 "most memorable events and programs from the first fifty years of television history." Covering 1945 through 1995, Bianculli discusses the significance of the program or event and gives his personal take on its quality. Includes an extensive bibliography, indexes to names and titles, and a scattering of black-and-white stills.

766.   Brown, Les. 1992. *Les Brown's Encyclopedia of Television.* 3rd ed. Detroit: Gale Research.

Media journalist Les Brown has produced one of the standard dictionaries of television. Now in its third edition, there are over 3,000 entries on television programs, actors, producers, writers, companies, and technology. Entries for shows provide brief descriptions, while other entries go into more depth in describing a person's or company's impact on television. Although international in scope, the primary emphasis is on American and some British television. After a brief bibliography, appendixes list top-rated feature films, sporting events, network programs, number of households owning television and subscribing to cable, FCC commissioners, worldwide advertising expenditures by country, European satellite broadcasters (the United States did not have enough in 1991 to be included), and hours of television viewed per day. The index includes both the main entries as well as names included within entries.

767.   Newcomb, Horace, Cary O'Dell, Noelle Watson, and Museum of Broadcast Communications. 1997. *Encyclopedia of Television.* Chicago: Fitzroy Dearborn Publishers.

With over 300 expert contributors and more than 1,000 articles, the *Encyclopedia of Television* is a monumental overview of television. But it is not so much the quantity as it is the quality that makes this three-volume set the premier encyclopedia in the field. Entries cover the people who make and study television, programs aired in the English-speaking world, and articles on topics relating to the historical, cultural, economic, political, and technical aspects of television. Biographical entries contain descriptions of the individual's contribution to television, a biography, and credits. Program entries include a description of the show and its impact on culture, a cast and producer list, and programming history. All entries include a list of further readings. The index points to the main entries for articles as well as people and shows named within articles. If the encyclopedia has any shortcoming, it would be the lack of thesaurus underlying the organization of the topic entries and the resulting lack of see also entries in the articles and in the index. The Museum has now made many of the articles available online at <http://www.museum.tv/archives/etv/index.html>.

768.　　Smith, Anthony, and Richard Paterson. 1998. *Television: An International History*. 2nd ed. Oxford, England; New York: Oxford University Press.

The first three parts of this encyclopedia cover the origins of television, its various genres, and the relation between television and society. The fourth and largest part is a region-by-region description of the development of television. Larger countries with developed television industries receive their own entries, while smaller countries are lumped into regions. The bibliographies for each section are given in a separate chapter at the end of the book, along with a list of television museums and archives and an index. The international scope and the detailed articles on national television make this a nice complement to the *Encyclopedia of Television* (see entry 767).

TELEVISION MOVIES AND MINISERIES

769.　　Canton, Maj. 1994. *Maj Canton's the Complete Reference Guide to Movies and Miniseries Made for TV and Cable, 1984–1994: 10 Years of TV Movies*. Fair Oaks, Calif.: Adams-Blake.

770.　　Canton, Maj. 2000. *Maj Canton's the Complete Reference Guide to Movies and Miniseries Made for TV and Cable, 1994–2000*. Venice, Calif.: Maj Canton.

Canton has compiled a list of 1,706 movies and miniseries made for TV or cable from 1984 to 1994. For each movie, she lists genre, air date, principal crew and cast, and a brief synopsis. For television productions, she also includes rating and audience share data. Appendixes list programs by subject, network, and Emmy awards; rank programs by rating; and list "movies based on books, plays and articles." Indexes list programs by writer, director, producer, and cast. This book is one-stop shopping for anything to do with movies and miniseries aired during the decade covered.

771.　　Marill, Alvin H. 1987. *Movies Made for Television: The Telefeature and the Mini-Series, 1964–1986*. New York: New York Zoetrope.

Marill has compiled a list of almost 2,100 movies and miniseries made for television from 1964 through 1986 for one of the three major U.S. networks, for cable, or for wide syndication. In alphabetical order by title, each entry includes principal cast and crew followed by a brief synopsis. An appendix lists the movies in chronological order. The index serves as a filmography for more than 22,000 producers, writers, and actors.

TELEVISION PILOTS

Fifty Years of Television: A Guide to Series and Pilots, 1937–1988 (see entry 784)

772.   Goldberg, Lee. 1990. *Unsold Television Pilots: 1955 through 1988.* Jefferson, N.C.: McFarland.

This is a book of flops—pilots that were made but that for one reason or another never became series. The book is arranged chronologically, divided into comedy and drama pilots. Reflecting how the television industry works, the early years are represented by both networks and production companies, and beginning in 1968, they are represented solely by the networks. Goldberg gathered his information from press releases, interviews, and articles in the entertainment industry, but mostly from the files of the Leo Burnett Agency. Each entry lists the pilot title, length, air date, production company, director, producers, and writers. The synopsis describes the premise, summarizes the plot, and lists the cast. The index gives access to the pilots and people who made them, which may be the most useful feature of the book.

773.   Terrace, Vincent. 1997. *Experimental Television, Test Films, Pilots, and Trial Series, 1925 through 1995: Seven Decades of Small Screen Almosts.* Jefferson, N.C.: McFarland.

Television researcher Terrace has compiled a unique guide to 3,016 experimental shows aired during the earliest days of broadcast television in the 1920s through the 1940s as well as aired and unaired pilots made between 1946 and 1995. For each show, he lists the premise, the characters, and a synopsis plus principal crew and cast. Includes a name index. Oddly, pilots are not cross-listed by series title—in other words, you can't look up Columbo to find its two pilots because they had different titles. Instead, you would need to look in the index under Peter Falk. Despite this one major shortcoming, the book is useful both for its coverage of early television (although there is no simple way to separate these entries from the rest) and the pilots for unaired television series.

TELEVISION PROGRAMS

774.   *Classic TV Database* [World Wide Web Resource]. Address: http://www.classic-tv.com. [Accessed: March 2005].

The *Classic TV Database* lists 79 American television shows that have achieved classic status. The Web site is not clear on the criteria, but the shows listed seem to have achieved both critical and popular acclaim. Shows may be searched or browsed by alphabet or decade. Records for individual shows usually include a summary, a list of cast and characters, the broadcast history, and the theme song. Additional sections list the top 100 shows and the top 60 theme songs of all time.

775.   Davis, Anthony. 1988. *TV's Greatest Hits.* London: Boxtree in association with Independent Television Books.

Davis lists 200 British and American television series that were popular around the world. He culled his information from "lists obtained from production and distribution companies" but doesn't explain the criteria that were used to determine which shows to include. The book is divided into 16 genres. Each chapter consists of descriptions of the genre (speculating about its international appeal) and the shows and their actors. The narratives make for interesting reading, but the most useful part of the book is the alphabetical list of the most popular shows in the index. Unfortunately, Davis does not list the countries or even the number of countries where the shows were aired.

776. Dintrone, Charles V. 2003. *Television Program Master Index: Access to Critical and Historical Information on 1,927 Shows in 925 Books, Dissertations, and Journal Articles.* 2nd ed. Jefferson, N.C.: McFarland.

In this second edition, film and television librarian Dintrone has greatly expanded his index to writings about individual American television shows. While the first edition featured 1,002 shows from 341 books and was 133 pages long, the second edition almost doubles the number of shows and almost triples the number of resources. Organized alphabetically by program title, each entry points to the book author and page numbers where the show is discussed. Readers then may turn to the substantial list of "sources used" at the end of the book to find the full citation. Sources used include "books on broad subjects but containing references to specific shows," books on one show, and books that list many shows in alphabetical order, as well as dissertations and select scholarly journal articles. An appendix lists books by groups or classes of people such as Asian Americans or the rich or scientists. An additional appendix lists programs by genre. This unique and valuable book will be most useful to researchers interested in seeing what has been written about individual television shows, but can also serve as a collection development guide.

777. Halliwell, Leslie, and Philip Purser. 1987. *Halliwell's Television Companion.* 3rd ed. London: Paladin.

Purser and the highbrow, highly opinionated, and nostalgic Leslie Halliwell have produced a list of television movies and programs aired on British and American television through 1985. Each title includes the country of origin, the year of release, the running time, production and cast credits, a synopsis, and an appraisal. Halliwell writes the entries for U.S. programs, and Philip Purser does the same for the British programs. Selected programs also may receive a one- to four-star rating or include critical quotes. Mixed in with the shows are names of people, companies, technical terms, and topics. As Halliwell did for film in his *Filmgoer's Companion* (see entry 993), Halliwell and Purser have created an interesting and informative guide to television.

778. Hawes, William. 2001. *Live Television Drama, 1946–1951.* Jefferson, N.C.: McFarland.

779. Hawes, William. 2002. *Filmed Television Drama, 1952–1958.* Jefferson, N.C.: McFarland.

Professor Hawes chronicles the history of television drama in its earliest years. The first volume covers live dramas that aired from 1946 to 1951, and the second volume covers dramas filmed from 1952 through 1958. In both volumes, the main part of the book consists of narrative chapters analyzing television drama. The reference guides appear in the appendixes, listing BBC, CBS, and NBC live dramas and the three major filmed anthologies and series along with the DuMont network dramas. The index covers both the chapters and the appendixes.

780.   Holst, Jerome A. *TV ACRES* [World Wide Web Resource]. Address: http://www. tvacres.com. [Accessed: March 2005].

Holst, a librarian and television fan, has spent over 25 years compiling facts about the characters, places, and things that have appeared on U.S. prime-time and Saturday-morning television programs from the 1940s to the present. The facts are organized into TV character bios and approximately 500 subject headings in such categories as addresses, animals, ethnic group, nationality, occupations and lifestyles, and places. While browsing is the best way to explore the site, Holst also offers a keyword search function. *TV ACRES* serves not only television fans, but researchers seeking patterns in popular culture.

781.   Lance, Steven. 1996. *Written out of Television: The Encyclopedia of Cast Changes and Character Replacements, 1945–1994.* Lanham, Md.: Scarecrow Press.

Lance, an entertainment industry critic and occasional participant, has written of 2,000 actors from more than 375 programs who were written out of a series and replaced with another actor. In some cases different actors played the same role; in other cases a new character filled the vacated spot. In alphabetical order by show title, each entry lists dates aired, network, and characters and actors who were replaced. Each show is described in detail, with particular attention to the circumstances that led to replacing characters. Includes a bibliography and index. Although of limited use, the book does fill a unique niche, helping answer questions such as "how many different people played the Lone Ranger on TV?"

782.   Marcus, Laurence, and Stephen Hulse. *Television Heaven* [World Wide Web Resource]. Address: http://www.televisionheaven.co.uk. [Accessed: January 2005].

Marcus and Hulse launched *Television Heaven* "to preserve the memory of tele-vision programmes both past and present" that they consider classics. To date, they and their team of writers have written good summaries and reviews of over 500 shows. The vast majority of the shows are from Great Britain, where the authors are based, or from the United States. In addition to a review, the record for a show will also usually list the length and total number of episodes, the network, and the years it aired. Other features include a history of television, biographies of influential people, interviews, and weekly news reports from the United States and the United Kingdom (this last through a link to a companion Web site).

783.   *Memorable TV* [World Wide Web Resource]. Address: http://www.memorabletv. com. [Accessed: January 2005].

Memorable TV, an Australian-based company that sells DVDs and CDs, offers one of the largest Web compilations of television shows that have been broadcast in Australia, Canada, Great Britain, and the United States. Organized by country as well as select genres, each of the thousands of programs includes the show's premise with cast and production credits. For just over 100 shows, the site provides episode guides. *Memorable TV* also reviews several hundred recent DVDs and features a "hall of fame" that provides biographies of a handful of artists from "in front of and behind the camera who have made a lasting contribution to the world of Television." Note that the search box was not functioning in January 2005—it was necessary instead to browse the alphabetical lists of programs.

784. Terrace, Vincent. 1991. *Fifty Years of Television: A Guide to Series and Pilots, 1937–1988.* New York: Cornwall Books.

Terrace has assembled a guide to more than 4,800 television series and pilots. Entries include series title, genre, length, dates aired, a very brief description, and the regular cast and producers. Once useful for its unique coverage of unaired pilots, that information is now better covered in Terrace's book *Experimental Television, Test Films, Pilots and Trial Series, 1925 through 1995* (see entry 773).

785. Terrace, Vincent. 1993. *Television Character and Story Facts: Over 110,000 Details from 1,008 Shows, 1945–1992.* Jefferson, N.C.: McFarland.

Need to know Laura Petrie's maiden name? How Archie and Edith met? The first song played on "WKRP in Cincinnati"? The addresses of the characters in "Beverley Hills 90210"? Prolific television writer Terrace has gathered a massive compendium of these types of facts for over 1,000 television shows. Organized alphabetically by program title, each entry lists the cast and then gives a synopsis of the show complete with names, dates, numbers, and biographies for each character. Also included are facts about alternate pilots and missing or lost episodes. The index lists series, alternate titles, and actor and character names. The book serves fans of television, people devising and answering trivia questions, and researchers seeking patterns in popular culture.

Episode Guides

786. *epguides.com* [World Wide Web Resource]. Address: http://epguides.com. [Accessed: March 2005].

epguides.com lists titles and air dates for over 2,500 television shows. The records for most shows also include guest stars, recurring characters, a snippet of the theme song, and a link to descriptions of each episode provided by *TV.com* (see entry 68). Fans may browse by alphabet, prime-time schedule, new and recently added shows, and year, or they may use the search function. As in *TV Tome,* volunteer editors and contributors from across the Internet suggest the content for the database, meaning it is only as complete and as accurate as its contributors make it. Most of the episode guides for science fiction, fantasy, and horror television series were removed by Alan Morton, one of the original contributors, so he could publish *The Complete Directory to Science Fiction, Fantasy and Horror Television Series* (see entry 649).

787. *Episode List* [World Wide Web Resource]. Address: http://www.episodelist.com/shows. [Accessed: January   2005].

Episode List provides episode guides for some 140 American and British television programs. Because the information is entered by fans, completeness varies. A complete record contains a show overview, cast portraits, season-by-season and show-by-show episode synopses with original air date, and a plot tracker. Incomplete records vary in their contents and often include only episode titles. Because episode guides can be difficult to find, the usefulness of the site to individual users will depend on whether it includes the show being sought.

788. *Garn's Guides* [World Wide Web Resource]. Address: http://www.geocities. com/Area51/Vault/4144. [Accessed: January 2005].

Garn has developed episode guides for more than 400 television shows. All guides include season and episode number, air date, and title. Complete guides provide links from the episode titles to a page listing regular cast and show creator and episode guest stars, writers, and directors for each season—but no synopsis. Although the guide includes all types of series, its greatest strength lies in the coverage of science fiction, fantasy, and horror.

789. *ShowGuide: TV Guide Online* [World Wide Web Resource]. TV Guide Online. Address: http://www.tvguide.com/tv/showguide. [Accessed: March 2005].

TV Guide provides episode guides for shows aired on American television from the earliest years to the present. Organized alphabetically by show, each record includes premier and air dates, stars, premise, honors, and classic episodes, along with related stories from the pages of *TV Guide*. Episodes are listed by season, with each entry including air date, episode title, a one-sentence synopsis, and guest stars. Although its descriptions are brief, *ShowGuide* is the most comprehensive episode guide for American television.

790. *Television without Pity* [World Wide Web Resource]. Address: http://www. televisionwithoutpity.com. [Accessed: March 2005].

Television without Pity, formerly known as *Mighty Big TV,* recaps episodes of current television shows. The recaps are well written, detailed, and usually witty, probably because the site employs paid writers. Although this is nice for the shows covered, the result is that shows that don't attract interest from Internet fans aren't covered, and many shows are placed on permanent hiatus with only a handful of episodes described. For the same reasons, the site does not cover sitcoms. Currently, it covers 30 current shows and has placed nearly 200 shows on hiatus. In addition to the reviews, *Television without Pity* also lists season, episode number, and air date. Viewers may browse shows by title or search by keyword.

TELEVISION SPECIALS

Animated TV Specials: The Complete Directory to the First Twenty-Five Years, 1962–1987 (see entry 477)

791. Einstein, Daniel. 1987. *Special Edition: A Guide to Network Television Documentary Series and Special News Reports, 1955–1979.* Metuchen, N.J.: Scarecrow Press.

792. Einstein, Daniel. 1997. *Special Edition: A Guide to Network Television Documentary Series and Special News Reports, 1980–1989.* Lanham, Md.: Scarecrow Press.

Television archivist Einstein has compiled data on "commercial network news documentary, newsmagazine, and news special programming. Volume 1 covers over 7,000 individual programs and 120 series aired between 1955 and 1979, and volume 2 covers almost 2,500 individual programs and 38 series aired in the 1980s. For individual specials, Einstein gives the title, the air date, the network, a description, and the producer, director, writer, and anchor. Series such as "60 Minutes" receive the same treatment for each and every newscast. Separate indexes cover personalities and crew. Unfortunately, only volume 2 includes an index to subjects and places. Einstein has created an excellent source for finding television news documentaries.

793.   Terrace, Vincent. 1995. *Television Specials: 3,201 Entertainment Spectaculars, 1939–1993.* Jefferson, N.C.: McFarland.

Prolific television writer Terrace has compiled a list of 3,201 television specials made between 1939 and 1993. He excludes "news specials, non-celebrity documentaries, sports, religious projects, awards, beauty pageants, and parades." Entries for each show are brief, including title, genre, length, broadcast station, and title of series (for example, "ABC Afterschool Special") followed by a brief synopsis with cast and character names and above-the-line production credits. Includes a name index.

MISCELLANEOUS

794.   Bennett, Mark. 1996. *TV Sets: Fantasy Blueprints of Classic TV Homes.* New York: TV Books: Distributed by Penguin USA.

Bennett's hobby is drafting blueprints of the homes where fictional television families dwell. For years, he closely observed the shows to determine the layout for the homes featured in 34 popular series. Each blueprint shows not only the architecture of the home and its surroundings, but also the placement of furniture and standard props, a narrative description, and the home's address. A curious compilation, this book is strictly for fans who want a map of Gilligan's Island or the plans to their favorite TV family's home.

WAR (SEE ALSO *HISTORICAL FILMS* AND *BIOPICS*)

795.   Davenport, Robert Ralsey. 2004. *The Encyclopedia of War Movies: The Authoritative Guide to Movies about Wars of the Twentieth Century, The Facts on File Film Reference Library.* New York: Facts on File.

A soldier, lawyer, and writer, Davenport has compiled a survey of over 800 films about wars "from the Boxer Rebellion of 1900 to the Persian Gulf War and the campaigns in the Balkans." Organized alphabetically by film title, it is necessary to use the index to locate films by war. All entries include producer, director, screenwriter, distributor, location, principal cast, and a brief synopsis. Entries for more prominent films also contain historical background, critical comments, interesting facts, the military service record of lead actors, mistakes made in filming (including errors in continuity, anachronisms, and historical inaccuracies), quotes, and awards. The index lists films, filmmakers, and wars.

796.   Evans, Alun. 2000. *Brassey's Guide to War Films.* 1st ed. Washington, D.C.: Brassey's.

Evans, a member of the British Film Institute, has compiled a dictionary of over 2,000 war films that "portray battles, the effects of war, the psychology of waging war and the psychology of war on people." Films are in alphabetical order by title, listing director, country of origin, date of release, principal stars, and a plot summary with editorial comment. Scattered black-and-white stills illustrate selected films. Indexes list films by time period and director. *Brassey's* is the most complete guide to war films, but the longer discussions make it worthwhile to also consult *VideoHound's War Movies* (see entry 799).

797.　Freitas, Gary. 2004. *War Movies: The Belle & Blade Guide to Classic War Videos.* Bandon, Ore.: R.D. Reed.

Freitas, a war movie fan, a former soldier, and an expert on violence, has written reviews for 347 mostly English-language combat films. Each one-page entry provides war and genre, year, country, director, a rating on a five-point scale, a review discussing the merits of the film and its combat scenes, and a summary of its critical reception. Supplementary materials include lists of the 25 greatest action war movies and the 25 greatest war dramas and over a dozen 10-best lists for various subgenres. Separate essays describe the four main wars in which the United States was involved over the last century and the films about them. The index lists films by war. Although not as comprehensive as some of the other guides in this section, the fine analysis make Freitas's guide worth consulting.

798.　Langman, Larry, and Ed Borg. 1989. *Encyclopedia of American War Films, Garland Reference Library of the Humanities; Vol. 873.* New York: Garland.

Writer of film books Langman and writer and war buff Borg reviewed "virtually every war-related feature and most of the documentaries, short subjects, serials and cartoons" to come up with an alphabetical list of 2,000 American films dealing with war. Entries list the director, writer, and principal cast and include a synopsis with commentary. Appendixes list biographical films and Academy Award winning films; the most useful appendix lists films by 76 wars. Although *The Encyclopedia of War Movies* (see entry 795) is more up-to-date, it only covers twentieth-century wars, so this *Encyclopedia of American War Films* remains one of the best sources for all films about wars from every time period and every place.

799.　Mayo, Mike. 1999. *VideoHound's War Movies: Classic Conflict on Film.* Detroit: Visible Ink Press.

Mayo has compiled a list of over 200 war films. The book is organized by war, beginning with American, British, French, Japanese, and Russian wars, and then moving on to the great wars of the twentieth century, with by far the largest section on World War II. Mayo writes lengthy evaluations and plot summaries of each film. Illustrations and quotes enhance virtually every entry, and the author recommends other similar films. He includes the standard VideoHound rating of one to four bones and lists the principal cast and crew. Indexes list titles, cast, directors, writers, cinematographers, composers, and categories.

800.　Mulay, James J. 1989. *War Movies: A Guide to More Than 500 Films on Videocassette.* 1st ed, *Cinebooks Home Library Series; No. 6.* Evanston, Ill.: CineBooks.

War Movies is a guide for movie fans that looks "at war from all sides." Most of the nearly 400 films listed are in English, but there are some foreign-language films included as well. In alphabetical order by title, each entry "offers a concise plot synopsis, star rating (zero to five), critical appraisal, anecdotal material, actors and roles played, production credits" and now dated cassette availability notes. Lists at the beginning of the book sort the films by rating (from masterpiece to without merit), by parental recommendation, and by year of release. Indexes list principal actors, cinematographers, directors, editors, composers, producers, screenwriters, and source authors. Although designed for movie fans deciding what war movie to add to their movie collection or to rent, *War Movies* also is a good starting point for researchers of the genre.

801. Parish, James Robert. 1990. *The Great Combat Pictures: Twentieth-Century Warfare on the Screen.* Metuchen, N.J.: Scarecrow Press.

Parish, a prolific filmographer, has compiled a list of English-language combat films featuring twentieth-century wars. As in his other filmographies, he lists the major cast and crew and writes an engaging plot summary and discussion. Appendixes organize films by war and list television series. There is no index to personal names, limiting the book's usefulness.

802. Wetta, Frank Joseph, and Stephen J. Curley. 1992. *Celluloid Wars: A Guide to Film and the American Experience of War, Research Guides in Military Studies, No. 5.* New York: Greenwood Press.

Not content to merely list war films, Professors Wetta and Curley examine the influence of war on film and the influence of film on war. After two general essays, the book takes a chronological look at American wars and films made about them. Entries include title, a one- to four-star rating, technical data, director, and principal cast. Only four-star (and very rarely three-star) movies are discussed in depth. Includes an annotated bibliography, lists of top 10 war films and best war film by war, and a general and title index. The book will be of interest primarily to professors planning classes or film programmers.

WORLD WAR I

803. Campbell, Craig W. 1985. *Reel America and World War I: A Comprehensive Filmography and History of Motion Pictures in the United States, 1914–1920.* Jefferson, N.C.: McFarland.

More than half of this book is an analysis of the way World War I was portrayed in the movies of the time. It is included here for its filmography of films made during the war. The filmography is divided into sections on feature films, short films, documentaries, newsreels, and cartoons related to the war. It also includes the Liberty Loan Specials urging the purchase of bonds, other military films, and "Bolshevik" films. Each film entry includes the title, distributor, director, cast, and a brief synopsis. While limited in scope, the book is definitely useful for those analyzing war on film.

WORLD WAR II

804. Basinger, Jeanine. 2003. *The World War II Combat Film: Anatomy of a Genre.* Updated and expanded ed. Hanover, N.H.; London: Wesleyan University Press; Eurospan.

Film Professor Basinger has written an analysis of the war film genre. Although the book is not a reference book, it does contain a chronological filmography of over 1,000 American World War II and Korean War combat films made between 1941 and 1980 as well as a second chronology by Jeremy Arnold listing all combat films released in the United States between 1981 and 2003. For each film, the author describes the plot and places it in context—unless she discusses the film in the body of the work, in which case it is necessary to look up the film in the index to read about the film in the text. For each year, Basinger includes notes on war films made outside the United States, films with related themes such as saboteurs or prison escapes or comedies, and films with titles that could cause them to be mistaken for war films. An appendix lists World War I films. Most useful to researchers for its comprehensive list of World War II and Korean War films.

805.   Shull, Michael S., and David E. Wilt. 1996. *Hollywood War Films, 1937–1945: An Exhaustive Filmography of American Feature-Length Motion Pictures Relating to World War II.* Jefferson, N.C.: McFarland.

The authors analyze feature films released in the United States during World War II. The book is divided into two parts: films produced before the United States joined the war and films produced after. Each part includes an extensive filmography that not only lists the films, but provides a statistical analysis of the number of films, the amount of bias found in them, and the frequency of topical and pejorative references. Each film entry includes the title, distributor, director, genre, location, several descriptors, and a relevance ranking. A synopsis highlights all of the references to the war. Useful for studying war and film.

KOREAN WAR

806.   Lentz, Robert J. 2003. *Korean War Filmography: 91 English Language Features through 2000.* Jefferson, N.C.: McFarland.

Lentz, a film distributor, exhibitor, and reviewer, has written a guide to "Hollywood's depictions" of the Korean War. For 91 English-language films, he lists cast and crew credits, comments on the level of historical accuracy and propaganda, notes combat and plot "elements," and writes a lengthy review that summarizes the plot, places it in historical context, and examines its quality. Appendixes list films chronologically, by production company and distributor, by levels of accuracy and propaganda, and by subject and theme. An additional appendix lists "films with incidental Korean War references." Lentz has written the only reference guide devoted solely to the Korean War, and it is a nice addition to the literature. Includes a bibliography and an index.

VIETNAM WAR

807.   Devine, Jeremy M. 1995. *Vietnam at 24 Frames a Second: A Critical and Thematic Analysis of Over 400 Films about the Vietnam War.* Jefferson, N.C.: McFarland.

Devine writes filmographic essays examining nearly 400 films made about the Vietnam War. Ten chronological chapters cover the films in the context of the times they were made and the themes they explored. Appendixes list feature films and documentaries alphabetically and feature films chronologically. Supplementary materials include a smattering of black-and-white illustrations, a dated distributor directory, and an index.

808. Lanning, Michael Lee. 1994. *Vietnam at the Movies.* 1st ed. New York: Fawcett Columbine.

Lanning, a Vietnam veteran, has written a guide to films featuring the Vietnam War and its aftermath. The first half of the book provides an overview of how the war was portrayed, contrasting the coverage with films about previous wars. Chapters explore villains and heroes, soldiers and veterans, combat, and the Vietnamese. The second half of the book lists 380 films, including director and cast and offering a summary and commentary on whether the film accurately portrays the war and its soldiers. The film is rated on a scale of one to four for overall quality and for accuracy and believability. There is no index.

809. Malo, Jean-Jacques, and Tony Williams. 1994. *Vietnam War Films: Over 600 Feature, Made-for-TV, Pilot, and Short Movies, 1939–1992, from the United States, Vietnam, France, Belgium, Australia, Hong Kong, South Africa, Great Britain, and Other Countries.* Jefferson, N.C.: McFarland.

As the subtitle of the states, Malo and Williams have compiled an international list of films and made-for-TV movies on the Vietnam War. Films are included if they represent Southeast Asia before or after the war, show images of the war or the home front (including the antiwar movement) during French or American involvement, or show the aftermath of the war by depicting veterans or refugees. Each film receives a detailed synopsis followed by comments that analyze the film's relation to the war. Appendixes include a chronology, countries of origin, directors, writers, and actors, and a list of films the authors were unable to view. Includes a bibliography and index.

WESTERNS

810. Buscombe, Edward, and Christopher Brookeman. 1993. *The BFI Companion to the Western.* New ed. London: A. Deutsch: British Film Institute.

Buscombe and Brookeman have produced another fine film compendium on behalf of the British Film Institute, covering all aspects of the western. Part I is a history of the western genre, and Part II is a "dictionary of people, places, events and ideas which have made their mark on the Western" as well as actions, plot devices, and stereotypical characters. Part III is a selective guide to 300 representative westerns, each with a critical synopsis and a list of principal cast and crew. Part IV is a guide to the full spectrum of actors and filmmakers with career biographies and their western filmographies. Part V is a complete list of western TV series and made-for-TV movies, each briefly described. Appendixes include charts and tables on production, a bibliography, and cross-references for topics, people, and alternative titles that take the place of indexes. This excellent volume belongs in the library of all western film fans and researchers.

811. Lentz, Harris M. 1996. *Western and Frontier Film and Television Credits 1903–1995.* Jefferson, N.C.: McFarland.

Reference book writer Lentz compiled this index to the people who created films and television shows released in the United States that take place in the American West and feature cowboys, Indians, settlers, frontiersmen, and others "involved in the expansion of the United States' borders to the Pacific Ocean." Volume 1 lists credits for actors, directors, producers, and writers. Volume 2 lists films with credits and television series with general credits for the series as well as credits for individual episodes. A minor quibble: the television section has no guide words (just a letter), so it can be difficult to find the beginning of an entry.

812. Miller, Lee O. 1979. *The Great Cowboy Stars of Movies & Television.* New Rochelle, N.Y.: Arlington House.

Miller makes it clear throughout his biography of 44 western stars that he is first and foremost a fan. His book is a paean to the actors who brought westerns to life. Divided into sections on the living, TV stars, and the dead, each entry includes a multipage biography covering life and career followed by a list of western film credits. Additional western stars are named in two appendixes. Names and movies are listed in the index.

813. Pitts, Michael R. 1997. *Western Movies: A TV and Video Guide to 4200 Genre Films, McFarland Classics; 1.* Jefferson, N.C.: McFarland.

Pitts compiled a list of nearly 4,200 westerns available to the public in 1986, and he updated the video sources section for the 1997 edition. The entry for each feature film includes production company, year of release, technical data, director and producer, cast credits, and a brief critical review. Appendixes list cowboys and their horses, screen names, and video sources. Although somewhat dated for video sources, the thorough list of films, the complete name index, and the fact that very few westerns have been produced in recent years means this guide is still useful for fans and researchers interested in the western film genre.

FILM

814. Adams, Les, and Buck Rainey. 1978. *Shoot-Em-Ups: The Complete Reference Guide to Westerns of the Sound Era.* New Rochelle, N.Y.: Arlington House.

815. Rainey, Buck, and Les Adams. 1990. *The Shoot-Em-Ups Ride Again. A Supplement to Shoot-Em-Ups.* Metuchen, N.J.: Scarecrow Press.

Adams and Rainey produced the first comprehensive guide to "every sound Western made since 1928" through 1977. Organized into 12 eras, each chapter features a lengthy essay followed by year-by-year chronological lists of over 3,000 films made, complete with title, production data, cast, director, writer, and producer. The final chapter is a selective list of spaghetti westerns, listing only title, company, U.S. release date, star, and country where produced. The supplement updates for the years 1978–1989, includes 430 overlooked westerns and 100 made-for-television movies, and adds credits for the spaghetti westerns and additional credits for films listed in the original volume. Both volumes have title indexes. Although somewhat dated, the *Shoot-Em-Up* guides are useful because of their comprehensive coverage of the golden era of westerns, particularly the hard-to-research "B" movies.

816.   Fagen, Herb. 2003. *The Encyclopedia of Westerns.* New York: Facts on File.

Western film expert Fagen's goal was "to present the most comprehensive and annotated volume of Westerns available to the public." He has largely succeeded, with over 3,500 feature films listing title, technical data, and principal crew and cast. Synopses are usually brief, but are up to several pages for the most important westerns. "Master entries" list entire series. Appendixes list spaghetti westerns (most do not have separate entries), Oscar-worthy westerns, literary sources, and additional sound and silent films not listed in the body of the filmography. The well-conceived name and title index also serves as a western filmography because it attaches films to names. Fagen has created an excellent western filmography.

817.   Garfield, Brian. 1982. *Western Films: A Complete Guide.* 1st ed. New York: Rawson.

Garfield, a writer of western films and novels, has compiled a one-volume encyclopedia about "A" westerns. After introductory chapters on the western genre as well as discussions of silents, programmers, talkies, directors, writers, crews, and actors, most of the book is devoted to almost 2,000 films entries that list director, writer, and principal cast followed by a plot summary interwoven with the author's opinions. Appendixes cover documentaries, westerns made for children, and made-for-TV and spaghetti westerns. There is no index, reducing the research value of the introductory chapters. Includes a bibliography.

818.   Hardy, Phil, and Kobal Collection. 1995. *The Overlook Film Encyclopedia. The Western.* 2nd ed. Woodstock, N.Y.: Overlook Press.

Hardy, a popular film writer, has compiled one of the most comprehensive guides to westerns. Arranged chronologically by year and then alphabetically by film title, the encyclopedia includes more than 1,800 films. The description of each film weaves Hardy's evaluation around the plot and ends with a list of the above-the-line crew and cast. He writes an overview of westerns for each decade from the 1930s through the 1980s. Appendixes rank western films and stars by the money they made (including one list that adjusts for inflation), critics' top 10 lists, Oscar winners and nominees, and novels from which westerns were adapted. A final appendix lists hundreds of additional westerns for which no details were available. Includes a bibliography. The index lists only films; the encyclopedia would have been even more useful if the index had also included cast and crew. Revised edition of *The Western* (2nd edition 1991). The British edition is entitled *The Aurum Film Encyclopedia.*

819.   Hanfling, Barrie. 2001. *Westerns and the Trail of Tradition: A Year-by-Year History, 1929–1962.* Jefferson, N.C.: McFarland.

Hanfling, a writer on westerns and the West, produced a year-by-year guide to trends and innovations in the film industry, advances in technology, and evolution of plots as they reflect on the western and on American culture. Each chapter and essay focuses on one year, primarily describing and illustrating the principal players and films. This is not a filmography, although the index does include titles and names.

820.   Hoffmann, Henryk. 2000. *"A" Western Filmmakers: A Biographical Dictionary of Writers, Directors, Cinematographers, Composers, Actors and Actresses.* Jefferson, N.C.: McFarland.

Hoffman has written a biographical dictionary of the actors and filmmakers who made "A" westerns—those western films with high budgets and production values that are defined mostly by not being "B" westerns. He offers separate chapters on writers, screenwriters, directors, cinematographers, composers, leading men, leading ladies, supporting actors, and supporting actresses. To be included, the filmmaker must have appeared in at least three westerns or written at least two. Entries provide a basic biography, a discussion of the work, and a filmography. Appendixes list actors who appeared in one or in two westerns. The index lists film titles and personal names.

821.   Holland, Ted. 1989. *B Western Actors Encyclopedia: Facts, Photos, and Filmographies for More Than 250 Familiar Faces.* Jefferson, N.C.: McFarland.

Holland has compiled a list of the heroes, sidekicks, cowgirls, and bad guys featured in "B" westerns. Arranged alphabetically within the categories just listed, each entry includes a career biography that reflects Holland's lifelong affection for Westerns followed by a complete filmography. For heroes, he lists horses, sidekicks, and leading ladies. For sidekicks, leading ladies, and bad guys, he lists heroes. Appendixes list miscellaneous players, "B" western film series filmographies, and a bibliography. Includes a name index.

822.   Katchmer, George A. 2002. *A Biographical Dictionary of Silent Film Western Actors and Actresses.* Jefferson, N.C.: McFarland.

After 20 years of work, silent film historian Katchmer completed this biographical guide to silent film western actors just before he died in 1997. He includes every actor who appeared in at least three feature westerns or who appeared regularly in shorts. Unlike his earlier book, *Eighty Silent Film Stars* (see entry 729), he includes women as well as men. In alphabetical order by screen name, each entry includes a biography of life and career followed by a silent film filmography—most also include a portrait. In place of an index, an appendix lists films along with the featured actors.

Kid Kowboys: Juveniles in Western Films (see entry 1044)

823.   Lahue, Kalton C. 1971. *Winners of the West: The Sagebrush Heroes of the Silent Screen.* South Brunswick, N.J.: A.S. Barnes.

Popular culture writer Lahue has written in-depth and opinionated explorations of the lives and careers of 38 western stars from the silent era. The book is well illustrated, with each star being featured in portraits and stills. A final chapter features an additional 16 stars, each with a portrait captioned with a brief biography. There is no index.

824.   Langman, Larry. 1992. *A Guide to Silent Westerns, Bibliographies and Indexes in the Performing Arts, No. 13.* New York: Greenwood Press.

Langman, a film historian and writer, has compiled a list of over 5,400 silent westerns. Listed in alphabetical order by title, he includes the date of release, director, cinematographer, and cast. Except in those cases in which the film is unavailable for viewing, he also includes a brief synopsis. Appendixes list serials, series, epics, and westerns from the Northwest. The index lists personal names.

825. Magers, Boyd, and Michael G. Fitzgerald. 1999. *Westerns Women: Interviews with 50 Leading Ladies of Movie and Television Westerns from the 1930s to the 1960s.* Jefferson, N.C.: McFarland.

826. Fitzgerald, Michael G., and Boyd Magers. 2002. *Ladies of the Western: Interviews with Fifty More Actresses from the Silent Era to the Television Westerns of the 1950s and 1960s.* Jefferson, N.C.; London: McFarland.

Magers and Fitzgerald interviewed 50 female western stars to write interesting and extensive biographies of each with selective lists of the films in which they appeared. The index points to the stars, the films, and the people mentioned in the interviews. The companion volume *Ladies of the Western* contains 50 more interviews.

827. McClure, Arthur F., and Ken D. Jones. 1972. *Heroes, Heavies and Sagebrush; a Pictorial History of the "B" Western Players.* South Brunswick, N.J.: A.S. Barnes.

McClure has written a biographical guide to the actors who appeared in "B" westerns before the 1970s. Divided into chapters on heroes, sidekicks, heavies, Indians, and assorted players, each entry includes at least one illustration followed by a career biography and a list of principal films. The book will be of most interest to western fans.

828. Nachbar, John G. 1975. *Western Films: An Annotated Critical Bibliography, Garland Reference Library of the Humanities; Vol. 17.* New York: Garland.

829. Nachbar, John G., Jackie R. Donath, and Chris Foran. 1988. *Western Films 2: An Annotated Critical Bibliography from 1974 to 1987, Garland Reference Library of the Humanities; Vol. 638.* New York: Garland.

Nachbar, Donath, and Foran have compiled an annotated bibliography of scholarly books and articles written about the western. Categories include reference books, criticism, history, and films, filmmakers, and performers. The first volume contains "just under 400 entries that covered almost 75 years of film scholarship." Although it covers only 12 years, the second volume contains more than 700 entries. Appendixes list books published too late to be incorporated into the bibliography and western fan magazines, which are not included in the bibliography at all. Indexes list author, subject, and title. The bibliographies will be of most use to researchers interested in seeing what has been written about westerns.

831. Parish, James Robert, and Michael R. Pitts. 1976. *The Great Western Pictures.* Metuchen, N.J.: Scarecrow Press.

832. Parish, James Robert, and Michael R. Pitts. 1988. *The Great Western Pictures II.* Metuchen, N.J.: Scarecrow Press.

The prolific duo of Parish and Pitts have compiled a list of several hundred feature-length and serial westerns. As with most books they have coauthored, each film entry includes extensive cast and crew information, a detailed plot summary, and a brief discussion of the film. Appendixes list the titles of radio and television westerns and a bibliography of western novels. Unfortunately, there are no actor or character name indexes, reducing the book's usefulness somewhat.

833. Rainey, Buck. 1987. *Heroes of the Range: Yesteryear's Saturday Matinee Movie Cowboys.* Metuchen, N.J.: Scarecrow Press.

Rainey has compiled the complete screen credits for 15 "B" movie cowboy stars. For each, the author includes a photograph, a lengthy biography focusing on the movie star's career, and a chronological filmography. The filmography does more than list the films; it also includes the production company and date of release, the cast, the director, and the screen writer. Indexes list names and film titles.

834. Rainey, Buck. 1996. *The Reel Cowboy: Essays on the Myth in Movies and Literature.* Jefferson, N.C.: McFarland.

Although it is more of a scholarly analysis of the western film genre than a reference guide, Rainey's book is included here for the 200 pages in Part II that list western novelists and the film adaptations that have been made of their works. The most prominent writers, from Zane Grey to James Oliver Curwood, are given their own chapters. The rest are grouped under "others," but each author entry includes a filmography with title, release company and date, and cast and crew credits. *Reel Cowboys* will be of interest to fans and researchers interested in adaptation. Includes a name and title index.

835. Rainey, Buck. 1992. *Sweethearts of the Sage: Biographies and Filmographies of 258 Actresses Appearing in Western Movies.* Jefferson, N.C.: McFarland.

Rainey has compiled the complete screen credits for 258 actresses who were featured in at least eight westerns. Organized by decade, each entry includes a photograph, a biography focusing on career, references, and a chronological filmography. The filmography lists films as well as serials, and includes the production company and date of release, the cast, the director, and the screen writer. Includes a bibliography and a film title index.

836. Rothel, David. 1978. *The Singing Cowboys.* South Brunswick, N.J.: A.S. Barnes.

Rothel interviewed actors who starred as singing cowboys to write biographies of their lives and careers. Seven chapters feature biographies of the most renowned stars complete with a select filmography and discography, while an eighth chapter looks at some lesser-known actors. The indexes list titles and names but do not include the names listed in the credits for the filmographies.

837. Rothel, David. 2001. *Those Great Cowboy Sidekicks.* Rev. and updated ed. Madison, N.C.: Empire.

Rothel writes biographies of 40 actors who played sidekicks in westerns. The in-depth biographies—based on interviews with the actors and the people who knew them—cover lives and careers with portraits and filmographies of their works. Includes a bibliography, a title index, and a general index.

838. Rutherford, John, and Richard B. Smith. 1992. *More Cowboy Shooting Stars: The Encyclopedic Film Credits Tribute to 240 "A" and "B" Western Saddle Heroes Plus 24 Low-Budget Series of the Sound Era.* Madison, N.C.: Empire.

Western historians Rutherford and Smith have compiled western film credits for 240 mostly male western stars. Arranged by name, each entry includes a chronological list of sound films with release year, studio, and running time. The "index" lists studio abbreviations—there is no film title index. Note that *More Cowboy Shooting Stars* completely replaces the authors' original book from 1988 entitled *Cowboy Shooting Stars.*

Universal-International Westerns, 1947–1963: The Complete Filmography (see entry 877)

839.   Weisser, Thomas. 1992. *Spaghetti Westerns: The Good, the Bad, and the Violent: A Comprehensive, Illustrated Filmography of 558 Eurowesterns and Their Personnel, 1961–1977.* Jefferson, N.C.: McFarland.

Many guides to westerns relegate the spaghetti western—westerns made in Europe—to an appendix or do not include them at all. Weisser compiled the first complete guide to spaghetti westerns made between 1961 and 1977 to fill a gap in the literature. Five hundred fifty-eight films are listed in alphabetical order and include English and original language title, release date, principal crew and cast, and a synopsis with brief commentary on the film and the filmmaker. The sections on performers, directors, composers, writers, and cinematographers contain complete lists of the spaghetti westerns they made. Appendixes list Django and Sartana films (two of the more popular series in Europe), American westerns designed to look spaghetti, and top 10 and 20 lists. The filmography is lightly illustrated with stills and posters and includes an index.

Western Movie Quotations (see entry 1105)

TELEVISION

840.   Aaker, Everett. 1997. *Television Western Players of the Fifties: A Biographical Encyclopedia of All Regular Cast Members in Western Series, 1949–1959.* Jefferson, N.C.: McFarland.

Aaker has written biographies of every actor who had a regular role on a western television series during the 1950s. Organized alphabetically by last name, Aaker provides extensive information about each actor, including vitals, family life, show business career, critical reception as an actor, and a complete filmography. An appendix lists the television series; a bibliography lists the sources used; and there is an index to shows and individuals.

841.   Jackson, Ronald. 1994. *Classic TV Westerns: A Pictorial History, Citadel Press Film Series.* Secaucus, N.J.: Carol.

Jackson's heavily illustrated book covers more than 120 westerns from the earliest days of television through the early nineties. Arranged chronologically, each entry includes program credits, cast, and a description of the western. The index points to the shows and to the people named in the text and pictured in photographs. The photographs make this a nice companion to Lentz's *Television Westerns Episode Guide* (see entry 842).

842.   Lentz, Harris M. 1997. *Television Westerns Episode Guide: All United States Series, 1949–1996.* Jefferson, N.C.: McFarland.

This most complete guide to American westerns on television covers 180 series ranging from the earliest days of television to 1996. Arranged alphabetically by series name, each entry begins with the network, length, and broadcast history followed by the regular cast and series premise. Each episode of the series includes title, original air date, guest stars, and a synopsis. The storyline index is an interesting feature offering access to episodes by character and historical names, tribes, institutions, places and locations, and subjects. The personnel index matches people to the shows and episodes on which they worked.

843.   West, Richard. 1987. *Television Westerns: Major and Minor Series, 1946–1978.* Jefferson, N.C.: McFarland.

West lists all 119 westerns that aired on American prime-time television between 1946 and 1978. For each series, he writes about the show, with as much attention paid to its making as to its premise, characters, and stars. Appendixes list shows with cast and character credits, Emmy Award winners, season-by-season ratings winners, alternate titles (usually for syndication), and air times. Includes an index.

7
Formats

One format makes way for another. Each time a new way to screen movies and television shows comes along, technophiles write books in homage. Since DVD is relatively new, there are a handful of resources listed here, but there are no guides to videorecorders. Nor are there guides to tools used to project or broadcast unless they had a direct impact on the film or show.

3-D

844.   Hayes, R. M. 1989. *3-D Movies: A History and Filmography of Stereoscopic Cinema.* Jefferson, N.C.: McFarland.

Hayes has written a history and compiled a filmography of 3-D movies. The first six chapters cover the history of 3-D from its early years through each of its iterations. The largest part of the book is the most comprehensive international filmography of 3-D movies available. Listed in alphabetical order by original title, each entry includes year of release, 3-D technique, credits for crew and cast, and a commentary on the move and its artistry. As might be expected, illustrations don't do justice to the 3-D process. The final chapter lists "all currently available stereoscopic formats and from whom they can be secured." Includes an index.

DVD

845.   Bracke, Peter M. 2004. *Ultimate DVD: The Essential Guide to Building Your DVD Collection.* Berkley trade pbk. ed. New York: Berkley Books.

Bracke recommends the best 100 films available on DVD, not just for the film itself, but for the quality of the visual, aural, and extra presentations. For each film, he writes a summary, describes the extra "goodies,", and discusses the technical quality. A dozen interviews are scattered through the book, along with a description of aspect ratios and a glossary of terms. For fans who love the technology behind the movie as much as the movie itself.

846.   Hunt, Bill, and Todd Doogan. 2004. *The Digital Bits Insider's Guide to DVD.* Special ed. New York: McGraw-Hill.

Hunt and Doogan, reporters for the *Digital Bits* Web site <http://www.thedigitalbits.com>, have written a guide to DVD technology and the best films available in the format. After chapters that explain DVD technology and how to build a home theater system, they list over 100 of the best films by genre. Each entry describes the film, but focuses primarily on the visual, aural, and extras that qualified the film for inclusion on the list. The *Digital Bits* Web site has reviews for over 2,000 DVDs at <http://www.thedigitalbits.com/dvdmenu.html>. For fans who love the technology behind the movie as much as the movie itself.

847.   Scheuer, Steven H., and Alida Brill-Scheuer. 2003. *The Pocket Guide to Collecting Movies on DVD: Building an Essential Movie Collection.* New York: Pocket Books.

The Scheuers have compiled a guide to some 150 of the best films available on DVD. To be included, a DVD must be a high-quality transfer and should offer worthwhile supplementary materials. Films are listed in alphabetical order by title, and entries contain principal cast, director, writer, release year, rating, and a critical summary and overview of the extras. Includes an actor index.

SOUND

848.   Kay, Jonathan, Kimber Ghent, Brian Chumney, and Erik Lutkins. *Film Sound History* [World Wide Web Resource]. Address: http://www.mtsu.edu/~smpte/timeline.html. [Accessed: March 2005].

Members of the Society of Motion Pictures and Television Engineers of Middle Tennessee State University have developed a timeline of film sound from the 1920s through the 1990s. Organized by decade, most developments are covered in one paragraph that describes the technology and its significance. More significant developments are given more in-depth coverage. Although the site as a whole gives a nice overview of sound in cinema, it would benefit from an introductory overview of its own.

WIDE-SCREEN

849.   Carr, Robert E., and R. M. Hayes. 1988. *Wide Screen Movies: A History and Filmography of Wide Gauge Filmmaking.* Jefferson, N.C.: McFarland.

Carr and Hayes have written an excellent overview of wide-screen movies. The first half of the book is a history of the various wide-screen processes and the films that were made with them. The second half of the book is a filmography of wide- and large-screen movies. For each entry, the authors list title, date of release, wide-screen process, and principal crew and cast. The index includes everything but the film titles in the filmography.

850.   Hart, Martin B. *American Widescreen Museum* [World Wide Web Resource]. Address: http://www.widescreenmuseum.com. [Accessed: January 2005].

Hart's lavishly illustrated Web site describes the history of wide-screen technology as well as the development of color cinematography and milestones in sound technology. The wide-screen portion of the museum is divided into nine wings, each describing one technology with specs, references, and a filmography. Because the Web site deals only with older technologies, there is a useful set of links to pages that describe wide- and large-screen systems in use today. The color and sound portions are newer additions to the pages and are not as comprehensive, offering overviews of various color and sound processes.

8
Studios

There are published filmographies of the complete oeuvre of virtually all U.S. studios, including major early studios, the Big Five studios, the Little Three studios, and the Poverty Row studios. Studios outside of the United States aren't as well represented, but a handful of filmographies have been published.

Hollywood on the Palisades: A Filmography of Silent Features Made in Fort Lee, New Jersey, 1903–1927 (see entry 722)

852.   Pitts, Michael R. 1997. *Poverty Row Studios, 1929–1940: An Illustrated History of 53 Independent Film Companies, with a Filmography for Each.* Jefferson, N.C.: McFarland.

This most complete guide to independent movie making in the thirties and forties lists 53 different companies. For each, Pitts writes a short history that includes a sampling of its movies followed by complete filmographies. Most films receive the standard treatment, listing cast and crew with a short synopsis, but a handful of films receive detailed plot summaries and discussion. Because they were already covered by Okuda (see entry 853), Pitts left out several Poverty Row studios.

853.   Okuda, Ted. 1989. *Grand National, Producers Releasing Corporation, and Screen Guild/Lippert: Complete Filmographies with Studio Histories.* Jefferson, N.C.: McFarland.

Okuda continues his complete history and filmographies of independent film production companies by covering Grand National, Producers Releasing Corporation, and Screen Guild/Lippert. For each of these "poverty row" studios, he writes a brief history of the company and its films followed by a complete filmography. For each film, he lists director, producer, story credits, and cast followed by a one-sentence description. A short bibliography is followed by name and title indexes. The book will be most useful to readers as a quick reference when researching minor studios or their "B" films and nicely supplements Pitts's book on 53 other studios (see entry 852).

ALLIED ARTISTS

854.   Martin, Len D. 1993. *The Allied Artists Checklist: The Feature Films and Short Subjects of Allied Artists Pictures Corporation, 1947–1978.* Jefferson, N.C.: McFarland.

Martin has compiled a catalog of all the films produced by Allied Artists. For each of the 452 films—most of them feature films—he lists technical information, principal crew and cast, and a brief plot synopsis. Appendixes list film titles by release date, movie series, western players and their movies, and Academy Award nominees. Includes a personal name index.

AMERICAN INTERNATIONAL PICTURES

855.   Ottoson, Robert. 1985. *American International Pictures: A Filmography, Garland Reference Library of the Humanities; Vol. 492.* New York: Garland.

Ottoson has created a catalog of all of the mostly "B" movies made by American International Pictures from 1954 until it went out of business in 1979. Arranged chronologically, each film entry includes director, screenwriter, cinematographer, above-the-line cast, and a one-paragraph plot summary with only occasional evaluative comments. Includes title and name indexes.

BIOGRAPH COMPANY

856.   Bowser, Eileen. 1973. *Biograph Bulletins, 1908–1912.* New York: Octagon Books.

857.   Niver, Kemp R., and Bebe Bergsten. 1971. *Biograph Bulletins, 1896–1908.* Los Angeles: Locare Research Group.

Niver has compiled a set of reproductions of all but a dozen bulletins distributed by the Biograph Company. They are arranged chronologically, beginning in the first volume with handbills advertising the studio's earliest attempts with thumb books, flip cards, peep shows, and Vitascopes from 1896 through 1908. The second volume continues with the films D. W. Griffith made between 1908 and 1912 (1908 is duplicated in each volume). The handbills generally include a title, a subtitle, length and price per foot, a still, a detailed plot summary, and contact information. The bills can be useful for researchers analyzing the plots of the earliest films. They are of limited value for identifying actors, because the earliest films did not list credits, although Griffith's cameraman, G. W. (Billy) Bitzer, did annotate by hand many of the stills with names. Indexes in the first volume list name, title, and cameramen; the second volume indexes only titles.

COLUMBIA PICTURES CORPORATION

858.   Hirschhorn, Clive. 1999. *The Columbia Story.* London; New York: Hamlyn; Distributed in the United States and Canada by Sterling.

Part of the excellent *Story* series on studio histories, Hirschhorn's compilation is a chronological list of the films produced by Columbia between 1928 and 1988. Columbia was not known for its silents, so most films released between 1922 and 1930 are briefly listed in a sidebar. For select films from that period and all subsequent years, films are treated to a summary laced with commentary and a narrative of credits. The book is lavishly illustrated with over 1,000 stills and publicity photos. Appendixes list serials, series, westerns, cartoons, shorts, Oscar winners, documentaries, British films, and foreign and independent films. Researchers interested in the studio will benefit from the historical overview and the extensive film and personnel indexes.

859.   Martin, Len D. 1991. *The Columbia Checklist: The Feature Films, Serials, Cartoons, and Short Subjects of Columbia Pictures Corporation, 1922–1988.* Jefferson, N.C.: McFarland.

Martin has compiled a catalog of all of the films produced by Columbia Pictures between 1922 and 1988. For each of the 3,111 feature films, serials, and cartoons, he lists technical information, principal crew and cast, and a brief plot synopsis. Appendixes list movie series, western stars and their movies, shorts, and Academy Award nominees. Includes a personal name index.

860. Okuda, Ted, and Edward Watz. 1986. *The Columbia Comedy Shorts: Two-Reel Hollywood Film Comedies, 1933–1958.* Jefferson, N.C.: McFarland.

Based on interviews with the original filmmakers, archival research, and viewing, Okuda and Watz pay homage to the two-reel shorts made by Columbia between 1933 and 1958. Although best known for the *Three Stooges,* Columbia made dozens of series for a total of 526 shorts. The book begins with a historical review of Columbia's short subjects department and the people who made the films. The largest section describes each series in great detail and then lists all the films in the series by name with date released, complete cast, and a one-sentence synopsis. The final section provides biographical sketches of the performers featured in at least 10 films. Includes a bibliography and a name and title index.

861. Perry, Jeb H. 1991. *Screen Gems: A History of Columbia Pictures Television from Cohn to Coke, 1948–1983.* Metuchen, N.J.: Scarecrow Press.

In the second of his books about a television studio, Perry lists the television shows produced by Screen Gems and Columbia Pictures. He begins with an extensive corporate history beginning with the founding of Columbia Pictures in 1924 and continuing with the incorporation of Screen Gems as its television production arm in 1948. The history chronologically covers finances and production highlights. Sections on programming include series, telefeatures, pilots, and specials. Each entry contains title, network, broadcast history, number of episodes, length, sponsors, a synopsis, cast, and credits. Perry provides a separate program chronology and a list of Emmy Award nominees and winners. The name index is described as "selective"—it is not clear who is omitted, but it seems like regular cast, directors, and production crew are listed.

EALING STUDIOS

862. Barr, Charles. 1998. *Ealing Studios.* 3rd ed. Berkeley: University of California Press.

Barr's essays chronologically examine the films produced by Ealing Studios from 1938 until it closed down in 1959. He reviews each film individually and also in the context of the times. The book includes numerous black-and-white stills. One appendix chronologically lists production data and credits for each film while the other offers biographies and filmographies of the Ealing "creative elite." Includes a title index.

EDISON MOTION PICTURES

863. Musser, Charles. 1997. *Edison Motion Pictures, 1890–1900: An Annotated Filmography.* Gemona (UD) Italy; Washington, D.C.: Giornate del Cinema Muto; Smithsonian Institution Press.

Professor Musser has compiled a complete list of all known Edison films made between 1890 and 1900. The book begins with a history of early motion pictures. The filmography is then arranged chronologically by release date; each of the 936 entries includes title, length, copyright, producer, camera, cast, production date, location, source, and a description of the action. Most are illustrated with a still. Added materials include a timeline of Thomas Edison and his film company, a bibliography, and film, name, and subject indexes.

GRAND NATIONAL PICTURES

Grand National, Producers Releasing Corporation, and Screen Guild/Lippert: Complete Filmographies with Studio Histories (see entry 853)

HAMMER FILM PRODUCTIONS

864.   Hunter, Jack. 2000. *House of Horror: The Complete Hammer Films Story.* New ed. London: Creation.

House of Horror traces the history of Hammer Films, with chapters covering its schlock science fiction, monster, and psycho movies. The appendixes provide the most reference value, including biographies of filmmakers and actors who worked regularly for Hammer, lists of unfinished films, and a complete filmography. The filmography lists the movies chronologically, including title, year of release, and principal cast and crew. For a summary of the film, it is necessary to use the title index to find the chapter in which the film is discussed. Lavish black-and-white illustrations give a feel for the Hammer oeuvre.

865.   Johnson, Tom, and Deborah Del Vecchio. 1996. *Hammer Films: An Exhaustive Filmography.* Jefferson, N.C.: McFarland.

Hammer devotees Johnson and Del Vecchio have compiled an exhaustive list of Hammer Films that were made from the time the studio was formed in 1935 until it closed its doors in 1979 (Hammer has since resumed production). Organized chronologically by release date, each entry includes film title, complete cast and crew credits, a critical plot summary, and one or more stills or posters. Added materials include lists of short subjects and television productions, a bibliography, and an index. With separate entries for each film, *Hammer Films* is easier to use as a reference than *House of Horror* (see entry 864).

LIPPERT PICTURES

Grand National, Producers Releasing Corporation, and Screen Guild/Lippert: Complete Filmographies with Studio Histories (see entry 853)

MGM

866.   Eames, John Douglas, and Ronald Bergan. 1993. *The MGM Story: The Complete History of Sixty-Nine Roaring Years.* Rev. ed. London: Hamlyn.

Part of the excellent *Story* series on studio histories, Eames and Bergan have compiled a chronological list of all the films produced by MGM in the United States and in Great Britain. Each year begins with a historical overview. Each film is treated to a paragraph describing its plot, naming its stars, and commenting on its production and quality. The book is lavishly illustrated with over 1,000 stills and publicity photos and includes an index.

MONOGRAM PICTURES CORPORATION

867.   Okuda, Ted. 1987. *The Monogram Checklist: The Films of Monogram Pictures Corporation, 1931–1952.* Jefferson, N.C.: McFarland.

Okuda has compiled a catalog of all of the films produced by Monogram Pictures. For each of the 727 films—most of them feature films—he lists technical information, principal crew and cast, and a brief plot synopsis. Indexes list film titles and personal names.

PARAMOUNT PICTURES CORPORATION

868.   Eames, John Douglas. 1985. *The Paramount Story.* 1st ed. New York: Crown.

Part of the excellent *Story* series on studio histories, Eames has compiled a chronological list of the approximately 2,800 films produced by Paramount between 1916 and 1984. Most films released between 1916 and 1925 are briefly listed in a separate section at the back. For select films from that period and all subsequent years, films are treated to a summary laced with commentary and a narrative of credits. A handful of films each year are relegated to an "other releases" sidebar that includes only principal cast, director, producer, and a one-sentence description. The book is lavishly illustrated with over 1,000 stills and publicity photos. Researchers interested in the studio will benefit from the historical overview, lists of Academy Award nominations and winners, and the extensive film and personnel indexes.

869.   Parish, James Robert. 1972. *The Paramount Pretties.* New Rochelle, N.Y.: Arlington House.

Although there is no introductory material whatsoever to explain his purpose, Parish follows the format of his many other biographical books by devoting substantial space to 16 women featured by Paramount during the Studio years. In each chapter, Parish physically describes the actress and then describes in great detail her life and career. Chapters conclude with a filmography and a series of black-and-white publicity stills. Again without explanation, an appendix gives career biographies for nine directors who presumably directed many of the Paramount films. Useful for the depth of the essays, the lack of an index makes this primarily of use to researchers interested in one of the 16 stars featured in the book.

870.   Waldman, Harry, and Anthony Slide. 1998. *Paramount in Paris: 300 Films Produced at the Joinville Studios, 1930–1933, with Credits and Biographies.* Lanham, Md.: Scarecrow Press.

Waldman and Slide have written a dictionary of the foreign-language films made by Paramount Pictures at the Joinville Studios in France between 1930 and 1933. Chapters cover films and filmmakers in 11 languages. The entries for filmmakers and actors discuss life, career, and list films. The entries for films include the original title, major crew and cast, a brief synopsis, and notes on the film's reception. Unfortunately, there are no cumulative indexes and no cross-references from the English-language titles, making it necessary to know the language in which a film was made.

PRODUCERS RELEASING CORPORATION

871.   Dixon, Wheeler W. 1986. *Producers Releasing Corporation: A Comprehensive Filmography and History.* Jefferson, N.C.: McFarland.

Dixon has compiled a list of all of the films made by Producers Releasing Corporation (PRC), one of the "poverty row" studios in the 1940s. The book includes chapters on the studio's history, corporate structure, industry statistics, and the "B" movie structure. Of most reference value are the sections that provide career biographies of key personnel with filmographies and a checklist of all films produced by PRC. The index is complete, but it is necessary to look under "PRC, Works of" to see where films are mentioned in the text.

Grand National, Producers Releasing Corporation, and Screen Guild/Lippert: Complete Filmographies with Studio Histories (see entry 853)

REPUBLIC PICTURES CORPORATION

872.   Hayes, R. M. 1991. *The Republic Chapterplays: A Complete Filmography of the Serials Released by Republic Pictures Corporation, 1934–1955.* Jefferson, N.C.; London: McFarland.

Hayes, a producer and writer, has compiled a complete list of the serials produced by Republic Pictures. He provides the complete credits for every serial, listing title, credits, and chapter titles. The index points to titles of serials and chapters and to personal names.

873.   Martin, Len D. 1998. *The Republic Pictures Checklist: Features, Serials, Cartoons, Short Subjects, and Training Films of Republic Pictures Corporation, 1935–1959.* Jefferson, N.C.: McFarland.

Martin has compiled a catalog of all the films produced by Republic Pictures. For each of the 1,084 feature films, serials, shorts, and training films, he gives technical information, principal crew and cast, and a brief plot synopsis. Appendixes list film titles by release date, Academy Awards, movie series, and western stars and their movies. Includes a personal name index.

RKO RADIO PICTURES

874.   Jewell, Richard B., and Vernon Harbin. 1982. *The RKO Story.* 1st ed. New York: Arlington House.

Part of the excellent *Story* series on studio histories, Jewell has compiled a chronological list of the films produced by RKO from 1929 until the studio ceased production in 1960. Films are treated to a summary laced with commentary and a narrative of credits. The book is lavishly illustrated with hundreds of stills and publicity photos. Researchers interested in the studio will benefit from the historical overview of the company, the information on RKO films that were produced and distributed in Great Britain, lists of Academy Award nominations and winners, and the extensive film and personnel indexes.

875. Neibaur, James L. 1994. *The RKO Features: A Complete Filmography of the Feature Films Released or Produced by RKO Radio Pictures, 1929–1960.* Jefferson, N.C.: McFarland.

Neibaur has produced a comprehensive guide to the feature films released by RKO Pictures from 1929 to 1960. After a brief historical overview of the studio, films are listed in alphabetical order by title. Each entry includes title, release year, genre, technical data, above-the-line production credits, complete cast credits, and a plot synopsis. Includes a name index.

SCREEN GUILD PRODUCTIONS

Grand National, Producers Releasing Corporation, and Screen Guild/Lippert: Complete Filmographies with Studio Histories (see entry 853)

20TH CENTURY FOX

876. Thomas, Tony, and Aubrey Solomon. 1985. *The Films of 20th Century-Fox: A Pictorial History.* Rev. and enl. ed. Secaucus, N.J.: Citadel Press.

Thomas and Solomon have compiled a complete guide to the films produced by 20th Century Fox between 1935 and 1979. Organized by year and then by film title, each entry includes principal crew and cast and a plot summary with a one-sentence commentary. An appendix lists the title, director, and stars for Fox Films productions made from 1914 to 1935. The book is lightly illustrated and includes a title index.

UNIVERSAL PICTURES AND
UNIVERSAL-INTERNATIONAL

877. Blottner, Gene. 2000. *Universal-International Westerns, 1947–1963: The Complete Filmography.* Jefferson, N.C.: McFarland.

Blottner has compiled a complete list of the 114 westerns made by Universal-International studios. In alphabetical order by title, entries include an advertising blurb, cast and credits, location, source, and a story summary followed by notes and commentary and excerpts from reviews. Blottner includes a superfluous appendix that lists the films alphabetically by title and a more useful chronological listing. Includes a bibliography and index.

878. Braff, Richard E. 1999. *The Universal Silents: A Filmography of the Universal Motion Picture Manufacturing Company, 1912–1929.* Jefferson, N.C.: McFarland.

Braff has compiled a catalog of all the silent films produced by the Universal Motion Picture Manufacturing Company between 1912 and 1929. For each of the 9,397 silent movies, he lists technical information and principal crew and cast. An appendix lists serials and episodes. Includes a personal name index.

879. Fitzgerald, Michael G. 1977. *Universal Pictures: A Panoramic History in Words, Pictures, and Filmographies.* New Rochelle, N.Y.: Arlington House.

Fitzgerald has compiled a complete guide to the films produced by Universal Pictures between 1930 and 1976 and the stars who appeared in them. A 120-page history describes the company and explores its musicals, comedies, westerns, and horror films. The next section lists all the studio's awards. A biography section contains career highlights and filmographies for its leading stars. The largest section of the book chronologically lists Universal's films, shorts, and cartoons with above-the-line crew and cast and character credits, genre, length, month of release, and a one-sentence synopsis. Songs are listed for musicals. The book is lavishly illustrated throughout and includes a name and title index.

880. Perry, Jeb H. 1983. *Universal Television: The Studio and Its Programs, 1950–1980.* Metuchen, N.J.: Scarecrow Press.

Media historian Perry has compiled a complete "catalog of more than 200 series, 250 telefeatures, 20 pilots and 20 specials" produced by Universal Television and its predecessor Revue Productions from the earliest days of television through 1980. Each entry includes where and when the show was aired, a brief synopsis, and cast and credits. Includes an introduction documenting the history of Universal Television, a section listing Emmy Award winners, appendixes on "theatrical films edited from series episodes" and "theatrical films based on series," and a comprehensive name index. Due to the diligence with which Perry gathered information, this is the most complete guide to the Universal Television shows.

881. Soister, John T. 1999. *Of Gods and Monsters: A Critical Guide to Universal Studios' Science Fiction, Horror, and Mystery Films, 1929–1939.* Jefferson, N.C.: McFarland.

Soister has written a guide to the more than 40 monster films Universal Studios made between 1929 and 1939. For each film, he writes a detailed plot summary replete with commentary, production notes, illustrations, production data, and cast and crew credits. Appendixes list the Shadow Detective and the Radio Murder Mystery shorts. Includes a bibliography and an index.

VITAGRAPH COMPANY OF AMERICA

882. Slide, Anthony, and Alan Gevinson. 1987. *The Big V: A History of the Vitagraph Company.* New and rev. ed. Metuchen, N.J.: Scarecrow Press.

Slide has written a comprehensive reference guide to the Vitagraph Company. After chapters covering the company's history, its two cofounders, its major stars, and its major films, the appendixes offer the true reference materials. The "who's who" contains career biographies for 50 prominent Vitagraph filmmakers and players not previously mentioned in the book. The filmography chronologically lists all Vitagraph Company films made between 1910 and 1915 complete with release date, length, and director. It is necessary to consult the name and title index to supplement the lists in the appendixes.

WALT DISNEY COMPANY

883.   Cotter, Bill. 1997. *The Wonderful World of Disney Television: A Complete History.* 1st ed. New York: Hyperion.

Cotter provides an insider's look at the television shows made by Disney. He begins with a history of the early days and a description of the specials that launched Disney on television. He follows with the anthology series, the "Mickey Mouse Club" and "Zorro," and the later series. Cotter devotes whole sections to Disney animation, the Disney Channel on cable, and Touchstone Television. For each episode of each show, Cotter provides the title, air dates, a complete cast list, and a description of the show. Separate appendixes lists the production credits for each episode of all Disney productions except the Touchstone shows, for which the author provides summarized credits for each season. Strangely, there is no index. The table of contents points readers toward the shows, but it is impossible to find episodes by title or to look up cast and crew by name. Aside from this lamentable limitation, the book is useful in that it provides the only episode-by-episode look at Disney's television output.

884.   Holliss, Richard, and Brian Sibley. 1988. *The Disney Studio Story.* 1st ed. New York: Crown.

Holliss and Sibley have written a lavishly illustrated historical guide to everything Disney. Part I looks at the history of film, cartoons, television, and theme parks. Part II offers a chronological filmography of all shorts and features made by Disney through 1987. Each entry includes title, featured characters, and a short description. Supplementary materials include a list of Academy Award winners, a bibliography, a title index, and a general index.

885.   Maltin, Leonard. 2000. *The Disney Films.* 4th ed. New York: Disney Editions.

Maltin describes in detail every Disney feature film. Organized chronologically, each film entry includes title, release date, cast and crew credits, song lists, a critical review that places the film in the context of its times, and plenty of black-and-white illustrations. Films made after Disney's death are surveyed in chapters by era, as are cartoon shorts and TV shows. Maltin has produced a nice guide, especially for the years Disney himself ran the show. Includes an index.

886.   Smith, Dave. 1998. *Disney A to Z: The Updated Official Encyclopedia.* Updated ed. New York: Hyperion.

Smith has compiled the official dictionary of everything Disney, including the movies and cartoons, the television shows, the theme parks, the characters, and the people who made them happen. All entries are interfiled alphabetically, with a complete list of feature films, animated features, television shows, Academy Awards, and characters such as Mickey Mouse and Goofy. Entries provide plot summaries or describe park attractions. Biographies focus exclusively on work with Disney. Includes illustrations and a bibliography.

WARNER BROS.

887. Hirschhorn, Clive. 1979. *The Warner Bros. Story.* New York: Crown.

Part of the excellent *Story* series on studio histories, Hirschhorn has compiled a chronological list of the feature films released by Warner Bros. in the United States between 1918 and 1978. Each decade and each year receives a brief introduction, and films are treated to a summary laced with commentary and a narrative of credits. The book is lavishly illustrated with over 1,000 stills and publicity photos. An appendix lists the Warner Bros. Teddington Studios productions. Includes an extensive film and personnel index.

The Warner Brothers Cartoons (see entry 467)

888. Woolley, Lynn, Robert W. Malsbary, and Robert G. Strange. 1985. *Warner Bros. Television: Every Show of the Fifties and Sixties, Episode by Episode.* Jefferson, N.C.: McFarland.

Woolley, Malsbary, and Strange have compiled a guide to every episode of every television series produced by Warner Bros. for ABC television during the 1950s and 1960s. After a brief introductory section, each chapter is devoted to one series. The chapters describe in detail the series and their stars and contain a one-sentence synopsis of each episode. Includes a name index.

9
Portrayals

The resources in this chapter focus on how groups of people are portrayed in film and television. People are listed by ethnic group, gender, sexual orientation, physical challenge, and occupation. In some cases, the books also focus on filmmakers and performers from each group. (See also the section on characters.)

ETHNIC GROUPS (SEE ALSO *NATIONAL CINEMA*)

889.   Abrash, Barbara, and Catherine Egan. 1992. *Mediating History: The MAP Guide to Independent Video by and about African American, Asian American, Latino, and Native American People.* New York: New York University Press.

The Media Alternatives Project (MAP) is dedicated to introducing "multicultural perspectives into American history teaching in colleges and universities through the use of independent film and video." Its guide lists 126 independent videos made by African Americans, Asian Americans, Chicanos, Puerto Ricans, and Native Americans about themselves. Entries list title, director, length, production company, and a summary with commentary. The guide also contains essays, a guide to alternative media sources, a list of distributors, and title, subject, and chronological indexes.

890.   Gevinson, Alan. 1997. *Within Our Gates: Ethnicity in American Feature Films, 1911–1960.* Berkeley: University of California Press.

The American Film Institute has compiled a catalog of "2,464 films made between 1911 and 1960 that portray the experiences and perspectives of the many ethnic groups comprising America's rich cultural fabric." The films are arranged in alphabetical order by title, making it necessary to consult the ethnic category index to research movies about a particular ethnic group. The entries follow the same format as the *AFI Catalog* (see entries 391 to 393); they provide technical information, exhaustively listing cast and crew credits, and describe the plot in great detail. In addition to the ethnic category index, there are chronological, personal name, subject, and foreign-language indexes—all are superb.

891.   Oshana, Maryann. 1985. *Women of Color: A Filmography of Minority and Third World Women.* New York: Garland.

Oshana has compiled a list of "English-language films whose characters include a woman of color, specifically an American woman character who belongs to a minority group or a woman of the Third World." Nearly 850 films made between 1930 and 1983 are listed alphabetically by title and include a minority or Third World/country of origin classification, year of release, principal crew and cast, and a synopsis describing the plot and the character. Indexes list films by actress and by classification. Useful in locating films that feature minority or Third World women as long as researchers keep in mind the publication date.

892.   Parish, James Robert, and T. Allan Taylor. 2003. *The Encyclopedia of Ethnic Groups in Hollywood, The Facts on File Film Reference Library.* New York: Facts on File.

Reference book writers Parish and Taylor have written an excellent guide to "the treatment and progress of five ethnic groups" in American cinema: African Americans, Asian Americans, Hispanic Americans, Jewish Americans, and Native Americans. Parish examines "not only how each group was represented or *not* represented on screen but also how the U.S. entertainment industry dealt with talent from each of these minority communities." Each of the five chapters consists of an interfiled list of films, filmmakers, and topics. Film entries include director, writer, cast, and a summary discussing the treatment of characters as well as the ethnic group in general. Filmmaker entries provide a career biography that highlights prominent works. Topical entries provide history and context and describe examples from films. Most entries include extensive cross-references, and there is a good index as well. Parish and Taylor have made no attempt to seek commonalities across the five ethnic groups, but the separate chapters warrant consultation in and of themselves.

893.   Signorielli, Nancy, Elizabeth Milke, and Carol Katzman. 1985. *Role Portrayal and Stereotyping on Television: An Annotated Bibliography of Studies Relating to Women, Minorities, Aging, Sexual Behavior, Health, and Handicaps, Bibliographies and Indexes in Sociology; No. 5.* Westport, Conn.: Greenwood Press.

The Corporation for Public Broadcasting sponsored this bibliography of 423 scholarly articles and book chapters that examines "women and sex-roles, racial and ethnic minorities, age-roles, sexual behavior and orientations, and health and handicaps." Entries include a standard bibliographic citation and an annotation describing the results of the study. Although dated, the focus on scholarship makes this a nice addition to the literature. Includes author and subject indexes.

AFRICAN AMERICANS

894.   Black Film Center/Archives. *Black Film Center/Archive Holdings and Collection Information* [World Wide Web Resource]. Black Film Center/Archive Department of Afro-American Studies Indiana University. Address: http://www.indiana.edu/~bfca/collection.html. [Accessed: March 2005].

The Black Film Center/Archive (BFC/A) at Indiana University in Bloomington is a "repository of films and related materials by and about African Americans." On its Web site, the BFC/A lists over 1,000 films in alphabetical order by title with release year, genre, length, format, director, and a description of the film with special attention to its portrayal of African Americans. Descriptions usually mention the lead actors' names. The BFC/A does not lend its holdings, so the filmography is best used as a guide to films. The Black Film Center/Archive also sponsors events, publishes the journal *Black Camera,* and hosts a handful of stereotypical shorts from the first years of cinema.

Blacks in Film and Television: A Pan-African Bibliography of Films, Filmmakers, and Performers (see entry 251)

895.   Bogle, Donald. 1988. *Blacks in American Films and Television: An Encyclopedia, Garland Reference Library of the Humanities; Vol. 604.* New York: Garland.

Bogle, a researcher and writer on African Americans in the media, has created an illustrated guide to black performers and filmmakers and the widely distributed mainstream American films and television shows they made. The first section of the encyclopedia lists films in alphabetical order with principal crew and cast and a detailed critical synopsis and discussion of its critical reception and black themes, characters, and stereotypes. The second section gives a similar treatment to television shows and miniseries. A third section profiles black actors and filmmakers with career biographies. Although the encyclopedia could do with an update, it is still one of the best sources for information about African Americans in film and television.

896.   Hill, George H., and Sylvia Saverson Hill. 1985. *Blacks on Television: A Selectively Annotated Bibliography.* Metuchen, N.J.: Scarecrow Press.

The Hills have compiled a bibliography of more than 2,800 books, dissertation and theses, and journal, magazine, and newspaper articles spanning "forty-five years of black involvement in television" from 1939 through the 1983–1984 season. Organized first by format and then by topic, entries are annotated for books and theses (although not for biographies), but are not annotated for journal, magazine, or newspaper articles. This last is unfortunate, because topical headings are broad and article titles are not always self-explanatory. The subject and name index alleviates this problem somewhat, making this a useful guide for researchers interested in the era before television periodicals were well indexed.

897.   Hill, George H., Lorraine Raglin, and Chas Floyd Johnson. 1990. *Black Women in Television: An Illustrated History and Bibliography, Garland Reference Library of the Humanities; Vol. 1228.* New York: Garland.

After 20 pages of photographs and 25 pages of history, the rest of the book is a bibliography of books and articles about African American women with sections on personalities and programs. Only the books and dissertations are annotated. The articles, which come primarily from popular magazines and newspapers, are not. The book would have benefited from annotations throughout and the inclusion of scholarly journals. There are appendixes for awards and starring roles and indexes by author/subject, program and film, and station.

898.   Hyatt, Marshall. 1983. *The Afro-American Cinematic Experience: An Annotated Bibliography & Filmography.* Wilmington, Del.: Scholarly Resources.

The first half of this book is an annotated bibliography of almost 1,000 articles from scholarly journals, popular magazines, and newspapers covering "the black image and the participation of blacks in American films." Although fairly comprehensive on performers, directors, and social commentary, Hyatt only included reviews that "illuminate controversies, clarify intentions, and analyze art." Because the bibliography is in order by author, it is necessary to use the name, title, and subject index. In the second half of the book, Hyatt compiled a filmography of full-length films featuring black directors, performers, or themes. Divided into sections such as "blacks in stereotyped roles" and "black independent films," the first category is films Hyatt considers significant enough to annotate.

The other 10 sections merely list the films. Although now more than 20 years old, the book is still useful for finding older publications and for its lists of films.

899.   James, Darius. 1995. *That's Blaxploitation! Roots of the Baadasssss 'Tude (Rated X by an All-Whyte Jury).* New York: St. Martin's Griffin.

James (AKA Dr. Snakeskin, AKA fan of blaxploitation) has written an entertaining book about blaxploitation films and the people who made them. Most of the chapters are organized by filmmaker; the exceptions being chapters on Shaft (which he disliked), pimps, and panthers. This is not a reference book or a scholarly treatise (there is, in fact, no index) but a praise song to the genre. It is included here because of its lavish illustrations and the films interspersed through each chapter that include producer, director, screenwriter, story, and cast followed by brief commentary.

900.   Jones, G. William. 1991. *Black Cinema Treasures: Lost and Found.* Denton: University of North Texas Press.

Jones, archivist for the Southwest Film-Video Archives at Southern Methodist University, has written a guide to the Tyler, Texas, Black Film Collection, an archive of approximately 100 films made from the 1920s through the 1950s featuring all-black crews and casts. After an introduction and a discussion of some of the most prominent of the filmmakers, the book provides synopses to the nine films in the archive that have been transferred from nitrate to safety film. Each entry includes complete credits, and each synopsis runs several pages and is accompanied by numerous stills. Particularly useful is the appendix that provides a complete list of "all black-cast films meant primarily for black audiences" made by independent filmmakers. A second appendix is a bibliography of books about black independent filmmaking published between 1910 and 1960. Includes a name and title index.

901.   Klotman, Phyllis Rauch. 1979. *Frame by Frame: A Black Filmography.* Bloomington: Indiana University Press.

902.   Klotman, Phyllis Rauch, and Gloria J. Gibson. 1997. *Frame by Frame II: A Filmography of the African American Image, 1978–1994.* Bloomington: Indiana University Press.

Frame by Frame is a project developed by the Black Film Center/Archive in the Department of Afro-American Studies at Indiana University. The aim of the editors was to compile the most comprehensive list of films featuring contributions from African Americans, and in this they were quite successful. Volume 1 covers films made through 1978, and volume 2 extends the list through 1994. Each volume consists of an alphabetical list of film titles. Each entry lists the principal cast and crew and usually includes a brief annotation summarizing the film with emphasis on black themes and characters. Indexes include cast, directors, producers, musicians, and screenwriters. In volume 2, additional sections list distributors, archives, and award winners and include a bibliography.

903.   Koven, Mikel J. 2001. *The Pocket Essential Blaxploitation Films.* Harpenden, England: Pocket Essentials.

Professor Koven's analysis of blaxploitation films focuses on just a few of the key films in the genre. Organized first by lead character and then by theme, he describes each film, discusses its subtext, states his verdict on its quality—including a one- to five-point rating—and lists director, writer, and cast. With just under 40 films, this works better as an exploration of the genre than as a reference book.

904.   Moon, Spencer. 1997. *Reel Black Talk: A Sourcebook of 50 American Filmmakers*. Westport, Conn.: Greenwood Press.

Filmmaker and scholar Moon pays homage to 50 black filmmakers. Each chapter covers an individual filmmaker in depth, giving background, describing the career and its success, discussing film style and techniques, citing influences, and placing careers in context. Moon interviewed the contemporary filmmakers who make up half of the book, adding valuable depth. Each chapter also provides a complete filmography, bibliography, and list of sources consulted along with awards won and select memberships. An appendix lists sources for ordering films, and an index points to names, titles, and subjects. Moon's sourcebook will be helpful to anyone researching black filmmakers because of the depth of information and the primary information from interviews.

905.   Ogle, Patrick, and Facets Multimedia (Chicago). 1994. *Facets African-American Video Guide*. Chicago: Facets Multimedia/Academy Chicago Publishers.

Facets Video, a large video rental store (see entry 88), commissioned a guide to films and videos with a "substantial African-American theme and significant participation by African-American artists." Chapters cover classic recent, blaxploitation, foreign, children's, nonfiction, and Civil Rights films and documentaries about Africa and music. Each film entry includes technical data, credits, a description, information on mid-nineties availability, and price. Indexes point to director, performer, and title.

906.   Parish, James Robert, and George H. Hill. 1989. *Black Action Films: Plots, Critiques, Casts, and Credits for 235 Theatrical and Made-for-Television Releases*. Jefferson, N.C.: McFarland.

Film writer Parish and scholar Hill have compiled a list of 235 action films featuring black performers from the earliest days of filmmaking through the blaxploitation films of the seventies and eighties. Listed in alphabetical order by title, each entry includes production information, principal cast and crew, and an in-depth summary with commentary based both on critical reception and the authors' own evaluation. Includes a name index.

907.   Powers, Anne. 1974. *Blacks in American Movies; a Selected Bibliography*. Metuchen, N.J.: Scarecrow Press.

Powers has compiled a bibliography whose focus is "on general commentary on Blacks in American films," with emphasis on the "social significance of Black involvement in films." Organized by format, there is one short chapter on non-periodical citations; the rest of the book lists magazine and journal articles by subject or name, by periodical, and by date. The bibliography relies on titles for most entries, but Powers does add parenthetical explanations when she deems a title insufficient. Includes an author and subject index. Although dated, the coverage of the 1920s through the early 1970s makes the bibliography useful because that was an era before film periodicals were well indexed.

908.   Richards, Larry. 1998. *African American Films through 1959: A Comprehensive, Illustrated Filmography*. Jefferson, N.C.: McFarland.

Based not only on published scholarly research, but also on articles and ads in African American newspapers, Richards—a librarian and host of a television show showcasing African American films—has compiled the most comprehensive list of 1,324 films and documentaries featuring black casts or stories made between 1895 and 1959. Films are listed in alphabetical order by title and include year of release, director, producer, production and distribution companies, cast, citations to reviews, and a brief plot synopsis. The appendixes could serve as a reference book in their own right, listing credits for actors, film companies, directors, and producers, as well as a film chronology. The book is illustrated throughout with posters from Richards's own collection. Includes a name and title index. Richards credits *Blacks in Black and White* (see entry 909) as a source for some of his information.

909. Sampson, Henry T. 1995. *Blacks in Black and White: A Source Book on Black Films.* 2nd ed. Metuchen, N.J.: Scarecrow Press.

Sampson, an engineer who also writes and lectures on African Americans in film and the performing arts, has written a guide to "the all-Black cast films that were independently produced in the United States between 1910 and 1950." Based on black newspapers, interviews with performers, and collections of memorabilia, he begins with chapters on the overall history, blackface, the Lincoln Motion Picture Company, Oscar Micheaux, and other independent companies before listing the films chronologically by decade. Each entry includes year of release, the company, the cast, and a synopsis. A separate chapter contains career biographies with select filmographies. Appendixes list films in alphabetical order by title, individuals and companies that produced black-cast films, theaters that catered to black patrons, soundies (three-minute musicals), and film credits for performers. The book is illustrated with poster, publicity stills, and memorabilia from private collections and includes a name and title index.

ASIAN AMERICANS

910. Pak, Greg, and Mark Manalo. *Asian American Film & Video Database* [World Wide Web Resource]. Address: http://www.asianamericanfilm.com/filmdatabase. [Accessed: January 2005].

Pak and Manalo designed their *Asian American Film* Web site "to build an engaged, involved, active, and excited audience for Asian American films." They developed a list of over 250 independent films with either Asian American directors or that featured Asian American characters and themes. Organized by film and by filmmaker, each record includes title, genre, director, producer, a synopsis, and contact and distributor information.

HISPANIC AMERICANS

911. Keller, Gary D. 1997. *A Biographical Handbook of Hispanics and United States Film.* Tempe, Ariz.: Bilingual Press/Editorial Bilingüe.

Professor Keller wrote this biographical guide as a companion to his book *Hispanics and United States Film: An Overview and Handbook,* which documented how Hispanics have contributed to filmmaking and how they have been portrayed in cinema.

Assisted by his researcher mother, Keller compiled a list of actors and filmmakers of Hispanic origins. For each person, Keller lists career specialty, dates and places of birth and death, a career biography, and a selective filmography that includes select television credits. The guide is well illustrated, so images are available for many of the actors. The bibliography and the name and title indexes refer to both this handbook and his original study, so it is useful to have both books available while conducting research.

912. Reyes, Luis, and Peter Rubie. 2000. *Hispanics in Hollywood: A Celebration of 100 Years in Film and Television.* Hollywood, Calif.: Lone Eagle.

Reyes and Rubie have written a well-illustrated guide to films and television shows and the Hispanic actors and filmmakers who made them. The "term Hispanic American refers to all people living in the United States who can trace their background to Spain, Portugal or Latin America." After an excellent introduction, the first section of the book describes some 400 films and television shows. Film entries contain title, director, writer, producer, cast, and a plot synopsis. Television show entries contain title, cast, and a summary of the series premise. Both highlight Hispanic themes, characters, and settings. The second section provides career biographies for approximately 500 actors and filmmakers, devoting anywhere from one paragraph to a couple of pages to an exploration of their lives and works. Although lacking an index, this is still an excellent resource for both fans and researchers. The earlier edition of this work was entitled *Hispanics in Hollywood: An Encyclopedia of Film and Television.*

913. Richard, Alfred Charles. 1992. *The Hispanic Image on the Silver Screen: An Interpretive Filmography from Silents into Sound, 1898–1935, Bibliographies and Indexes in the Performing Arts, No. 12.* New York: Greenwood Press.

914. Richard, Alfred Charles. 1993. *Censorship and Hollywood's Hispanic Image: An Interpretive Filmography, 1936–1955, Bibliographies and Indexes in the Performing Arts, No. 14.* Westport, Conn.: Greenwood Press.

915. Richard, Alfred Charles. 1994. *Contemporary Hollywood's Negative Hispanic Image: An Interpretive Filmography, 1956–1993, Bibliographies and Indexes in the Performing Arts, No. 16.* Westport, Conn.: Greenwood Press.

Richard has compiled a chronological list of over 7,000 films that portray Hispanics in the United States or south of the border. Volume 1 covers 1,814 films made between 1898 and 1935 that, for the most part, portrayed Hispanics in a negative light. Volume 2 covers 2,139 films made between 1936 and 1955 during the time of the Hays Code and "Hollywood's Latin love affair" when images of Hispanics were more positive. Volume 3 covers 3,085 films made between 1956 and 1993, when negative images once again abounded. Filmographic essays on the image of Hispanics introduce each volume. In chronological order by year and then alphabetically, each film entry includes original and English-language title, a critical plot summary that discusses "stereotype, a historical interpretation, specific nation, associated behavior and attitudes, and a list of the Hispanic actors and actresses," cross-references, and lists of critical reviews. There are indexes to film titles, actors, locations, and subjects. Richard's monumental work is of interest to researchers investigating the image of Hispanics in film as well as anyone interested in film.

JEWS (SEE ALSO HOLOCAUST)

916.   Anklewicz, Larry. 2000. *Guide to Jewish Films on Video.* Hoboken, N.J.: KTAV.

Anklewicz's list of feature films that have "recognizably Jewish characters" or story lines begins with a chronological history of Jewish film portrayals. The films are listed alphabetically, each including the year of release, director, principal cast, language, and a brief idiosyncratic description of the film and its Jewish elements. Appendixes list the films alphabetically (again) and chronologically, by director, genre, and language, and also provide a list of distributors.

917.   Bernheimer, Kathryn. 1998. *The 50 Greatest Jewish Movies: A Critic's Ranking of the Very Best.* Secaucus, N.J.: Carol.

Bernheimer defines a Jewish movie as "a film that examines an aspect of the Jewish experience and features at least one clearly defined Jewish central character." She has selected films that are of high quality or great influence as well as personal favorites and has made a conscious effort to represent the most prominent Jewish directors and actors. Drawn from over 250 films, she pared the list to 50 and presents them in order from 1 to 50. Her lengthy reviews are engaging, nicely blending plot, Jewish elements, and her evaluation. Many of the reviews discuss other films with similar themes worth watching. The bibliography is extensive, and the index points to names and films that are main entries as well as those mentioned in the text.

918.   Fox, Stuart, Arkhiv Seratim be-Nos'im Yehudiyim 'al Shem Avraham F. Rad, University of Southern California., and World Zionist Organization. Organization and Information Dept. 1976. *Jewish Films in the United States: A Comprehensive Survey and Descriptive Filmography.* Boston: G.K. Hall.

Film scholar Fox has compiled a list of approximately 4,000 feature films, documentaries, and television shows made or released in the United States "having anything to do, in any manner, shape, or form, with Jews and Judaism." Feature films are listed by decade, and entries include title, technical details, producer and distributor, above-the-line cast, and a plot synopsis. Fox included films even if there is no evidence that copies still exist, so not all films include synopses. Additional sections include Yiddish films, films related to Israel, newsreels, documentaries, and television shows. A supplement adds over 400 "films on which information came in after the major survey had been completed." Includes indexes to film titles and subjects. Although dated, *Jewish Films in the United States* is still a significant filmography.

919.   Luterman, Wendy, and Hillel Tryster. *Steven Spielberg Jewish Film Archive* [World Wide Web Resource]. Hebrew University of Jerusalem. 2002 Address: http://spielbergfilmarchive.org.il. [Accessed: March 2005].

The *Steven Spielberg Jewish Film Archive* "holds over 3,000 titles on film and video, constituting the largest collection of Jewish documentary film footage in the world." The catalog is searchable by author, title, and subject. Films may also be searched by producer, technical staff, genre, and language. The *Archive* is in the process of making 500 of its films available online. Listed under the categories that echo its collections covering

Jewish communities, the Holocaust, pre-state, state of Israel, and Hebrew University of Jerusalem, more than 200 documentaries may now be viewed online.

920. Plotkin, Janis, Caroline Libresco, Deborah Kaufman, Sam Ball, and Peter Jacobson. 2000. *Independent Jewish Film: A Resource Guide.* 4th ed. San Francisco: San Francisco Jewish Film Festival.

The editors, organizers of the San Francisco Jewish Film Festival, have compiled a list of independently made feature films and documentaries with Jewish themes and characters. The book begins with six articles on Jewish cinema, including coverage of Holocaust films and American, Arab, and Israeli Jewish cinema. Most of the book is a catalog of films that were featured in the first 20 years of the festival. Listed in alphabetical order, each film includes the country of origin, date released, format, director, and source of the print. The capsule summaries and reviews highlight the Jewish elements in each film. The subject index lists topics such as anti-Semitism, humor, and Sephardic culture. Other indexes list films by country and distributor, and appendixes list Jewish film organizations and programmers. Earlier editions were entitled *Guide to Films Featured in the Jewish Film Festival.*

921. Stevens, Matthew. 1992. *Jewish Film Directory: A Guide to More Than 1200 Films of Jewish Interest from 32 Countries over 85 Years.* Westport, Conn.: Greenwood Press.

The *Jewish Film Directory* is the most comprehensive international list of Jewish films. Films are in alphabetical order by English title and include country of production, date of release, length, format, genre, principal cast and crew, and a very brief synopsis. See references point readers from original title to English-language title. Indexes list director, country of production, subjects, and source material.

NATIVE AMERICANS

922. American Indian Film Institute. 2001. *Films of the American Indian Film Festival 1975–2000.* San Francisco: American Indian Film Institute.

Since 1975, the American Indian Film Institute has held an annual film festival "dedicated to Native Cinema." All 626 films and documentaries screened between 1975 and 2000 are listed in alphabetical order, offering country and year, producer and director, and a description of the film and its making. Most entries include a black-and-white still. If the film is available for rent or purchase, the entry also includes the distributor's address. There is no index. For information about the Institute and its upcoming film festivals, see its Web site at <http://www.aifisf.com>.

923. Bataille, Gretchen M., and Charles L.P. Silet. 1985. *Images of American Indians on Film: An Annotated Bibliography, Garland Reference Library of Social Science; Vol. 307.* New York: Garland.

Bataille and Silet have compiled an annotated bibliography of 194 books and journal articles that discuss the image of American Indians in film, an annotated collection of 170 movie reviews, and a chronological list of 361 films that deal with American Indians. The filmography lists director and principal cast but does not include any summary or discussion, somewhat limiting its use. The bibliography, despite its age, is still useful to researchers seeking information on what has been written on the image of American Indians in film.

924. Hilger, Michael. 1995. *From Savage to Nobleman: Images of Native Americans in Film.* Lanham, Md.: Scarecrow Press.

Hilger has compiled a chronological list of films featuring American Indian characters and themes. After an excellent introduction, filmographic essays introduce chapters on silent films, early sound films, and each decade from the 1950s through the 1990s. Each film includes production company, release year, director, and a summary that pays particular attention to Indian characters, names actors, and includes quotes from reviews. The book concludes with an essay on new images, a bibliography, and general and film title indexes. An earlier edition entitled *The American Indian in Film* had a separate name index that included symbols indicating Indian and non-Indian actors portraying Indians.

925. Weatherford, Elizabeth, Emelia Seubert, and Museum of the American Indian Heye Foundation. 1981. *Native Americans on Film and Video.* New York: Museum of the American Indian/Heye Foundation.

926. Weatherford, Elizabeth, Emelia Seubert, and Museum of the American Indian Heye Foundation. 1988. *Native Americans on Film and Video, Volume II.* New York: Museum of the American Indian/Heye Foundation.

On behalf of the Museum of the American Indian's Film and Video Project, Weatherford and Seubert compiled a list of approximately 400 documentaries and ethnographic films featuring the "Inuit and Indians of North, Central and South America." Selected for their quality, issues covered, and input of Native Americans, most of the documentaries were made in the 1970s. Entries are in alphabetical order by title and include technical data, information about the filmmaker, and a summary. Because it is dated, the resource section on how to acquire the films is, for the most part, useless, but a handy classified subject index pointing to the thoughtful selection of documentaries means this could still be useful to teachers and programmers interested in Native American studies.

GENDER AND SEXUAL ORIENTATION

GAY, LESBIAN, BISEXUAL, TRANSGENDER

Bijou Video: The Complete Reference Guide of Gay Adult Films (see entry 714)

927. Daniel, Lisa, and Claire Jackson. 2003. *The Bent Lens: A World Guide to Gay & Lesbian Film.* 2nd ed. Los Angeles: Alyson Books.

Daniel and Jackson's guide to over 1,700 films that depict gay men or lesbians begins with a series of essays covering lesbians, musicals, and the cinemas of Europe, Asia, and Australia. The book lists movies in alphabetical order by title, including the title, director, technical information, major cast and crew, genre, and a synopsis that summarizes the plot and highlights gay and lesbian elements. Appendixes list films of interest to lesbians, gay men, genres, country of origin, director, distributor, and film festivals, plus a bibliography.

928.   Darren, Alison. 2000. *Lesbian Film Guide.* London; New York: Cassell.

Darren has compiled a list of easily available films that feature lesbian themes or characters. The films are in alphabetical order by title, each including director, screenwriter, production company, and featured cast. A brief synopsis is followed by a longer discussion of the lesbian themes and characters. Indexes list directors, countries of origin, and actors.

929.   Hadleigh, Boze. 2001. *The Lavender Screen: The Gay and Lesbian Films: Their Stars, Makers, Characters, and Critics.* Rev. and updated. ed. New York: Citadel Press.

Hadleigh's history of gay and lesbian films and filmmakers is organized thematically, with almost 50 chapters on such topics as roomies, transsexuals, and dress reversal—featuring just two or three films each. Although the writing is excellent and the book is packed with information, its usefulness is limited as a reference, because there are no indexes.

High Camp: A Gay Guide to Camp and Cult Films (see entry 527)

930.   Howes, Keith. 1993. *Broadcasting It: An Encyclopaedia of Homosexuality in Film, Radio and TV in the UK, 1923–1993, Cassell Lesbian and Gay Studies.* London; New York: Cassell.

Howes's dictionary is chock-full of entries describing how homosexuality was broadcast on British television and radio between 1923 and 1993. Over 3,000 entries describe actors, filmmakers, fictional characters, names, groups of people, jobs, activities, meeting places, politics, songs, words, phrases, and the "secret passages which broadcasting has allowed homosexuals" in series, films, plays, and documentaries (but excluding sports and news). Entries often draw connections between seemingly disparate ideas and are extensively cross-referenced, which is useful, because there is no index. There is nothing quite like this dictionary in its breadth of scope and detailed coverage of British media.

931.   Murray, Raymond. 1998. *Images in the Dark: An Encyclopedia of Gay and Lesbian Film and Video.* Rev. and updated. ed. London: Titan Books.

Murray, a video store operator and gay activist, put together a list of gay and lesbian actors and filmmakers and videos with gay or lesbian themes or characters. The first three chapters cover directors and independent filmmakers, actors, and other behind-the-scenes artists. While international in scope, the majority of the people included are either American or British. Each entry analyzes the body of work, includes quotes from other sources, and lists their most prominent films. Gay icons are highlighted for each decade from the 1930s through the 1980s. Subsequent chapters list films of queer, lesbian, gay male, and transgender interest and camp movies. A chapter on "honorable and dishonorable mentions" covers films featuring gay and lesbian characters in bit roles. Film entries throughout the encyclopedia include technical data, capsule reviews, and commentary on gay themes and characters. Indexes list film titles, directors, personalities, and themes such as adolescence, AIDS, and parenting. Illustrated throughout, the guide is of most interest to film buffs.

932.   Olson, Jenni. 1996. *The Ultimate Guide to Lesbian & Gay Film and Video.* New York: Serpent's Tail.

Begun as a thesis project to create a lesbian filmography, Olson ended up creating a complete list of films and videos shown at the San Francisco Lesbian & Gay Film Festival. Arranged alphabetically by title, each film includes the director, technical details, and a description written by the festival programmers for the festival catalogs. The book also features critics' lists of top films, now dated directories of film and video distributors and festivals, and a festival programming checklist. Indexes point to directors and to broad topics. Although the list of films is not intended to be comprehensive, the more than 2,000 movies provide an excellent overview of lesbian and gay videos and films produced from 1976 through 1996 and decent coverage of earlier cinema. Olson now takes care of the *PopcornQ* Web pages (see entry 934), which contain newer films.

933. Parish, James Robert. 1993. *Gays and Lesbians in Mainstream Cinema: Plots, Critiques, Casts and Credits for 272 Theatrical and Made-for-Television Hollywood Releases.* Jefferson, N.C.: McFarland.

The ever-prolific Parish has compiled a list of mainstream films made between 1914 and 1992 featuring gay or lesbian characters. An introductory filmographic essay places the films in a historical and cultural context and provides a history of the censorship codes. The films are described in great detail with particular attention to gay and lesbian characters and how they are portrayed. Also included are quotes from reviews and cast and crew credits. Includes illustrations, a film chronology, and a name index.

934. *PopcornQ Movies* [World Wide Web Resource]. PlanetOut. Address: http://www.planetout.com/popcornq. [Accessed: March 2005].

PlanetOut hosts *PopcornQ,* a Web site of news, reviews, and previews of gay, lesbian, bisexual, and transgender movies. Movies may be browsed by alphabet, subject, year, or country. Viewers may also search by title, director, or star. Additional pages feature new releases, online cinema, film festivals, short movie awards, and the "Queer Top 10."

935. Stewart, Stephen. 1994. *Gay Hollywood Film & Video Guide: 75 Years of Gay & Lesbian Images in the Movies.* 2nd ed. Laguna Hills, Calif.: Companion Publications.

Stewart has compiled a list of more than 1,000 films "that feature gay and lesbian subject matter." Organized by title, each film includes a one- to five-star rating, technical data, director, cast, genre, and a plot summary that focuses on gay themes and characters. Films "with minor gay characters; drag; shorts; non-gay films featuring gay actors" and other films are listed in a separate section. Supplementary materials include a list of gay and lesbian film festivals, director and actor filmographies, and a name index.

MEN

936. Parish, James Robert. 2002. *Hollywood Bad Boys: Loud, Fast, and Out of Control.* Chicago: Contemporary Books.

Parish, a prolific writer of film reference books, has written a guide to 70 of the most infamous male movie stars, from the silent era to today. Each chapter provides a comprehensive biography focusing on the personal lives of the stars. An index makes it possible to trace connections between actors. The book is of most interest to starstruck fans.

937. Neibaur, James L. 1989. *Tough Guy: The American Movie Macho.* Jefferson, N.C.: McFarland.

Neibaur profiles a dozen actors known for appearing as "tough guys" on film. Each chapter begins with an in-depth filmographic essay exploring the various roles that made the actor appear tough followed by a complete filmography that includes film title, year of release, length, and production and acting credits. Additional materials include an introductory chapter on the early genres and the tough actors they featured, a brief bibliography, and an index.

WOMEN

Black Women in Television: An Illustrated History and Bibliography (see entry 897)

An Encyclopedic Dictionary of Women in Early American Films: 1895–1930 (see entry 739)

938. Foreman, Alexa L. 1983. *Women in Motion.* Bowling Green, Ohio: Bowling Green University Popular Press.

Foreman writes a guide to the films made by "women who have been active within the motion picture industry as well as independent filmmakers." Selective in scope, the book is divided into chapters on independent and avant-garde filmmakers, directors, editors, and screenwriters. For each filmmaker, she lists the films she made with technical data and a brief description quoted from books and articles. The filmography cannot be relied upon as complete, because Foreman includes only films that were available in 16mm for rent or purchase at the time the book was published in the early 1980s. Select filmmakers are represented by complete filmographies in an appendix.

939. Foster, Gwendolyn Audrey. 1995. *Women Film Directors: An International Bio-Critical Dictionary.* Westport, Conn.: Greenwood Press.

Professor Foster has compiled a guide to women directors and the films they have made. She includes women who direct films (not videos) based on the availability of information. While international in scope, she admits a bias toward Western filmmakers. The introduction provides a historical framework for the individual entries for directors that make up the rest of the book. For each director, Foster includes birth and death date, country where she works, a critical career biography, and selected filmographies and bibliographies. Appendixes list directors by nationality and decade of influence, a bibliography points out further reading, and indexes list film titles and general information. *Women Film Directors* is an excellent guide to researchers interested in women film directors and their work.

940. Foster, Gwendolyn Audrey, Katrien Jacobs, and Amy L. Unterburger. 1998. *Women Filmmakers & Their Films.* Detroit: St. James Press.

Women's film scholar Foster has selected nearly 200 directors and other behind-the-scenes women filmmakers to receive in-depth treatment from a team of film experts. Entries include facts of nationality, birth and death, education, family, career, awards, a filmography, a bibliography, and a signed essay exploring the body of work. Agent names and addresses are included for filmmakers who are still active. An additional 50 entries cover "films in which women filmmakers have had a major role" and include production data, cast and crew credits, a bibliography, and a critical essay. Added materials include a chronology of women filmmakers, a nationality index covering over 30 countries, and indexes for occupation, awards, and film title. The complete filmographies and select bibliographies as well as the scholarly essays make this an excellent place to research prominent women directors and filmmakers.

Frankly, My Dear: More Than 650 of the Funniest, Smartest, Gutsiest, Nastiest, Sexiest, and Simply Greatest Quotes in Celebration of Women in the Movies (see entry 1095)

941.　Kowalski, Rosemary Ann Ribich. 1976. *Women and Film: A Bibliography.* Metuchen, N.J.: Scarecrow Press.

Librarian Kowalski compiled this mostly annotated bibliography of 2,302 books and articles covering "any and all aspects of women's contributions to the development of film." Sections on performers, filmmakers, images of women, and columnists and critics are further subdivided into reference and historical works, catalogs, and specific works. A subject index guides researchers to relevant works. The section on performers excludes the years covered by Schuster's *Motion Picture Performers* (see entries 1010 and 1011), meaning it covers only some very early works and works from the first half of the 1970s. With major research on women and film written after this bibliography was published in 1976, it is mostly useful in looking at earlier viewpoints.

942.　Kuhn, Annette, and Susannah Radstone. 1990. *The Women's Companion to International Film.* London: Virago.

Film theorist and critic Kuhn has edited an international feminist film dictionary with articles written by a panel of 80 expert contributors. Like other film dictionaries, entries cover history, national cinemas, theory, movements, genres, filmmakers, and technical jargon. Unlike other film dictionaries, all of the entries take a feminist perspective. Entries are extensively cross-referenced, and there is an index of films directed, written, or produced by women.

943.　Lowe, Denise. 1999. *Women and American Television: An Encyclopedia.* Santa Barbara, Calif.: ABC-CLIO.

Noticing a large gap in the literature as she conducted her research, historian Lowe decided to create a dictionary of women "who were trendsetters or groundbreakers or cultural icons" and television shows that "featured a female character in a lead role that lasted at least six months." The biographical entries focus on careers, and the series entries focus on the show's premise and plot. Just as interesting are the topical sidebar articles (listed in a separate table of contents) that cover events and developments having an impact on women in television. Appendixes list directors, writers, Emmy winners, and the 12 women and one show in the Television Hall of Fame. Includes an extensive bibliography and index.

944.　Pallister, Janis L. 1997. *French-Speaking Women Film Directors: A Guide.* Madison, N.J.; London; Cranbury, N.J.: Fairleigh Dickinson University Press; Associated University Presses.

Professor Pallister has compiled this guide for "French professors teaching women's studies and film courses." The first chapter lists directors and occasional other filmmakers with their films. At minimum, each entry consists of a select list of films made. Most entries also include a brief career biography and descriptions of the major films. The second chapter groups the films by concepts or themes such as friendship between women, prostitution, or racism. Additional sections include a glossary of film terms, questions to ask for film analysis, an annotated bibliography, sample syllabi for film courses, and an index.

945. Parish, James Robert. 2002. *Hollywood Divas: The Good, the Bad, and the Fabulous.* New York; London: McGraw-Hill.

The ever-prolific Parish has written tell-all biographies of over 70 of the best known and most notorious Hollywood actresses. Focusing as much on their personal lives as their careers, this book is of most interest to fans of the stars. An index makes it possible to trace connections between actors.

946. Segrave, Kerry, and Linda Martin. 1990. *The Post-Feminist Hollywood Actress: Biographies and Filmographies of Stars Born after 1939.* Jefferson, N.C.: McFarland.

In writing biographies of 50 actresses who made their name after the beginning of the women's movement, Segrave and Martin set out to illustrate the varied treatment male and female actors receive in Hollywood. Divided into chapters on superstars, leading ladies, new screen stars, and up-and-coming actresses, all of the women receive the star treatment, with in-depth biographies covering life and career and a complete filmography of leading roles. Appendixes list percentage differences by gender in American cinema in the categories of popularity of stars by era, men versus women in lead roles in Academy Award winning films, nominations by age, gender of producers, directors, and screenwriters in Hollywood, and first five billed. Includes an index.

947. Smith, Ronald L. 1989. *Sweethearts of '60s TV.* 1st ed. New York: St. Martin's Press.

Smith, a popular culture writer, has written a biographical guide to 16 women who became stars by appearing on 1960s television series. Divided into the categories "girls next door," "dream wives," "comic cuties," "fantasy figures," and "women of action," each biography discusses career and the secrets behind each actor's appeal, answers the question of where they are now, and offers several illustrations. Includes an index.

948. Sullivan, Kaye. 1980. *Films for, by, and About Women.* Metuchen, N.J.: Scarecrow Press.

949. Sullivan, Kaye. 1985. *Films for, by, and About Women. Series II.* Metuchen, N.J.: Scarecrow Press.

Film consultant Sullivan largely succeeded in her goal of creating an international guide that will help researchers explore women's role in society through film and in identifying women filmmakers and their films—at least for films made through 1985. In alphabetical order by title, each of the nearly 3,000 films and documentaries include technical data, a synopsis, producer and director, and production company. Of particular use to researchers are the index of women filmmakers with filmographies and the solid subject index. Series II covers approximately 3,200 films released between 1980 and 1985 and adds personal names to the subject index.

950.   Unterburger, Amy L. 1999. *The St. James Women Filmmakers Encyclopedia: Women on the Other Side of the Camera.* Detroit: Visible Ink Press.

Women's film scholar Unterburger has selected 200 directors and other behind-the-scenes filmmakers from the larger-in-scope *Women Filmmakers & Their Films* (see entry 940). Similar in style and format to *The St. James Film Directors Encyclopedia* (see entry 1055), which includes fewer than 10 women, each entry includes facts of nationality, birth and death, education, family, career, awards, a filmography, and a signed essay exploring the body of work. Agent names and addresses are included for filmmakers who are still active. Added materials include a chronology of film history, a nationality index covering over 30 countries, and a director and film title index. The complete filmographies and scholarly essays make this an excellent place to research prominent women directors and filmmakers—but note that the content of each entry is identical to those in the larger *Women Filmmakers & Their Films,* so it is not necessary to consult both.

Women in Horror Films, 1930s (see entry 663)

Women in Horror Films, 1940s (see entry 664)

951.   *Women Make Movies* [World Wide Web Resource]. Women Make Movies Inc. Address: http://www.wmm.com. [Accessed: March 2005].

Women Make Movies is "a multicultural, multiracial, non-profit media arts organization which facilitates the production, promotion, distribution and exhibition of independent films and videotapes by and about women." Its database lists more than 400 carefully selected films, documentaries, and animated works by title, maker, and more than 70 subjects. Other sections include news, events, and links to Web sites devoted to women and film. Services include a production assistance program and a distribution program.

Women of Color: A Filmography of Minority and Third World Women (see entry 891)

Working Women on the Hollywood Screen: A Filmography (see entry 757)

OCCUPATIONS (SEE ALSO *GENRE*)

JOURNALISM

952.   Langman, Larry. 1997. *The Media in the Movies: A Catalog of American Journalism Films, 1900–1996.* Jefferson, N.C.: McFarland.

Langman has compiled a list of feature films that cover journalism and journalists from every media. His introduction describes the genre and the stock characters that inhabit the films. The films are listed in alphabetical order by title and list date of release, distributor, director, screenwriter, and principal cast. The descriptions mostly convey the plots but also include brief evaluative comments. Appendixes list series, serials, and films in which newspapers are in the periphery. The book includes a brief bibliography and a name index.

953.   Ness, Richard. 1997. *From Headline Hunter to Superman: A Journalism Filmography.* Lanham, Md.: Scarecrow Press.

Ness has compiled a list of films that deal with "the practice of the journalism profession, and works in which the journalist plays a contributing role in the events." After the silent film section, each chapter is devoted to a decade through 1996. Ness introduces the book and each chapter with lengthy, in-depth introductions to the genre and to the films. Within each chapter, the film are listed alphabetically by title and include the standard technical information, principal crew and cast, and a plot summary. An appendix lists films that did not meet selection criteria but still had journalistic elements. Additional appendixes list British films, serials and miniseries, and a brief bibliography. The index lists film titles.

LIBRARIANS

954.   Raish, Martin. *Librarians in the Movies: An Annotated Filmography* [World Wide Web Resource]. Brigham University Harold B. Lee Library. Address: http://emp. byui.edu/RAISHM/films/introduction.html. [Accessed: March 2005].

Raish presents four lists of some 550 films featuring librarians as characters. The first group of films clearly identifies the character as a librarian; the second group features the library as a place; the third group mentions a librarian or library in passing; and the final group consists of movies with librarians in the credits that Raish has not yet seen. The entry for each film includes title, year of release, and a brief summary with special attention to the role of the librarian or library in the film. Additional pages list actors who have portrayed librarians and cite articles written about librarians in the movies.

MEDICINE

955.   Flowers, John, and Paul Frizler. 2004. *Psychotherapists on Film, 1899–1999: A Worldwide Guide to Over 5000 Films.* Jefferson, N.C.: McFarland.

Professors Flowers and Frizler compiled a list of 5,000 films and made-for-TV movies made between 1899 and 2000 depicting psychotherapists. Their definition is broad, including not only appearances by psychiatrists and psychologists, but also by hypnotherapists, parapsychologists, mental therapists, group therapy leaders, religious counselors, and the various forms of early mental health workers. After an introduction discussing the positive and negative portrayals of psychotherapists over time, films are listed in alphabetical order by title; each entry contains year of release, studio, country of origin, length, director, writer, source, cast, and plot summary with special attention to the role of the psychotherapist. The authors watched just over 3,000 of the films. Appendixes list films by decade, by alternate and foreign titles, made from 2000 to 2002, and adult films. Includes a name index.

956.   Paietta, Ann Catherine, and Jean L. Kauppila. 1999. *Health Professionals on Screen.* Lanham, Md.: Scarecrow Press.

Paietta and Kauppila have compiled a list of over 1,600 films and television series that portray health professionals. Films are included if the "physicians, psychiatrists, nurses, dentists, psychologist, pharmacists, and other health professionals" play a lead character or make an impact on the plot. The book is divided into separate sections on film and television series, but the vast majority of the listings are movies. Within each category, the entries are in alphabetical order by title and include technical information, listing producer, director, writer, cast, and a brief synopsis. As one might expect of authors who are librarians, the bibliography is extensive, and the subject and name indexes are quite good.

957.   Rabkin, Leslie Y. 1998. *The Celluloid Couch: An Annotated International Filmography of the Mental Health Professional in the Movies and Television, from the Beginning to 1990.* Lanham, Md.: Scarecrow Press.

Rabkin, a clinical psychologist and movie lover, has amassed a list of American films that portray mental health professionals (MHPs). The book is organized by decade, providing the opportunity to discuss the changing image of MHPs over the course of the twentieth century. For each film, the author lists technical information, director, producer, cast, and a synopsis that summarizes the plot and discusses the role of the MHP in the film. Coded letters describe the professional specialization of the MHP and the form of therapy presented. The bibliography is an excellent resource for further research. The index lists film titles.

PHYSICALLY CHALLENGED

958.   Klobas, Lauri E. 1988. *Disability Drama in Television and Film.* Jefferson, N.C.: McFarland.

An interest in "attitudes and influences that negatively affect society" led Klobas to compile this guide to dramatic films and television shows about people with disabilities. The book is not intended to be comprehensive; instead, it includes films and television programs that came to her attention over an 11-year period as she compiled the book. The sections are organized by disability in order of visibility: blindness, wheelchair-users, deafness, amputation, developmental disability, small-stature, other, and multiple disabled characters. Each section introduces the disability with particular attention to the standard misconceptions and stereotypes as well as a list of adaptive equipment and is followed by a chronological list of films and programs. Each item lists the film or episode, the principal crew, the disability, the character's gender, race, and disability, and a plot summary complete with relevant quotes. Klobas then describes how realistically and sensitively the disability is portrayed in the context of the story. The appendix lists additional television programs and feature films that came to the author's attention and regular or recurring characters with disabilities on televisions shows. The index includes movies, television shows and episodes, and filmmakers.

959.   Schuchman, John S. 1988. *Hollywood Speaks: Deafness and the Film Entertainment Industry.* Urbana: University of Illinois Press.

Schuchman has written an analysis of how deafness and the deaf are portrayed in film and television. After five chapters exploring the portrayals of various eras, he lists films and television programs made from 1902 through 1987 "that deal with deafness or that includes a deaf character in a major or pivotal role." In chronological order, each entry includes title, distributor, release year, actor portraying the deaf character, and a synopsis that discusses the portrayal of deafness. The filmography also lists 27 sign-language films made especially for the deaf. Includes name and subject and title indexes.

10
Filmmakers

Biographies in this section provide information about the lives of people who make and perform in film and television, usually focusing on career more than personal life. People are listed first in general biographies and then by career specialty. The biographies are often accompanied by lists of credits, with some books specializing in credits only. Other books cumulate obituaries. Many of the general, national cinema, and genre dictionaries and encyclopedias in other parts of this guide also offer biographies. (See also chapters on National Cinema, Genres, Format, Studios, and Portrayals.)

Because this guide does not include books devoted to an individual filmmaker or performer, it is necessary instead to consult local library catalogs or union catalogs such as *WorldCat* (see entry 64) or *RedLightGreen* (see entry 63). In most library catalogs, people involved in making films and television shows are listed as authors, so when seeking a book about directors or performers, it is generally best to use an author or subject search rather than a keyword search.

BIOGRAPHY

960. Langman, Larry. 2000. *Destination Hollywood: The Influence of Europeans on American Filmmaking.* Jefferson, N.C.: McFarland.

In this unusual book, Professor Langman focuses on how European immigrant filmmakers influenced American cinema. Organized by country of origin, each chapter provides an overview of that country's cinema and the conditions that led to emigration followed by entries for individual filmmakers. Divided into categories according to film specialty (director, screenwriter, art director, cinematographer, or composer), each film-maker's biography covers the standard ground of career and prominent films, but pays particular attention to the perspectives and themes informed by being an "outsider." Includes a name index.

961. Morgan, Robin, and George C. Perry. 1997. *The Book of Film Biographies: A Pictorial Guide of 1000 Makers of Cinema.* 1st Fromm international ed. New York: Fromm International.

Morgan and Perry led a team of film experts in compiling a list of 1,000 international filmmakers they "felt had made the biggest contribution" to filmmaking in the first 100 years of cinema. Each entry includes screen name, a portrait, nationality, specialty, years of birth and death, and a career biography with the most prominent films highlighted. Filmographies are listed separately at the end of the book along with a sidebar that contains a very small glossary of film terms. The *Book of Film Biographies* is of most interest to fans and is sure to prompt debate on who was included and who was left out.

962.   Pendergast, Tom, and Sara Pendergast. 2000. *International Dictionary of Films and Filmmakers.* 4th ed. Detroit: St. James Press.

A team of film scholars has written this dictionary of the most prominent North American and Western European films and filmmakers. Volume 1 presents 683 films, covering production data, crew and cast credits, a bibliography of works about the film, a critical essay, and, in many cases, a still from the film. Indexes list film by director and country of production. Volume 2 covers 483 directors, volume 3 covers 615 actors, and volume 4 covers 545 writers and other production artists. Each filmmaker entry includes a brief career biography with nationality, place and date of birth and death, family, a complete filmography, a bibliography of works about the artist, and a critical essay. Indexes list filmmakers by nationality, and all volumes include a film title index. Intended to be selective rather than comprehensive, the *Dictionary* is highly recommended for its high-quality essays, the representative bibliographies, and the complete filmographies. Earlier editions were entitled *The Macmillan Dictionary of Films and Filmmakers.*

963.   Quigley, Martin, and Barry Monush. 1995. *First Century of Film.* 1st ed. New York: Quigley.

Using the biographies in the *International Motion Picture Almanac* (see entry 1176), Quigley and Monush have compiled a list of 1,300 of the most prominent American filmmakers from the first 100 years of cinema who died before August 31, 1994. After a history of cinema and its makers, filmmakers and actors are listed in alphabetical order by last name. Each entry includes specialty, date and place of birth, a career biography, a filmography, and date of death. Glossy black-and-white publicity stills are drawn mostly from Georgetown University's Quigley Photo Archives and are blocked together in a separate section. Monush was later asked to compile a similar guide just for actors for *Screen World* entitled *Encyclopedia of Hollywood Film Actors* (see entry 1001).

964.   Roud, Richard. 1980. *Cinema: A Critical Dictionary: The Major Film-Makers.* New York: Viking Press.

Film scholars write critical analyses of the most prominent filmmakers of the first 80 years of filmmaking. Because the dictionary takes critical stances, Roud occasionally includes more than one entry for a filmmaker. As one might expect, the majority of the entries are for directors, but there are also essays written about the full range of filmmakers as well as individual films, movements, and national cinemas. The essays vary in length, but most provide several pages of in-depth critical analysis that will be of use to beginning film students. Lightly illustrated, the dictionary also includes a comprehensive index. Because the coverage outside of North America, Europe, and Japan is paltry, it is best to use other dictionaries for the rest of the world.

965.   Sadoul, Georges, and Peter Morris. 1972. *Dictionary of Film Makers.* Berkeley: University of California Press.

In 1965, Sadoul wrote one of the first dictionaries listing filmmakers as a companion to his *Dictionary of Films* (see entry 174), listing 1,000 "directors, scriptwriters, cinematographers, art directors, composers, producers, inventors—but not actors and actresses" from over 60 countries. For each filmmaker, Sadoul writes an evaluative career biography followed by an abridged filmography—films marked with an asterisk are described in great detail in the companion volume. The book was updated by Morris as he translated from French into English.

966. Scheuer, Steven H. 1983. *Who's Who in Television and Cable.* New York: Facts on File.

Scheuer has edited this first and only edition of a television who's who that profiles over 2,000 executives, producers, writers, journalists, and actors currently working in television and cable. Since the first edition was published in 1983, the dictionary is now dated, but it could still be used to look up career highlights up to that point. Includes indexes for corporations and job title.

967. Smith, Scott. 1998. *The Film 100: A Ranking of the Most Influential People in the History of the Movies.* Secaucus, N.J.: Carol.

In consultation with film critics, scholars, and filmmakers, Smith has selected the 100 individuals who "created significant changes in the way films are made, seen, distributed, and appreciated." Ranked in order from 1 to 100, Smith writes lengthy biographies featuring the ideas and innovations that make the person influential. Originally conceived as a now-defunct Web site, the book shares greater detail and the research behind the ranking. *The Film 100* list is now hosted by the *Greatest Films* Web site (see entry 206) at <http://www.filmsite.org/film100.html>.

968. Tibbetts, John C., James Michael Welsh, and Gene D. Phillips. 2002. *The Encyclopedia of Filmmakers.* New York: Facts on File.

969. Tibbetts, John C., and James Michael Welsh. 2002. *The Encyclopedia of Great Filmmakers.* New York: Checkmark Books.

In this guide to some 350 filmmakers from around the world, each filmmaker is treated to two or three pages of engaging writing on career and most prominent films. Films not mentioned in the body are selectively listed at the end of the essay under "other films" along with a list of references. Unfortunately, the index lists only those films mentioned in the body of the essay. The set is of most value to beginning film students. The smaller *Encyclopedia of Great Filmmakers* takes 150 directors from the set to provide a less expensive alternative.

970. Waldman, Harry, and Anthony Slide. 1996. *Hollywood and the Foreign Touch: A Dictionary of Foreign Filmmakers and Their Films from America, 1910–1995.* Lanham, Md.: Scarecrow Press.

Waldman has written a dictionary of foreign filmmakers and actors who worked in Hollywood between 1910 and 1995 and the foreign-language films they made. The entries for filmmakers and actors discuss life and career. Hollywood studios made Spanish, French-, and German-language films between 1930 and 1935. Waldman includes these in the dictionary, providing the original title, a brief synopsis, major cast, and notes on the film's reception. Unfortunately, there is no index and no cross-references from the English-language titles, nor is there an index listing country of origin. Both would have improved the book.

CREDITS

971. Academy of Motion Picture Arts and Sciences. *Annual Index to Motion Picture Credits.* Westport, Conn.: Greenwood Press.

The Academy of Motion Picture Arts and Sciences (AMPAS) compiles an annual index to films released in Los Angeles that lists credits for actors, art direction, casting, cinematography, costume designers, directors, editors, makeup, music, producers, sound, visual effects, writers, and releasing company. Each section lists filmmakers by last name and lists the films they made that year. The names are cumulated in the alphabetical index of individual credits and, beginning in 1985, a cumulative index to film titles. Oddly enough for an AMPAS publication, the index did not begin listing Academy Awards until 1997.

972. *Credits.* 1985. Wallington, N.J.: Magpie Press.

Credits lists the complete production credits for over 900 English-language films made from 1979 to 1985. Volume 1 lists credits by film title. Volume 2 lists credits by production categories such as editor or screenplay. Volume 3 lists credits by individual. Note that there are no cast credits listed. Intended as a biennial publication, there is no indication that another edition was ever published.

973. Goble, Alan. 2003. *The Complete Index to World Film since 1895.* 5th ed. East Sussex, England: Valan.

974. Goble, Alan. 1991. *The International Film Index, 1895–1990.* London; New Jersey: Bowker-Saur.

I was not able to review this CD-ROM, but I did examine its print predecessor, *The International Film Index, 1895–1990.* If the database is anything like the book, it remains one of the most complete lists of credits for international films available. Publicity for the CD-ROM claims that it provides credits for "more than 359,000 films from more than 170 countries" with keyword searching and hypertext links.

975. Michael, Paul. 1980. *The Great American Movie Book.* Englewood Cliffs, N.J.: Prentice-Hall.

The Great American Movie Book lists complete cast and crew credits for American sound films made from *The Jazz Singer* through 1980. Although the selection criteria are not explicit, all the films seem to have been produced by major studios. Each film is illustrated with a black-and-white still. Includes an appendix listing Academy Award winners, a bibliography, and a name index.

976. Pettifer, Arthur G. *AGP Films* [World Wide Web Resource]. Address: http://www.agpfilms.com. [Accessed: January 2005].

In the early 1980s, Pettifer began noting the air dates and credits for films aired on Australian television. By 2005, he had more than 16,000 films in his database. The database is searchable by film, actor, crew member, company, and supplier. Entries are labeled either complete (every person listed in the credits is included) or incomplete. Film records include title, release year, and links to credits; records for individuals include name, role, and a link to other films. More often than not, the credits are incomplete, but even the incomplete records offer a lot of information, so this is nonetheless a resource worth consulting when looking for names deep in the credits—I can attest to this personally, because this is the only freely accessible database that lists even one of my few credits.

OBITUARIES

977.   Donnelly, Paul. 2003. *Fade to Black: A Book of Movie Obituaries.* Rev. and updated ed. London: Omnibus.

Donnelley has written new obituaries for over 1,100 actors, filmmakers, and other prominent Hollywood personalities. Most of the entries are straightforward biographies of life, career, and death, but many focus on the darker, seedier aspects of their lives.

978.   Doyle, Billy H., and Anthony Slide. 1995. *The Ultimate Directory of the Silent Screen Performers: A Necrology of Births and Deaths and Essays on 50 Lost Players.* Metuchen, N.J.: Scarecrow Press.

Based on extensive research, Doyle records the date and place of birth and death for over 7,000 silent film performers. In addition, he writes obituaries of 50 "lost players" whose deaths eluded the notice of the press.

979.   Doyle, Billy H., and Anthony Slide. 1999. *The Ultimate Directory of Film Technicians: A Necrology of Dates and Places of Births and Deaths of More Than 9,000 Producers, Screenwriters, Composers, Cinematographers, Art Directors, Costume Designers, Choreographers, Executives, and Publicists.* Lanham, Md.: Scarecrow Press.

This book "documents the births and deaths, and the places where they occurred, for more than 9,000 men and women who labored behind the camera in both the American and international film industries, and who died prior to 1997." Doyle has researched and created a true necrology—the entire book is an alphabetical list of filmmakers with date and place of birth and death. Parentheses indicate occupation.

980.   Keylin, Arleen, and Suri Boiangiu. 1977. *Hollywood Album: Lives and Deaths of Hollywood Stars from the Pages of the New York Times.* New York: Arno Press.

981.   Keylin, Arleen. 1979. *Hollywood Album 2: Lives and Deaths of Hollywood Stars from the Pages of the New York Times.* New York: Arno Press.

Hollywood Album reprints movie star's obituaries from the *New York Times,* complete with illustrations. Each volume features over 200 of the "greats." Although they admit that choosing which actors to include was "difficult," the editors do not share their selection criteria. The table of contents lists the stars in alphabetical order, while the index is a filmography for each star drawn from the *New York Times Film Reviews* (see entry 170).

982.   Parish, James Robert. 2001. *The Hollywood Book of Death: The Bizarre, Often Sordid, Passings of Over 125 American Movie and TV Idols—From Rudolph Valentino and Clara Bow to James Dean and Marilyn Monroe to River Phoenix and Phil Hartman.* 3rd ed. Lincolnwood, Ill.: St. Albans, England: Contemporary; Verulam.

Parish takes a ghoulish look at how 125 of our favorite stars died. Organized by cause of death (such as accident or murder or suicide), each biography focuses on life and career with special attention to the circumstances of the death. Appendixes include a necrology with month, day, and year of birth and death for many more actors and a list of cemeteries where celebrities are buried.

983. Stewart, William T., Arthur F. McClure, and Ken D. Jones. 1981. *International Film Necrology, Garland Reference Library of the Humanities; V. 215.* New York: Garland.

The *International Film Necrology* is one of the most complete and accurate guides to when actors and filmmakers were born and died—at least if they died before 1978 in California. Stewart spent 22 years searching California public records and secondary literature to come up with accurate dates and places for actors' births and deaths. Each entry lists name, career specialty, date and place of birth, date and place of death, and age at death.

984. Vazzana, Eugene Michael. 2001. *Silent Film Necrology.* 2nd ed. Jefferson, N.C.: McFarland.

Vazzana conducted extensive research to compile the dates and places of birth and death for over 18,500 filmmakers and actors from the silent era. When available, he also includes cause of death. Unique among necrologies, he also includes an annotated bibliography of articles appearing in the *New York Times, Variety,* and *Movie Weekly,* among others, covering an entire career as well as the obituaries.

ACTORS

BIOGRAPHY

985. Aylesworth, Thomas G., and John Stewart Bowman. 1987. *The World Almanac Who's Who of Film.* New York: World Almanac.

Aylesworth and Bowman have written brief biographies for hundreds of actors featured in English-language films. Each biography features career highlights and a selective filmography. The authors do not explain their selection criteria or sources of information, and the only index points to the black-and-white stills, so the audience for this book is film fans watching a movie and wondering "who was that?"

986. Brode, Douglas. 1997. *Once Was Enough: Celebrities (and Others) Who Appeared a Single Time on the Screen.* Secaucus, N.J.: Carol.

The one-hit wonders of the movie world are presented here in 31 categories. These stars were for the most part celebrities from other fields who made exactly one movie. They include musicians, athletes, models, and family members hired through nepotism. For each actor, Brode gives a brief biography and explains why there were no more movies. Unique in its coverage, this book fills a niche in celebrity biography.

987. Cawkwell, Tim, and John Milton Smith. 1972. *The World Encyclopedia of Film.* London: Studio Vista.

At the time of its publication in 1972, *The World Encyclopedia of Film* was the most comprehensive international biographical film encyclopedia available. Editors Cawkwell and Smith led a team of film experts in compiling and writing the entries, including the full range of filmmakers and actors, but giving the greatest emphasis to directors. Entries list career specialty, birthplace and date, date of death, and career highlights. Filmographies for directors are complete through 1971. Filmographies for other people include only films that are already listed under a director. One-third of the book consists of an index to films, which makes the encyclopedia suitable as an international guide to films. Includes over 900 black-and-white stills.

988.   Chapman, Peter. 1994. *The Players: Actors in Movies on Television and Video-cassette.* New York: Windsor Press.

Chapman, a movie fan and former actor, has created a guide designed to help movie fans identify actors. Drawn from over 4,000 films likely to be seen on television, the book features lesser-known actors rather than the stars that every fan knows. Listed in alphabetical order by last name, there are two entries per page featuring a large publicity still, a career biography, and a character filmography. If the filmography doesn't fit on the page, it is continued in a separate section at the back. The index lists films, so film viewers can reach for the book, look up the film, and turn to the pages with the photos.

989.   Cohen, Daniel, and Susan Cohen. 1985. *Encyclopedia of Movie Stars.* New York: Gallery Books.

The Cohens compiled a list of stars from every era and then "consulted with editors, friends, even enemies" to create a glossy illustrated guide to 400 movie stars. Each entry describes life and career and includes one or more illustrations and a filmography. Most of the stars are American or British, but a few foreign actors are included. The *Encyclopedia* is intended primarily for movie fans rather than researchers.

990.   Ellrod, J.G. 1989. *Hollywood Greats of the Golden Years: The Late Stars of the 1920s through the 1950s.* Jefferson, N.C.: McFarland.

991.   Ellrod, J.G. 1997. *The Stars of Hollywood Remembered: Career Biographies of 82 Actors and Actresses of the Golden Era, 1920s–1950s.* Jefferson, N.C.: McFarland.

Film fan Ellrod's guide to the stars of the Golden Age of studio system sound films covers 81 stars who had all passed away by the time the book was published. For each star, Ellrod writes a brief career biography, lists credits, and provides one or more stills from his or her films. The sequel volume, *The Stars of Hollywood Remembered* covers 82 more stars. Both books include name indexes.

992.   *Filmbug* [World Wide Web Resource]. Address: http://www.filmbug.com. [Accessed: January 2005].

Filmbug provides biographies for "over 8,000 actors, directors, screenwriters and other celebrities." Searchable or browsable by name, each entry includes a career biography followed by birth name, birthday, birthplace, occupation, height, awards, and a selective filmography. *Filmbug* also includes a database for films, listing genre, director, cast, release dates, MPAA rating, excerpts, and links to reviews from other Web sites.

993.   Halliwell, Leslie, and John Walker. 2003. *Halliwell's Who's Who in the Movies.* 15th ed. New York: HarperResource.

Walker and venerable film critic Halliwell wrote this guide "for people who like movies." Formerly entitled *Halliwell's Filmgoer's Companion* and *Halliwell's Filmgoer's & Video Viewer's Companion, Halliwell's Who's Who in the Movies* has been published every two to four years from its inception in 1965 until Halliwell's death in 1989 and biennially since film critic Walker took over in 1993. The dictionary lists more than 11,000 actors, directors, producers, writers, and other prominent filmmakers. Filmmakers receive career synopses, lists of their most prominent films and television series, and occasional quotes from the filmmakers themselves or from their critics. Appendixes point readers to entries that cover characters, series, remakes, and themes. Additional appendixes list prizes for the Academy Awards, British Academy of Film and Television Arts, European Film Awards, and the Berlin, Cannes, and Venice Film Festivals. Includes a bibliography and a chronology.

994.   Hofstede, David. 1996. *First Appearances.* Las Vegas, Nev.: Zanne-3.

Hofstede has written a guide to the film debut and star-making performances of 150 film stars. Each entry fills a couple of pages and contains the actor's first appearance in a feature film, the role that made him or a star, and an engaging essay on both early efforts. An appendix lists "more first appearances," devoting a couple of sentences to each actor. There is no index, so this book is primarily of interest to fans who are curious to learn how their favorite stars got their starts.

995.   Houseman, Victoria. 1991. *Made in Heaven: The Marriages and Children of Hollywood Stars.* Chicago: Bonus Books.

Houseman, a fan of movies and movie stars, has written family biographies of over 700 film stars. Each biography dryly describes the names and dates for marriages, divorces, and children. As one might expect, the book is extensively cross-referenced. An appendix lists stars who had never married as of 1991 and a name index lists as many as four entries per individual. The book is of interest not just to fans, but to librarians attempting to answer sometimes difficult questions about a star's family life.

996.   Karney, Robyn. 1984. *The Movie Stars Story.* New York: Crescent Books.

A companion volume to the Hollywood studio *Story* series (see the Studios chapter), *The Movie Stars Story* is a lavishly illustrated guide to 500 movie stars from the 1920s through the 1980s. Each chapter covers a decade of filmmaking, beginning with an overview of the industry that covers the major events and people followed by an alphabetical list of the stars who had the greatest impact. Each article includes real name, place and date of birth, date of death, an overview of career and life, and at least one photograph. There is a name index, but no film index.

997.   Karney, Robyn. 1993. *Who's Who in Hollywood.* London: Bloomsbury.

Eleven film journalists have written biographies of approximately 600 contemporary filmmakers and actors. Each entry lists real name, occupation, and date of birth. The bios are well written and often engaging and the filmographies are complete. Although it has fewer entries, the longer biographies make *Who's Who in Hollywood* a nice complement to *Quinlan's* (see entries 1008, 1025, and 1053).

998.   Lloyd, Ann, Graham Fuller, and Arnold Desser. 1987. *The Illustrated Who's Who of the Cinema.* New York: Portland House: Distributed by Crown Publishers.

Lloyd and Fuller led a team of researchers in creating this lavishly illustrated biographical guide to over 2,000 actors and filmmakers. Coverage is international and includes the entire era of filmmaking, but the Golden Age of the 1920s and 1930s receives the most emphasis. In alphabetical order by name, each entry includes a career biography and a selective filmography. With both color and black-and-white stills and publicity photos on every page, this is an excellent, although dated, biographical film guide.

999.   Maltin, Leonard, Spencer Green, and Luke Sader. 1994. *Leonard Maltin's Movie Encyclopedia.* New York: Dutton.

Maltin and his editorial team have compiled a biographical dictionary of filmmakers and actors. Each entry includes occupation, date and place of birth and death, and a researched biography with filmography interspersed in the text. The book is a nice complement to Maltin's *Movie Guide* (see entry 163).

1000.   Marx, Kenneth S., and Geraldine Gonzales Eckert. 1979. *Star Stats: Who's Whose in Hollywood.* Los Angeles: Price/Stern/Sloan.

Star Stats is a computer printout of vital statistics for over 1,000 actors. Although dated, it contains information not readily available elsewhere, listing all family members, marriages, friendships and romances, birth and death dates, city of residence, written memoirs, awards, and select credits. The cross-reference index connects actors with the people close to them. One appendix lists past and current top management of film studios. A second appendix is a calendar of birth dates.

1001.   Monush, Barry. 2003. *Screen World Presents the Encyclopedia of Hollywood Film Actors.* New York; Milwaukee: Applause Theatre and Cinema Books; Sales and distribution by Hal Leonard.

On behalf of *Screen World,* editor Monush has conducted extensive research to write accurate biographies of the most prominent film actors around the world. Each entry includes a black-and-white portrait, date and place of birth and death, where educated, and a critical analysis of life and career. Filmographies are complete for films released in the United States but selective for television movies, stage appearances, and films released only abroad. This first volume covers actors who gained prominence by 1965; a second volume covering actors who gained prominence after 1965 is in the works.

1003.   *The Movie Book.* 1999. London: Phaidon.

This lavishly illustrated oversized book serves as a paean to "500 people from around the world who have made a landmark contribution to the medium of film." Nowhere does the publisher explain the criteria by which they were selected, but there is no doubt that each person included has made a great impact on film. Included are actors, directors, screenwriters, animators, composers, producers, and more. Each page is devoted to one person. A photograph designed to highlight the person's work fills the page—a caption describes the still. A brief text provides a biography that discusses the impact the person has had in the world of film, with cross-references to related people. The book includes a glossary of film terms and a directory of film festivals and museums. There are no indexes. As a reference book, its greatest use will be for the photographs and the list of 500 icons.

1004.   Parish, James Robert, Don E. Stanke, and Michael R. Pitts. 1977. *The All-Americans*. New Rochelle, N.Y.: Arlington House.

Parish, a prolific writer of film reference books, Stanke, a film journalist, and Pitts, a journalism professor, have written a biographical homage to seven actors who "captured the essence of America": Gary Cooper, Henry Fonda, William Holden, Rock Hudson, Fred MacMurray, Ronald Reagan, and James Stewart. Each entry is a lavishly illustrated biography of life and career complete with a filmography that lists cast and crew credits. Includes an index. *The All-Americans* is of most interest to those interested in the in-depth biographies of these seven American movie stars.

1005.   Parish, James Robert, and William T. Leonard. 1976. *Hollywood Players, the Thirties*. New Rochelle, N.Y.: Arlington House.

1006.   Parish, James Robert, and Lennard DeCarl. 1976. *Hollywood Players: The Forties*. New Rochelle, N.Y.: Arlington House.

Parish, a prolific writer of film reference books, and Leonard, a librarian and film researcher, have written a guide to 71 of the most prominent stars of the 1930s. After a paragraph placing the actor's career in context, each chapter provides a comprehensive career biography chock-full of quotes from interviews and reviews, numerous black-and-white photographs, and a complete list of film credits. Unlike Parish's books featuring movies, *Hollywood Players* includes an index to filmmakers and films. The book is of most interest to those interested in the in-depth biographies of the biggest names in film. *Hollywood Players: The Forties* adds 70 additional stars.

1007.   Parish, James Robert. 1974. *Hollywood's Great Love Teams*. Carlstadt, N.J.: Rainbow Books.

Parish, prolific writer on films and filmmakers, has written a guide to 28 romantic on-screen pairs. To be included, it seems actors must have been teamed in three or more films. Each chapter provides brief biographies, release dates, physical descriptions, astrological sign, stills, and complete filmographies for each pair with sections on the films in which they starred together. For each film, Parish includes selected crew and complete cast credits, a synopsis, and an evaluation of the film with particular attention to the romance. The index lists names, films, and photographs. The book is most useful in its study of the now rare practice of featuring romantic couples in several movies.

1008.   Quinlan, David. 2000. *Quinlan's Film Stars*. 5th ed. Washington, D.C.: Brassey's.

Quinlan, a film critic and writer, has compiled a biography of actors, mostly from the English-speaking world. Covering over 2,000 actors from the first 100 years of cinema, each entry includes a physical description, "a picture of the star, a full career overview, and a complete list of all films, TV movies, and cameo appearances." Vital data such as date of birth, cause and date of death, and marriages to other stars are also included. The book does not have a film title index, so it is best used for its capsule biographies and complete filmographies.

The Post-Feminist Hollywood Actress: Biographies and Filmographies of Stars Born after 1939 (see entry 946)

1009. Ragan, David. 1992. *Who's Who in Hollywood: The Largest Cast of International Film Personalities Ever Assembled.* New York: Facts on File.

In this biographical guide to actors, Ragan made a concerted effort to include "all players who could be found, those still living and those not." He acknowledges that he did not succeed, but he has still produced an excellent guide to the lives and careers of several thousand actors from all over the world. The first edition included actors who performed from 1900 until its publication in 1976. This second edition is updated through April 1991. Each entry lists names; whether they played lead, character, or support roles; a physical description with biography and career highlights; and a representative list of credits. Entries for supporting actors usually include only the name and year of death if passed away. Probably the largest print collection of biographies, *Who's Who in Hollywood* is an excellent place to find biographical information on film performers.

1010. Schuster, Mel. 1971. *Motion Picture Performers: A Bibliography of Magazine and Periodical Articles, 1900–1969.* Metuchen, N.J.: Scarecrow Press.

1011. Schuster, Mel. 1976. *Motion Picture Performers: A Bibliography of Magazine and Periodical Articles: Supplement No. 1, 1970–1974.* Metuchen, N.J.: Scarecrow Press.

Schuster compiled a bibliography of biographical magazine articles by consulting the collections of the Library & Museum of the Performing Arts (now the New York Public Library of Performing Arts) of the New York Public Library. Although these are among the premier film libraries, they are by no means complete. The effort led to a very good collection of articles written about 2,900 film actors appearing in magazines between 1900 and 1969. The supplement went well beyond the original, consulting libraries outside New York to fill gaps missed in the original time period, adding magazines, and updating through 1974. The result is an additional 2,600 actors, including those active in television as well as in film. Although most fan magazines are excluded, the emphasis on popular magazines over scholarly journals makes these books useful to fans and researchers interested in popular culture.

1012. Segrave, Kerry, and Linda Martin. 1990. *The Continental Actress: European Film Stars of the Postwar Era—Biographies, Criticism, Filmographies, Bibliographies.* Jefferson, N.C.: McFarland.

Segrave and Martin have written a guide to 41 European actresses who became international stars sometime after World War II. Divided into chapters on Italian, Greek, French, German, and Scandinavian actresses, each entry includes one or more black-and-white stills, an excellent in-depth critical essay on life and career, and a complete filmography of feature films that covers 1,799 films in all. Includes an index.

1013.   Shipman, David. 1993. *The Great Movie Stars: Vol. 1 The Golden Years; Vol. 2 The International Years.* New ed. London: Warner.

1014.   Shipman, David. 1991. *The Great Movie Stars: Vol. 3 The Independent Years.* 1st U.S. ed. Boston: Little, Brown.

Shipman has written one of the best collective biographies of movie stars. Although he can't define what makes a star, because they "were all originals and any description more precise founders on their individuality," he includes actors based on box office, popularity polls, and critical reputation. Each volume covers approximately 200 stars, with *The Golden Years* including stars who "made their names before the start of World War II" and *The International Years* including not only those who made their names after the war, but all foreign performers as well. These first two volumes were originally published in 1970 and 1972 and were reprinted into one volume in 1993 (see entry 1013). *The Independent Years* was published later to cover approximately 100 stars of the eighties and early nineties. The entries are well-researched multipage essays on the career, inter-weaving critical comments, description of roles and movies, and illustrations. The books will be of most use for the excellent introductions and biographies, because they include a title change index but no full title index. Includes a bibliography of sources consulted.

1015.   Thomson, David. 2003. *The New Biographical Dictionary of Film.* 4th ed. London: Little, Brown.

Thomson has written an opinionated biographical dictionary of filmmakers. He has selected the directors, writers, producers, and actors he thinks have made the greatest impact on the cinema. His biographies are lively and engaging, and he has succeeded in his goal of including accurate information in the framework of his strongly prejudiced overviews of each filmmaker's career. Films are not listed separately, but instead are inter-spersed throughout the biographies. The first three editions were called *A Biographical Dictionary of Film.*

1016.   Truitt, Evelyn Mack. 1983. *Who Was Who on Screen.* 3rd ed. New York: R.R. Bowker.

Truitt has compiled a list of over 13,000 American, British, French, and German actors (including animal stars!) who died between 1905 and 1982. Filmmakers are included only if they also appeared on screen. Listed alphabetically by last name, each biography includes date of birth and death, cause of death, family information, career specialty, and a list of film credits. The book has a selected bibliography but no index. A condensed edition was published in 1984.

1017.   Ward, Jack. 1996. *The Supporting Players of Television, 1959–1983: Illustrated.* Cleveland, Okla.: Lakeshore West.

Ward has written a visual guide to 500 supporting actors who made their mark on television between 1959 and 1983. Designed for television fans who can't place a character, each entry contains a portrait, a career biography, and a list of credits. Unfortunately, there is no index, meaning fans will need to either wait for the credits or skim the book for portraits. Ward has written a complementary book entitled *Television Guest Stars* (see entry 1018).

1018. Ward, Jack. 1993. *Television Guest Stars: An Illustrated Career Chronicle for 678 Performers of the Sixties and Seventies.* Jefferson, N.C.: McFarland.

Ward has written a visual guide to 678 actors who appeared as guests at least 15 times on network television programs aired in the 1960s and 1970s. Each entry contains a portrait, a career biography, and a list of guest credits. Supplementary materials include an appendix listing air dates for series, a bibliography, and a show index. Ward has written a complementary book entitled *The Supporting Players of Television* (see entry 1017).

CHARACTER ACTORS

1019. Cadden, Tom Scott. 1984. *What a Bunch of Characters! An Entertaining Guide to Who Played What in the Movies.* Englewood Cliffs, N.J.: Prentice-Hall.

Cadden has written a guide to the characters played by 50 actors. All the performers are well known, but the selection criteria are not stated. For each actor, Cadden includes real names, date and place of birth, and a film-by-film description of the characters the performer played. Characters are very briefly described in the context of the plot. There is an index by film title, but not by character name. For a dictionary by character name, try *Memorable Film Characters* (see entry 1088).

1020. Jones, Ken D., Arthur F. McClure, and Alfred E. Twomey. 1976. *Character People.* South Brunswick, N.J.: A.S. Barnes.

1021. McClure, Arthur F., Alfred E. Twomey, and Ken D. Jones. 1984. *More Character People.* 1st ed. Secaucus, N.J.: Citadel Press.

Jones, McClure, and Twomey have written three biographical volumes on character actors featured in films from 1930 to 1955. The first volume was called *The Versatiles,* but it is sufficient to refer to these two volumes, because *Character People* is a sequel and *More Character People* "is an updated, revised, and corrected version of *The Versatiles* with additional materials." To be included, the actors must have played numerous character roles; subsequent stardom in film or television does not exclude them from the book. The listings are very brief, including dates of birth and death, a brief biography, and selected credits. Despite of the brevity of the entries, these books were the first biographies to feature character actors. The authors were able to contact many of the actors who have since passed away, making the biographies useful not only for listing and describing character actors, but for the unique tidbits included in some of the bios. There are no indexes, so it is necessary to consult both volumes to find an actor.

1022. Juran, Robert A. 1995. *Old Familiar Faces: The Great Character Actors and Actresses of Hollywood's Golden Era.* 1st American ed. Sarasota, Fla.: Movie Memories.

Journalist and movie fan Juran has written a biographical guide to 89 character actors featured in the films of the 1930s. Each illustrated entry discusses the characteristics expected from the actor followed by a career biography and a complete filmography. Includes a bibliography and an index.

1023. Mazor, Dave. *What a Character* [World Wide Web Resource]. Address: http://www.what-a-character.com. [Accessed: January 2005].

Mazor's site features hundreds of character actors from film and television. Each entry includes a portrait, a career biography, and a list of appearances in films and as featured or guest roles in television shows. The index lists actors by last name but may be resorted by first name, age, film, or television show. Unfortunately, the search function looks only at names and works, making it impossible to search for words from the biography.

1024. Parish, James Robert. 1978. *Hollywood Character Actors.* New Rochelle, N.Y.: Arlington House.

The prolific Parish and his team of researchers provide brief biographies for almost 400 character actors. A who's who–style entry that includes birth, marriage, children, and death is followed by a few sentences describing the type of character and most noticeable roles along with a quote spoken by the character in a film. The filmographies list all feature-length films, but exclude television roles, even if they are described in the biography. As with most of Parish's books, there is no index.

1025. Quinlan, David. 2004. *Quinlan's Character Stars.* Rev. and updated ed. Richmond, England: Reynolds & Hearn.

Quinlan, a film critic and writer, has compiled a biography of character actors, mostly from the English-speaking world. Covering 1,100 character actors and bit players, each entry includes a portrait; a physical description; a career biography including "type"; and a complete list of all films, shorts, and TV movies appearances. Vital data such as birth date, cause and date of death, and marriages to other stars are also included. As in *Quinlan's Film Stars* (see entry 1008), there is no film title index, so the book is best used for its capsule biographies and complete filmographies. Originally titled *The Illustrated Directory of Film Character Actors.*

1026. Young, Jordan R. 1986. *Reel Characters: Great Movie Character Actors.* 1st ed. Beverly Hills, Calif.: Moonstone Press.

Popular culture writer Young has written biographies of a dozen prominent character actors. Based on interviews with each actor, he has written well-illustrated in-depth biographies of their lives and careers with the most accurate and complete filmographies available (in many cases correcting filmographies published elsewhere). Includes an index.

CHILD ACTORS (SEE ALSO CHILDREN)

1027. Aylesworth, Thomas G. 1987. *Hollywood Kids: Child Stars of the Silver Screen from 1903 to the Present.* 1st ed. New York: Dutton.

Aylesworth, a popular culture writer, has created a biography of more than 150 child stars featured in the earliest movies through the 1980s. *Hollywood Kids* is not a traditional biography—each lavishly illustrated chapter is an essay covering not only individual child actors, but also examining film history, the place of child actors in the film industry, and individual movies. In order to find the stars, it is necessary to use the index, which also lists films. A separate section lists selected filmographies for each child star. Useful for its histories and biographies, the book will also help answer the common question "what ever happened to…?"

1028. Best, Marc. 1971. *Those Endearing Young Charms; Child Performers of the Screen.* South Brunswick, N.J.: A.S. Barnes.

1029. Best, Marc. 1975. *Their Hearts Were Young and Gay.* South Brunswick, N.J.: A.S. Barnes.

Best wrote these two volumes as a paean to child stars. Covering 50 actors in *Those Endearing Young Charms* and 40 more in *Their Hearts Were Young and Gay,* each entry devotes approximately one page to a biography complete with childhood credits and several more pages to black-and-white publicity photographs and stills from their films.

1030. Dye, David. 1988. *Child and Youth Actors: Filmographies of Their Entire Careers, 1914–1985.* Jefferson, N.C.: McFarland.

For 618 child stars, Dye includes names, dates and places of birth, and chronologies (extending into adult careers) listing movies, television series, and stage appearances. Some entries include trivia—often interesting biographical tidbits or notes on how they were discovered. Dye gathered most of the information from movies and teen magazines, but he does include a brief bibliography of books consulted. The extensive index points to films and made-for-television movies, television series and individual episodes, and plays.

1031. Goldstein, Ruth M., and Edith Zornow. 1980. *The Screen Image of Youth: Movies about Children and Adolescents.* Metuchen, N.J.: Scarecrow Press.

Goldstein and Zornow have compiled an international filmography of "more than 350 films in which a child or an adolescent is a significant character." Although it contains films made as early as 1921, most films were made in the fifties, sixties, and seventies. The authors were selective according to their own taste, choosing representative films and made-for-TV movies and excluding cult, exploitation, and occult horror films. They begin with a descriptive filmographic essay describing cultural attitudes toward children and their image in film. The filmography is divided into 15 categories such as Growing Pains, Generation Conflicts, and Delinquency and Crime. Each film includes technical data, principal crew and cast, and a critical synopsis. The classified arrangement makes it necessary to consult the category index and title indexes. The book will be most useful to researchers interested in how children were portrayed on film in the middle of the twentieth century.

1032. Holmstrom, John. 1996. *The Moving Picture Boy: An International Encyclopaedia from 1895 to 1995.* Wilby, Norwich: Michael Russell.

Holmstrom has written an international biography and filmography of boy actors—actors with speaking roles whose voices have not yet broken. Arranged chronologically, each boy merits a brief description of looks and type of roles followed by a complete filmography. Most entries are illustrated with a black-and-white still. Indexes include an alphabetical list of boy actors, film titles, and a broader name index.

1033. Nareau, Bob. 2003. *Kid Kowboys: Juveniles in Western Films.* Madison, N.C.: Empire.

Western genre film historian Nareau has written profiles of more than 70 juvenile actors who were featured in westerns. The loving essays are informative, based on interviews, articles, and studio publicity. Includes a bibliography but no index. The book is of interest to fans and any who wonder "what ever happened to" their favorite child star.

CREDITS

1034. *BaselineFT* [World Wide Web Resource]. Address: http://baseline.hollywood.com or http://filmtracker.com. [Accessed: January 2005].

Baseline claims to host the largest database of cast and crew credits based on tracking each film and television show from development to release since 1982. Complete credits are listed for 1.1 million artists. *Baseline* also offers celebrity biographies, directories for both celebrities and companies, and box office grosses. *Filmtracker* tracks projects from beginning to end. Both of these services are fee-based, with options to subscribe (over 1,500 clients), pay by the search, or license the database. Web portals such as *Lycos* and *Yahoo!* take advantage of this last option to create their film and television databases (see entries 79, 84, and 85). A portion of the database is also available on *Hollywood.com* (see entry 77). Because I did not pay to search the database, this description is based purely on the parts of the Web site that are freely accessible.

Film

1035. Corey, Melinda, and George Ochoa. 1992. *A Cast of Thousands: A Compendium of Who Played What in Film.* New York: Facts on File.

Corey and Ochoa list year of release, production company, director, and cast for nearly 10,000 films. Part I, which takes up two volumes, lists the films in alphabetical order. The cast lists are not complete, rarely listing more than 10 to 15 cast members and their character names. Part II serves as an index and filmography of directors. Part III, which takes up all of the third volume, serves as an index and filmography for 40,000 actors. Neither comprehensive for films nor complete for casts, the compilation is still impressive in scope and worth consulting to see who appeared in what.

1036. Dimmitt, Richard B. 1967. *An Actor Guide to the Talkies; A Comprehensive Listing of 8,000 Feature-Length Films from January, 1949, until December, 1964.* Metuchen, N.J.: Scarecrow Press.

1037. Aros, Andrew A., and Richard B. Dimmitt. 1977. *An Actor Guide to the Talkies, 1965 through 1974.* Metuchen, N.J.: Scarecrow Press.

Dimmitt conceived *An Actor Guide to the Talkies* as the first of two volumes that would complement *A Title Guide to the Talkies* (see entries 1071 to 1073). This first volume covers 1965 to 1974, and the never-published volume was supposed to cover 1928 to 1948. As a result, these books cover half the number of films that the *Title Guide* does. Volume 1 lists 8,000 films with production company, year of release, and a complete cast list, frequently with character names. Volume 2 is an index and filmography of credits for over 30,000 actors. Aros wrote a supplement covering 1965 to 1975.

1038.   Monaco, James. 1987. *Who's Who in American Film Now.* 2nd ed. New York: New York Zoetrope.

Originally intended as a serial publication, *Who's Who in American Film Now* was published in 1981 and again in 1987. Film critic Monaco published this guide to film credits from the *BaselineFT* database (see entry 1034). Separate sections provide filmographies listing films and the year they were released for writers, producers, directors, actors, designers, costumers, cinematographers, sound people, choreographers, stunts, music, special effects, and editors. This *Who's Who* is out of date, but viewers can go online to *Hollywood.com* (see entry 77) for updated filmographies.

1039.   Oliviero, Jeffrey. 1991. *Motion Picture Players' Credits: Worldwide Performers of 1967 through 1980 with Filmographies of Their Entire Careers, 1905–1983.* Jefferson, N.C.: McFarland.

Oliviero has compiled a complete list of film credits from 1905 to 1983 for 15,000 actors active between 1967 and 1980. Other than making reference to an "artistic 'renaissance'" that began in the 1960s, it's not clear why the information is limited to this particular 13-year period of activity. The result is a comprehensive list of credits including a brief career profile, lists of films and select television shows, and contact information when available.

1040.   Parish, James Robert. 1977. *Film Actors Guide: Western Europe.* Metuchen, N.J.: Scarecrow Press.

Parish compiled lists of credits for actors "based in Western Europe exclusive of Scandinavia—who have performed in feature length films." Actors who got their start in Europe and then made films in the United States are also included. In alphabetical order by actor, each entry lists name, real name, date and place of birth and death, and a filmography listing films with country and year of production. Later volumes intending to cover Eastern Europe, Asia, Africa, and Australia were never published.

1041.   Stewart, John. 1975. *Filmarama.* Metuchen, N.J.: Scarecrow Press.

Originally intended to be a six-volume set listing actor filmographies through 1969, the series ended after two volumes: *Volume I: The Formidable Years, 1893–1919* and *Volume II: The Flaming Years, 1920–1929.* The two volumes, however, are quite useful because the era was not well documented. Stewart scoured records and came up with lists of films performed by actors for the first part of each book and an index of films made for the second part.

1042.   Weaver, John T. 1970. *Forty Years of Screen Credits 1929–1969.* Metuchen, N.J.: Scarecrow Press.

Weaver lists credits for approximately 4,000 actors and animal stars. After Academy Award nominees and winners and cast lists for Our Gang, the Dead End Kids, and WAMPAS Babies, individual entries list years of birth and death followed by year-by-year film credits. Along with his *Twenty Years of Silents* (see entry 750), Weaver has compiled a reliable source for film credits.

Television

1043. Inman, David. 2001. *Performers' Television Credits, 1948–2000.* Jefferson, N.C.: McFarland.

Inman took over 15 years to compile this massive three-volume list of television credits. Organized alphabetically by last name, with crosss-references when needed, each entry includes a list of shows and made-for-TV movies in which the actor appeared as a regular or as a guest, along with where and when aired. Excluded are award shows, sports, news broadcasts, and some talk shows ("The Tonight Show" is in, "Entertainment Tonight" is out). When available, Inman includes date and place of birth and death, best known roles, and Emmy Awards won. Very useful in its comprehensiveness. Originally published in 1991 under the title *The TV Encyclopedia.*

1044. Parish, James Robert, and Vincent Terrace. 1989. *The Complete Actors' Television Credits, 1948–1988.* 2nd ed. Metuchen, N.J.: Scarecrow Press.

Cumulating the earlier *Actors' Television Credits* and its three supplements, Parish and Terrace give the credits for 1,587 actors, listing every television program in which they appeared between 1948 and 1988, including pilots, series, variety shows, specials, and documentaries. This book offers the most comprehensive list of television credits through 1988.

STUNTS

1045. Freese, Gene Scott. 1998. *Hollywood Stunt Performers: A Dictionary and Filmography of over 600 Men and Women, 1922–1996.* Jefferson, N.C.: McFarland.

Freese has compiled a biography of over 600 stunt men and women who appeared in at least 10 films. Listed in alphabetical order by last name, each entry includes a brief biography and as complete a filmography as possible, considering that stunt doubles were not credited in early films. An appendix lists stunt organizations, a bibliography lists sources for further reading, and an index points to people and films.

ART DIRECTORS

1046. Stephens, Michael L. 1998. *Art Directors in Cinema: A Worldwide Biographical Dictionary.* Jefferson, N.C.: McFarland.

Stephens has written a biographical dictionary of art directors, the people who design movie sets. Covering the entire history of cinema, he lists mostly art directors from the United States and Europe, with only a few from Asia. For each art director, he writes a biography featuring career and style followed by a filmography. Unfortunately, the book contains only a handful of illustrations. Includes a bibliography and comprehensive index.

CINEMATOGRAPHERS

1047. Darby, William. 1991. *Masters of Lens and Light: A Checklist of Major Cinematographers and Their Feature Films.* Metuchen, N.J.: Scarecrow Press.

Darby has compiled film credits for over 700 cinematographers. For each cinematographer, he lists their feature films along with date of release, country of origin, and distributor. To be included, a cinematographer must have worked on at least five films, so Darby created a miscellaneous films section that "includes entries for notable films that are not included among the works of major cinematographers." A film title index points to both sections.

COSTUME DESIGNERS

1048. Leese, Elizabeth. 1991. *Costume Design in the Movies: An Illustrated Guide to the Work of 157 Great Designers, Dover Books on Fashion.* New York: Dover.

Leese wrote the first reference book on motion picture costume designers. After a historical overview, she provides lavishly illustrated career biographies for 157 designers with credits updated through 1988 in the second edition. Appendixes list Oscar and BAFTA nominations and winners for costume, and an index lists 6,000 film titles.

1049. Perez Prichard, Susan. 1981. *Film Costume, an Annotated Bibliography.* Metuchen N.J.: Scarecrow Press.

Perez Prichard has compiled a bibliography of 3,627 books and articles that discuss costumes for film and the designers who make them. Organized by author, each entry includes the standard bibliographic data and an annotation. The index lists names, titles, and subjects.

DIRECTORS
BIOGRAPHY

1050. Allon, Yoram, Del Cullen, and Hannah Patterson. 2002. *Contemporary North American Film Directors: A Wallflower Critical Guide.* 2nd ed. London; New York: Wallflower.

The *Wallflower Critical Guides* feature biographies of "well-established and emerging directors." In this volume, the focus is on 500 directors currently working in the United States and Canada. The articles are written by film critics and scholars and discuss the director's life, career, and films. Films and year of release are listed in the margins. No cast or crew is included, as the *Guides* are intended to be biographies rather than filmographies. The "filmography" is actually the film title index. *The Wallflower Guide* is useful in its wide-ranging coverage (even one-time film directors are included) of contemporary directors.

1051.   Andrew, Geoff. 1999. *The Director's Vision: A Concise Guide to the Art of 250 Great Filmmakers.* North American ed. Chicago: A Cappella.

Andrew has selected 250 film directors from all over the world who he thinks have distinct visual styles. Each director is given one full page, with half the page devoted to an image from a film that is representative of the filmmaker's oeuvre. Beginning with an analysis of the image, the rest of the page discusses the "composition, lighting, camera-movement, colour and cutting" and themes that define the director's style. The caption identifies the film and actors in the still, includes a selective list of films by the director, and recommends other directors with similar styles. The focus on visual style makes Andrew's book a nice complement to other guides to directors and their work, including his own *Film Handbook* (see entry 1052).

1052.   Andrew, Geoff. 1990. *The Film Handbook, The G.K. Hall Performing Arts Handbooks.* Boston: G.K. Hall.

Andrew takes a critical look at 200 of the best known directors from around the world whose works were widely available for viewing at the time of the book's publication. Entries include dates of birth, direction, and death, a critique of their work, a discussion of influences called "lineage," suggested reading, and suggested viewing in the form of a list of representative films. Supplementary materials include a glossary of genre and style, lists of film books and other resources, and an index. Andrew later wrote a complementary book entitled *The Director's Vision* (see entry 1051) focusing on visual style.

1053.   Finler, Joel W. 1985. *The Movie Directors Story.* New York: Crescent Books.

A companion volume to the Hollywood studio *Story* histories (see Studios chapter), *The Movie Directors Story* is a lavishly illustrated guide to 140 American and British film directors who were active from the 1920s through 1985. Each chapter covers 15 to 20 years of filmmaking. Overviews of the industry and the major events and people are followed by alphabetical lists of the directors who had the greatest impact. Each article includes real name, place and date of birth, and date of death, an overview of career and life, and stills and publicity photos. There is a list of Academy Award nominees and winners and indexes by director, other personnel, and film title.

1054.   Quinlan, David. 2001. *Quinlan's Film Directors.* London: Batsford.

Quinlan, a film critic and writer, has compiled an illustrated guide to directors and the films they made. Covering over 850 directors, each entry includes a biography focusing primarily on the career, although vital data such as birth date, cause and date of death, and marriages are also included. He does not include a film title index, diminishing somewhat the book's usefulness.

1055.   Sarris, Andrew. 1998. *The St. James Film Directors Encyclopedia.* Detroit: Visible Ink Press.

Sarris—a film professor, critic, and early proponent of the auteur theory—has selected 200 directors from the 500 listed in the *International Dictionary of Films and Filmmakers* (see entry 962) for reprinting in this guide. Each entry includes facts of nationality, birth, education, family, career, awards, and death, a filmography, and a signed essay exploring the body of work. Agent names and addresses are included for directors who are still active. Added materials include a chronology of film history, a nationality index covering nearly 30 countries, and a director and film title index. The complete filmographies and scholarly essays make this an excellent place to research prominent directors—but note that the content of each entry is identical to those in the larger *International Dictionary of Films and Filmmakers,* so it is not necessary to consult both.

1056. Sennett, Ted. 1986. *Great Movie Directors.* New York: Abrams.

Created in association with the Directors Guild of America and the American Film Institute, Sennett has created an excellent guide to the careers of more than 200 film directors "who have contributed indelibly or substantially to the development of film." For each of these mostly American directors, Sennett writes a career biography that features common thematic elements and best known films. The book is lavishly illustrated with stills. An appendix lists DGA Award winners, a bibliography lists sources consulted, and a complete filmography lists all feature-length films and documentaries by each director. The index is comprehensive. *Great Movie Directors* is of interest to both casual movie fans and serious film researchers.

1057. Tasker, Yvonne. 2002. *Fifty Contemporary Filmmakers, Routledge Key Guides.* London; New York: Routledge.

Professor Tasker led a team of experts in writing biographical and critical articles on 50 filmmakers (mostly directors) currently working in Europe, North America, and Asia. In some cases, some more established filmmakers are excluded in favor of filmmakers just beginning to make their mark. Each essay explores and critiques career and works from a variety of theoretical perspectives, most often focusing on authorship. Each entry also includes a filmography and bibliography of further readings. Well indexed, this is a guide that is useful not only to film buffs, but is of special interest to film professors and students.

1058. Wakeman, John. 1987. *World Film Directors.* New York: H.W. Wilson.

Wakeman led a team of writers in compiling information on the "work and lives of about four hundred of the world's best-known film directors." Volume 1 covers directors born before 1920 who made films between 1890 and 1945, while Volume 2 covers more recent directors who made films between 1945 and 1985. Like H.W. Wilson's similar books on authors, the entries gather in one place information on life and career, a representative critical response to the films, a filmography, and a bibliography. Although the entries do not represent original research, the fact that they bring together so much information from multiple sources makes these books an excellent place to begin investigating directors who made their mark before 1985.

CREDITS

1059. Bushnell, Brooks. 1993. *Directors and Their Films: A Comprehensive Reference, 1895–1990.* Jefferson, N.C.: McFarland.

Bushnell has compiled an international filmography of theatrical feature films by their directors. Part I lists directors and their films by year. Part II lists 108,000 films by year and director. Although Bushnell does not explain his selection criteria, the inclusion of both prominent and more obscure directors indicate comprehensive coverage. Because of its international scope and massive size, this is a useful guide for researchers seeking the most complete lists possible of director credits.

1060. Krautz, Alfred, Hille Krautz, and Joris Krautz. 1993. *Encyclopedia of Film Directors in the United States of America and Europe.* München; New Providence, N.J.: K.G. Saur.

The authors have compiled the filmographies of approximately 3,300 comedy directors and 3,600 crime directors. *Volume 1: Comedies to 1991* lists over 19,000 comedies, and *Volume 2: Crime Films to 1995* lists over 9,500 crime films. Each volume includes American and European directors, beginning with a one-sentence biography that lists other specialties and types of films made and a complete filmography naming film, release date, and country. Each volume includes film title indexes and chronological listings of films. Useful because of their systematic coverage.

1061. Parish, James Robert, and Kingsley Canham. 1976. *Film Directors Guide—Western Europe.* Metuchen, N.J.: Scarecrow Press.

Parish and Canham compiled lists of credits for directors "based in Western Europe—who have contributed feature-length productions to the cinema." In alphabetical order by director, each entry lists name, real name, date and place of birth and death, and a filmography listing films with country and year of production. Later volumes intending to cover Eastern Europe, Asia, Africa, and Australia were never published.

WRITERS (SEE ALSO *ADAPTATION*)
BIOGRAPHY

1062. Morsberger, Robert Eustis, Stephen O. Lesser, and Randall Clark. 1984. *American Screenwriters, Dictionary of Literary Biography; Vol. 26.* Detroit: Gale Research.

1063. Clark, Randall. 1986. *American Screenwriters: Second Series, Dictionary of Literary Biography; Vol. 44.* Detroit: Gale Research.

The *Dictionary of Literary Biography,* designed to serve teachers and scholars by making literature accessible to their students, gives the same treatment to screenwriters as it does to other authors in these two volumes. Screenwriter entries begin with a complete list of the films, television shows, plays, books, and periodical articles they authored. A critical career biography is followed by a list of published interviews and references consulted. Entries are illustrated with a portrait, posters, and publicity stills. With only 129 screenwriters covered, the books are not comprehensive, but they do provide excellent introductions and overviews to the most prominent American screenwriters.

CREDITS

1064. Academy of Motion Picture Arts and Sciences and Writers Guild of America West. 1970. *Who Wrote the Movie and What Else Did He Write? An Index of Screen Writers and Their Film Works, 1936–1969.* Los Angeles.

The Academy of Motion Picture Arts and Sciences and the Screen Branch of the Writers Guild of America collaborated to compile this index to the films of approximately 2,000 screenwriters and the nearly 13,000 films they wrote between 1936 and 1969. The first section lists the writers and their credits, while the second section lists film titles with screenwriter credits. A separate index lists films that were nominated for or won Academy Awards for writing. Although now dated, this work of scholarship is still valuable for its thoroughly researched lists of credits.

1065. Langman, Larry. 1984. *A Guide to American Screenwriters: The Sound Era, 1929–1982, Garland Reference Library of the Humanities; Vol. 501.* New York: Garland.

Langman, a prolific producer of film reference books, has compiled credits for the "complete works of American screenwriters—their features, full-length documentaries, and animated films from 1929 through 1982." Excluded are short subjects, X-rated films, and made-for-TV movies. Volume 1 lists the credits for nearly 5,000 screenwriters by year and title. Volume 2 lists more than 20,000 films with complete screenwriting credits. The *Guide* is useful for seeing who wrote what.

11
Screenplays

This chapter lists adaptations of novels, plays, short stories, and other source materials as well as novelizations of films and television shows. This chapter also includes guides to characters, lists of quotes, and collections of scenes and scripts.

ADAPTATIONS

1066. *Based on the Book* [World Wide Web Resource]. Mid-Continent Public Library. Address: http://www.mcpl.lib.mo.us/readers/movies. [Accessed: March 2005].

The librarians at the Mid-Continent Public Library in Independence, Missouri, have compiled a list of over 1,100 feature films released in the United States since 1980 that have been based on books. Readers may browse the lists by movie title, movie release year, book title, or book author. These same four elements make up the tables for each list. The films are drawn from the *IMDb* (see entry 66), but it is nice to have one source that updates the many print resources that are now out-of-date.

1067. Baskin, Ellen, and A.G.S. Enser. 2003. *Enser's Filmed Books and Plays: A List of Books and Plays from Which Films Have Been Made, 1928–2001.* 6th ed. Aldershot, Hant, England; Burlington, Vt.: Ashgate.

Enser's Filmed Books and Plays lists films adapted from books or plays between 1928 and 2001. The first half of the book points from the film title to the author and publisher of the book or play. The second half of the book points from the author and title to the film, production company, and year of release. An index lists changes filmmakers made to the book titles.

1068. Costello, Tom. 1994. *International Guide to Literature on Film.* London; New Jersey: Bowker-Saur.

Costello has compiled a comprehensive list of all films made from significant novels, short stories, or plays between 1930 and 1991. Literary significance was determined by literary scholars and the editors of several standard reference works in the field of literature as well as the merits of the films made. Arranged across two-page spreads, the left-hand "literature" page lists the author, nationality, format, title, and date; the right-hand "film" page lists the film title, the country of production, the date of release, the director, and the length of the film. Indexes list film titles and literary titles. The *Guide*'s strength lies in its excellent coverage of authors from around the world and will be of interest to researchers comparing literature and film.

1069. Daisne, Johan. 1971. *Dictionnaire Filmographique de la Littérature Mondiale. Filmographic Dictionary of World Literature. Filmographisches Lexikon Der Weltliteratur. Filmografisch Lexicon Der Wereldliteratuur.* Gand: E. Story-Scientia.

1070.   Daisne, Johan. 1978. *Dictionnaire Filmographique de la Littérature Mondiale = Filmographic Dictionary of World Literature = Filmographisches Lexikon Der Weltliteratur = Filmografisch Lexicon Der Wereldliteratuur.* Suppl. (A–Z). ed. Gand: E. Story-Scientia.

Johan Daisne, a pseudonym of noted Belgian writer and librarian Herman Thiery, published a two-volume set listing international films adapted from books by authors from all over the world (including himself). Organized by author, entries include book title, film title if different, country and year of production, director, and lead actors. While the introduction is in French, English, German, and Dutch, entries for films are written in each respective language, and entries for other languages default to French. The second half of each book offers over 400 pages of black-and-white plates from the films listed. A supplement was published in 1978. A title index points to authors. The book is most useful in its coverage of some lesser-known authors.

1071.   Dimmitt, Richard B. 1965. *A Title Guide to the Talkies; a Comprehensive Listing of 16,000 Feature-Length Films from October, 1927, until December, 1963.* New York: Scarecrow Press.

1072.   Aros, Andrew A., and Richard B. Dimmitt. 1977. *A Title Guide to the Talkies, 1964 through 1974.* Metuchen, N.J.: Scarecrow Press.

1073.   Aros, Andrew A., and Richard B. Dimmitt. 1986. *A Title Guide to the Talkies, 1975 through 1984.* Metuchen, N.J.: Scarecrow Press.

Dimmitt wrote this book to guide readers who have seen a movie and now wish to read the "novel, play, poem, short story, or screen story which was used as a basis for the movie." In alphabetical order by title, 16,000 entries include copyright owner, producer, and a bibliographic citation for the work on which the movie is based. Cross-references are used when the titles of the movie and the original work are different. Aros compiled supplements for 1964–1974 and 1975–1984 in which he added distribution company, year of release, director, and novelizations. Both volumes include name indexes. *An Actor Guide to the Talkies* (see entries 1036 and 1037) complements the *Title Guide.*

1074.   Fenton, Jill. 1990. *Women Writers, from Page to Screen, Garland Reference Library of the Humanities; Vol. 687.* New York: Garland.

This compilation lists more than 2,200 American and British films made from 1913 through 1988 "inspired by women's writings." Writings include not only short stories, novels, and plays, but articles, diaries, poems, and songs as well. Organized first by author and then by literary work, each film includes title, production information, and release date. Indexes to film titles and literary sources complete the filmography.

1075.   Gifford, Denis. 1991. *Books and Plays in Films, 1896–1915: Literary, Theatrical, and Artistic Sources of the First Twenty Years of Motion Pictures.* Jefferson, N.C.; London; New York: McFarland; Mansell.

Many guides to literary sources neglect the silent era, either because it's difficult to uncover sources or because it is assumed that films without sound are not worthy of literary analysis. Gifford fills this gap by listing 861 authors and the more than 2,000 films they inspired during the first 20 years of cinema. Sources include "novels, plays, non-fiction books, short stories, biographies, poems, operas, songs, cartoons and comic strips," and even dance. Organized alphabetically by author and then chronologically by film title (if different from the source, original titles are given in parentheses), each film lists the production company and the type of source. A title index lists films and literary sources, and an appendix lists film production companies by country.

1076. Goble, Alan. 1999. *The Complete Index to Literary Sources in Film.* London; New Providence, N.J.: Bowker-Saur.

Goble has compiled by far the most complete index to literary sources for film with 12,122 authors and 30,572 works from which movies in 83 different countries were adapted. The first half of the book is the author index, listing author, original work, and films adapted from each work. The literary source index and the film index point from each work to the author.

1077. Langman, Larry. 1986. *Writers on the American Screen: A Guide to Film Adaptations of American and Foreign Literary Works, Garland Reference Library of the Humanities; Vol. 658.* New York: Garland.

Langman has compiled a list of authors whose "poems, short stories, plays and novels have been made into motion pictures." He selects writers who have been recognized in major literary reference works. Organized first by author and then by literary work, each entry lists the films with release date and distributor. An index lists literary and film titles.

1078. Parlato, Salvatore J. 1980. *Films Ex Libris: Literature in 16 MM and Video.* Jefferson, N.C.: McFarland.

Parlato has compiled a list of 1,410 16mm films inspired by novels, "poetry, short stories, fairy tales, fables, legends, drama, mythology, and non-fiction" made between 1903 and 1979. Classified by type of literature such as the Bible, biography, and the categories above, each entry includes film title, a brief summary, and the literary source. Indexes list 645 authors and 1,012 literary works. Parlato originally designed the book as a guide to films available on 16mm. That aspect of the book is dated, but the list of literary sources could still be useful to researchers.

1079. Ross, Harris. 1987. *Film as Literature, Literature as Film: An Introduction to and Bibliography of Film's Relationship to Literature, Bibliographies and Indexes in World Literature, No. 10.* New York: Greenwood Press.

Ross, an English professor, has compiled a bibliography of almost 2,500 English-language books and articles that examine the relationship of "film to drama, prose fiction, and poetry" written between 1908 and 1985. Seventeen chapters focus on such issues as adaptation, writers (Shakespeare gets an entire chapter), and regional influences. Ross includes brief annotations only if the title of the article is vague, doesn't name the film, or uses a different title for a film. The bibliography is intended to be comprehensive, but it excludes film reviews and newspaper articles. Provides an author index and a subject index that names individual films and filmmakers.

1080. Tibbetts, John C., and James Michael Welsh. 2005. *The Encyclopedia of Novels into Film.* 2nd ed. New York: Facts on File.

Professors Tibbetts and Welsh have compiled a series of scholarly essays on the adaptation of literature to film. Organized by the novel titles, each entry compares the novel to the film and provides references to critical works. Appendix A is an essay on novelists turned screenwriters, and Appendix B provides brief biographies of the writers. The index lists names and subjects, but does not include film titles, making it difficult to find films that do not share the name of the source material. The detail and comparative essays make this encyclopedia a nice complement to the reference books that merely list sources without comment. The companion *Encyclopedia of Stage Plays into Film* (see entry 1086) is also worth exploring.

1081.   Welch, Jeffrey Egan. 1981. *Literature and Film: An Annotated Bibliography, 1909–1977, Garland Reference Library of the Humanities; Vol. 241.* New York: Garland.

1082.   Welch, Jeffrey Egan. 1993. *Literature and Film: An Annotated Bibliography, 1978–1988, Garland Reference Library of the Humanities; Vol. 1114.* New York: Garland.

Welch has compiled a bibliography of 1,235 works written between 1909 and 1977 "published in North America and Great Britain having to do with the special relationship between films and works of literature." The main section of the bibliography is in alphabetical order by author and annotates books and articles on issues relating to adaptation, influence, and teaching. A separate section lists dissertations chronologically without annotations. The appendix lists the authors of the works of literature that have been adapted, be they novelists, playwrights, poets, or short-story writers. Includes an index. The supplement covers works published between 1978 and 1988. Although dated, the bibliography is still of use to students interested in older films and older research methods relating to film and literature.

NOVELIZATIONS

1083.   Peer, Kurt. 1997. *TV Tie-Ins: A Bibliography of American TV Tie-in Paperbacks.* 1st ed. Tucson, Ariz.: Neptune.

Peer has compiled a bibliography of mass market paperbacks and Whitman hardbacks that were "based on or issued in conjunction with a TV show" and published by 1990. Organized by program, each entry lists air dates and broadcaster followed by a list of the tie-ins with all the standard bibliographic elements. Indexes list tie-ins by author and by publisher, which actors are pictured on the covers of the tie-ins, and episodes that have been novelized. *TV Tie-Ins* includes a block of black-and-white plates that show sample book covers. A collector himself, Peer adds an appendix on physical condition. This unique guide, however, is not just for collectors, but for the fans of the shows and popular culture researchers as well.

PLAYS

1084.   Erskine, Thomas L., and James Michael Welsh. 2000. *Video Versions: Film Adaptations of Plays on Video.* Westport, Conn.: Greenwood Press.

Erskine and Welsh have compiled a list of films adapted from plays. Organized by play title, each entry lists the film adaptations and a summary of each. The index lists films, plays, and names. The book is very similar to the slightly better *Encyclopedia of Stage Plays into Film* (see entry 1086), both of which Welsh coauthored.

1085. Rothwell, Kenneth S., and Annabelle Melzer. 1990. *Shakespeare on Screen: An International Filmography and Videography.* New York: Neal-Schuman.

Professors Rothwell and Melzer have compiled a guide to 750 "film and video treatments of Shakespeare's cannon" produced between 1899 and 1989. They include "not only the major film adaptations but also modernizations, spin-offs, musical and dance versions, abridgements, travesties and excerpts," as well as filmed plays and documentaries about Shakespeare and his plays. After an overview, the filmography is organized first alphabetically by play and then chronologically by film. Each film includes production data, quotes from critics, format, and credits. Because *Shakespeare on Screen* is intended primarily for educators, the authors also list supplementary materials and availability (as of 1990). Includes indexes by film, series, date, names, and distributor.

1086. Tibbetts, John C., and James Michael Welsh. 2001. *The Encyclopedia of Stage Plays into Film, Facts on File Film Reference Library.* New York: Facts on File.

Tibbetts and Welsh have compiled a series of scholarly essays on the adaptation of plays into film. Organized by the title of the play, each entry compares the play to the film and provides references to critical works. The book has separate sections for Shakespeare and musical theater. An appendix explores adapting Shakespeare to the screen. Unlike their *Encyclopedia of Novels into Film* (see entry 1080), the authors have included film titles in the index as well as personal names and subjects. Like the *Encyclopedia of Novels into Film,* the detail and comparative essays make this encyclopedia a nice complement to the reference books that merely list sources without comment.

SHORT STORIES

1087. Emmens, Carol A. 1985. *Short Stories on Film and Video.* 2nd ed. Littleton, Colo.: Libraries Unlimited.

Emmens lists "all the films produced between 1920 and 1984 that are based on short stories by American authors or outstanding international authors well known in America." Arranged alphabetically by author and then by short story, each of the 1,375 entries includes the title of the film, production information, director, principal cast, and, in most cases, a one-sentence synopsis. The book also includes distributor information that is now too dated to be useful. Film title and short story title indexes point readers to the appropriate page. With its exclusive focus on short stories, Emmens's guide is useful to researchers interested in issues of adaptation.

CHARACTERS (SEE ALSO *PORTRAYALS*)

1088. Lieberman, Susan, and Frances Cable. 1984. *Memorable Film Characters: An Index to Roles and Performers, 1915–1983, Bibliographies and Indexes in the Performing Arts, No. 1.* Westport, Conn.: Greenwood Press.

Librarian Cable completed her colleague Lieberman's work by compiling an index to over 1,500 memorable characters featured in films. They selected memorable characters from films and actors who were nominated for major international film awards, a survey of 75 film buffs, and their own experiences. Organized by character name, each entry includes a physical description and personality profile in the context of the plot followed by the name of the film and the actor. Indexes list films and actors. There are occasional omissions of characters from nominated films, but this remains a good place to find who portrayed whom or to merely browse for fun.

1089.   Nowlan, Robert A., and Gwendolyn Wright Nowlan. 1990. *Movie Characters of Leading Performers of the Sound Era.* Chicago: American Library Association.

Writers of several film reference books, the Nowlans have compiled lists of the most prominent characters played by approximately 450 lead actors during their careers. Each actor is represented by a brief career biography, a list of key roles describing the character and placing it in the context of the plot, and a list of other roles. There are no indexes, so this guide is most useful for researchers and fans curious to see the roles that made their favorite actors famous.

1090.   Nowlan, Robert A., and Gwendolyn Wright Nowlan. 1993. *The Name Is Familiar: Who Played Who in the Movies? A Directory of Title Characters.* New York: Neal-Schuman.

This strange reference book lists movies whose characters are featured in the film title. Characters can be real or fictional or even obliquely referred to in the title. The book is divided into three parts. The first part covers the performers, the second the title characters, and the third the films. Although interesting, its use is limited as a reference book. The character lists might be useful in seeing whether a movie has been made that features a real person or a fictional character, and perhaps it could be used to trace a series that names its lead character in each title. But because the book is limited to characters when named in the title, there can be no assurance that the results will be complete.

1092.   Pickard, Roy. 1988. *Who Played Who on the Screen.* London: Batsford.

Designed to answer questions such as "who has played Marilyn Monroe?" or "how many times has Dracula been seen in the movies?" Pickard has written an illustrated dictionary of major fictional characters and prominent real people who have been portrayed on screen in sound films through 1987. The entries for each person or character provide a brief biography, a list of actors who portrayed him or her, and occasional notes on other (most often silent or television) portrayals. The reference use of the book could have been improved by including indexes to actors and to films, but the book still serves readers who wants to know (as the first edition was entitled) *Who Played Who in the Movies.*

1093.   Sharp, Harold S., and Marjorie Z. Sharp. 1973. *Index to Characters in the Performing Arts: Part 4, Radio and Television.* Metuchen, N.J.: Scarecrow Press.

The first three parts of the Sharp's compilation list characters that appear in plays, musicals and operas, and ballets. Part IV identifies characters from radio and television programs that aired from the earliest days of television through 1972. Organized by character, there is only one entry per television (or radio) program, with one character designated as main with cross-references to other characters and the show's title. The entry then lists all regular characters with brief descriptions of each.

QUOTATIONS

1094. Bainbridge, Jim. 1999. *"Show Me the Money": A Century of Great Movie Lines.* 1st ed. Emeryville, Calif.: Woodford Press.

Bainbridge, a sports writer and "movie hound," has compiled a list of his favorite quotes from films. He begins with his own top 10, and then arranges the rest of the quotes into 18 categories. Unlike many compilations, this one isn't limited to lighthearted banter and includes such categories as death, justice, and religion. In each category, quotes are organized by film and include the writer and the year. There is no index, so it's of most interest to movie buffs and quote seekers willing to browse.

1095. Bloch, Jeff. 1993. *Frankly, My Dear: More Than 650 of the Funniest, Smartest, Gutsiest, Nastiest, Sexiest, and Simply Greatest Quotes in Celebration of Women in the Movies.* Secaucus, N.J.: Carol.

Popular culture writer Bloch spent a year watching movies in order to compile this list of more than 650 film quotes by (mostly) women. Divided into 17 chapters, each entry includes the quote, the speaker, the film, and the year released. Bloch includes actor and film title indexes, but no keyword index, so it is necessary to browse the chapters to locate quotes. This is fun, because the quotes are well selected, but it diminishes the reference value somewhat.

1096. Chesher, R. Donna. 1992. *"The End": Closing Lines of Over 3,000 Theatrically-Released American Films.* Jefferson, N.C.: McFarland.

Chesher has compiled the last spoken lines from over 3,000 American films through 1990. Each film entry lists the title, release date, production company, the line, and the character's and actor's name. Unique in scope, the lack of an index somewhat reduces the book's usefulness.

1097. Corey, Melinda, and George Ochoa. 1995. *The Dictionary of Film Quotations: 6,000 Provocative Movie Quotes from 1,000 Movies.* 1st ed. New York: Crown Trade Paperbacks.

Film reference writers Corey and Ochoa have compiled a list of memorable quotes from 1,000 of the "most acclaimed popular, and characteristic films of the day." Organized in alphabetical order by film, entries typically include year of release, studio, director, screenwriter, and up to 15 quotes with the characters who spoke them and the context in which they were spoken. Speaker and subject indexes guide readers to quotes.

1098. Crawley, Tony, and W. & R. Chambers Ltd. 1991. *Chambers Film Quotes.* Edinburgh: Chambers.

Crawley has compiled over 2,000 quotes and anecdotes about movies and life by stars and filmmakers—there are no quotes from films. Arranged under 260 topics, each quote lists the speaker and cites the source. Includes an author index. *Chambers* has an interesting selection, so it's of value to both fans as well as anyone seeking a quotable.

1099. Douglas, D.C. *Useless Movie Quotes* [World Wide Web Resource]. Address: http://www.uselessmoviequotes.com. [Accessed: January 2005].

Working under the assumption that a "movie quote unused is a useless movie quote," Douglas compiled "more than 2600 quotes from more than 220 movies." Quotes are organized by film but may also be browsed by actor or searched by keyword. Each record quotes a dozen or so lines from a film and lists the actors and the characters they played. Most of the films cited were made during the last 20 to 30 years, with only a handful from the 1960s.

1100.   Fennell, John P. 1989. *"You Ain't Heard Nothin' Yet!" 501 Famous Lines from Great (and Not-So-Great) Movies.* Secaucus, N.J.: Carol.

Fennell compiles a list of his favorite quotes from movies. He presents them in chronological order, making an effort to proportionately represent each era. Without an index, the book is more browsable than useful as a reference source. But as is true for all books of quotations, the best is the one that has the quote the reader is seeking.

1101.   Forget, Carol, and Hilary Weber. 1996. *VideoHound's Movie Laughlines: Quips, Quotes, and Clever Comebacks.* Detroit: Visible Ink Press.

Carol Forget and Hilary Weber led a team of editors in gathering humorous quotes from throughout movie history. Divided into 100 categories, quotes are listed in chronological order and include character and actor name, film, and year of release. Of the greatest value in this collection are the seven indexes covering film title, keywords, decades, and names of actors, characters, directors, and writers.

1102.   Gardner, Gerald C. 1992. *I Coulda Been a Contender.* Warner Books ed. New York: Warner Books.

Gardner quotes the wit and wisdom to be found in movie dialogue. The book contains 22 chapters on themes such as sex and sin, wealth and poverty, and death. The last chapter quotes lines censored by the Hays Office. Quotes list just the movie, with no citation to speaker. Writers, directors, and cast for each film are listed in the appendix. There is no index, so the collection is mostly a browser's delight.

1103.   Haun, Harry. 1980. *The Movie Quote Book.* 1st ed. New York: Lippincott & Crowell.

Haun, a movie reporter, has compiled a list of over 4,000 quotes taken from movies. Arranged by dozens of broad subjects from Accuracy to Youth and including headings such as Bravado, Humility, Regrets, and Truth, each entry includes the quote, the speaker, and the context in which it was spoken. It seems Haun has selected quotes he likes rather than working from any systematic selection strategy, but the quotes can still be useful when mining for wisdom or clever turns of phrase. Includes a list of films, but no keyword index.

1104.   Jarski, Rosemarie. 1999. *Wisecracks: Great Lines from the Classic Hollywood Era.* Lincolnwood, Ill.: Contemporary Books.

Screenwriter Jarski watched 1,000 movies to compile this list of witty one-liners taken from movies made mostly, but not exclusively, during the days of the studio system. Organized into nine broad categories and further subdivided into 76 narrower categories, each wisecrack includes the line, the actor who spoke it, the film in which it was said, and the year the film was released. Includes a name, film title, and topic index. This fun read is also useful for tracking down humorous film quotes.

1105.   Kane, Jim. 1999. *Western Movie Quotations*. Jefferson, N.C.: McFarland.

Kane has compiled "over 6,000 quotations from more than 1,000 western movies." The book is arranged according to broad topics such as bad guys, gambling, and lawmen. Most of the entries are not stand-alone quotes, but are snippets of dialogue placed in context. Indexes list actor and character names, films, and keywords and subjects.

1106.   Langman, Larry, and Paul Gold. 2001. *Comedy Quotes from the Movies: Over 4,000 Bits of Humorous Dialogue from All Film Genres, Topically Arranged and Indexed.* Jefferson, N.C.; London: McFarland.

The title says it all. Film professor Langman and math teacher Gold have compiled funny quotes from the advent of talkies through movies made in the early 1990s. Divided into over 100 categories such as the battle of the sexes, religion, and villains, quotes are then organized in chronological order. Each quote is placed in the context of the plot and lists the actors and the movie title along with the year of release. The authors include name and title indexes, but there is no keyword index that can so often complete a book of quotations. Nonetheless, the nice selection of quotes and the large number of subject classifications make this an excellent addition to film quotation books.

1107.   Nowlan, Robert A., and Gwendolyn Wright Nowlan. 1994. *Film Quotations: 11,000 Lines Spoken on Screen, Arranged by Subject, and Indexed.* Jefferson, N.C.: McFarland.

Professors Nowlan and Nowlan have compiled the largest and most systematic collection of quotes from films. They have organized 11,420 quotes into 900 subject categories. Within each category, quotes are organized chronologically and include the quote, the speaker, the context, the film, and the year. Indexes point to performers and film titles. A keyword index would have been ideal, because this is the premier film quote collection.

1108.   Petras, Ross, and Kathryn Petras. 1999. *Stupid Movie Lines: The 776 Dumbest Things Ever Uttered on the Silver Screen.* 1st ed. New York: Villard Books.

Petras and Petras, siblings who have made a career of publishing stupid comments, have compiled a list of 776 bad movie lines—"non-sequiturs, cloyingly awful romantic lines, terrible jokes, moronic monologues, failed comebacks, awful dialogue." Organized alphabetically by keyword (sort of), each quote is introduced by a caption-like headline and finished off with the speaker and the context of the dialogue. Of virtually no reference use, the book is mild entertainment at best.

1109.   Rees, Nigel. 2000. *Cassell's Movie Quotations*. London: Cassell.

Rees has compiled a list of "not only quotable lines of dialogue from films but also quotable remarks by and about film-makers and, indeed, filmgoers." Rees interfiles two types of entries. Entries for films include screenwriters, cast and characters, and quotes from the dialogue. Entries for individuals include quotes about film as well as quotes about them. The index lists significant keywords and people who are the subject of quotes who don't have their own entries. Cassell's is one of the more systematic quote books, and its inclusion of quotes both from films and about film makes it well worth consulting for readers seeking quotes.

1110.   Ringler, Stephen M. 2000. *A Dictionary of Cinema Quotations from Filmmakers and Critics: Over 3400 Axioms, Criticisms, Opinions, and Witticisms from 100 Years of the Cinema.* Jefferson, N.C.: McFarland.

Filmmaker Ringler takes a different approach to movie quotations. Instead of drawing quotes from movies, he has mined the film literature for quotes from filmmakers on filmmaking. Divided into 31 chapters on such topics as audience, genre, critics, and the various aspects of making a movie, each of the 3,408 quotes are connected to 1,850 different speakers or writers. The selection represents everyone from the most prominent filmmakers to the unknown who panned actors such as Fred Astaire during his screen test. Includes a resource bibliography and source names and movie title and keyword indexes.

1111.   Rutledge, Leigh W. 1999. *Nice Girls Don't Wear Cha-Cha Heels!* 1st ed. Los Angeles: Alyson Books.

Rutledge collects memorable lines from films. The categories range from insults to catty remarks to dating to pure camp. A very small book with few quotations, it still might be useful for having quotes not included in other collections.

1112.   Shalit, Gene. 2002. *Great Hollywood Wit: A Glorious Cavalcade of Hollywood Wisecracks, Zingers, Japes, Quips, Slings, Jests, Snappers & Sass from the Stars.* 1st ed. New York: St. Martin's Press.

Movie critic Shalit has compiled a list of quotes by movie stars made in movies and off screen. Divided into two dozen chapters, each entry includes the quip and the speaker. Not the least bit scholarly or systematic, and with no index, this is nonetheless a fun read that could provide quotables for movie fans.

SCENES

1113.   Leff, Leonard J. 1983. *Film Plots: Scene-by-Scene Narrative Outlines for Feature Film Study.* Ann Arbor, Mich.: Pierian Press.

Film Plots gives scene-by-scene descriptions of 117 of the most popular and critically successful films. For each film, Leff lists the director, screenwriter, composer, cinematographer, and principal cast. The film is then divided into scenes, each of which lists the location and describes the characters and the action. The scenes are numbered in order to standardize and facilitate communication between film scholars.

SCRIPTS

1114.   *American Film Scripts Online* [World Wide Web Source]. Alexander Street Press. Address: http://www.alexanderstreet2.com/afsolive. [Accessed: March 2005].

American Film Scripts Online (*AFSO*) provides the full text of well-known screenplays. When first launched, the Web site host expected to have 1,000 scripts representing 100,000 scenes by fall of 2004. In March of 2005, the site advertises 386 scripts by 484 writers with no date for completion. I have not viewed the database, but the idea is a sound one, indexing scripts down to the scene and character level. Researchers may search by title, year, script version, genre, writer, producer, actor, and director. In addition, it is possible to search by character gender, nationality, race, ethnicity, sexual orientation, or occupation. Researchers may browse by writer, by script and scenes, by subject, or by character. *AFSO* also offers brief biographies of the writers and lists awards.

1115.   Center for Motion Picture Study, Margaret Herrick Library, and Academy of Motion Picture Arts and Sciences Foundation. 2003. *Motion Picture Scripts: A Union List.* 2002–2003 ed. Beverly Hills, Calif.: Margaret Herrick Library and Academy Foundation Academy of Motion Picture Arts and Sciences.

The Academy of Motion Picture Arts and Sciences (AMPAS) coordinates the publication of a union list of working motion picture scripts held by six libraries in southern California. Holdings come from libraries at AMPAS, the American Film Institute, the Goldwyn Hollywood Regional Library, the University of California, Los Angeles, the University of Southern California, and the Writers Guild of America. Now published biennially, the cumulative alphabetical listing of scripts includes title, releasing company and date, screenwriter, and holding libraries. An index lists screenwriters. Most collections are noncirculating and require that scripts be read on the premises.

1116.   *Drew's Script-O-Rama* [World Wide Web Resource]. Address: http://www.script-o-rama.com. [Accessed: March 2005].

Drew's Script-O-Rama offers links to hundreds of draft and final scripts and transcripts from films and television shows. Links are listed in alphabetical order and list title, type, size, and provider for films and show, type, and provider for television shows. The scripts that come in both draft and final form are particularly useful for aspiring scriptwriters studying the craft.

1117.   McCarty, Clifford. 1971. *Published Screenplays; a Checklist.* 1st ed., The Serif Series: Bibliographies and Checklists, No. 18. Kent, Ohio: Kent State University Press.

McCarty compiled one of the earlier lists of 388 screenplays published in whole or in part or that have been rewritten as novels. Each screenplay is listed by title, with production company and date, director, writer, original source, and a citation. Includes an index. Although most screenplays will have long been out of print, it still can be useful to know that they are potentially available.

1118.   Poteet, G. Howard. 1975. *Published Radio, Television, and Film Scripts: A Bibliography.* Troy, N.Y.: Whitston.

Poteet has compiled a bibliography of "radio, television, and film scripts which have appeared in print." Entries are organized first by format and then by program or film title and include the standard bibliographic data. An index points to names only. While dated, the citations are still valid for finding published scripts.

1119.   Samples, Gordon. 1974. *The Drama Scholars' Index to Plays and Filmscripts: A Guide to Plays and Filmscripts in Selected Anthologies, Series, and Periodicals.* Metuchen, N.J.: Scarecrow Press.

1120.   Samples, Gordon. 1980. *The Drama Scholars' Index to Plays and Filmscripts, Volume 2: A Guide to Plays and Filmscripts in Selected Anthologies, Series, and Periodicals.* Metuchen, N.J.: Scarecrow Press.

1121.   Samples, Gordon. 1986. *The Drama Scholars' Index to Plays and Filmscripts, Volume 3: A Guide to Plays and Filmscripts in Selected Anthologies, Series, and Periodicals.* Metuchen, N.J.: Scarecrow Press.

Samples's play index is unusual in that it also includes screenplays. He indexes anthologies, series, and periodicals for complete plays and scripts as well as fragments. For films, scripts are listed under both screenwriter and director with cross-references to the film title. Entries cite the journal or point readers to the list of anthologies. The first volume is complete through 1972, Volume 2 is complete through 1977, and Volume 3 is complete through 1983—but it is necessary to consult all three because of the uncertainty of when a screenplay might have been published.

12
Making Films and Television Programs

The resources in this chapter include guides for aspiring filmmakers, taking them through the entire process, from financing to pre-production to work on the set to editing to distribution and exhibition. It begins with guides for film studies aimed at teaching film faculty and students, offering lists of film schools and resources. The next section offers general guides to filmmaking and television production and continues with guides and handbooks for the various specialties. Resources for professional filmmakers are listed in the next chapter.

FILM STUDIES

1122. Corrigan, Timothy. 2004. *A Short Guide to Writing about Film.* 5th ed. New York: Pearson/Longman.

Film professor Corrigan has written a guide for students on how to place their ideas about a film into an essay. In addition to chapters on writing, he explains how to analyze a film, terms and topics for film analysis, six approaches to film, and researching primary and secondary literature. Includes a glossary of film terms, a list of works cited, and an index. Corrigan's book is of most use to beginning film writers.

1123. *Cyber Film School Encyclopedia CD-ROM* [CD-ROM]. Internet Film Group. Address: http://www.cyberfilmschool.com. [Accessed: March 2005].

The *Cyber Film School Encyclopedia CD-ROM* teaches film history, screenwriting, planning, budgeting, producing, directing, shooting, lighting, and editing. If the free Web preview available at the time I write this is any indication, the *Encyclopedia* provides a solid basic grounding in film history and techniques. Coupled with practice and feedback, the *Encyclopedia* can certainly guide beginning filmmakers through the filmmaking process. *Cyber Film School* also provides links to other Web sites that teach filmmaking.

1124. *Film Schools* [World Wide Web Resource]. Address: http://www.cinema.com/industry. [Accessed: January 2005].

Cinema.com, a general purpose film Web site, lists 149 film schools located in over 50 countries. Organized by country, links take browsers to a directory of addresses, telephone numbers, e-mail addresses, and Web sites. Although it's not comprehensive, the *Film Schools* page is still useful for locating a number of film schools around the world.

Film Study: An Analytical Bibliography (see entry 12)

1125. Jacobson, Ronald L. 1995. *Television Research: A Directory of Conceptual Categories, Topic Suggestions, and Selected Sources.* Jefferson, N.C.: McFarland.

Although not explicitly stated in his brief introduction, Jacobson obviously intends his book for students. He has divided the topic of television into 29 categories such as advertising, minorities, and social aspects. For each category, he provides a one- to two-page overview, topic suggestions for research, and a selective list of sources. There is a small list of reference sources in television at the end. Teachers will find the book useful for assigning research topics.

1126. *Library of Annotated Film Schools* [World Wide Web Resource]. Address: http://filmmaker.com/reviews.html. [Accessed: January 2005].

Filmmaker.com offers a list of film schools from all over the world with comments from students who have attended. This is not a directory—it is a place for students to share experiences with other students considering film school.

1127. Mackaman, Julie. 1997. *Filmmaker's Resource: The Watson-Guptill Guide to Workshops, Conferences & Markets, Academic Programs, Residential & Artist-in-Residence Programs, Getting Your Act Together.* New York: Watson-Guptill.

"Filmmaker's Resource looks at traditional and alternative paths for learning how to make and write films and videos" in the United States. Although not comprehensive, the book is a good place for aspiring filmmakers to explore options. In addition to the expected list of academic programs, the book also lists workshops, conferences, and residential artist programs. Interesting sidebars answer questions not covered elsewhere. The general index points to these and more, while specialized indexes cover the categories listed above plus programs that emphasize film, video, television, or multimedia and that offer handicapped access or financial aid

FILMMAKING AND DIRECTING (SEE ALSO *SPECIALIZED DICTIONARIES* AND *ENCYCLOPEDIAS*)

1128. Ascher, Steven, and Edward Pincus. 1999. *The Filmmaker's Handbook: A Comprehensive Guide for the Digital Age.* Completely rev. and updated. ed. New York: Plume.

The Filmmaker's Handbook is one of the standard guides for students learning how to make movies. Most of the book focuses on shooting and editing—with chapters on topics such as the camera, sound recording systems, and lighting—but there is also a chapter on producing and distributing movies. Supplementary materials include appendixes with tables necessary to filmmakers, a bibliography, and an index.

1129. Blumenthal, Howard J., and Oliver R. Goodenough. 1998. *This Business of Television.* Rev. and updated 2nd ed. New York: Billboard Books.

Blumenthal and Goodenough have produced a handy reference guide for people working in television and video. Most of the book is a well-written guide to the business and legal aspects of television, from distribution to programming and advertising to audience measurement. Appendix A comes on a compact disc and excerpts U.S. statutes and regulations applicable to the television industry (in Microsoft Word). Appendix B includes 19 different sample contracts in seven categories—of particular interest is the checklist of issues under each category. Appendix C includes a bibliography, directories, television organizations and stations, and Web sites. The guide is of most use to industry newcomers and students interested in entering the television business.

1130. Collier, Maxie D. 2001. *The IFILM Digital Video Filmmaker's Handbook.* Hollywood, Calif.: Lone Eagle.

Collier's guide to making digital films cheaply takes aspiring filmmakers from preproduction to distribution, focusing on the processes and the equipment needed to complete a project. Added materials include a case study of one of the author's films, a resource directory, and a glossary.

1131. Harmon, Renee. 1994. *The Beginning Filmmaker's Business Guide: Financial, Legal, Marketing, and Distribution: Basics of Making Movies.* New York: Walker.

In addition to working as an actor, writer, director, and producer, Harmon is president of her own production company. Her guide focuses on marketing a film: from concept and packaging through financing and distribution. Intended for beginning filmmakers, she covers the basics in an easy-to-understand writing style that makes it clear that selling a film is more business than art. Appendixes list film festivals, associations and labor organizations, and include sample release forms, distribution plans, contracts, and grant applications. Includes an index.

1132. International Documentary Association. *IDA Survival Guide & Membership Directory.* Los Angeles: IDA.

The International Documentary Association exists to "promote nonfiction film and video, to support the efforts of documentary film and video makers around the world, and to increase public appreciation and demand for the documentary." In addition to the list of members, the directory lists resources for documentary filmmakers, archives and stock footage libraries, broadcasters, distributors, and festivals. Indexes list members by profession and by geography.

1133. Jolliffe, Genevieve, and Chris Jones. 2004. *The Guerilla Film Makers Handbook.* New York: Continuum.

By interviewing over 150 people who work in every aspect of the film industry, independent filmmakers Jolliffe and Jones have created a fun and useful guide for aspiring filmmakers. Chapters cover education, developing a project, film organizations, finance, talent, production, post-production, and sales. Sidebars provide details, clarify answers given in the interviews, and often include illustrations. The index is necessary, because the interview format can make it difficult to locate answers to specific questions. Although the writers are British, the handbook will be just as useful to American filmmakers—in fact, any beginning filmmaker will benefit from the words of experienced filmmakers.

Women Make Movies (see entry 951)

JOBS

1134. Hines, William E. 1999. *Job Descriptions for Film, Video & CGI: Responsibilities and Duties for the Cinematic Craft Categories and Classifications.* 5th ed. Los Angeles, CA: Ed-Venture Films/Books.

Hines, who has worked in many of the jobs he describes in this book, has created the most comprehensive guide to who does what in the process of making films, videos, and CGI. Chapters cover 21 different craft categories representing 250 different jobs. Each chapter gives an overview of the category. Each job includes responsibilities, duties, and considerations. Responsibilities include reporting lines and the role the position plays in making a movie. Duties list the tasks for which each position is responsible during pre-production, production, and post-production. "Considerations" is a miscellaneous category that usually includes the circumstances under which a position would be used and how many from that position might work on a production. Essential knowledge and skills for each category are listed in a separate appendix. Additional appendixes cover animation, professional societies and associations, and guilds and unions. The glossary is thorough, organized by terms used in each craft category, general definitions, and operational definitions—the glossary even has its own index. The general index points not only to the job description, but also to other places where the job is mentioned. A bibliography lists books that provide more in-depth information on selected craft categories.

1135. Rachlin, Harvey. 1991. *The TV and Movie Business: An Encyclopedia of Careers, Technologies, and Practices.* 1st ed. New York: Harmony Books.

This dictionary provides in-depth definitions and descriptions of the television and film business from initial idea to production to distribution to marketing and the careers involved at each stage. The introduction provides an overview of the film and television industries. The best articles describe the roles played by the people who make movies and television shows and would be particularly useful to students considering a career in the industry.

1136. Reed, Maxine K., Robert M. Reed, and Lee Phenner. 1999. *Career Opportunities in Television, Cable, Video, and Multimedia.* 4th ed. New York: Facts on File.

The Reeds have written an excellent guide to more than 100 jobs in television for students exploring future careers. For each job, they describe the duties, the salary range, employment and advancement prospects, prerequisites, and career path. Additional sections speak of opportunities for minority and women and the need to join unions or associations. The position descriptions give prospective employees a good sense of what a job is like. The appendix listing degree and non-degree programs is only marginally useful, as it is overly selective. The list of unions and associations is much more complete. Includes a bibliography and an index.

DIRECTORIES

1137. *HCD Online.* 2004. 51st ed. Hollywood, Calif.: Hollywood Creative Directory. [World Wide Web Resource]. Address: http://www.hcdonline.com. [Accessed: January 2005].

HCD Online combines the *Hollywood Creative Directory,* the *Hollywood Representation Directory,* the *Hollywood Music Industry Directory,* and the *Hollywood Distributors Directory* into one database. These guides include "addresses, phone and fax numbers, emails and Web sites, staff names and titles, and select television and film credits" for virtually everyone working in the film industry. Available by subscription only.

1138. Hollywood Creative Directory. *Below-the-Line Talent: The Most Complete Directory of Cinematographers, Production Designers, Costume Designers, Film Editors, Set Directors, and Art Directors.* Hollywood, Calif.: IFILM.

This is an annual directory of cinematographers, production designers, and film editors. In each section, filmmakers are listed alphabetically by last name, including their representation and a list of the films on which they have worked. All information is provided by the filmmaker. Indexes list film titles and Academy Awards and nominations. Unions and guilds are listed on the last page. Now available for online searching by subscription as a subset of *HCD Online* at <http://www.hcdonline.com> (see entry 1137).

1139. *Hollywood Creative Directory's Film Directors.* Los Angeles: Lone Eagle.

In this biannual directory, directors are listed alphabetically by last name, including their representation and a list of the films they have directed. A separate section lists notable directors of the past. All information is provided by the director. Indexes list film titles and directors by name and country as well as Academy Awards and nominations. Now available for online searching by subscription as a subset of *HCD Online* at <http://www.hcdonline.com> (see entry 1137).

ACTING

1140. *Hollywood Creative Directory's Film Actors: Over 6,000 Film Actors and 15,000 Film Titles.* Hollywood, Calif.: IFILM.

In this biennial directory, actors are listed alphabetically by last name, including their representation and a list of the films in which they have acted. All information is provided by the filmmaker. Indexes list film titles and Academy Awards and nominations. Now available for online searching by subscription as a subset of *HCD Online* at <http://www.hcdonline.com> (see entry 1137).

1141. Kondazian, Karen, and Eddie Shapiro. 1999. *The Actor's Encyclopedia of Casting Directors: Conversations with over 100 Casting Directors on How To Get the Job.* Los Angeles: Lone Eagle.

Kondazian, an actor, writer, and producer, collected interviews of casting directors previously published in *Drama-Logue* or *Back Stage West* to create a directory and biographical dictionary that also serves as a guide for aspiring actors. The entry for each casting director begins with a brief career biography and is followed by the transcript of the interview. Questions vary from person to person, but all focus on what a casting director does and what it takes for actors to get roles in movies or television shows. Not intended as a comprehensive guide, check the *C.D. Directory* at <http://www.castingsociety.com/Members> for a searchable list of casting directors.

1142. Kozlowski, Rob. 2000. *The Actor's Guide to the Internet.* Portsmouth, N.H.: Heinemann.

Actor, writer, and Web designer Kozlowski has created an Internet guide for actors. Opening chapters describe the basics of Internet searching, and subsequent chapters provide links to sites specifically for actors on training, online trade magazines, monologues and plays, unions and organizations, and some early feeble attempts at casting Web sites. Additional chapters focus on dance, stagecraft, and the catchall "other" category. An appendix conveniently lists in one place all of the URLs mentioned in the chapters, and an even more convenient CD-ROM links straight to the sites. With the rapid changes on the Internet, the guide is already somewhat dated, but will still be useful to actors for at least a couple of years.

1143.   *The National Casting Guide.* 1998. New York: G. James.

The National Casting Guide is a directory of casting directors, talent agencies, acting schools, production companies, state film commissions, and any other contacts actors might need—from answering services to plastic surgery to photographers.

CINEMATOGRAPHY

1144.   Box, Harry C. 2003. *Set Lighting Technician's Handbook: Film Lighting Equipment, Practice, and Electrical Distribution.* 3rd ed. Amsterdam; Boston: Focal Press.

Box, a gaffer and director of photography, has written a technical guide to set lighting. He begins with the basics, describing the various jobs involved in lighting and then covers preproduction, supplies and equipment, types of lighting, stands and rigging, lighting objectives and techniques, electrical wiring and power sources, and labor organizations and union agreements. Appendixes include the tables and formulas needed to light the set, directories of resources, checklists, and power and television systems in use around the world. Includes a glossary, a bibliography, and an index. Box's handbook is as useful to aspiring students as it is to professionals on the set.

1145.   Carlson, Sylvia, and Verne Carlson. 1994. *Professional Cameraman's Handbook.* 4th ed. Boston: Focal Press.

The Carlsons wrote this handbook to "help the professional and student cinematographer to function efficiently" in the film industry. The handbook describes equipment, techniques, and reports cinematographers will need to do their work. Includes a glossary.

1146.   Elkins, David E. 2005. *The Camera Assistant's Manual.* 4th ed. Burlington, Mass.: Elsevier Focal Press.

Elkins describes every aspect of the work expected of the first and second camera assistants, from the basics of cinematography to responsibilities, cameras, techniques, and reports. Appendixes list film stock, equipment, tools, tables and provide checklists. Includes a glossary and an index.

1147.   Ferncase, Richard K. 1995. *Film and Video Lighting Terms and Concepts, Focal Handbooks.* Boston: Focal Press.

Ferncase, a filmmaker and professor, has written a dictionary of "all the terms that cinematographers, lighting directors, camera operators and assistants, gaffers, electricians, and grips may encounter on a typical day on the set." His dictionary is a good resource for students as well, including clear definitions and illustrated when needed.

1148.   Hummel, Rob, and American Society of Cinematographers. 2001. *American Cinematographer Manual.* 8th ed. Hollywood, Calif.: ASC Press.

The American Society of Cinematographers has compiled a manual that covers equipment, lighting, visual effects, and techniques for working cinematographers. Includes index.

1149.   Ryer, Alex. *Light Measurement Handbook* [World Wide Web Resource]. International Light Inc. 1997. Address: http://www.intl-light.com/customer/handbook. [Accessed: March 2005].

International Light has made available the complete text of Ryer's *Light Measurement Handbook* as either HTML or a downloadable PDF. The book's 12 chapters cover everything needed to measure light, from how light behaves to principles of light measurement to choosing detectors, filters, input optics, and radiometers (all of which International Light sells). The *Handbook* is useful to cinematographers and lighting crews.

EDITING

1150.   *Motion Picture Film Timing Tables.* 1972. Syracuse, N.Y.: Tyo Productions.

Tables give "exact feet and frames up to one hour and thirty-nine seconds of running time, by seconds" for 8mm, 16mm, and 35mm film. Intended for use by cinematographers and editors.

PRODUCING

1151.   Chater, Kathy. 1998. *Production Research: An Introduction.* Oxford, England: Boston: Focal Press.

In this slim book, Chater undertakes the daunting task of characterizing all of the skills needed to be a production researcher. After an overview of the production process, she describes gathering information, locating experts, finding visual and audio materials, scouting locations, checking facts, and following up during recording and post-production. Appendixes include copyright considerations, legal and ethical issues, and further reading. The chapter on information gathering does not provide a detailed guide on how to do research, but instead recommends basic strategies.

1152.   Gates, Richard. 1999. *Production Management for Film and Video.* 3rd ed. Oxford, England; Boston: Focal Press.

Gates, a producer and production manager, has written a basic guide to managing the production of films, television shows, animated features, documentaries, and ads. From pre-production to post-production, he covers script breakdowns, scheduling, budgeting, and the shoot. Although the third edition was published in the late nineties, it does not address the many computer tools now available to production managers—this might make it useful for independent filmmakers on a budget who cannot afford the software, but it does limit the book's overall usefulness. In addition, Gates writes from a British perspective, which means the cost and the legal aspects are most relevant to filmmakers in Great Britain. Still, the book is useful as a primer on the duties of a production manager.

1153.   Houghton, Buck. 1991. *What a Producer Does: The Art of Moviemaking (Not the Business).* 1st ed. Los Angeles; Hollywood, Calif.: Silman-James Press; Distributed by Samuel French Trade.

Houghton, a television and film producer, has written a guide on how to produce. The subtitle is a little misleading, because he does discuss business aspects of making movies. His emphasis, however, is not on the details of fundraising and budgets, but on explaining the functions of a producer. The book is structured to parallel the filmmaking process, beginning with the story and moving through the director, cast, and crew and continuing with the production and post production needs. The chapters are clearly written and contain engaging overviews of what it takes to bring a movie or television show to the screen. Houghton's book will be most useful to students learning the craft and to new producers.

1154.   Singleton, Ralph S. 1991. *Film Scheduling, or, How Long Will It Take To Shoot Your Movie? The Complete Step-by-Step Guide to Professional Motion Picture Scheduling.* 2nd ed. Los Angeles: Lone Eagle.

This is one of several books Singleton, a film and television producer, has written on the production process. Using one film as an example, *Film Scheduling* covers the process of breaking down a script to create a shooting schedule. One chapter covers the use of computer programs, but Singleton prefers good old-fashioned production boards with cardboard strips to create paper lists and day-out-of-days, because the process ensures the production manager knows the project inside and out. The book will be of most use to neophyte filmmakers. Includes a glossary and an index. There is a companion volume entitled the *Film Scheduling / Film Budgeting Workbook.* These books work best in conjunction with *Film Budgeting, or, How Much Will It Cost To Shoot Your Movie?* (see entry 1156).

Budgeting

1155.   Simon, Deke, and Michael Wiese. 2001. *Film & Video Budgets.* 3rd ed. Studio City, Calif.: M. Wiese Productions.

Writers, producers, and directors Simon and Wiese have written the most complete guide to creating budgets for films and videos. The first half of the book covers setting up a production company, pre-production planning, and lists of possible line items. The second half of the book offers sample budgets for feature films, documentaries, digital films, video-to-film transfers, "no budget" films, industrial and music videos, and student films. They include ballpark costs, but readers are expected to research actual local costs. The third edition also makes the budgets available on Excel spreadsheets. Numerous appendixes cover a variety of resources for filmmakers plus commercial budget forms, a sample series budget, and things to keep in mind when creating budgets for grants or donations. Without an index, readers must rely on the table of contents. The book will be useful for anyone who wants to create a realistic budget for a film or video, especially if making a proposal to clients or potential investors.

1156.   Singleton, Ralph S., Alain Silver, and Robert Koster. 1996. *Film Budgeting, or, How Much Will It Cost To Shoot Your Movie?* Los Angeles: Lone Eagle.

This is one of several books Singleton, a film and television producer, has written on the production process. *Film Budgeting* gives aspiring producers the tools needed to estimate the cost of a film, with chapters on above-the-line, below-the-line, post-production, and contractual costs. Figures are based on Los Angeles union scale circa 1996, so it is important to consult up-to-date agreements. One chapter covers use of computer programs (which are now out-of-date), but Singleton recommends at least double-checking everything the computer produces using the knowledge garnered here. The book will be of most use to neophyte filmmakers. Includes a glossary and an index. This book works best in conjunction with *Film Scheduling, or, How Long Will It Take To Shoot Your Movie?* (see entry 1154).

Financing

1157.   Cones, John W. 1998. *43 Ways to Finance Your Feature Film: A Comprehensive Analysis of Film Finance.* Updated ed. Carbondale: Southern Illinois University Press.

Cones, an entertainment lawyer, has written a guide for independent filmmakers on how to finance a film. Chapters are organized into sections on industry, lender, investor, securities, and foreign financing opportunities. Chapters explain the type of financing, the related laws, and the advantages and disadvantages of each.

1158.   Curran, Trisha. 1986. *Financing Your Film: A Guide for Independent Filmmakers and Producers.* New York: Praeger.

Curran, a professor of cinema and an independent filmmaker, has written a book designed to guide novice producers through the morass of film financing. Based on her own experiences and input from film financiers, the book is easy to follow, moving from planning and packaging to signing with a distributor to securing financing. The author offers money-saving tips and a series of worksheets designed to put the fundraising process in motion. Although somewhat dated, the book is an excellent primer to film financing.

1159.   Levison, Louise. 2004. *Filmmakers and Financing: Business Plans for Independents.* 4th ed. Amsterdam; Boston: Elsevier.

Levison, a consultant "specializing in business plan packaging and venture capital financing," has written a guide for independent filmmakers on how to develop a business plan to make a film. The book follows the standard format for a business plan, including chapters on the executive summary, the company, the product, marketing, selling, and financing. There are sample business plans for a fictional filmmaking company and for an Internet start-up firm. Levison's book is for independent filmmakers who have an idea for a movie and wonder "what now?"

SCRIPT READING

1160.   Katahn, Terri. 1990. *Reading for a Living: How to Be a Professional Story Analyst for Film and Television.* 1st ed. Los Angeles: Blue Arrow Books.

Katahn's guide describes the job of the story analyst, the person who reads scripts on behalf of the busy executive producer. Chapters cover reading, summarizing, breaking down characters, and evaluation of the script as well as getting and keeping a job as a reader. Katahn provides samples, standard formats, a glossary, and an index.

STUNTS

1161. Baur, Tassilo, and Bruce Scivally. 1993. *Special Effects and Stunts Guide.* 2nd ed. Los Angeles: Lone Eagle.

Baur, a special effects supervisor, and Scivally have compiled a directory of physical effects, optical effects, makeup effects, and stunt coordinators. For each coordinator or company, the authors list address and telephone number, awards, and a filmography with the role on each film described. Indexes list film titles and special effects and stunt coordinators.

1162. Cann, John. 1992. *The Stunt Guide: Comprehensive Stunt Reference Book for the Motion Picture and Television Industry.* New, rev., exp. 3rd ed. Van Nuys, Calif.: Action P.A.C. International.

Cann, a professional stuntman, has written a handbook for stunt professionals. Much of the book, especially the directory, is too old to be of much use, but some of the articles in the general section covering emergency procedures, safety bulletins, risk factors, contracts, and basic stunt recommendations may still be useful. Consult one of the general purpose directories in this section for more up-to-date stunt organizations and professionals.

WRITING

1163. Argentini, Paul. 1998. *Elements of Style for Screenwriters.* 1st ed. Los Angeles: Lone Eagle.

Argentini, a screenwriter and playwright, has written a style manual for writers of screenplays. The key to this book is its brevity, simply telling the standards for formatting a script. He begins with a sample screenplay, which he annotates to illustrate and explain the format. The rest of the book is a dictionary of terms, one page per item, that includes the vocabulary a screenwriter will need while writing a screenplay and communicating in Hollywood. Part 2 does the same thing for playwriting. Strangely, Argentini includes a separate glossary of terms used in the definitions but not defined in the dictionary. Appendixes list literary agents and managers.

1164. Berry-Fortner, Deidre. 2001. *Screenwriter's Marketing and Resource Directory: Over 2,000 Industry Contacts to Help Get Your Script Sold and Produced.* San Jose, Calif.: Writer Club Press.

Designed for screenwriters who would like to sell scripts, this directory lists agents, actors, directors, attorneys, and producers who might be interested, as well as film commissions, contests, internships, and film festivals. Each entry includes name, address, telephone number, e-mail address, and Web site. Because the information is somewhat dated, consulting the online databases in this section would be recommended.

1165.   Hollywood Creative Directory. *Film Writers.* Hollywood, Calif.: IFILM.

The *Hollywood Creative Directory* produces a biennial directory of film writers. The largest part of the book lists writers alphabetically by last name, including their representation and a list of the films they have written. All information is provided by the writer. A second section lists notable film writers of the past. Indexes list film titles and Academy Awards with nominations. The directory is more complete than the annual *Writers Guild of America Directory,* which is available on the Internet at <http://www.wga.org/agency/MemAgency. asp>, because it includes writers who are not members. Now available for online searching by subscription as a subset of *HCD Online* at <http://www.hcdonline.com> (see entry 1137).

1166.   Lewinski, John Scott. 2001. *The Screenwriter's Guide to Agents and Managers.* New York: Allworth Press.

Screenwriter Lewinski's guide describes the day-to-day work of agents and managers and the different types of agencies. Most important to new screenwriters is advice on how to get an agent and what to do with the screenplay while waiting. Appendixes list production companies and agents. A glossary defines terms, and the book includes an index.

1167.   Naylor, Lynne. 1996. *Television Writers Guide.* 4th ed. Los Angeles: Lone Eagle.

The first part of this directory lists television show writers and their credits from 1974 through the 1994–1995 season. Included are the writer's name, agent's name and telephone number, and a list of shows with their networks. The index of television titles has entries for each writer involved in a show. In between are separate listings of shows by genre for comedy and drama series, movies of the week and miniseries, specials, and variety shows—note that these do not directly list writers. Additional indexes list Emmy Award nominations and winners, guilds, and agents and managers.

1168.   Press, Skip. 2001. *Writer's Guide to Hollywood Producers, Directors, and Screenwriter's Agents, 2002–2003.* Rocklin, Calif.: Prima.

Press has written a guide for aspiring screenwriters on the business of getting a script produced. Chapters explain every step of the process, from concept to script, from developer to independent producer, from agents and managers to Hollywood. The second half of the book is a directory of agents and producers. A glossary defines terms, a bibliography lists books on screenwriting, and an index ties the book together. The book is useful to beginning screenwriters.

1169.   Reichman, Rick. 1994. *Formatting Your Screenplay.* 1st ed. Lexington, Ky.: BookSmiths.

Reichman, a screenwriting professor, has created a guide to writing and formatting screenplays. The book takes aspiring writers through the entire process, beginning with a sample script and then breaking it down into its elements. He includes a glossary and a list of suggested readings for more about the art of screenwriting.
The Screenwriter's Legal Guide (see entry 1189)

1170.   Suppa, Ron. 1999. *This Business of Screenwriting: How To Protect Yourself as a Screenwriter.* Los Angeles: Lone Eagle.

Suppa, a screenwriter and lawyer, has written a guide for aspiring screenwriters that explains the business of screenwriting from concept to script to marketing and covers representation, writing as part of a team, and legally protecting the work. The appendix is a complete list of Writers Guild of America signatory agents and agencies.

1171.   Wilson, John M. 1998. *Inside Hollywood: A Writer's Guide to Researching the World of Movies and TV.* 1st ed., *Behind the Scenes.* Cincinnati, Ohio: Writer's Digest Books.

Wilson, a writer, producer, and reporter, has created a guide for writers on how Hollywood works. Chapters cover the movie and television industries, the role of various filmmakers, how a movie or television show gets made and marketed, and Hollywood as a place and as a lifestyle. One appendix serves as a glossary, while another list organizations and research tools. There is an index, but it does not point to the lists in the appendixes.

The Writer Got Screwed (but Didn't Have to): A Guide to the Legal and Business Practices of Writing for the Entertainment Industry (see entry 1195)

1172.   Zaza, Tony. 1993. *Script Planning: Positioning and Developing Scripts for TV and Film.* Boston: Focal Press.

Zaza, a writer and reviewer, has written a guide for screenwriters on how to sell their scripts. Chapters cover the script as a product, script development, marketing, and the various markets. Appendixes cover festivals, banks that lend money for entertainment projects, independent production companies, unions, MPAA and USCC ratings, cable programmers, and sponsors.

13
Film and Television Industry

The resources in this chapter contain annuals and handbooks about the film and television industry. Among the types of resources available are box office charts, film festival directories, legal guides, and directories of services and resources available to producers.

ANNUALS

1173. Australian Film Commission. 2002. *Get the Picture: Essential Data on Australian Film, Television, Video, and Interactive Media.* 6th ed. Sydney: Australian Film Commission.

Since 1989, the Australian Film Commission has gathered statistics related to the Australian film, television, and new media industries. Now in its sixth edition, this book covers new media, production, release, distribution, trade, audience, and top films and programs. Published every two years, the volumes are not cumulative. Useful for studying the Australian film and television industries.

1174. Dyja, Eddie, and British Film Institute. 2003. *BFI Film and Television Handbook 2004.* London: British Film Institute.

Known simply as the *Film and Television Handbook* from 1990 to 1992, the *BFI Film and Television Handbook* is an annual guide to the U.K. film and television business. The early sections highlight production, revenue, and audience statistics and awards. Most of the book is a directory of 32 categories of companies and organizations that serve the film and television industries. The book is essential to filmmakers and television producers working in the United Kingdom.

1175. *Film TV Daily Yearbook of Motion Pictures and Television.* New York: Film TV Daily.

The *Film Daily* newspaper covered the film and television industries from 1915 through 1970. From 1918 to 1969, it published an annual guide under the titles *Wid's Year Book* and *Film Daily Yearbook of Motion Pictures.* The yearbook survived the newspaper. Now titled the *Film TV Daily Yearbook of Motion Pictures and Television,* the annual serves as both a directory and a guide to the year's films and personalities. The international directory portion lists film and television companies and organizations. The guide portion lists credits for the films released by title (with a separate cumulative title index), company, filmmaker, actor, and awards.

1176. *International Motion Picture Almanac.* annual. New York: Quigley.

Originally a biennial publication (from 1929 to 1936) titled *Motion Picture Almanac* and briefly (from 1952 to 1955) titled *Motion Picture and Television Almanac,* the now annual *International Motion Picture Almanac* is intended to be a one-stop source for people in the film industry. Approximately half of each volume covers the year in review, including statistics, earnings, awards, festivals, biographies and obituaries, and films released between October 1 and September 30 of the prior year in all parts of the world. Biographical entries provide career overviews and a complete list of credits. Film entries list producer and distributor, release dates, running time, rating, and all above-the-line crew and cast. The second half of each volume consists of directories of companies and organizations that serve the film industry, from casting directors to film stock to independent theaters to guilds and unions. The index lists companies, agencies, and organizations, but only selectively, so it is often necessary to scan individual sections.

1177.   *International Television & Video Almanac, 2004.* 49th ed. New York: Quigley.

First published as the *International Television Almanac* in 1956, this annual guide to the television industry has been published under its current title since 1987. Each volume begins with the "Year in Review" and goes on to cover virtually every aspect of the business of television. The largest section is a current who's who of people who work both behind and in front of the camera. Other sections list current prime-time series, movies and miniseries, television stations and network affiliates, networks, cable and satellite companies, and production service companies. The almanac covers primarily the United States; Canada and Great Britain receive the most international coverage in a separate section entitled "The World Market." Includes a selective index to companies and organizations. Later volumes include a Web site guide to URLs for companies.

BOX OFFICE

1178.   *Art Murphy's Boxoffice Register.* 1995. Hollywood, Calif.: Art Murphy's Boxoffice Register.

Beginning in 1982, when film distributors began reporting box office proceeds to the media, Murphy published an annual compilation of how much money movies grossed. Section A is an alphabetical list of all films released in the United States and Canada. For each movie, he lists the distributor, the opening and closing dates, the number of weeks and days in theaters, and the total box office receipts. Section B ranks movies by box office receipts. Section C is a week-by-week listing—otherwise unavailable without perusing the Hollywood trade publications. Also provided are the number of weeks in release and the week's receipts. The *Boxoffice Register* ceased publication in 1995.

1179.   *Box Office Champions.* 1999. Carmel, Calif.: Kagan Moviedata, for hollywood.com.

Formerly *Paul Kagan's Box Office Champion,* now published for *Hollywood. com,* this serial compiled box office figures for the most recent year as well as cumulative figures back to 1985 (the 2000 edition has data through 1998/1999). Volume 1 covers actors, and volume 2 covers directors, producers, and writers—for each film, the book lists release date, number of screens, and domestic and worldwide box office dollars. Separate tables rank the top 100 in each category. *BaselineFT* of *Hollywood.com* <http://baseline. hollywood.com> now sells box office statistics to regular clients and individuals.

1180. *The Numbers* [World Wide Web Resource]. Address: http://www.the-numbers. com. [Accessed: January 2005].

The Numbers tracks U.S. and international box office figures for movies each week. Weekly charts consist of ranked movies listing distributor, genre, gross, percentage change, number of theaters, per theater grosses, total gross, and number of days in release. Archives to the weekly box office figures are available back to 1980, but the number of movies and the information included in each chart is inconsistent over the years. The Web site lists records such as all-time U.S. and international grosses back to 1977, biggest openings, and fastest-earning movies. *The Numbers* is a useful guide for box office figures for the past 25 years, but the all-time records as adjusted for inflation are suspect, because they don't include the first 80 years of cinema.

1181. Pandya, Gitesh. *Box Office Guru* [World Wide Web Resource]. Box Office Guru. Address: http://www.boxofficeguru.com. [Accessed: March 2005].

Pandya maintains charts of the box office performance of American movies. The film database tables list gross, first week percentage, number of theaters and per theater gross, and the distributors for 2,700 titles released since 1989. The worldwide tables list international, domestic, and worldwide gross in dollars and percentages. *Box Office Guru* also lists grosses by season, opening weekend, and all-time champs. Archives of weekend performance are available back to July 1997.

FILM FESTIVALS

1182. British Council. 1994. *Directory of International Film and Video Festivals 1995 and 1996.* 8th ed. London: British Council.

1183. Britfilms.com. *Directory of International Film and Video Festivals* [World Wide Web Resource]. Address: http://www.britfilms.com/festivals. [Accessed: March 2005].

Britfilms "acts as a gateway to a world of useful information published on the internet about the British film industry." Perhaps the most useful feature is the *Directory of International Film and Video Festivals* listing 600 festivals taking place around the world. Filmmakers and fans may browse by country or search by festival title, category, requirement, country, town, month of the year, or deadline. Britfilms also offers a catalog of shorts made since 1998, a list of films in progress, and a database of directors. A specialized Web search engine seeks British film and television industry pages. The British Council published a print directory biennially from 1985 through 1995.

1184. Coe, Michelle E., and Association of Independent Video and Filmmakers. 2004. *The AIVF Guide to International Film & Video Festivals.* New York: Foundation for Independent Video and Film.

On behalf of the Foundation for Independent Video and Film and the Association of Independent Video and Filmmakers, Coe has compiled a list of over 500 U.S. and foreign festivals to help independent filmmakers hoping to showcase their films. The information on each festival is based on a survey questionnaire and includes festival name, address and telephone number, and a description of the number and type of each film presented.

Also included are the formats accepted, entry fees, and dates held. Supplementary materials include U.S. and foreign directories as well as lists of festivals sorted by deadline, by date held, and by category.

1185. *FilmFestivals.com* [World Wide Web Resource]. Multimedia Partners. Address: http://www.filmfestivals.com. [Accessed: March 2005].

FilmFestivals.com is one of the premier portal sites for film festivals. Its goal is "showcasing film festivals around the world and fostering new film and filmmaking talent." Festival fans and filmmakers may browse by country, month, or current festivals and search by festival, film, or video. Included are approximately 1,900 festivals ranging from major festivals such as Cannes, Berlin, Sundance, and Venice to lesser known festivals such as Cineme or the Hong Kong Jewish Film Festival. For each festival, information is given about the venue, the hours, and the price, and, in rare cases, the rules and regulations for submission. There is always an e-mail link to the person who submitted the festival so that filmmakers have a contact for their questions. There is a section for festival-goer comments, but it is usually empty. Entries for films and videos include credits, a synopsis, the director, and, in some cases, a review. The site's archives go back to 1995, with sparse coverage in the earlier years.

1186. Langer, Adam. 2000. *The Film Festival Guide: For Filmmakers, Film Buffs, and Industry Professionals.* Rev. ed. Chicago: Chicago Review Press.

Langer, an independent filmmaker, compiled this guide while looking for places to submit his own work. Now in its second edition, the book covers over 500 film festivals around the world. The author begins with a description of the 16 film festivals he considers "worth the trip." For these 16 and the festivals that introduce each of the regional chapters, he provides where, when, and how to enter along with award winners, quantity, and ticket prices. Descriptions vary in length according to the prominence of the festival. Each chapter lists incomplete listings under "more" festivals, most often including only contact information. The book includes a submission calendar and a title index. There is no subject index, making it necessary to read every listing to see if a film will be of interest to a festival.

1187. Litwak, Mark. *Film Festivals* [World Wide Web Resource]. M. Litwak. Address: http://www.marklitwak.com/film_festivals/festival.php. [Accessed: March 2005].

Litwak hosts a directory linking to a couple hundred film festival Web sites. The list may be displayed alphabetically, by month, or by region. Entries are submitted by the festival organizer and include title, description, date, address, and links to e-mail and Web site.

1188. Nowlan, Robert A., and Gwendolyn Wright Nowlan. 1988. *An Encyclopedia of Film Festivals, Foundations in Library and Information Science; Vol. 23.* Greenwich, Conn.: JAI Press.

Professors Nowlan and Nowlan have written a guide to putting on a film festival. The first brief chapter covers financing, film selection, publicity, facilities, equipment, and evaluation. Most of the book consists of a guide to "suggested film festivals." Divided into genres such as westerns and science fiction, each chapter is further broken down into subgenres such as pioneers or evil scientists. The authors describe each subgenre and then provide a list of some of the films that best represent it. Although intended to serve potential film festival organizers interesting in programming, the guides can also serve as an indication of some of the best or most prominent films by genre. Appendixes include a bibliography, lists of film periodicals, associations, film festivals, companies, and a glossary. Indexes list movie titles and moviemakers.

LEGAL GUIDES

1189. Breimer, Stephen F. 2004. *The Screenwriter's Legal Guide.* 3rd ed. New York: Allworth Press.

Breimer is a lawyer in an entertainment law firm and has written a straightforward guide to the law for screenwriters. After a brief history of Hollywood screenwriting and an overview of contracts, Breimer presents chapters on negotiation, rights, compensation, types of screenplays, copyright, and the Writers Guild. Appendix A is a sample option/ purchase agreement. The book is indexed. Breimer does not recommend that readers use the book to write contracts, but rather use it as a guide to understanding the process.

1190. Erickson, J. Gunnar, Harris Tulchin, and Mark E. Halloran. 2005. *The Independent Film Producer's Survival Guide: A Business and Legal Sourcebook.* 2nd ed. New York: Schirmer Trade Books.

The authors of this guide to the legal aspects of producing a film use their background as entertainment lawyers to explain to independent filmmakers topics such as development and deal making, finance agreements, hiring contracts, locations, releases, and delivery and distribution. Each section includes sample forms and contracts. Includes an index.

1191. Litwak, Mark. 1998. *Contracts for the Film & Television Industry.* 2nd ed. Los Angeles: Silman-James Press.

Litwak, an entertainment lawyer, provides sample boilerplate contracts governing releases, literary submissions and sales, employment, collaboration, music, financing, production, distribution, merchandising, and agent and attorney agreements within the entertainment industry. He defines and explains the terms used in each contract in the text and in a glossary. An appendix includes the text of the applicable California code. The compilation is a companion to his book *Dealmaking in the Film & Television Industry* (see entry 1192).

1192. Litwak, Mark. 2002. *Dealmaking in the Film & Television Industry: From Negotiations to Final Contracts.* 2nd expanded and updated ed. Los Angeles: Silman-James Press.

Litwak, an entertainment lawyer, has written a guide to the legal aspects of making a film or television program. Chapters cover not only the deal making, but permissions, clearances, literary acquisitions, employment contracts, music, copyright, and more. The book is full of checklists and advice on how independent filmmakers can protect themselves and their work. Litwak wrote a companion volume with sample contracts entitled *Contracts for the Film & Television Industry* (see entry 1191).

1193. Moore, Schuyler M. 2002. *The Biz: The Basic Business, Legal and Financial Aspects of the Film Industry.* 2nd ed. Los Angeles: Silman-James Press.

Moore is a lawyer in an entertainment law firm and has written a guide to the film industry intended for independent filmmakers. The book begins with a chapter decoding legal jargon. Subsequent chapters cover every aspect of the business from a legal perspective—from contracts and negotiation to distribution and taxation to financing and guilds and more. Moore offers 11 sample forms for independent filmmakers to use as a guide to negotiating contracts.

1194.   Muller, Peter. 1991. *Show Business Law: Motion Pictures, Television, Video.* New York: Quorum Books.

Muller presents the essential elements of film and television contracts for people in show business who will be asked to sign contracts. Sixteen chapters examine topics ranging from the acquisition of rights to agreements by each of the filmmakers to licensing agreements. Appendix A contains sample contracts. Appendix B lists labor organizations and associations. From the perspective of a non-lawyer, it seems this book is more useful for understanding contracts than it is for creating them.

1195.   Wharton, Brooke. 1996. *The Writer Got Screwed (but Didn't Have to): A Guide to the Legal and Business Practices of Writing for the Entertainment Industry.* 1st ed. New York: HarperCollins.

Wharton's book is intended to help screenwriters understand the "basic concepts that must be considered if (they) plan to write for the entertainment industry." Her engaging book covers intellectual property, representation, and the various types of screenwriting. It is not intended to take the place of attorneys, agents, and managers, but to guide screenwriters through the business side of the film industry.

RENT AND PURCHASE (SEE ALSO *PORTALS*)

1196.   Frank, Sam. 1999. *Buyer's Guide to Fifty Years of TV on Video.* Amherst, N.Y.: Prometheus Books.

Frank has compiled a list of over 50,000 American network, cable, and syndicated television programs and specials available for purchase on video. Each entry includes the name of the program, a one- to four-star rating, technical data, purchase information, production and cast credits, a critical summary, and an episode guide. Supplementary materials include a directory of distributors, recommended family shows, the most wanted shows that are not available on video, a bibliography, and an index. In addition to a buyer's guide, Frank's book can also serve as an episode guide for series not covered elsewhere, at least if the shows are available for purchase.

1197.   *Television Programming Source Books.* 1989. New York: BIB/Channels.

Published every two years, this guide is the standard reference book on television programming available for rental or purchase. Volumes 1 and 2 list theatrical films, direct-to-video films, and made-for-television movies. Each entry includes film title, running time, genre, year of release, MPAA rating with explanation, cast, director, producer, and plot. Also included is a star rating from the *New York Times* and awards won. The current distributors are listed at the end of each entry. Volume 3 lists films available in packages.

Volume 4 lists television series organized by length. Appendixes list films and television series without distributors, top grossing films, top rated and most syndicated television programs, and films in the U.S. National Film Registry. All volumes include contact information for distributors and indexes to cast, director, and language. The television series volume also includes a holiday and theme index.

SERVICES AND RESOURCES (SEE ALSO *JOBS*)

1198.   Andersen, Arthur. 1996. *The European Film Production Guide: Finance, Tax, Legislation.* London; New York: Routledge.

As stated in its introduction, the *European Film Production Guide* "sets out in one comprehensive volume the major economic, financial and business considerations which independent producers need to bear in mind when making films" in Europe. The book's organization follows the process of developing a film, beginning with incorporation and discussing issues such as accounting and taxes and funding. Each chapter begins with an overview and then describes the variations and resources within each country. To pull together all the information on one country, it is necessary to consult the index. The *Guide* is an excellent resource for independent filmmakers planning to make a film in Europe.

1199.   Animation World Network. *AIDB: Animation Industry Database* [World Wide Web Resource]. Animation World Network. Address: http://www.aidb.com. [Accessed: March 2005].

Animation World Network (AWN) hosts *AIDB: Animation Industry Database,* a list of more than 5,000 international animation and visual effects companies, distributors, schools, advertising agencies, and supply companies in 80 categories. *AIDB* offers several databases including an animation business directory, directories of computer and production companies, and a school directory that lists "more than 550 schools that offer courses and programs in animation and related fields in 42 countries." In addition, AWN hosts an animation newswire, a calendar of events, professional publications, career resources, discussion forums for animators, and a list of upcoming theatrical releases. AWN with its *AIDB* directory is an excellent starting place for animators and animation fans.

1200.   Bay Area Video Coalition. 2000. *Mediamaker Handbook: The Essential Resource for Making Independent Film, Video, & New Media.* Millennial ed. San Francisco: BAVC.

The *Mediamaker Handbook* is a directory for independent filmmakers who are making, distributing, and exhibiting their projects. Chapters cover festivals, distributors, exhibitors, funders, broadcasters, and schools. There are separate general and subject indexes. With the exception of the funding section, the directory is more useful for filmmakers with a completed project than for those still in the creative stages.

1201.   Bension, Shmuel. 2000. *The Producer's Masterguide, 2000/2001: The International Production Manual for Motion Picture, Broadcast-Television, Commercials, Cable/ Satellite, Digital & Videotape Industries.* 18th ed. New York: Producer's Masterguide.

Bension has published an international directory of resources for filmmakers and television producers since 1982. Each issue begins with professional and financial overviews and contains directories for countries around the world. The most detailed information is available for the United States and Canada, with information by state and province. For each, he lists government agencies and locations of special interest. For other countries, he profiles the country and its climate and scenery and covers film commissions and issues of interest to filmmakers such as financing and labor. The next part of the book covers unions and their standard agreements, festivals and awards, and major film markets. The book concludes with a list of companies providing every kind of service for film and television production.

1202. *Blu-Book Production Directory.* 2004. Hollywood, Calif.: Hollywood Creative Directory in association with the Hollywood Reporter.

The annual *Blu-Book* is a standard directory of resources needed by film, television, and commercial producers. The contents range from accent removal to writing workshops and divide every aspect of production into 12 broad categories. The index lists companies. Added information include the top box office films and actors of the year, film festivals, and Academy and Emmy Award winners. Formerly entitled the *Hollywood Reporter Blu-Book.*

1203. *Directory of the Canadian Film, Television, Multimedia and Video Industry* [World Wide Web Resource]. Telefilm Canada. 2000. Address: http://www.canadashow. com. [Accessed: March 2005].

Telefilm, the federal agency charged with developing and promoting the Canadian film and television industry, has produced a bilingual directory of "companies, government departments, agencies and associations connected with the Canadian film, television and video industry." The directory also includes a list of festivals and special events and provides indexes to individual and corporate names. As with the *Film Canada Yearbook* (see entry 1205), the directory is most useful to filmmakers working in Canada. The directory is now available online as part of the larger *Canadian Culture and Communications Database* at <http://www.canadashow.com>.

1204. *Film and Media Related Web Sites in Canada* [World Wide Web Resource]. Address: http://www.film.queensu.ca/Links.html. [Accessed: March 2005].

The Department of Film Studies at Queen's University in Kingston, Ontario, Canada, has compiled a subject guide to film and television resources in Canada. Categories cover both the film and television industries and the study of film and media, offering links with very brief descriptions.

1205. *Film Canada Yearbook.* 1986. Toronto: Cine-Communications.

Each year, Moving Pictures Media gathers information from companies and individuals who make films and television shows and compiles the information into a directory of production and post-production companies, broadcasters, financial and legal services, talent representatives, unions, equipment suppliers, distributors, and exhibitors. For a similar work with a more complete list of government agencies, refer to Telefilm's *Directory of the Canadian Film, Television, Multimedia and Video Industry* (see entry 1203). The directory is most useful to filmmakers working in Canada.

1206. *411 Online: L A and New York* [World Wide Web Resource]. LA 411. Address: http://www.la411.com and http://www.newyork411.com. [Accessed: March 2005].

L A 411 is a standard business-to-business directory for the film, television, and commercial industry in southern California. Searchable by keyword, entries provide address, telephone number, e-mail, and Web site for just about anything a producer might need to make a movie from pre-production to post-production, including crew, facilities, equipment, props and wardrobe, financial services, and even a city guide. The newer *New York 411* provides the same service for New York. Registration is not required, but those who register receive "exclusive discounts and first peeks at new offerings designed to better serve your production business' needs." I am not a registered user, so I can't tell you what these are.

1207. *Kemps International Film, Television and Commercials Handbook.* East Grinstead, West Sussex, England: Reed Information Services.

1208. *Kemps Film and Television Production Services Handbook Online* [Worldwide Web Resource]. Reed Elsevier. Address: http://www.kftv.com. [Accessed: March 2005].

Kemps is an international directory to film, television, and commercial services, with everything a producer might need to film on location—from equipment rental and production service companies to hotels, transportation, communication, and weather. In the print annual, listings from 70 countries "provide details on equipment rental, production services, crew, climate and much more." The print version is organized first by region, including U.S. states and Canadian provinces, and then by production service. *Kemps* is available on the Web as a freely searchable online source called *Kemps Film and Television Production Services Handbook Online* at <http://kftv.com> that features "37,000 production services companies from 115 countries worldwide." The Web version is searchable by product and service, by company and crew, and by country, city, U.S. state, and Canadian province. Entries in both the print and online versions list address, telephone and fax numbers, e-mail address, and Web address. One of the categories is festivals, which is a good way to keep tabs on what is out there, although it will take further investigation to see when they are screened. *Kemps* is an essential directory for producers planning to film outside the region with which they are familiar.

1209. *The Knowledge* [World Wide Web Resource]. Miller Freeman. Address: http://www.theknowledgeonline.com. [Accessed: March 2005].

The Knowledge is a directory of film, television, and commercial services available in the United Kingdom. The directory contains "over 18,300 contacts, including over 10,800 freelance crew & technicians." The "Know How" section contains studio and post-production charts, as well as production guidelines and articles and maps. Free registration provides limited access to the directory. Full access to the directory and to the "Know How" portion requires an annual subscription or purchase of the print version of *The Knowledge.*

1210. *Motion Picture, TV and Theatre Directory for Services and Products.* Tarrytown, N.Y.: Motion Picture Enterprises.

Motion Picture Enterprises publishes a semi-annual guide to products and services for the motion picture and television industries. The directory is divided into dozens of categories that range from accents to wireless microphones. Entries contain the standard directory information of name, address, and telephone number, but do not yet include Web pages. The "alphabetical section" is a company name index. The directory is freely available online at <http://www.mpe.net>.

1211. *New York Production Guide* [World Wide Web Resource]. NYPG. Address: http://www.nypg.com. [Accessed: March 2005].

The *New York Production Guide* is a production directory for the film, television, and commercial industries in New York. Searchable by AICP codes, entries provide contact information and a description of services offered. The directory is also available in a print version.

1212. *Production Index: Hawaii, Louisiana, Northwest* [World Wide Web Resource]. Media Index. Address: http://www.hawaiifilm.com and http://www.louisianaproductionindex. com and http://www.nwfilm.com. [Accessed: March 2005].

Media Index produces the standard business-to-business directories for the film, television, and commercial industries in Hawaii, Lousiana, and Oregon and Washington. Searchable by keyword or category and subcategory, entries provide address, telephone number, e-mail, Web site, and, in some cases, a personal statement from the individual or company that provides services that range from pre-production to post-production, including crews, unions, companies, equipment, and stage, props, and wardrobe. The directory also comes in a printed version.

1213. *Reel Directory* [World Wide Web Resource]. Address: http://www.reeldirectory. com. [Accessed: January 2005].

The *Reel Directory* is a standard directory of resources needed by film, television, and commercial producers working in Northern California. The contents are searchable by keyword and browsable by alphabet from "1st Assistant Directors" to "Writers," including anything producers might need to make a film. Each entry includes an address and telephone number, and most entries include a link to the company's Web site and an e-mail address.

1214. *Spectrocom Producer's Masterguide* [World Wide Web Resource]. Spectrocom. Address: http://www.producers.masterguide.com. [Accessed: March 2005].

The *Producer's Masterguide* is an international directory to film, television, and commercial services, listing products and services from pre-production to distribution and everything in between. On its web site, it sells a print directory and provides links to Web sites from its online directory via broad categories in an alphabetical list. Although the copyright is up to date, many of the links on the online version are outdated, making this a less useful resource than some of its competitors.

1215. *United States Film Commission* [World Wide Web Resource]. Address: http:// www.redbirdstudio.com/AWOL/filmcomms.html. [Accessed: January 2005].

The Acting Workshop On-line (AWOL), a "place for beginning actors and actresses to learn about acting and the acting business," hosts a list of U.S. state film commissions as well as a second larger alphabetical list that includes international film commissions. Each entry includes address, telephone and fax number, and, for select commissions, a link to their Web page.

STOCK FOOTAGE

1216. *Footage: The Worldwide Moving Image Sourcebook.* 1997. New York: Second Line Search.

The introduction defines stock footage as "any piece of film or video photographed by an outside source that is licensed to a producer in a separate, secondary production." *Footage* is the standard guide to film and video archives and stock footage companies. The directory is divided into US/Canada and International Sources. Each entry includes the name and type of organization or company and an address followed by contact names, access information, the physical materials, and whether they are accessible by catalog, rights, licensing, and restrictions to use of materials, publications, and a description of the collections. An extensive subject index points to archives, while additional indexes cover source and collections and place. A separate section covers just about any service related to stock footage such as research, screening, rights and clearances, film labs, archival management, and online resources. An almanac covers issues and trends in the footage industry.

1217. *PhotoGraphicLibraries.com* [World Wide Web Resource]. Address: http://www. photographiclibraries.com. [Accessed: March 2005].

PhotoGraphicLibraries.com contains a directory of stock libraries, archives, moving image collections, and libraries and museums that make images available to photographers and filmmakers freely or at a cost. Records include the name of the organization, a Web link, and a brief description. The collections include all formats, not just digital, making it an excellent resource for finding images of all types.

THEATERS (SEE ALSO *TICKETS*)

1218. National Association of Theatre Owners (U.S.). 1976. *Encyclopedia of Exhibition.* New York: NATO.

NATO—the National Association of Theatre Owners—has published the *Encyclopedia of Exhibition* for theater owners each September since1976. The largest section is a guide to coming attractions. Designed to help exhibitors select films they would like to show, each entry includes the film title, a synopsis, the production company, and, if known, writer, director, and above-the-line cast. The next largest section is a statistical compilation of the number of theaters and films and how much money they make along with a demographic profile of who goes to the movies. In addition to the annual compilations going back several years, the annual also lists the all-time statistical leaders among U.S. releases. Directories cover domestic and international exhibitors, distributors, cinema associations, and trade publications. Resource lists include award winners, profiles of exhibitors, and the rules of the classification and rating system. The 2000–2001 edition includes guidelines from the exhibition of motion pictures recommended for adoption by the Theatre Alignment Program. Included as a part of membership in the Association, but also available for purchase.

14
Fans and Audience

This chapter lists resources about the film and television audience, including fans. It includes guides for contacting celebrities and touring locations. There are also guides on ratings and censorship.

AUDIENCE

1219.   Austin, Bruce A. 1983. *The Film Audience: An International Bibliography of Research with Annotations and an Essay.* Metuchen, N.J.: Scarecrow Press.

Professor Austin has systematically gathered an international list of over 1,200 studies examining film audiences. Although most are empirical, he does include some advocacy and speculative works. Organized alphabetically by author, each entry provides standard citation information and a brief annotation. The book contains indexes to titles and secondary authors as well as a very useful subject index. While intended primarily for social scientists and film producers, the bibliography will also be useful to film scholars.

1220.   Beville, Hugh Malcolm. 1988. *Audience Ratings: Radio, Television, and Cable.* Rev. ed. Hillsdale, N.J.: Lawrence Erlbaum.

Beville was one of the most prominent researchers of television and radio ratings. In 1988, he revised his definitive book on how broadcasters measure their audiences. The book begins with a history of ratings services such as Crossley's *Cooperative Analysis of Broadcasting* and Nielsen and then explains the various ratings methodologies and how ratings are used. Appendixes provide basic definitions and formulas, a directory of national rating companies, highlights of audience size from 1970 to 1986, and studies of the strengths and weaknesses of various rating techniques. Although dated, the historical section remains superb, and the overview of techniques can still serve as a primer. Includes a bibliography and index.

CELEBRITIES

1221.   *CelebrityEmail.com* [World Wide Web Resource]. Address: http://www.celebrityemail.com. [Accessed: January 2005].

CelebrityEmail.com has collected street or e-mail addresses for over 22,000 actors, musicians, athletes, and politicians. For a subscription fee, it will forward messages from subscribers to their favorite celebrities. For free, fans can post public messages on a bulletin board. (Note: I did not pay to subscribe to this service; I only examined its Web pages.)

1222.   *Contact Any Celebrity* [World Wide Web Resource]. Address: http://contactanycelebrity.com. [Accessed: January 2005].

Contact Any Celebrity claims that they maintain "the largest online database of over 45,000 accurate celebrity contacts," in many cases also listing "the agent, manager, publicist, attorney, business manager and production company" as well as the charitable causes to which they donate. For a monthly fee, subscribers gain access to the entire database. The Web site provider also publishes the *Celebrity Black Book* with over 40,000 of the addresses from its database. (Note: I did not pay to subscribe to this service; I only examined its Web pages.)

LOCATIONS (SEE ALSO *NATIONAL CINEMA*)

1223. Reeves, Tony. 2003. *The Worldwide Guide to Movie Locations.* Rev. ed. London: Titan.

Reeves has compiled a list of movies and the places where they were filmed. Unlike other location guides, the book is organized by movie instead of by location, making the book useful for finding out where a movie was filmed. The selection criteria are not clear, although the book does emphasize American and British films. The book concludes with a gazetteer of locations listing the films made there.

EUROPE

1224. Adams, Mark. 2004. *Location London.* Northampton, Mass.: Interlink.

Adams, a film programmer and journalist, has written an illustrated guide for fans interested in seeing the locations in London where their favorite movies were filmed. Organized by region, each section begins with an introduction describing the area's appeal to filmmakers followed by descriptions of smaller neighborhoods and the films made there. Additional sections locate commemorative plaques, identify pubs, bars, restaurants, and hotels, and list films where London stands in for another place. With a bibliography and an index, the book is ideal for tourists who love movies.

UNITED STATES

1225. Barth, Jack. 1991. *Roadside Hollywood: The Movie Lover's State-by-State Guide to Film Locations, Celebrity Hangouts, Celluloid Tourist Attractions, and More.* Chicago: Contemporary Books.

By contacting local film commissions, Barth created this guide for tourists that lists movie locations by region, state, and city. There is a history of filming in each state, a list of filmmakers and actors born there, and a list of the cities and the movies filmed in each. There are separate indexes of films and people. The book is of interest primarily to tourists.

1226. Gelbert, Doug. 2002. *Film and Television Locations: A State-by-State Guidebook to Moviemaking Sites, Excluding Los Angeles.* Jefferson, N.C.: McFarland.

Gelbert, a writer specializing in tourist locations, has compiled a guide to 1,500 places outside of Los Angeles where movies were made. Organized by state, each chapter lists movies with title, year, lead actors, a synopsis, and a description of the filming locations. Gelbert confirmed that the site still exists before including it in the book. For states with a much-used location, he makes a special note at the end of the chapter. Covering just over 1,100 movies, the book is certainly not comprehensive, but it is a nice guide for tourists and fans who want to see where their favorite movies were made.

1227. Gordon, William A. 1995. *Shot on This Site: A Travelers Guide to the Places and Locations Used To Film Famous Movies and TV Shows.* Secaucus, N.J.: Carol.

Gordon has compiled a guide for tourists that lists movie locations by region, state, and location. He gathered information by contacting local film commissions and, based on his research, excluded Idaho and North Dakota. He selected movies based purely on popularity. For each state, he lists often-used locations and the movies and television shows filmed there. Movies filmed in the state that used other locations are listed at the end of each state entry. Separate indexes cover film, television, and names. The book is of interest primarily to tourists.

California

1228. Fleming, E. J. 2000. *Hollywood Death and Scandal Sites: Sixteen Driving Tours with Directions and the Full Story, from Tallulah Bankhead to River Phoenix.* Jefferson, N.C.: McFarland.

Fleming's guide for morbid tourists contains 16 Los Angeles driving tours that "include over 500 sites relating to celebrity deaths and scandals." An extensive bibliography lists the resources consulted, and an index points to names, locations, types of scandals, and causes of death.

1229. Gordon, William A. 2002. *The Ultimate Hollywood Tour Book: The Incomparable Guide to Movie Stars' Homes, Movie and TV Locations, Scandals, Murders, Suicide, and All the Famous Tourist Sites.* 3rd ed. El Toro, Calif.: North Ridge Books.

Gordon has compiled a tourist guide to stars' homes and filming locations in greater Los Angeles. Arranged by region, each section includes a map and entries that either describe the history of a star's home, the location used in a film or television show, or hot spots where celebrities hang out. Includes an index.

1230. *Seeing Stars* [World Wide Web Resource]. Address: http://seeing-stars.com. [Accessed: January 2005].

Designed for tourists who would like to see a movie star during their travels, *Seeing Stars* claims to be "the ultimate guide to stars & Hollywood." The site includes a calendar of events and lists places where stars perform and play, places they own, even where they go to church. Readers can find out where stars died and were buried as well as spots where they are immortalized. For those wanting to contact their favorite celebrity, there is a free directory of mailing addresses. An index lists 150 of the biggest stars. The site also lists Hollywood landmarks and locations.

1231. Smith, Leon. 1993. *Famous Hollywood Locations: Descriptions and Photographs of 382 Sites Involving 289 Films and 105 Television Series, McFarland Classics.* Jefferson, N.C.: McFarland.

Smith has compiled a list of locations in the greater Los Angeles area where film and television series have been filmed. He divides the city into regions, describes the location, and then lists a selection of the movies and shows filmed in each place. The index covers locations, movies, shows, and people. The book is of interest primarily to tourists.

1232. Smith, Leon. 2000. *Movie and Television Locations: 113 Famous Filming Sites in Los Angeles and San Diego.* Jefferson, N.C.: McFarland.

Smith has compiled a list of locations used in films and television series in southern California designed to complement his earlier book *Famous Hollywood Locations* (see entry 1231). The 113 sites named in the title are categorized into 24 different types of locations such as bridges, caves, or mansions. He describes each location and then lists the movies and shows filmed there. The book is illustrated with black-and-white photographs of many of the locations. The index lists locations, movies, shows, and names. The book is of interest primarily to tourists.

Hawaii

1233. Langman, Larry. 1998. *Return to Paradise: A Guide to South Sea Island Films.* Lanham, Md.: Scarecrow Press.

Langman has gathered information on approximately 600 American films of a genre he calls South Sea island films. Connected by both place and thematic elements, these films are arranged chronologically by decade. Each chapter is introduced by a lengthy discussion of "how American culture influenced American South Sea island films both in theme and content." Individual films list the director, screenwriter, and principal cast followed by a paragraph summarizing the film and describing how it reflects American society. Langman includes a brief bibliography, appendixes listing documentaries, serials, and alternate titles, and title and name indexes.

1234. Reyes, Luis, and Ed Rampell. 1995. *Made in Paradise: Hollywood's Films of Hawai'i and the South Seas.* Honolulu: Mutual.

Reyes explores Hollywood films based or shot in Hawaii and in the South Pacific. After chapters describing myths versus realities and the development of the Hawaiian film industry, Reyes lists films and television shows made about Hawaii and the South Seas made in Hawaii and elsewhere as well as films made in Hawaii about other places. Each film entry is illustrated with several stills and includes director, writer, producer, cast, a plot summary, a review, and a list of locations. One chapter is devoted to the careers of Hawaiian actors. Although the book is a guide to the films and how they portrayed the islands, the index lists locations as well as names and titles, so it can also serve to a lesser extent as a location guide for tourists.

1235. Schmitt, Robert C. 1988. *Hawaii in the Movies, 1898–1959.* Honolulu: Hawaiian Historical Society.

Schmitt, a movie fan and employee of the Hawaii Chamber of Commerce, has compiled a list of feature films made in or about Hawaii before statehood in 1959. The introduction covers the dates and places, themes and titles, technical details, quality, casts, and a discussion of other categories of non-feature films. Most of the book lists the films in chronological order. Each entry lists the title, distributor, technical information, principal cast, and frequently mentions "local supporting cast." The plot summary features Hawaii's role in the picture. The book is extensively researched with endnotes and includes indexes to titles and personal names.

New Mexico

1236. New Mexico Magazine and New Mexico Film Office. 1998. *100 Years of Film-making in New Mexico 1898–1998.* Santa Fe: New Mexico Department of Tourism.

New Mexico Magazine and the New Mexico Economic Development Department commissioned this illustrated narrative guide to the first 100 years of film in New Mexico. Eight chapters explore various aspects of the New Mexico film history, filmmaking, and locations, but the most useful portion for reference purposes is the year-by-year chronology at the end of the book listing "films shot partially or wholly in New Mexico."

New York

1237. Katz, Chuck. 1999. *Manhattan on Film: Walking Tours of Hollywood's Fabled Front Lot.* 1st Limelight ed. New York: Limelight Editions.

1238. Katz, Chuck. 2002. *Manhattan on Film 2: More Walking Tours of Location Sites in the Big Apple.* 1st Limelight ed. New York: Limelight Editions.

Katz's walking tours for tourists explore exterior locations of movies filmed in New York. Each tour begins with a street map and directions. The locations are numbered in walking order and list movies filmed at each place. The book is of interest primarily to tourists.

North Carolina

1239. Henderson, Jenny. 2002. *The North Carolina Filmography: Over 2,000 Film and Television Works Made in the State, 1905 through 2000.* Jefferson, N.C.: McFarland.

Henderson took several years to compile a list of "every feature film, made-for-TV film, documentary, short, television program, newsreel, and promotional video" shot even briefly in North Carolina through the year 2000. Organized by film, each entry includes film format, release year, complete production and cast credits, a synopsis, and a list of places where filming took place. The book includes a location index for those interested in seeing what was filmed where as well as a personnel index.

RATINGS AND CENSORSHIP (SEE ALSO *CHILDREN*)

1240. Buhle, Paul, and David Wagner. 2003. *Blacklisted: The Film-Lover's Guide to the Hollywood Blacklist.* 1st Palgrave Macmillan ed. New York: Palgrave Macmillan.

Buhle and Wagner have compiled a list of over 2,000 "films written, directed or produced, all or in part, by victims of the Hollywood blacklist." They also include those who escaped the blacklist by testifying before Congress. The entries are inconsistent in the amount of information they supply. Most include producer, director, writer, cast credits, and a critical review focusing on the work of the blacklisted artist, but many entries merely mention the role played by a filmmaker in the making of the film. The blacklisted artists are highlighted by bullets within the text, but there is, unfortunately, no index, severely limiting the book's usefulness as a reference work. Still, the book is unique and provides a nice approach to the blacklist.

1241.   Catholic Church. United States Conference of Catholic Bishops. *Movie and Family Video Reviews* [World Wide Web Resource]. United States Conference of Catholic Bishops. Address: http://www.nccbuscc.org/movies. [Accessed: March 2005].

The Office of Film and Broadcasting of the United States Conference of Catholic Bishops (USCCB) review movies "according to artistic merit and moral suitability." Acceptable movies are rated for general patronage, adults and adolescents, adults, or adult with reservations. Unacceptable movies are rated morally offensive. Each film includes USCCB and MPAA ratings with an explanation and a brief synopsis and review. Movies are grouped by new and upcoming films in theaters, on television, and on DVD/video. There is an archive of reviews going back to the silent era. One page lists movies appropriate for the family. The site also includes the top 10 movies for each year since 1965 and the top 45 movies in the categories of religion, values, and art that the Vatican released in 1995.

1242.   The Classification and Rating Administration. *Reasons for Movie Ratings* [World Wide Web Resource]. Address: http://www.filmratings.com. [Accessed: January 2005].

The Classification and Rating Administration, the organization responsible for rating films G, PG, PG-13, R, or NC-17 for the Motion Picture Association of America and the National Association of Theatre Owners, explains how the rating system works and offers a database of film ratings going back to 1968, when the rating system began. The database is searchable by title and may be limited by rating. Records list the reasons the film received its rating, including such aspects as theme, language, violence, nudity, sex, or drug use. Reasons are not included for R-rated films released prior to September 27, 1990.

1243.   Motion Picture Association of America. *Movie Ratings* [World Wide Web Resource]. MPAA. Address: http://www.mpaa.org/home.htm. [Accessed: March 2005].

The Motion Picture Association of America (MPAA) provides a database of the ratings for all movies made since the MPAA rating system began in 1968. A search retrieves the film title, its rating, and a summary of the themes, language, nudity and sex, violence, and other elements that viewers might want to take into consideration. A link leads to explanations of the purpose of the rating system, how it works, and what each rating means.

1244.   Sova, Dawn B. 2001. *Forbidden Films: Censorship Histories of 125 Motion Pictures, Facts on File Library of World Literature.* New York: Facts on File.

Professor Sova analyzes 125 films that were censored in the United States on sexual, social, political, or religious grounds or for violent content. She succeeds admirably in her goal to examine "representative films and the means by which they have been suppressed in whole or in part." Each film entry includes the standard production data along with the producer, director, writer, awards, genre, and cast. The author summarizes each film and describes the history behind its censorship. Each entry lists further readings, which are cumulated in a bibliography. Appendixes contain profiles of directors, group films by the reasons they were banned, and list 125 additional censored films. Includes an index.

Appendix A
Library of Congress Subject Headings

The *Library of Congress Subject Headings* are printed in four massive red books that describe all the subject headings used by the United States Library of Congress and most libraries. *Motion pictures* is the standard subject heading for film (*moving pictures* was used until 1978; use it for print materials published before 1978). *Television programs* and *television broadcasting* are the standard subject headings for television. See *Appendix C* for a large list. *Motion pictures* and *television programs* and *television broadcasting* are qualified by hundreds of subheadings; some of the most useful include:

FORM

Motion pictures—Bibliography
Motion pictures—Dictionaries
Television broadcasting—Encyclopedias

PLACE

Motion pictures—France
Motion pictures—New Mexico
Television programs—Australia

PRODUCTION

Motion pictures—Art direction
Motion pictures—Editing
Television acting

RELATION TO SOCIETY

Motion pictures—Censorship
Motion pictures—Influence
Television programs—Social aspects (Religious aspects, Political aspects, etc.)

STUDY

Motion pictures—Plots, Themes, etc.
Motion pictures—Reviews

Television—History and criticism
Television—Study and teaching

FOR FILM, GENRE USUALLY TAKES THE FORM *"GENRE" FILMS*. FOR TELEVISION, GENRE SUBJECT HEADINGS VARY (SEE *APPENDIX B* FOR GENRE/FORM HEADINGS).

Feature films
Comedy films
Documentary films
Film noir

THEME

African Americans in motion pictures
Devil in motion pictures
Ballet on television
Mothers on television

FILM AS IT RELATES TO THE OUTSIDE WORLD TAKES THE FORM *"SOCIETY" AND MOTION PICTURES* OR *MOTION PICTURES AND "SOCIETY."*

Art and motion pictures
Feminism and motion pictures
Television and baseball
Television and politics

Appendix B
Library of Congress Moving Image Genre/Form List

There is a special category of subject heading applied to films and television programs called the Genre/Form heading. The entire list developed by the Library of Congress Motion Picture Broadcasting and Recorded Sound Division for *The Moving Image Genre-Form Guide* (see entry 439) follows:

- Actuality
- Adaptation
- Adventure
- Adventure (Nonfiction)
- Ancient world
- Animal
- Art
- Aviation
- Biographical
- Biographical (Nonfiction)
- Buddy
- Caper
- Chase
- Children's
- College
- Comedy
- Crime
- Dance
- Dark comedy
- Disability
- Disaster
- Documentary
- Domestic comedy
- Educational
- Erotic
- Espionage
- Ethnic

- Ethnic (Nonfiction)
- Ethnographic
- Experimental
- Exploitation
- Fallen woman
- Family
- Fantasy
- Film noir
- Game
- Gangster
- Historical
- Home shopping
- Horror
- Industrial
- Instructional
- Interview
- Journalism
- Jungle
- Juvenile delinquency
- Lecture
- Legal
- Magazine
- Martial arts
- Maternal melodrama
- Medical
- Medical (Nonfiction)
- Melodrama

- Military
- Music
- Music video
- Musical
- Mystery
- Nature
- News
- Newsreel
- Opera
- Operetta
- Parody
- Police
- Political
- Pornography
- Prehistoric
- Prison
- Propaganda
- Public access
- Public affairs
- Reality-based
- Religion
- Religious
- Road
- Romance
- Science fiction
- Screwball comedy
- Show business
- Singing cowboy
- Situation comedy
- Slapstick comedy
- Slasher
- Soap opera
- Social guidance
- Social problem
- Sophisticated comedy
- Speculation
- Sponsored
- Sports
- Sports (Nonfiction)
- Survival
- Talk
- Thriller
- Training
- Travelogue
- Trick
- Trigger
- Variety
- War
- War (Nonfiction)
- Western
- Women
- Youth
- Yukon

Appendix C
Library of Congress Classification—By Subject

Libraries shelve books in classification order. They usually use one of two classification systems: the Library of Congress or the Dewey Decimal. The table below lists topics and corresponding Library of Congress call numbers, which readers can use to browse the shelves. See *Appendix D* for a table ordered by classification number.

Aboriginal Australians in motion pictures	PN1995.9.A835
Adventure television programs	PN1992.8.A317
Advertising—Television programs	PN1992.8.A32
African Americans on television	PN1992.8.A34
African Americans in the motion picture industry	PN1995.9.N4
AIDS (Disease) in motion pictures	PN1995.9.A435
Alcoholism in motion pictures	PN1995.9.A45
Alien labor in motion pictures	PN1995.9.A46
Alienation (Social psychology) in motion pictures	PN1995.9.A47
Aliens in motion pictures	PN1995.9.A48
Anarchism in motion pictures	PN1995.9.A487
Animals in motion pictures	PN1995.9.A5
Animals on television	PN1992.8.A58
Animated films	PN1997.5
Antisemitism in motion pictures	PN1995.9.A55
Appalachians (People) in motion pictures	PN1995.9.M67
Arabs in motion pictures	PN1995.9.A
Arabs on television	PN1992.8.A7
Archaeology in motion pictures	PN1995.9.A69
Architects in motion pictures	PN1995.9.A695
Armed Forces in motion pictures	PN1995.9.A72
Art on television	PN1992.8.A75
Arthurian romances in motion pictures	PN1995.9.A75
Asian Americans in the motion picture industry	PN1995.9.A77
Asian Americans on television	PN1992.8.A78
Asians in motion pictures	PN1995.9.A78
Auteur theory	PN1995.9.A837
Authors in motion pictures	PN1995.9.A84
Automobiles in motion pictures	PN1995.9.A85
Baseball films	PN1995.9.B28
Basques in motion pictures	PN1995.9.B29
Baths in motion pictures	PN1995.9.B3
Bible films	PN1995.9.B53
Bisexuality in motion pictures	PN1995.9.B57
Blind in motion pictures	PN1995.9.B59

Face in motion pictures	PN1995.9.F32
Family in motion pictures	PN1995.9.F35
Family on television	PN1992.8.F33
Film adaptations	PN1997.85
Film archives	PN1993.4
Film criticism	PN1995
Film hairstyling	PN1995.9.H25
Film noir	PN1995.9.F54
Film posters	PN1995.9.P5
Fire fighters on television	PN1992.8.F57
Flashbacks	PN1995.9.F56
Flight in motion	PN1995.9.F58
Foreign films	PN1995.9.F67
Frankenstein films	PN1995.9.F8
Geopolitics in motion pictures	PN1995.9.G39
Germans in motion pictures	PN1995.9.G45
Germany—On television	PN1992.8.G47
Girls in motion pictures	PN1995.9.G57
Hawaii—In motion pictures	PN1995.9.H38
Holocaust, Jewish (1939–1945), in motion pictures	PN1995.9.H53
Holocaust, Jewish (1939–1945), on television	PN1992.8.H63
Home in motion pictures	PN1995.9.H54
Homosexuality in motion pictures	PN1995.9.H55
Homosexuality on television	PN1992.8.H64
Hunting in motion pictures	PN1995.9.H84
Hypnotism in motion pictures	PN1995.9.H95
Impressionism in motion pictures	PN1995.9.I45
Indians in motion pictures	PN1995.9.I48
Indians on television	PN1992.8.I64
Interviewing on television	PN1992.8.I68
Invisibility in motion pictures	PN1995.9.I59
Irish Americans in motion pictures	PN1995.9.I67
Italian Americans in motion pictures	PN1995.9.I73
Jazz in motion pictures	PN1995.9.J37
Jewish-Arab relations in motion pictures	PN1995.9.J45
Jews in motion pictures	PN1995.9.J46
Journalists in motion pictures	PN1995.9.J6
Justice, Administration of, on television	PN1992.8.J87
Justice, Administration of, in motion pictures	PN1995.9.J8
Juvenile delinquency films	PN1995.9.J87
Kissing in motion pictures	PN1995.9.K57
Latin Americans in motion pictures	PN1995.9.L37
Latin lovers	PN1995.9.L38
Lesbianism in motion pictures	PN1995.9.L48
Love in motion pictures	PN1995.9.L6
Magazine format television programs	PN1992.8.M33
Man-woman relationships in motion pictures	PN1995.9.M27
Marriage in motion pictures	PN1995.9.M3

Martial arts films	PN1995.9.H3
Masochism in motion pictures	PN1995.9.M
Medicine on television	PN1992.8.M43
Melodrama in motion pictures	PN1995.9.M45
Men in motion pictures	PN1995.9.M46
Mental illness in motion pictures	PN1995.9.M463
Metaphor in motion pictures	PN1995.9.M472
Mexican Americans in motion pictures	PN1995.9.M49
Mexico—In motion pictures	PN1995.9.M5
Middle Ages in motion pictures	PN1995.9.M52
Miners in motion pictures	PN1995.9.M54
Minorities in motion pictures	PN1995.9.M23
Minorities on television	PN1992.8.M54
Money in motion pictures	PN1995.9.M59
Monsters in motion pictures	PN1995.9.M6
Mothers in motion pictures	PN1995.9.M63
Mothers on television	PN1992.8.M58
Motion picture	PN1995.9.S29
Motion picture authorship	PN1996
Motion picture industry in motion pictures	PN1995.9.M65
Motion picture industry—Public relations	PN1995.9.P79
Motion picture locations	PN1995.67
Motion picture plays	PN1996–1997
Motion picture plays—Women authors	PN1997
Motion picture remakes	PN1995.9.R45
Motion picture theater etiquette	PN1995.9.E86
Motion pictures	PN1993–1999
Motion pictures and history	PN1995.2
Motion pictures and language	PN1995.4
Motion pictures and literature	PN1995.3
Motion pictures and the arts	PN1995.25
Motion pictures, Yiddish	PN1995.9.Y54
Motion pictures—Art direction	PN1995.9.A74
Motion pictures—Biography	PN1998.2–.3
Motion pictures—Casting	PN1995.9.C34
Motion pictures—Collectibles	PN1995.9.C53
Motion pictures—Evaluation	PN1995.9.E9
Motion pictures—Moral and ethical aspects	PN1995.5
Motion pictures—Setting and scenery	PN1995.9.S4
Motion pictures—Social aspects	PN1995.9.S6
Motorcycle films	PN1995.9.M66
Mummy films	PN1995.9.M83
Music videos	PN1992.8.M87
Musical films	PN1995.9.M86
Mythology in motion pictures	PN1995.9.M97
National characteristics in motion pictures	PN1995.9.N33
National characteristics, American, in motion pictures	PN1995.9.N34
National characteristics, Australian, in motion pictures	PN1995.9.N35

National characteristics, British, in motion pictures	PN1995.9.N352
National characteristics, German, in motion pictures	PN1995.9.N354
National socialism in motion pictures	PN1995.9.N36
Nature in motion pictures	PN1995.9.N38
Nihilism (Philosophy) in motion pictures	PN1995.9.N55
Nonverbal communication on television	PN1992.8.N65
Nostalgia in motion pictures	PN1995.9.N67
Nurses on television	PN1992.8.N87
Occupations on television	PN1992.8.O27
Opera in motion pictures	PN1995.9.O64
Organizational behavior in motion pictures	PN1995.9.O75
Organizational behavior on television	PN1992.8.O72
Outlaws in motion pictures	PN1995.9.O84
People with disabilities on television	PN1992.8.H36
Periodicals. Societies. Serials	PN1992
Physicians in motion pictures	PN1995.9.P44
Pioneers in motion pictures	PN1995.9.P487
Politics in motion pictures	PN1995.9.P6
Prehistoric animals in motion pictures	PN1995.9.P67
Psychiatry in motion pictures	PN1995.9.P78
Puppet films	PN1995.9.P8
Puppets on television	PN1992.8.P86
Railroads in motion pictures	PN1995.9.R25
Rape in motion pictures	PN1995.9.R27
Rape on television	PN1992.8.R26
Realism in motion pictures	PN1995.9.R3
Realism on television	PN1992.8.R4
Rednecks in motion pictures	PN1995.9.R33
Regeneration in motion pictures	PN1995.9.R35
Religion in motion pictures	PN1995.9.R4
Rites and ceremonies in motion pictures	PN1995.9.R56
Road films	PN1995.9.R63
Romanies in motion pictures	PN1995.9.R67
Russians in motion pictures	PN1995.9.R87
Sadism in motion pictures	PN1995.9.S23
Schools in motion pictures	PN1995.9.S253
Science films	PN1995.9.S25
Scotland—In motion pictures	PN1995.9.S27
Sculpture in motion pictures	PN1995.9.S274
Sea in motion pictures	PN1995.9.S28
Sensationalism in motion pictures	PN1995.9.S284
Sensationalism on television	PN1992.8.S37

Appendix D
Library of Congress
Classification—By Classification

Libraries shelve books in classification order. They usually use one of two classification systems: the Library of Congress or the Dewey Decimal. The table below allows readers to browse the shelves by Library of Congress classification number. See *Appendix C* for a table listing classification numbers by subject heading.

PN1992 — Television

PN1992	Periodicals. Societies. Serials
PN1992.1	Yearbooks
PN1992.13	Congresses
PN1992.15	Collections
PN1992.16	Television archives
PN1992.3	By region of country
PN1992.4	Television actors and actresses
PN1992.56	Television and history
PN1992.6	Television and politics
PN1992.655	Television and literature
PN1992.66	Television and the performing arts
PN1992.7	Television authorship
PN1992.75	Television—Production and direction
PN1992.77	Television
PN1992.8.A317	Adventure television programs
PN1992.8.A32	Advertising—Television programs
PN1992.8.A34	African Americans in television
PN1992.8.A58	Animals on television
PN1992.8.A7	Arabs on television
PN1992.8.A75	Art on television
PN1992.8.A78	Asian Americans on television
PN1992.8.B64	Body, Human, on television
PN1992.8.B87	Businessmen on television
PN1992.8.C36	Television programs—Casting
PN1992.8.C46	Television programs for children—Plots, themes, etc.
PN1992.8.C66	Television comedies
PN1992.8.D4	Death on television
PN1992.8.D48	Detective and mystery television programs
PN1992.8.D74	Drinking on television
PN1992.8.E84	Ethnic television broadcasting

PN1992.8.F33	Family on television
PN1992.8.F5	Television broadcasting of films
PN1992.8.F57	Fire fighters on television
PN1992.8.G47	Germany—On television
PN1992.8.H36	People with disabilities on television
PN1992.8.H63	Holocaust, Jewish (1939–1945), on television
PN1992.8.H64	Homosexuality on television
PN1992.8.I64	Indians on television
PN1992.8.I68	Interviewing on television
PN1992.8.J87	Justice, Administration of, on television
PN1992.8.L5	Television—Lighting
PN1992.8.M33	Magazine format television programs
PN1992.8.M36	Television makeup
PN1992.8.M43	Medicine on television
PN1992.8.M54	Minorities on television
PN1992.8.M58	Mothers on television
PN1992.8.M6	Television broadcasting of animated films
PN1992.8.M87	Music videos
PN1992.8.N65	Nonverbal communication on television
PN1992.8.N87	Nurses on television
PN1992.8.O27	Occupations on television
PN1992.8.O72	Organizational behavior on television
PN1992.8.P86	Puppets on television
PN1992.8.R26	Rape on television
PN1992.8.R4	Realism on television
PN1992.8.S37	Sensationalism on television
PN1992.8.S4	Soap operas
PN1992.8.S64	Television specials
PN1992.8.T75	Travel on television
PN1992.8.T78	True crime television programs
PN1992.8.V3	Variety shows
PN1992.8.V55	Violence on television
PN1992.8.W65	Women on television
PN1992.8.Y68	Youth on television
PN1992.94	Video recordings—Production and direction
PN1992.95	Video recordings
PN1993–1999	**Motion pictures**
PN1993.4	Film archives
PN1995	Film criticism
PN1995.2	Motion pictures and history
PN1995.25	Motion pictures and the arts
PN1995.3	Motion pictures and literature
PN1995.4	Motion pictures and language
PN1995.5	Motion pictures—Moral and ethical aspects
PN1995.67	Motion picture locations

PN1995.7	Sound motion pictures
PN1995.9.A	Arabs in motion pictures
PN1995.9.A435	AIDS (Disease) in motion pictures
PN1995.9.A45	Alcoholism in motion pictures
PN1995.9.A46	Alien labor in motion pictures
PN1995.9.A47	Alienation (Social psychology) in motion pictures
PN1995.9.A48	Aliens in motion pictures
PN1995.9.A487	Anarchism in motion pictures
PN1995.9.A5	Animals in motion pictures
PN1995.9.A55	Antisemitism in motion pictures
PN1995.9.A69	Archaeology in motion pictures
PN1995.9.A695	Architects in motion pictures
PN1995.9.A72	Armed Forces in motion pictures
PN1995.9.A74	Motion pictures—Art direction
PN1995.9.A75	Arthurian romances in motion pictures
PN1995.9.A77	Asian Americans in the motion picture industry
PN1995.9.A78	Asians in motion pictures
PN1995.9.A835	Aboriginal Australians in motion pictures
PN1995.9.A837	Auteur theory
PN1995.9.A84	Authors in motion pictures
PN1995.9.A85	Automobiles in motion pictures
PN1995.9.B28	Baseball films
PN1995.9.B29	Basques in motion pictures
PN1995.9.B3	Baths in motion pictures
PN1995.9.B53	Bible films
PN1995.9.B57	Bisexuality in motion pictures
PN1995.9.B59	Blind in motion pictures
PN1995.9.B62	Body, Human, in motion pictures
PN1995.9.B64	Bondage (Sexual behavior) in motion pictures
PN1995.9.B69	Boxing in motion pictures
PN1995.9.B8	Bullfights in motion pictures
PN1995.9.B85	Bureaucracy in motion pictures
PN1995.9.B87	Business in motion pictures
PN1995.9.C333	Captivity in motion pictures
PN1995.9.C34	Motion pictures—Casting
PN1995.9.C35	Catholics in motion pictures
PN1995.9.C36	Characters and characteristics in motion pictures
PN1995.9.C39	Child sexual abuse in motion pictures
PN1995.9.C45	Children in motion pictures
PN1995.9.C47	China—In motion pictures
PN1995.9.C5113	Christmas in motion pictures
PN1995.9.C513	Cities and towns in motion pictures
PN1995.9.C52	Clergy in motion pictures

PN1995.9.C53	Motion pictures—Collectibles
PN1995.9.C543	College life films
PN1995.9.C546	Colors in motion pictures
PN1995.9.C55	Comedy films
PN1995.9.C553	Composers in motion pictures
PN1995.9.C58	Country life in motion pictures
PN1995.9.C65	Credit titles (Motion pictures, television, etc.)
PN1995.9.C85	Culture conflict in motion pictures
PN1995.9.C9	Cyborgs in motion pictures
PN1995.9.D35	Deaf in motion pictures
PN1995.9.D37	Death in motion pictures
PN1995.9.D44	Developing countries—In motion pictures
PN1995.9.D46	Devil in motion pictures
PN1995.9.D49	Dialogue in motion pictures
PN1995.9.D52	Dinners and dining in motion pictures
PN1995.9.D53	Dinosaurs in motion pictures
PN1995.9.D62	Documentary-style films
PN1995.9.D64	Dracula films
PN1995.9.D68	Drifters in motion pictures
PN1995.9.D75	Drinking in motion pictures
PN1995.9.D78	Drugs in motion pictures
PN1995.9.E44	Emigration and immigration in motion pictures
PN1995.9.E77	Entertainers in motion pictures
PN1995.9.E83	Eskimos in motion pictures
PN1995.9.E86	Motion picture theater etiquette
PN1995.9.E9	Motion pictures—Evaluation
PN1995.9.E95	Exoticism in motion pictures
PN1995.9.E96	Experimental
PN1995.9.F32	Face in motion pictures
PN1995.9.F35	Family in motion pictures
PN1995.9.F54	Film noir
PN1995.9.F56	Flashbacks
PN1995.9.F58	Flight in motion pictures
PN1995.9.F67	Foreign films
PN1995.9.F8	Frankenstein films
PN1995.9.G39	Geopolitics in motion pictures
PN1995.9.G45	Germans in motion pictures
PN1995.9.G57	Girls in motion pictures
PN1995.9.H25	Film hairstyling
PN1995.9.H3	Martial arts films
PN1995.9.H38	Hawaii—In motion pictures
PN1995.9.H53	Holocaust, Jewish (1939–1945), in motion pictures
PN1995.9.H54	Home in motion pictures
PN1995.9.H55	Homosexuality in motion pictures

PN1995.9.H84	Hunting in motion pictures
PN1995.9.H95	Hypnotism in motion pictures
PN1995.9.I45	Impressionism in motion pictures
PN1995.9.I48	Indians in motion pictures
PN1995.9.I67	Irish Americans in motion pictures
PN1995.9.I73	Italian Americans in motion pictures
PN1995.9.J37	Jazz in motion pictures
PN1995.9.J45	Jewish-Arab relations in motion pictures
PN1995.9.J46	Jews in motion pictures
PN1995.9.J6	Journalists in motion pictures
PN1995.9.J8	Justice, Administration of, in motion pictures
PN1995.9.J87	Juvenile delinquency films
PN1995.9.K57	Kissing in motion pictures
PN1995.9.L28	Working class in motion pictures
PN1995.9.L37	Latin Americans in motion pictures
PN1995.9.L38	Latin lovers
PN1995.9.L48	Lesbianism in motion pictures
PN1995.9.L6	Love in motion pictures
PN1995.9.M	Masochism in motion pictures
PN1995.9.M23	Minorities in motion pictures
PN1995.9.M27	Man-woman relationships in motion pictures
PN1995.9.M3	Marriage in motion pictures
PN1995.9.M45	Melodrama in motion pictures
PN1995.9.M46	Men in motion pictures
PN1995.9.M463	Mental illness in motion pictures
PN1995.9.M472	Metaphor in motion pictures
PN1995.9.M49	Mexican Americans in motion pictures
PN1995.9.M5	Mexico—In motion pictures
PN1995.9.M52	Middle Ages in motion pictures
PN1995.9.M54	Miners in motion pictures
PN1995.9.M59	Money in motion pictures
PN1995.9.M6	Monsters in motion pictures
PN1995.9.M63	Mothers in motion pictures
PN1995.9.M65	Motion picture industry in motion pictures
PN1995.9.M66	Motorcycle films
PN1995.9.M67	Appalachians (People) in motion pictures
PN1995.9.M83	Mummy films
PN1995.9.M86	Musical films
PN1995.9.M97	Mythology in motion pictures
PN1995.9.N33	National characteristics in motion pictures
PN1995.9.N34	National characteristics, American, in

	motion pictures
PN1995.9.N35	National characteristics, Australian, in motion pictures
PN1995.9.N352	National characteristics, British, in motion pictures
PN1995.9.N354	National characteristics, German, in motion pictures
PN1995.9.N36	National socialism and motion pictures
PN1995.9.N38	Nature in motion pictures
PN1995.9.N4	African Americans in the motion picture industry
PN1995.9.N55	Nihilism (Philosophy) in motion pictures
PN1995.9.N67	Nostalgia in motion pictures
PN1995.9.O64	Opera in motion pictures
PN1995.9.O75	Organizational behavior in motion pictures
PN1995.9.O84	Outlaws in motion pictures
PN1995.9.P44	Physicians in motion pictures
PN1995.9.P487	Pioneers in motion pictures
PN1995.9.P5	Film posters
PN1995.9.P6	Politics in motion pictures
PN1995.9.P67	Prehistoric animals in motion pictures
PN1995.9.P78	Psychiatry in motion pictures
PN1995.9.P79	Motion picture industry—Public relations
PN1995.9.P8	Puppet films
PN1995.9.R25	Railroads in motion pictures
PN1995.9.R27	Rape in motion pictures
PN1995.9.R3	Realism in motion pictures
PN1995.9.R33	Rednecks in motion pictures
PN1995.9.R35	Regeneration in motion pictures
PN1995.9.R4	Religion in motion pictures
PN1995.9.R45	Motion picture remakes
PN1995.9.R56	Rites and ceremonies in motion pictures
PN1995.9.R63	Road films
PN1995.9.R67	Romanies in motion pictures
PN1995.9.R87	Russians in motion pictures
PN1995.9.S23	Sadism in motion pictures
PN1995.9.S25	Science films
PN1995.9.S253	Schools in motion pictures
PN1995.9.S27	Scotland—In motion pictures
PN1995.9.S274	Sculpture in motion pictures
PN1995.9.S28	Sea in motion pictures
PN1995.9.S284	Sensationalism in motion pictures
PN1995.9.S29	Motion picture

PN1995.9.S297	Serial murderers in motion pictures
PN1995.9.S4	Motion pictures—Setting and scenery
PN1995.9.S45	Sex in motion pictures
PN1995.9.S47	Sex role in motion pictures
PN1995.9.S48	Shamanism in motion pictures
PN1995.9.S55	Sisters in motion pictures
PN1995.9.S554	Slasher films
PN1995.9.S557	Slavery in motion pictures
PN1995.9.S58	Smoking in motion pictures
PN1995.9.S6	Motion pictures—Social aspects
PN1995.9.S62	Social problems in motion pictures
PN1995.9.S63	Socialist realism in motion pictures
PN1995.9.S665	Soviet Union—In motion pictures
PN1995.9.S67	Sports films
PN1995.9.S69	Stage props
PN1995.9.S697	Strong men in motion pictures
PN1995.9.S7	Stunt performers
PN1995.9.S74	Suburbs in motion pictures
PN1995.9.S8	Supernatural in motion pictures
PN1995.9.S85	Surrealism in motion pictures
PN1995.9.S87	Suspense in motion pictures, television, etc.
PN1995.9.T4	Teachers in motion pictures
PN1995.9.T45	Telephone in motion pictures
PN1995.9.T46	Terrorism in motion pictures
PN1995.9.T55	Time in motion pictures
PN1995.9.T57	Titles of motion pictures
PN1995.9.T75	Trials in motion pictures
PN1995.9.U45	Ukrainians in motion pictures
PN1995.9.U6	Underground movements in motion pictures
PN1995.9.U62	Unidentified flying objects in motion pictures
PN1995.9.U64	United States—In motion pictures
PN1995.9.V44	Veterans in motion pictures
PN1995.9.V47	Villains in motion pictures
PN1995.9.V5	Violence in motion pictures
PN1995.9.V66	Voodooism in motion pictures
PN1995.9.W38	Werewolf films
PN1995.9.W45	Whites in motion pictures
PN1995.9.W6	Women in motion pictures
PN1995.9.W74	Wrestlers in motion pictures
PN1995.9.Y54	Motion pictures, Yiddish
PN1995.9.Y6	Youth in motion pictures
PN1995.9.I59	Invisibility in motion pictures
PN1996–1997	Motion picture plays
PN1996	Motion picture authorship

PN1997	Motion picture plays—Women authors
PN1997.5	Animated films
PN1997.85	Film adaptations
PN1998.2–.3	Motion pictures—Biography

Appendix E
Dewey Decimal Classification— By Subject

Libraries shelve books in classification order. They usually use one of two classification systems: the Library of Congress or the Dewey Decimal. The table below lists topics and corresponding Dewey Decimal numbers, which readers can use to browse the shelves. See *Appendix F* for a table ordered by Dewey Decimal classification number.

Actors	791.43028
Aesthetics, Audience, Criticism, Philosophy, Social Aspects, Theory	791.4301
Africa	791.43096
Animation	791.433
Asia	791.43095
Audience(s), Research, Interpreting Audiences, Audience Making	302.234072
Biography	791.43092
Broadcasting	384.54
Careers, Cinema Production	384.802341
Cinematography	778.5
Comedy Films	791.43617
Communication Studies, Cultural and Media Studies	302.2
Costume Design	791.43026
Criticism of Individual Films	791.4375
Culture, Media and Society	302.234
Directors	791.430233
Documentary Film	70.18
Europe	791.43094
Feminism	791.4365042
Film	791.43
Film Editing	778.535
Film Genres	791.435
Film Noir	791.43655
Gay Cinema	791.4369
Genres	791.43015
History, Reviews and Criticism	791.4309
Horror Films	791.43616
Industry	791.43097
Latin America	791.43098
Mass Media, Communication and Culture	302.234
Melodrama	791.43655
Music in Film	782.85

Appendix F
Dewey Decimal Classification

Libraries shelve books in classification order. They usually use one of two classification systems: the Library of Congress or the Dewey Decimal. The table below allows readers to browse the shelves by Dewey Decimal classification number. See *Appendix E* for a table listing classification numbers by subject heading.

70.18	Documentary Film
302.2	Communication Studies, Cultural and Media Studies
302.23082	Women and Media, Feminism, Media and Gender
302.234	Culture, Media and Society
302.234	Mass Media, Communication and Culture
302.234072	Audience(s), Research, Interpreting Audiences, Audience Making
384.54	Broadcasting
384.802341	Careers, Cinema Production
778.5	Cinematography
778.535	Film Editing
782.85	Music in Film
791.43	Film
791.4301	Aesthetics, Audience, Criticism, Philosophy, Social Aspects, Theory
791.43015	Genres
791.43019	Psychological Aspects
791.430232	Production
791.430233	Directors
791.43025	Set Design
791.43026	Costume Design
791.43028	Actors
791.4309	History, Reviews and Criticism
791.4309046	Politics and Cinema
791.4309093	Westerns
791.43092	Biography
791.43094	Europe
791.43095	Asia
791.43096	Africa
791.43097	Industry
791.430973	United States
791.43098	Latin America
791.432	Screenwriting
791.433	Animation
791.435	Film Genres

791.4352	Musicals
791.436	Women's Cinema
791.43615	Science Fiction Films
791.43616	Horror Films
791.43617	Comedy Films
791.4365042	Feminism
791.43655	Film Noir
791.43655	Melodrama
791.4369	Gay Cinema
791.437	Screenplays
791.4375	Criticism of Individual Films
791.45	Television

Author / Title Index

Reference is to entry number.

Subject Index

About the Author

MARK EMMONS is a Librarian and Associate Professor at the University of New Mexico. His lifelong passion for film led him to work briefly in the film and television industry immediately after graduating from UCLA in 1983. Realizing that he liked watching films more than making them, he explored a career in teaching before finding his niche as a librarian in 1990. As a librarian, he has selected books and films for the library collection, taught students how to conduct research, and answered reference questions about film and television. He has also written chapters on web-based film resources and how to teach film research to undergraduates. Mark lives with his family in Albuquerque.